ABHARLANNA COUNTAE F

A SOCIAL HISTORY OF
WOMEN IN IRELAND
1870–1970

A SOCIAL HISTORY OF WOMEN IN IRELAND 1870–1970

ROSEMARY CULLEN OWENS

Gill & Macmillan

Gill & Macmillan Ltd
Hume Avenue, Park West, Dublin 12
with associated companies throughout the world
www.gillmacmillan.ie
© Rosemary Cullen Owens 2005
0 7171 3681 7

Index compiled by Helen Litton
Typography design by Make Communication
Print origination by O'K Graphic Design, Dublin
Printed by Creative Print and Design (Wales)

This book is typeset in 11.75/14 pt Minion.

The paper used in this book comes from the wood pulp
of managed forests. For every tree felled, at least one
tree is planted, thereby renewing natural resources.

A CIP catalogue record for this book is available from the
British Library.

5 4 3 2 1

To Dr Margaret MacCurtain, mentor and friend

CONTENTS

ILLUSTRATIONS

Between pages 106 and 107

Mother with young children, *c.* 1890. *From* The Irish: A Photohistory *by Sean Sexton and Christine Kinealy, Thames & Hudson, London*

Members of the RIC with Excise 'gauger' and an old woman found with an illegal poitín still, Co. Mayo, 1890s. *Irish Picture Library*

The original company of the Girls' Brigade, Sandymount Presbyterian Church, 1893. *Private Collection*

Five women walking to church, Ahascragh, Co. Galway, *c.* 1890. *Courtesy of the National Library of Ireland*

'Coming home after shopping', Gorumna Island, Connemara, *c.* 1900. *Fáilte Ireland*

Women washing clothes, west of Ireland, 1910. *Photographer Philip G. Hunt. From* The Irish: A Photohistory *by Sean Sexton and Christine Kinealy, Thames & Hudson, London*

Shop girls, the Curragh, Co. Kildare, *c.* 1903. *Photographer Philip G. Hunt. From* The Irish: A Photohistory *by Sean Sexton and Christine Kinealy, Thames & Hudson, London*

Women in Claddagh, Co. Galway, wearing traditional costume, with the fish-catch, 1900–1910. *Courtesy of the National Library of Ireland*

Women curing fish at Downings Pier, Co. Donegal, 1906–14. *Courtesy of the National Library of Ireland*

The Congested Districts Board was established by the Chief Secretary for Ireland in the 1890s to alleviate poverty in the west of Ireland. *Courtesy of the National Library of Ireland*

Miss Crowe and Mr Gildea with their pupils at Kilglass National School, Ahascragh, Co. Galway, *c.* 1902. *Courtesy of the National Library of Ireland*

Members of the Irish Women Workers Union outside Liberty Hall, Dublin, 1913. *Courtesy of the National Library of Ireland*

Cumann na mBan recite the Rosary in their ranks outside Mountjoy prison, 25 April 1921. *Courtesy of the National Library of Ireland*

Miss Bloxham addressing a suffrage meeting in the summer of 1912. *Courtesy of the National Library of Ireland*

ABBREVIATIONS

1.	**Women's Organisations**

ACWW	Associated Country Women of the World
AWCS	Association of Widows of Civil Servants
BPWC	Business and Professional Women's Clubs
CAISM	The Central Association of Irish Schoolmistresses and other Ladies Interested in Education
CSW	Council for the Status of Women
CWFSSU	Catholic Women's Federation of Secondary School Unions
DUWGA	Dublin University Women Graduates Association
DWSA	Dublin Women's Suffrage Association
EEA	Employment Equality Agency
GFS	Girls' Friendly Society
IAW	International Alliance of Women
IAWGCG	Irish Association of Women Graduates and Candidate Graduates
ICA	Irish Countrywomen's Association
ICWPP	International Committee of Women for Permanent Peace
IHA	Irish Housewives Association
IIL	Irishwomen's International League
INO	Irish Nurses Organisation
IWCA	Irish Women's Citizens' Association
IWEL	Irish Women's Equality League
IWFL	Irish Women's Franchise League
IWLM	Irish Women's Liberation Movement
IWRL	Irish Women's Reform League
IWSA	International Woman Suffrage Alliance
IWSF	Irish Women's Suffrage Federation

IWSLGA	Irish Women's Suffrage and Local Government Association
IWSS	Irish Women's Suffrage Society
IWU	Irish Women United
IWWU	Irish Women Workers' Union
JCWSSW	Joint Committee of Women's Societies and Social Workers
LNA	Ladies' National Association for the Repeal of the Contagious Acts
MWFL	Munster Women's Franchise League
NAIW	National Association of Irish Widows
NCWI	National Council of Women of Ireland
NESWS	North of England Society for Women's Suffrage
NUWGA	National University Women Graduates Association
TOSI	Textile Operatives' Society of Ireland
UI	United Irishwomen
UWUC	Ulster Women's Unionist Council
WAC	Women's Advisory Council
WCA	Women Citizens' Association
WIL	Women's International League
WILPF	Women's International League for Peace and Freedom
WIZO	Women's International Zionist Organisation
WNCA	Women's National Council of Action
WNHA	Women's National Health Association
WPA	Women's Political Association
WRC	Women's Representative Committee
WSPL	Women's Social and Progressive League
WSPU	Women's Social and Political Union
YWCA	Young Women's Christian Association

2.	**General**

AGM	Annual general meeting
CCLAA	Committee on the Criminal Law Amendment Act
CDA	Contagious Diseases Acts
CPRSI	Child Protection and Rescue Society of Ireland
CSO	Central Statistics Office
CVO	Commission on Vocational Organisation
DAA	Drapers' Assistants' Association
DORA	Defence of the Realm Act
DTUC	Dublin Trade Union Council
EEC	European Economic Community
ESB	Electricity Supply Board
ESRI	Economic and Social Research Institute
FUE	Federated Union of Employers
FWUI	Federated Workers Union of Ireland
GAA	Gaelic Athletic Association
GPO	General Post Office
H.C.Deb.	House of Commons Debate
IAOS	Irish Agricultural Organisation Society
ICM	Irish Church Missions
ICTU	Irish Congress of Trade Unions
IFC	Irish Folklore Commission
IFS	Irish Free State
ILPTUC	Irish Labour Party and Trade Union Congress
INO	Irish Nurses Organisation
INTO	Irish National Teachers Organisation
INU	Irish Nurses' Union
IRB	Irish Republican Brotherhood
ITGWU	Irish Transport and General Workers' Union
ITUC	Irish Trade Union Congress
JCV	Joint Committee on Vocationalism
LPC	Lower Prices Council
MP	Member of Parliament
NAI	National Archives of Ireland
NAPSS	National Association for the Promotion of Social Science

NARCDA	National Association for the Repeal of the Contagious Diseases Acts
NFA	National Farmers' Association
NLI	National Library of Ireland
OEEC	Organisation for European Economic Cooperation
PAB	Prices Advisory Board
RTÉ	Radio Telefís Éireann
RUI	Royal University of Ireland
SSISI	Statistical and Social Inquiry Society of Ireland
TB	Tuberculosis
TCD	Trinity College Dublin
TD	Teachta Dála
TUC	Trade Union Congress
UCD	University College Dublin
UK	United Kingdom
UN	United Nations
US/USA	United States of America
VD	Venereal disease
WUI	Workers Union of Ireland

ACKNOWLEDGEMENTS

Reflecting as it does the work of some thirty years in the research and teaching of women's history, this book owes much to the help and encouragement of many people over time. While just over two years have been devoted to its writing, in effect the groundwork has been many years in the making.

It was Dr Margaret MacCurtain who suggested I write this book and kept me focused towards its completion. As always, she has been most generous with her time and advice to myself and my family. Maria Luddy is due particular thanks for her ongoing support, not least in coping with last minute panic phone-calls! The late Hilda and Robert Tweedy—both of whom died earlier this year—were most helpful to me in my research. I owe a debt of gratitude in particular to Hilda for her constant friendship and assistance. Other friends and colleagues who have been consistently supportive include Rosemary Raughter, Theresa Moriarty, Mary Cullen, Maryann Valiulis, Maeve Casey, Susan Parkes and members of the Women's History Association of Ireland.

My thanks also to Ailbhe Smyth and the staff of the Women's Education Research and Resource Centre at UCD who have been both staunch supporters of my work and stimulating colleagues. Particular thanks are due to Caitriona Crowe and the staff of the National Archives of Ireland. My thanks also to the staff of the National Library of Ireland, the staff of UCD library, and Beverley Cook, Museum of London. Siobhán McCrystal, Senior Librarian at Stewarts Hospital, was most adept at locating source material; my sincere thanks to her and her staff. My thanks to RTÉ for their co-operation; in particular the assistance of Peter Mooney and Fr Dermod McCarthy is much appreciated.

I wish to acknowledge those who assisted me in accessing photographic material, including Sara Smyth of the National Photographic Archive, Brian Walsh of the County Museum, Dundalk, Derek Cullen at Fáilte Ireland, Anne Kearney of the *Irish Examiner*, Clare Hackett and Eibhlín Roche at The Guinness Archive, Sergeant Pat Magee of the Garda Archives, David and Edwin Davison of The Irish Picture Library, Derek Speirs and Mary Jones.

My thanks to John Treacy, International Educational Services, Leixlip, for his constructive advice when I first started this project. I thank Seán Priestley for his unfailing support and encouragement throughout. Karen McElhinney not only provided original photographs, but is also due thanks for valued technical assistance with all photographic material. Thanks also to Sharon O'Connor and Brendan O'Connor for additional technical advice.

Two final groups remain to be acknowledged: the staff of Gill & Macmillan, and my long-suffering family. Fergal Tobin I thank not only for accepting my initial proposal, but also for his insightful suggestions as to areas needing further research. His support throughout has been a masterpiece of supervision: non-intrusive, yet always present, discreetly pointing to the deadline! Deirdre Rennison Kunz has been most supportive, and as with the rest of the team, Dearbhaile Curran and Helen Thompson, thoroughly professional.

My thanks to my family—particularly Jennifer, Michael and Aoife— for their care and understanding over the years. I have noted elsewhere that my sons Simon and David were weaned on women's history. It has always been part and parcel of their lives, and their constant support and encouragement of my various endeavours has been much appreciated. Once more, I would like to pay tribute to them for their moral support and for their practical help on the very many occasions when technology got the better of me!

Rosemary Cullen Owens
Dublin
August 2005

INTRODUCTION

Two reasons lie behind the writing of this book—(1) my experience of researching and teaching the history of Irish women, and (2) the consistent encouragement—and prodding—of Dr Margaret MacCurtain. My own particular journey into this field began in the mid-1970s. I wasn't quite sure where the journey would take me, but I was convinced that there had to be more to the lives of Irish women in the past than history text books then indicated. The late Professor R. Dudley Edwards adroitly steered me in the direction of the women's suffrage campaign in Ireland—in which his mother had been active. And, as the cliché goes, the rest is history, as I became and remain hooked on discovering, debating and disseminating information on the choices and challenges faced by women in Ireland.

Mary Robinson, in her contribution to the 1975 Thomas Davis series of lectures on *Women in Irish Society*, pointed to the significance of the series title and of her paper 'Women and the New Irish State'. Commenting on the unlikely chance of someone being asked to deliver a paper on 'Men and the New Irish State', she concluded that the significance of the title was in fact to highlight the absence of women as a significant force in the new state.[1] Answering the question 'What is history in Ireland', Maria Luddy and Cliona Murphy stated in 1990 that it was 'a narrative account of the doings of men, largely carried out by men, written by men and taught by men'.[2] Deirdre Beddoe noted in the 1980s that most of us had been conditioned to believe that the concrete body of facts taught us as history, *is* history, unaware that the package selected for us excluded working people and women.[3]

Over the past thirty years, publications on both labour and women's history have increased. It has been my experience, however, that difficulty is encountered by new readers in sourcing material, particularly in the area of women's history. Margaret MacCurtain commented in 1978: 'Many Irish women find it difficult to learn about their historical identity, or their role in the life of the country, because they have neither the information readily available, nor the skills of evaluation at their disposal.'[4] Excellent books (including MacCurtain's), now out of print, and articles scattered among journals, are not easy for the general reader or the new student of women's history to obtain. By incorporating the findings of such research and publications in a single volume, this book aims to amend that situation. Utilising a combination of primary research material and published works, this study proposes to explore the role and status of women in Ireland from 1870 to 1970. Examining lifestyle options available to women during this period, it will provide an overview of the forces working for change within Irish society, demonstrating the interaction between women's groups and other socio/political organisations. While certain chapters cover developments throughout the island of Ireland, the work centres primarily on the Republic.

Part 1 examines the movements and issues that formed the basis for women's gradual advancement by the turn of the century. Emanating from middle- and upper-class women, such campaigns initially sought parity of education and legal rights for women with their male peers. Both issues were fought against the prevailing ethos of the day regarding the accepted status of women. With both objectives ultimately achieved, the first concerted campaign for suffrage equality emerged. The nineteenth-century phase of this campaign was restrained and limited in nature, but did achieve the important break-through of local government and poor law guardianship rights for propertied women. Many of these early activists had started their public life in the area of philanthropy. The impact of religious endeavour on women's activity during the nineteenth century is discussed here, as are the differing results of such endeavour on the part of Catholic and Protestant women.

Part 2 looks at a new generation of Irishwomen from 1900 who had benefited from the work of earlier pioneers, particularly in the field of education. Confident, articulate, and in touch with international developments regarding women's demands, these women took up the fight for political equality in a more militant way. Publicly challenging male politicians and using militant tactics, many were arrested and imprisoned, some adopting hunger strike action in protest at their non-political prisoner status. Increasingly, current political developments within Ireland impinged on such activists. The radicalisation of Irish political life over the next decade or so produced intricate interaction between suffragists and other groups seeking change. Home Rule, Sinn Féin, Labour, the outbreak of War in 1914 and the Easter Rising of 1916—all would involve decisions and sometimes participation by women's groups, and/or individual women. The decision to ally suffrage commitment with one of these causes—or to prioritise another cause over that of suffrage—led to much soul-searching and disagreement.

Part 3 presents an overview of the social, economic and familial role of women in post-famine Ireland. Crucial to a determination of the status of Irish women throughout the period under review is an examination of the choices available to them regarding work, marriage and emigration. Class and land ownership remained key determinants for much of this period, with consequences for both rural and urban women. The distinguishing criterion for status within rural Ireland became ownership of land, forming the context for a patriarchal society in which strong father/farmer figures would dominate. The issues of class and available choice were significant for urban women also. During the early years of this study, limited female employment opportunities applied across all classes. Women who had to work were badly paid and generally unorganised, domestic service being the primary source of employment for single women. The lack of working class housing, overcrowded slum dwellings with inadequate sanitation and consequent health hazards posed particular problems for mothers. From the early 1900s, other employment opportunities emerged for women in shops, offices and services, although restrictions applied in most of these. In addition to a general review of the types of work available to women, attitudes towards the trade unionisation of women workers are also discussed.

Part 4 examines the status of women in the new Irish state from 1922 to 1970. Following the passing of the Free State Constitution of 1922, the new state guaranteed all its citizens full political rights and constitutional equality. Within a few years, however, a series of acts was passed restricting the employment and public equality of women, with the 1937 Constitution placing a firm emphasis on women's place within the home. Research cited by Mary Daly based on Irish society in the 1930s and 1940s makes sobering reading.[5] In the 1930s, Arensberg and Kimball found 'a rural female class who acquiesced in a subordinate status, eating separately after the men had been fed, and marrying partners chosen by parents to meet certain social aspirations rather than the woman's personal wishes'. In the 1940s, Humphreys depicted within urban life 'a strict demarcation of roles, separate socialising by men and women and a definitely subordinate status accorded to females'. Towards the end of the period examined, intimations of change appear. From the 1940s, small but significant groups of women emerge, challenging the status quo. Like earlier reform groups, most had a middle-class background, but they did not have a solely middle-class agenda. Over a fifteen-year period a wide range of reforms were debated and, increasingly, demanded. Beginning with pressure for price control and rationing during the war years, the list of issues expanded to cover other social concerns and discriminatory practices regarding the legal status and employment of women. From the late 1950s, intense debate developed on Ireland's possible entry into the EEC. Irish women's groups built up contacts and support within European women's organisations. Following a UN directive on the status of women in 1968, and sustained pressure by women's groups and female trade unionists, the Irish government—keen to be seen to meet EEC standards—established in 1970 the first government Commission on the Status of Women. The report of that Commission was published in December 1972, and formed the blueprint for radical change for Irish women.

V.H. Galbraith wrote in 1944 that 'History is the Past—so far as we know it. (It) is made by the historian who has not merely to continue it with the lapse of time but unceasingly to remake it.'[6] Based on the courses I have taught at the Women's Education Research and Resource Centre in UCD over the past fifteen years, and on personal research and other published works, this book aims to provide a step in 'remaking' the history of women in Ireland more accessible to students and general readers.

PART 1

Irishwomen in the Nineteenth Century

'A PROGRESSIVELY WIDENING SET OF OBJECTIVES'[1]—THE EARLY WOMEN'S MOVEMENT

A hundred years ago, women had not begun to make the vindication of their rights the prominent political and social problem it has become today (E.R. PENNELL, 1891).

So begins E.R. Pennell's introduction to an 1891 edition of *A Vindication of the Rights of Woman* by Mary Wollstonecraft.[2] First published in 1792, Mary Wollstonecraft's *Vindication* has been described by Deirdre Raftery as 'the work in which all previous arguments for the inferiority of the female mind are synthesised, and new ground was broken'.[3] Part of a young liberal and intellectual radical group seeking social and political reform in the revolutionary era, Mary Wollstonecraft argued in particular for female emancipation, having seen that those articulating demands for 'the rights of man' did not always wish to extend these rights to women. Her abiding commitment was to establish that human reason was the same in man and woman and, from this point, to argue that all humans are equal. She questioned the contemporary definition of woman's social role, arguing that the education of women was fundamental to the well-being of the state:

It is time to effect a revolution in female manners—time to restore to (women) their lost dignity—and make them, as a part of the human species, labour by reforming themselves to reform the world.[4]

Wollstonecraft was the first to link education with the idea of financial independence, arguing for change in the traditions and laws which prevented women from working in society:

How many women thus waste life away the prey of discontent, who might have practised as physicians, regulated a farm, managed a shop, and stood erect, supported by their own industry, instead of hanging their heads surcharged with the dew of sensibility ... I have seldom seen much compassion excited by the helplessness of females, unless they were fair ... How much more respectable is the woman who earns her own bread by fulfilling any duty, than the most accomplished beauty.[5]

The forceful views expressed in the *Vindication* led to vilification during her lifetime and for many years after her death. With historical reinterpretation of women's role in society, Wollstonecraft has been accorded her rightful position 'as the woman who dared to assume the doctrine of human rights for her own sex, and who wrote what may be seen as the first declaration of female independence'.[6]

In 1820 the English philosopher, economist and historian James Mill published a treatise *On Government* in which he argued that political rights could be removed without inconvenience from certain classes of people, including women, 'the interests of almost all of whom are involved in that of their fathers or in that of their husbands'.[7] In response, Tipperary-born Anna Wheeler—an admirer of Wollstonecraft —collaborated with William Thompson (originally from Cork) to produce a definitive work advocating female suffrage. While it was rare in early nineteenth-century England for a man to publicly acknowledge the collaboration of a woman in the writing of a major political work, Anna Wheeler was so acknowledged by Thompson in what Dolores Dooley has described as the 'first complete statement of a socialist defence of sexual equality'.[8] The rather unwieldy title of the work is in fact a synopsis of its content: *Appeal of one Half of the Human Race, Women, Against the Pretensions of the Other Half, Men, To Retain Them in Political, and Thence in Civil and Domestic Slavery*. Published in London in 1825, the work declared:

All women and particularly women living with men in marriage ... having been reduced by the want of political rights to a state of helplessness and slavery ... are more in need of political rights than any other portion of human beings.

Arguing for equal political, civil and domestic rights for women, the authors stated:

Without them (equal rights) they can never be regarded by men as really their equals, they can never attain that respectability and dignity in the social scale ... they could not respect themselves.[9]

Wheeler and Thompson did not claim that a change in laws would automatically lead to emancipation from oppression, accepting that cultural attitudes and public opinion would have to be changed. But legal changes were necessary precursors to such attitudinal change. These equality claims for women were articulated against a backdrop of much social unrest in Great Britain during the 1820s. Common to most western societies, extensive social and economic upheaval was taking place with the development of industrialised capitalism. Contemporaneously, a legacy of enlightenment philosophy and revolutionary ideals of equality synthesised into a liberal ideology. As the emerging middle classes began to play an increasingly prominent role in political and social life, they used their power to press for a voice in the nation's government through the creation of parliamentary institutions based on a property-qualified franchise (to exclude the lower classes) with full ministerial responsibility (to minimise aristocratic power exercised through court intrigue). They pleaded for the liberal principles of representative government, equality before the law and careers open to talent. As a result of such pressure a gradual democratisation of local and national government took place throughout Great Britain during the 1800s. The Franchise Reform Acts of 1832, 1868 and 1884 significantly shifted the power structure from the traditional wealthy landowning and aristocratic classes to 'newly rich' industrialist and professional groups. It was not until 1872 that secret balloting became law, enabling workers in towns and country to use their vote freely without fear of reprisals from employer or landlord. However, in spite of the added enfranchisement of many urban and rural workers towards the end of the century, the parliamentary vote retained two major disabilities. It was primarily property-based rather than person-based, leaving significant levels of the population without a vote. In addition all women, irrespective of whether or not they fulfilled the property qualifications, were excluded.

The passing of the Act of Union in 1800 established the United Kingdom of Great Britain and Ireland. This involved the loss of Ireland's native parliament and the absorption of Irish parliamentary representatives into the Westminster parliament. From 1800 until Ireland achieved independence in 1921, all laws governing Ireland would emanate from Westminster. During the nineteenth century a series of movements emerged in England and Ireland aimed at improving the social, economic and political status of women. A number of influences converged to bring such organisations into existence from the 1850s. Richard Evans has noted that it was out of the involvement of middle-class philanthropists in the debates over measures such as women's rights within marriage, extension of second- and third-level education to women, and the abolition of state regulation of prostitution that organised feminism began.[10] In addition, he cites John Stuart Mill's 1869 essay on *The Subjection of Women* as an incalculable influence on feminism.[11] During the 1850s in Britain, the forces of reform were realigning, and middle-class concern with social questions was growing after the Chartist challenges of the 1840s. Two other important influences on emerging women's groups were the experience of many within the anti-slavery movement earlier in the century, and with the Anti-Corn law agitation of the early 1840s. The tactics of the nascent women's suffrage campaign would be based on those of the Anti-Corn Law League, including the retaining of itinerant lecturers, the holding of indoor public meetings, the production of a steady stream of tracts, handbills and petitions to parliament, and the pressurising of candidates in parliamentary elections.[12] Another significant development was the emergence of a number of associations dedicated to social reform, of which the National Association for the Promotion of Social Science (NAPSS), the parent body of the early feminist movement, was perhaps the most important.[13] Women were active in many of these associations, and it is at meetings of such organisations, and in their journals, that we find the first debates of many reform issues related to women. Luddy has pointed out that the NAPSS provided an important platform for women activists, and offered a meeting ground for women from Ireland and England.[14]

Demands for better educational and employment opportunities for single, middle-class women provided a springboard for a series of further demands including property and child custody rights for married women, female representation on public boards and local authorities, the right to vote in local elections, and ultimately the right to the parliamentary vote. This process, paralleled in most western countries, has been described by R.J. Evans as 'the history of a progressively widening set of objectives'.[15]

It was in fact the 1832 Reform Act which specifically introduced sex discrimination into electoral qualifications with its use of the words 'male persons'. This was extended in 1835 to include local and municipal government franchises. This act has been described as planting the seed of later female suffrage agitation.[16] Up to 1832 women in England and Ireland had been prevented from voting by custom only, and in medieval times many qualified women had exercised their right to vote. From 1832, however, all women were prohibited from voting by law. The campaign for women's suffrage therefore took place against a backdrop of ever widening male eligibility for the vote with no recognition of equal rights for women with similar qualifications.

Between 1830 and 1860, the subject of woman and her 'place' was not entirely ignored in Irish publications. One such article in 1839 comparing Irish and French women noted approvingly that 'there is no free country where the women have less of a separate existence than in Ireland'.[17] While conceding the need for new avenues of employment for middle-class women, an article in *Dublin University Magazine* in 1859 stated: 'A woman's mission is to be true to her own womanhood, and surely no nobler portion of this mission is there than the exalting of men.'[18] Two years later it was reported that the issue of the Employment of Women in Ireland had been long and frequently discussed at recent meetings of the Statistical and Social Inquiry Society of Ireland (SSISI) in 1861; while accepting that educated women should not be limited to the profession of governess, the author advised that 'the sex of a woman, though it may be a misfortune, is not a crime'.[19] Reflecting these discussions, Andrew Rosen has written:

> In the 1850s and 1860s there was simply no career offering any degree of intellectual scope, pecuniary reward, and social respectability open to an unmarried middle-class woman. It was primarily as a reaction against the manifest lack of opportunities for unmarried middle-class women that organised feminism began in Britain.[20]

Similarly, George Dangerfield has commented: 'When a husband is a woman's career, the woman without a husband is as good as dead.'[21] Evans has pointed to the pattern that emerged from these demands:

> The rise of these pressure-groups for admitting women to the professions sparked off a kind of chain reaction, as these women found it necessary to campaign for admission into the universities in order to gain the necessary educational qualifications for admission to the professions, and then began to campaign for the vote in order to gain the necessary political power to force the legislative changes which would entitle them to enter the universities.[22]

Attainment of women's rights in the educational, legal and political arenas did not automatically occur at the same time in both countries. While the laws governing nineteenth-century Ireland and England were to a large extent similar, the social and political circumstances were quite different. Nineteenth-century Ireland was predominantly rural in character; in 1841 only 20 per cent of the population lived in towns. Unlike industrialised England, there were only three Irish towns with more than 50,000 inhabitants—Dublin, Belfast and Cork. The great famine of 1845–48 was a catalyst for lasting change in Irish society. In 1841, the population stood at just over 8 million; by 1851 this had been reduced to 6.6 million, through death and emigration. Population figures continued to decline throughout the nineteenth century—by 1911 the figure stood at 4.4 million.[23] A number of philanthropic women's groups worked to help families in the post-famine years; increasingly they sought to teach craftwork to the girls from such families so that they might have a source of income. One young Quaker woman so involved was Anna Fisher (Haslam) from Youghal. From the 1860s, interest developed on employment opportunities for unmarried middle-class women, and branches of like-minded English organisations were formed in Dublin. A somewhat similar chain-reaction to that described above by Evans occurred, although the big educational breakthrough for Irish girls did not occur until the late 1870s. Debates in Ireland on the employment and education of women were not formulated in a vacuum, but were affected by debates occurring in the English women's movement.[24] Activists in Ireland would seek extension of rights enjoyed by English women to Ireland, as well as demanding further equality in areas agreed by women in both countries.

STATUS OF WOMEN UP TO 1870s

- Women could not vote in local or parliamentary elections.
- Women could not be members of public boards or local authorities.
- Women were not expected or encouraged to earn their own living.
- Education for women was considered unnecessary and undesirable.
- On marriage a woman's property became her husband's.
- Women had legal custody of their children only to 7 years of age.

In 1866, when a new franchise reform bill to further extend the male franchise was imminent, the first petition seeking female suffrage was presented to the House of Commons. Ironically, it was presented by John

Stuart Mill, son of James Mill, who—unlike his father—was a lifelong champion of women's rights.[25] The petition, signed by 1,499 women, included the signatures of twenty-five Irish women, one of whom was Anna Haslam.[26] The following year, the first debate on female suffrage in the House of Commons occurred with Mill's proposed amendment to the 1867 Representation of the People Act. This proposed to replace the word 'man' in the act by the word 'person'. While the amendment failed, it had the effect of focusing various women's groups throughout England to form a permanent movement in the name of the National Society for Women's Suffrage. Private bills for women's suffrage continued to be presented to the House of Commons practically every year into the new century. By 1875 the majority voting against one such bill was only thirteen, despite two very stiff whips. This created so much unease amongst opponents of female suffrage in the House of Commons that a committee was formed 'for maintaining the integrity of the franchise'.[27]

It is clear from contemporary records of the late 1860s that the groundwork was being laid for an organised suffrage campaign in Ireland. Correspondence from John Stuart Mill to Thomas Haslam (Anna's husband) on the feasibility of starting such a society in Ireland shows initial disappointment in 1867 that 'the immediate prospects are not encouraging'.[28] Within a year, however, Mill was 'very happy to hear of the progress of the movement for women's suffrage in Dublin'.[29] It is clear from journals of the time that ideas of change were taking hold in some quarters. In December 1867, Mr Alfred Webb read a paper to the ssisi on 'The Propriety of Conceding the Elective Franchise to Women'. Webb, like most Quakers, was a strong supporter of women's rights. Responding to the argument that many women did not want the vote—an argument against granting women's suffrage that would be used frequently over the next fifty years—Webb stated succinctly: 'We should not refuse equal rights to some because others do not appreciate them.'[30] In 1870 a paper read to the Cork Literary and Scientific Society on the emancipation of women noted that 'an impending change is manifest in the present social and political position of women'.[31] It was reported that interest in the topic was so great that a debate which followed lasted four nights. That same year, the *English Women's Suffrage Journal* reported that numerous petitions had been received from Ireland at the House of Commons in support of women's franchise and the married women's property bill.

Over the next few years there are reports of suffrage meetings being held in various parts of the country, including Dublin, Cork, Belfast,

Carrickfergus, Dungannon, Bandon, Clonmel, Waterford and Limerick.[32] Two women in particular were responsible for these developments, Anne Robertson in Dublin and Isabella Tod in Belfast. Anne Robertson was particularly active in Dublin from the late 1860s, organising petitions to parliament and addressing many public meetings. One significant meeting she was involved in took place in April 1870 at Dublin's Molesworth Hall when the prominent English suffrage campaigner Millicent Fawcett addressed a large public meeting on 'The Electoral Disabilities of Women'. Among the distinguished audience were Sir William and Lady Wilde, Sir Robert Kane, Provost Lloyd of Trinity College and Sir John Gray MP.[33] Subsequent Dublin meetings addressed by Robertson are reported in English journals alternately as the 'Irish Society for Women's Suffrage' and the 'Dublin Committee for Women's Suffrage'. At one such meeting addressed by Robertson in Dublin's Blackrock in 1871, she pointed out that while women were often told that they should attend to their children rather than to politics, they had not the smallest legal rights as to the education or guardianship of their children:

> According to law, the father, whether he be Catholic or Protestant, was always of the right religion; and all his children, the girls as well as the boys, should be brought up to suit his views.[34]

Robertson argued that the cause of this injustice was the fact that women were not represented in parliament, where the laws were made or reformed, and where the interests of women were too often neglected. While there is some uncertainty as to whether there existed a formal suffrage committee in Dublin at this time, there is no doubt that Robertson was central to activating suffrage debate and laying the groundwork for an organised society.[35]

Isabella Tod established the Northern Ireland Society for Women's Suffrage in Belfast in 1871, and linked it to the London Women's Suffrage Society.[36] A seasoned campaigner for women's educational equality and property rights and repeal of the Contagious Diseases Acts, Tod travelled throughout Ireland addressing meetings on the suffrage issue. She argued for the vote on the basis of justice and on women's right to citizenship. Like most suffragists of the period, Tod sought a relatively restricted franchise, based on current property qualifications. Acquisition of the vote, she argued, would allow women to participate, as individuals, directly in society, not subordinate, but equal to men.[37] She sought not only political power for women, but their admission as citizens of the state, exercising moral responsibility and freedom of action. Her three-pronged approach to acquisition of political rights—Poor Law, Local Government and Parliamentary—would be the template followed by the Irish suffrage campaign for the remainder of the nineteenth century.

In 1876, Anna Haslam and her husband Thomas formed the Dublin Women's Suffrage Association (DWSA).[38] Like Tod, Anna Haslam had been prominent in the campaigns for female education, married women's property rights, and repeal of the Contagious Diseases Acts. She and her husband came from Quaker stock; both would remain active in the women's movement throughout their long lives. In her biography of the couple, Carmel Quinlan has written:

> The Haslams devoted their lives to reform. Thomas Haslam was a feminist theorist; his wife was an activist who put his theories into practice, and in her person epitomised his assertion that women, intellectually and morally, were deserving of equitable treatment in politics and before the law.[39]

Thomas published a number of pamphlets on a series of topics allied to the couple's work, including birth control, sexual morality and women's suffrage. In 1874, he wrote and published three issues of a periodical, *The Women's Advocate*, the first such Irish publication. While all three issues outlined Haslam's views on the suffrage question, issue one was primarily addressed to Irishmen. Referring to recent criticism of women degrading themselves by publicly claiming political rights, Haslam asked, 'If you are so grieved to see so many of our best and noblest women "unsex themselves"—as you affect to call it—what have you done to prevent (this) necessity ... Why have you not come forward, and insisted on their enfranchisement, before they were constrained to enter into the field of controversy on their own behalf?'[40] Issue 2 gave practical advice on organising local groups for effective political action. This issue was so highly regarded at the time that the leader of the English suffrage campaign, Lydia Becker, ordered five thousand copies of it for distribution.[41] Practical implementation of his advice would be seen in the methods of the DWSA.

Quinlan has pointed to a suffrage meeting held in Earlsfort Terrace in January 1876 as a possible catalyst for the formation of the DWSA.[42] Isabella Tod was among the speakers at this meeting. The following month, the first meeting of the DWSA was held in Leinster Hall, Molesworth Street (later renamed the Irish Women's Suffrage and Local

Government Association (IWSLGA)). Subsequently, an executive committee was formed. Anna would remain its secretary until 1913 when she stood down and was elected life-president. Mary Cullen has noted that 'throughout that entire period she did not miss a single meeting and was clearly the driving force in the organisation.'[43] Many of the early members and committee were Quaker. Membership was open to both men and women; Quinlan has pointed to the number of influential men associated with the DWSA from its formation; a 1918 retrospective report by the organisation noted: 'co-operation with men has been a distinguishing feature of the policy of the Association from the first.'[44]

The DWSA remained strictly non-militant in its methods, seeking to influence public opinion by use of petitions, public lectures, appeals to MPS, and letters to the press. Great emphasis was placed on the educational role of the society, and to this end regular meetings were held in members' homes; additionally larger public meetings were organised, frequently with prominent English and American suffrage speakers.[45] It sought reform of all legal and social measures discriminating against women, particularly emphasising the need for increased educational opportunities. Much of the society's time was involved in agitation for married women's property rights and the repeal of the Contagious Diseases Acts which regulated prostitution. With the parliamentary vote as its ultimate aim, initially it sought the local government vote for women, and their right to serve as poor law guardians. Regarding the latter two items, there was discrepancy between the rights accorded women in Ireland and England. The English Poor Law system had been extended to Ireland in 1838, with Boards of Guardians being established to supervise the running of workhouses and to administer poor relief. Rate-paying Irishwomen were eligible to vote for Poor Law guardians on the same terms as men, but unlike women in England and Wales, were not legally qualified to act as Poor Law guardians. Similarly, Irish women householders were not entitled to the municipal franchise—unlike their English counterparts—with the exception of Belfast city and the townships of Blackrock and Kingstown (Dún Laoghaire) where special charters applied. The DWSA argued that attainment of these two measures was essential if women were on the one hand to gain experience in public affairs, while simultaneously proving the value of their contribution.

This pragmatic approach was also reflected in its attitude towards qualification for the franchise. Nineteenth-century demands for women's franchise 'on the same terms as men' inevitably meant on the same property qualification then applicable to men. At a time when many men were without a vote, most women sought parity with their male colleagues, not adult suffrage. As eligibility for the male parliamentary vote was increasingly extended during the course of the century, so too was the potential for drawing more women into the franchise net. However, as women continued to be consistently excluded from any of the new franchise extensions, their anger grew. Cullen has pointed out that socialist feminists criticised suffragists as bourgeois women seeking votes for their own class,[46] and there is no doubt that many suffragists did have this perspective. However, citing Evans's description of 'a progressively widening set of objectives', it would appear pragmatic policy on the part of women's groups to proceed one step at a time, rather than demand adult suffrage at this point in time. Despite the quite radical changes in parliamentary structures and representation during the nineteenth century, Great Britain remained a class-structured society. Whereas previously power and representation had been held by an elite of landowning aristocracy, now it was vested in the wealthy middle classes and professional groups. While the nature of the property qualification had changed during the course of the century, it was deemed correct by the majority that representation be linked to property. Socialists would argue for adult suffrage; in time radical feminists would argue that all women should be included in such demands. Fundamentally, however, 'Nineteenth-century feminism was and remained an essentially middle-class movement.'[47]

In 1883, an act was passed which declared that canvassing and other election work could no longer be salaried. Suddenly, women found they were very much in demand as unpaid party workers, and women's auxiliaries of the main political parties were formed.[48] Clearly it was women's usefulness, rather than a sudden desire to see them involved in politics, that led to the formation of these societies. The Primrose League (Conservative) for example was always under male control, and the role of women in the League was essentially a social one 'acting as complements to the men'.[49] By including women in party work and using them as canvassers during elections, such organisations helped to divert attention away from the suffrage issue, and as Andrew Rosen notes, 'to make women feel that they were not altogether outcasts from the pole of the constitution'.[50] Significantly, between 1886 and 1892 the House of Commons did not once debate the issue of female suffrage. Within a nationalist perspective, the work of the Ladies Land League during the imprisonment of Charles Stewart Parnell and other leaders of the Land

League during the early 1880s, and their subsequent treatment by Parnell on his release can be seen as reflecting the pattern of political utilisation of women at times of difficulty allied to an unwillingness to treat them as equals.

The DWSA was not idle, however. Its general policy during 1881–94 is summarised in their 1918 Report:

> When any suffrage resolution or measure was before the House of Commons, letters were sent to all Irish members of Parliament urging them to support the measure. Letters were also sent to the Irish press, explaining the bearing of the particular measure, and asking all in sympathy with it to communicate with their local Parliamentary representative ... In 1886, twenty-seven petitions were sent to the House of Commons, and in 1890, seventeen.[51]

1884 saw a further extension of the male franchise. Attempts to secure an amendment to the bill seeking a measure of women's suffrage— supported by several Irish MPs—failed. Prime Minister Gladstone rejected such an amendment on the grounds that the proposed extension of the franchise already involved 'as much as ... it can safely carry'.[52] Increasingly the possibility of extending the franchise to women came to be viewed in terms of party politics over and above views on the status of women. The unknown effect of a new female electorate on the fortunes of political parties caused many politicians to hesitate.

In 1896 a bill was passed which allowed Irish women fulfilling certain property qualifications to serve as Poor Law guardians. There was some criticism of the bill in both houses. In the Commons one MP declared his opposition to bisexualism in public life,[53] while in the Lords, Viscount Clifden complained 'he did not like to see spouting women out of their place doing men's work', concluding that the effect of the bill would be to increase the power of priests on boards of guardians.[54] The bill—introduced by a supporter of the DWSA, William Johnston of Belfast—was subsequently enacted. In its Annual Report for 1896, the DWSA notes that already two lady guardians had been elected. The Association devoted much of its energies to informing women of their eligibility as electors and encouraging women to stand for election; in this regard in 1897 it published a leaflet 'Suggestions for Intending Lady Guardians'. In 1897, twelve women were elected as Poor Law Guardians; in 1898 the number rose to twenty-two. Membership and subscription numbers begin to increase from 1896, the report for 1897 advising members that 'this increase has been largely due to the inclusion of the Poor Law Guardian movement within your sphere of operations.' The organisation did not intend to sit on its laurels, however. Accepting the 1896 breakthrough as a welcome stepping stone, its report noted:

> There is nothing which has happened in our time that has imparted so powerful a stimulus ... to our fellow-countrywomen ... a stimulus (which) will be powerfully strengthened when in addition, they obtain the Country and the Municipal.[55]

During 1897, debate took place in the House of Commons on a proposed Local Government Bill for Ireland, and in particular on the proposed extension of the bill to include women. One MP, referring to the John Stuart Mill bill of 30 years earlier, commented that most MPs had considered women's franchise a huge joke. He objected to petticoat government, declaring that the vast majority of women recognised they were not fit to govern in the house, and did not wish to do so. A colleague warned that if ever women got into parliament, the end of the country was nigh.[56] Despite such reservations the Local Government bill introduced in February 1898 passed through both houses of parliament within six months. Local administration was to be distributed between County Councils, Urban District Councils, Rural District Councils and Boards of Guardians. The franchise for election to these bodies would be the parliamentary franchise, with the addition of Peers and Women, including lodgers. Under its terms, Irish women with certain property qualifications were granted the local government vote. As in England, women would be entitled to sit on district councils if elected, but *not* on county councils. The DWSA report for that year commented:

> It would be difficult to exaggerate the practical importance of this revolutionary measure. It has already enfranchised ... probably not fewer than one hundred thousand women; and there can be little doubt that in the course of the next few years a very large proportion of these will exercise the franchises now conferred on them.[57]

In the spring of 1899, eighty-five women were elected as Poor Law Guardians, thirty-one of these also being elected as Rural District Councillors. Four more were elected as Urban District Councillors. The DWSA had reason to be pleased and grounds for optimism. It pointed out that not just those newly elected, but also the new female electorate had participated in a significant new political experience. Like male Home Rulers, women would later point to their competency in local government as justification for greater responsibility. Events would show that women could not become complacent about their newly won rights. In 1903 attempts to have women Poor Law Guardians co-opted rather than elected 'to relieve them from the worry and turmoil of a popular election' reinforced the belief of suffragists that women must gain the parliamentary suffrage to ensure maintenance of existing rights.[58] The DWSA—under its new name of the Irish Women's Suffrage and Local Government Association (IWSLGA)—now set its sights firmly on attaining that goal. That crucial next step would prove difficult to attain, and twenty years would pass before a partial measure of parliamentary franchise was granted to women. Neither the Poor Law nor the Local Government provisions to Irishwomen had met with any serious opposition; both merely adjusted their position to that of their English counterparts. Nothing new or radical *per se* was involved. It could indeed be argued that the local government vote was granted with comparative ease to women throughout the British Isles precisely because it was a limited franchise. Significantly, women were disqualified from serving on county councils and boroughs in England and Wales until 1907, and in Ireland until 1911. In Ireland, these bodies were given the fiscal and administrative duties and powers formerly employed by Grand Juries.

It would appear that the more power connected with the office, the longer it was withheld from women. Despite the gradual admission of women to local government boards etc., their role on these was too often seen as an extension of their traditional role in the home. Their advice was welcomed in matters concerning the sick poor, and in the field of health, education and housing.[59] Undoubtedly, many women actively sought to change conditions in these areas, their philanthropic work and involvement in the women's movement having made them acutely aware of the appalling conditions endured by much of the population. But from a purely political point of view, within areas of finance and national politics, women's involvement was viewed as an encroachment on traditional male territory. With the explicit demand for parliamentary suffrage for women, attitudes on both sides became tougher and more emotional. Nonetheless, it is questionable whether even these limited franchises would have been introduced, had it not been for the constant agitation and pressure of the pioneer suffrage organisations during the nineteenth century.

Gains made for women 1859–1909

Year	Legislation
1870 1874 1882 }	Series of married women's property acts
1873	Mother allowed custody of children to 16 years
1859–1909	Series of educational gains: • Establishment of women's colleges • Intermediate Education Act • Admission to universities
1871 and 1876	Suffrage societies formed in Belfast and Dublin
1896	Women granted right to serve on Poor Law Guardian Boards
1898	Irishwomen granted Local Government vote

In addition to the campaigns for suffrage and for female education, there were two other significant issues which absorbed the time and energies of nineteenth-century activists—the campaign for the Repeal of the Contagious Diseases Acts, and the demand for Married Women's Property Rights.

MARRIED WOMEN'S PROPERTY RIGHTS

Nineteenth-century women of the middle and upper classes were not expected to earn their own living, but to remain dependent forever upon a man, initially their father, later their husband. Under the provisions of common law, a married woman could not own property in her own right; upon marriage a woman's property became her husband's. While many rich upper-class families could afford to arrange settlements for their daughters in advance of marriage to get around this provision, the majority of married women were not protected in this way. As with other laws affecting them, women's lack of a political voice left them unable to influence change in their favour; 'they were governed by laws made by men alone.'[60] From the mid-1850s, the embryonic women's movement developing in England included in its range of demands educational rights, expansion of employment opportunities, moral reform, and the right of married women to own property. One activist of the time summarised the legal position of married women in 1854 as follows, 'A man and wife are one person in law; the wife loses all her rights as a single woman, and her existence is, as it were absorbed in that of her husband.'[61] Thirteen years later, another woman involved with this pioneering group, Frances Power Cobbe (originally from Dublin), wrote:

> By the common law of England a married woman has not legal existence, so far as property is concerned, independently of her husband. The husband and wife are assumed to be one person, and that person is the husband. The wife can make no contract, and can neither sue nor be sued. Whatever she possesses of personal property at the time of her marriage, or whatever she may afterwards earn, or inherit, belongs to her husband, without control on her part.[62]

Cobbe went on to ask why this rule 'is generally considered expedient, yet invariably evaded by all who have means to evade it', pointing out that apart from those few able to evade its provisions, the law affected and left vulnerable 'the whole middle and lower ranks of women, and a certain portion of the upper ranks'. To Cobbe, the legal framework of marriage contributed to women's oppression. It was not just women's property that became their husband's; women themselves became part of their husband's property. Some reforms affecting married women emerged in Britain in the 1850s; an 1852 Act of parliament removed a husband's right to enforce cohabitation on his wife by issuing a writ of *habeas corpus* against anyone giving her shelter, and in 1857 a Divorce Act was passed. Prior to this, divorce was only possible through the costly process of obtaining a private Act of Parliament. Much remained to be attained, however. Until 1891 a husband retained the right to kidnap and imprison his wife, and the Divorce Act of 1857, while allowing a husband to divorce his wife on grounds of adultery, required a wife to prove a husband guilty of rape, sodomy or bestiality, or of adultery *in conjunction* with incest, bigamy, cruelty or desertion.[63]

Rafferty has pointed out that the legal system also deprived women of protection in cases of marital violence, noting that Cobbe saw such issues as inextricably linked with suffrage, 'It is one of the sore grievances of women in particular, that, not possessing representation, the measures which concern them are forever postponed.'[64] A committee of women was formed to petition for a Married Women's Property Bill in 1855. Eleven years later, some of this group were responsible for the first petition seeking female enfranchisement presented to the House of Commons by John Stuart Mill. Seeking as it did the extension of the franchise to 'all householders, without distinction of sex', the petition explicitly excluded married women, for married women could not be householders. Initial concern with franchise rights for widows and single women only, caused disagreement within early suffrage groups, some arguing that claims for voting rights on the same conditions as men logically excluded married women. Ultimately, the passing of a series of Acts allowing married women to own property in 1870, 1874 and 1882, removed this difficulty.

CONTAGIOUS DISEASES ACTS

While from the mid-nineteenth century women were becoming more active in a variety of campaigns as detailed above, Maria Luddy has pointed out that:

> It was not until the formation of an Irish branch of the Ladies' National Association for the Repeal of the Contagious Diseases Acts in 1870 that an organised and extended political campaign, based on a perception of sexual oppression and the rhetoric of gender difference, operated on a national scale.[65]

In an interview with Frank Sheehy Skeffington in 1914, Anna Haslam stated that the fight for repeal of the Contagious Diseases Acts (CDAS) 'threw the suffrage movement back for ten years, we were all so absorbed in it'.[66] In 1864 the first of three CDAS was introduced to control the spread of venereal disease among the soldiery; these allowed for the compulsory medical inspection of any woman suspected of being a prostitute in certain army camps in England and Ireland.[67] If found to be suffering from a venereal disease she was forcibly detained in a Lock Hospital (hospital for venereal diseases) for a period of up to nine months. There was no similar check on men. In Ireland the 'subjected districts' were Cork, Cóbh and the Curragh camp. Luddy has pointed out that:

> The acts subjected women who were on the street to arbitrary and compulsory medical examination. The introduction of the acts increased surveillance of the public activities of women; as there was no definition of the word prostitute made available to the police or the courts, all women were possible suspects.[68]

Quinlan has commented: 'the blatant double standard contained in the CDAS was the catalyst that moved women to organise and protest,' citing Keith Thomas that 'the Acts represented the high water mark of the double stand because of their bland assumption that prostitution was a permanent and necessary evil and by their direct application of the double standard in that all regulations and medical examination applied to the women alone'.[69] The use of the euphemism 'public woman' to describe prostitutes in the Acts, neatly illustrates the dominant 'separate sphere' ideology in which the woman was guardian of the private sphere with responsibility for the construction and maintenance of domestic and social order; the use of the word 'public' with 'woman' in the Acts signified the very antithesis of the feminine ideal.[70]

The acts heralded the beginning of the first women's organisation in Ireland. The Ladies' National Association for the Repeal of the Contagious Acts (LNA) was formed in England in 1869 by Josephine Butler; the National Association for the Repeal of the Contagious Diseases Acts (NARCDA) was formed the same year. Branches of both organisations were formed in Ireland; by 1871 the LNA had branches in Belfast, Dublin and Cork.[71] Although its membership was always small, the very existence of the LNA marked a new departure for Irish women. For the first time they were willing to discuss openly matters of sexual morality and to initiate a public campaign to question and alter the prevailing sexual double standard. There were a number of reasons for opposition to the acts; they were seen as an interference with civil liberties, as state recognition and support of vice, and the legitimisation of a double standard of sexual morality. Josephine Butler articulated the latter concern when she noted that the system ignored men, but treated women as commodities to be periodically cleansed and recycled as 'clean harlots for the army and navy'.[72] Both Isabella Tod and Anna Haslam were involved in the campaign from the beginning. Tod served on the executive of the London-based LNA until 1889 when Haslam took her place. Both women also served on the executive of the general council of the NARCDA. Women active in the movement in Ireland were predominantly Quaker (Isabella Tod was Presbyterian); very few if any were Catholic. There was considerable family support amongst repeal activists—many male members of the NARCDA were married or related to members of the LNA.[73]

In 1870 Thomas Haslam published a pamphlet on the Acts placing the blame for prostitution, 'one of the deadliest evils of our time', on male injustice and licentiousness. Analysing the causes of prostitution, he cited the lack of occupations open to women, the low pay of many men which did not allow them to marry, alcohol, and society's attitudes to women. Above all he maintained 'it is men's unchastity and men's injustice which are mainly responsible for this crying wrong.'[74] Quinlan has noted that the CDAS were not designed to rid the protected districts of commercial sex but rather to ensure that the concomitant venereal disease was held in check. Supporters of the Acts regarded prostitution as a necessary evil: 'Their concern was the provision of uninfected sex to military and naval consumers.'[75] The campaign continued in Ireland up to the mid-1880s, using similar methods to the suffrage campaign— petitions to parliament, distribution of pamphlets, fund-raising, and regular meetings. In 1878, the English founder of the LNA, Josephine Butler, addressed a public meeting at the Rotunda in Dublin. When Sir James Stansfield, MP, a leading advocate for repeal, rose to address the meeting, there were calls that women in the audience should be put out. The police had to be called and the meeting was abandoned due to disorderly conduct and heckling from the audience. Press coverage of this meeting revealed great unease with the involvement of 'ladies' in the movement, reaction ranging from the *Irish Times* shock at 'ladies taking part in the discussion of so unpleasant a subject' to the *Freeman's Journal* argument that 'we know little here about these Acts ... the necessity for them ... is happily not as great in Ireland as in England.'[76]

Anna Haslam quickly organised an alternate public meeting a few days later. At this meeting, Josephine Butler stressed the unity of women involved in the cause, a unity that levelled distinctions, commenting, 'We no more covet the name of ladies; we are all women.'[77] Generally Irish activists did not experience the same level of hostility as their English counterparts, Luddy noting however that the small number of LNA members in Ireland indicates how few were willing to be involved in such a campaign. Both Luddy and Cullen have pointed out that women who played an active role in the association were very courageous, having to breach many social and sexual taboos to campaign and speak at public meetings on an issue explicitly related to women's sexuality. When the wives of Henry Fawcett and P.A. Taylor addressed a suffrage meeting in 1869, the men were criticised in parliament for permitting their wives to behave in such 'advanced' and 'unsexing' a manner. That women now spoke out on such matters as venereal disease, prostitution and internal gynaecological examinations was unprecedented; one parliamentarian, referring to 'the revolt of women' as quite a new thing, asked 'what are we to do with such an opposition as this?'[78]

Summarising the effects of the campaign Luddy has noted:

For the women involved in the campaign there was an attempt made at a redefinition and representation of women and their relationship to men. The rhetoric of the campaign reveals the belief that it is 'womanhood' in the guise of the selfless, moral woman, which would bring change to society. For many activists women's moral nature, their imputed moral superiority, became the primary element in the concept of gender differences that emerged in the last decades of the nineteenth century.[79]

Another result of the repeal campaigns was the development of the Social Purity campaign. Initially seeking reform of male sexuality and the morals of the working classes, 'it eventually sought to regulate working-class behaviour—particularly that of working-class women —by methods ranging from philanthropic "rescue" work to vigilante activities.'[80] LNA supporters were initially involved, but as the movement became more repressive, many resigned. The Dublin White Cross Vigilance Association, formed in 1885 with Anna Haslam becoming its secretary, worked for 'the health and safety of women and girls and the purification of the moral atmosphere of society'.[81]

There is no doubt that the mobilisation of women in the campaign against the CDAS strengthened the campaign for women's suffrage. The acts were suspended in 1883, and repealed in 1886. The success of the campaign was cited by campaigners as proof of the effectiveness of women's activism. Isabella Tod wrote in 1885:

It was not only for the help which women must give to women, but even more, for the discharge of their special duty to the whole state (that) women are bound to demand their immediate admission within the electorate.[82]

Ironically, as Quinlan points out, by their protests against the CDAS, women activists were forced into the public arena, becoming 'public women', for which they were much criticised.

2

DEVELOPMENTS IN
FEMALE EDUCATION

*The restricted education offered to girls, at all social levels,
reflected society's attitude as to a woman's proper place.*
(MARIA LUDDY, *Women in Ireland 1880–1918*)

In 1790, the English historian Catherine Macaulay began a debate on
female education that would continue into the twentieth century. In
her *Letters on Education*, Macaulay advised parents: 'Confine not the
education of your daughters to what is regarded as the ornamental part
of it, nor deny the graces to your sons … Let your children be brought
up together; let their sports and studies be the same.'[1] This challenge to
Rousseau's theories on female education was continued by Mary
Wollstonecraft in her *Vindication of the Rights of Woman* when she wrote
in 1792:

> If women are in general feeble both in body and mind, it arises less
> from nature than from education. We encourage a vicious indolence
> and inactivity, which we falsely call delicacy; instead of hardening
> their minds by the severed principles of reason and philosophy, we
> breed them to useless arts, which terminate in vanity and sensuality.[2]

Four years later, the Rt Rev. George Horne, Bishop of Norwich, and
President of Magdalen College, Oxford, published in Dublin a work
entitled *Reflections on the importance of forming the female character by
education*. Arguing the case for the education of women, Horne stated
that if women are ignorant, it is through want of instruction, not of

capacity. His subsequent advice, however, that learned women exercise discretion and manage their learning— 'possess it as if they possessed it not'—and his argument that while different knowledge may be necessary for men and women, this should not mean that women are left in ignorance, pointed the way to the 'separate spheres' attitude that would dominate debate on female education into the twentieth century.

David Fitzpatrick has commented that 'Before the Famine most Irish women experienced neither education nor emigration. Later in the century, the majority experienced both.'[3] While men too experienced both phenomena, Fitzpatrick argues that for women the development over time was more remarkable. Key to such developments was a series of educational initiatives and economic developments during the course of the nineteenth century.

PRIMARY EDUCATION

1831 saw the introduction of the national school system in Ireland to provide basic literacy and numeracy at primary level to the poorer classes. The original intention that such schools be non-denominational did not find favour with either Catholic or Protestant clerics. Continuing a pattern of segregated education from the 'hedge-schools' and 'proselytising' school tradition of the eighteenth century, the majority of national schools developed as denominational. In fact, the national school quickly became the primary focus of religious instruction for girls and boys. By 1900 there were 8,684 national schools in operation, almost all of which were denominational.

Under this system, education became a right rather than a privilege, and was open to both girls and boys. The curriculum concentrated on reading, writing and arithmetic. While the initial programme drawn up in the 1830s held few gender differences, this soon changed with a strong emphasis emerging on domestic concerns and the acquisition of accomplishments for girls.[4] As a rule, girls were taught only basic arithmetical skills. Acceptance of the domestic sphere—whether in her own home or as a domestic servant—as the natural arena for girls dictated concentration on domestic skills. Girls' education was not deemed to be as important as that of their brothers, and they were more likely to be kept at home to help mothers with large families. Maria Luddy has pointed out:

The restricted education offered to girls, at all social levels, reflected society's attitudes as to a woman's proper place. Women's role was in the domestic sphere, and the care of children and husbands; cooking and cleaning did not, it was thought, require vast educational knowledge. Women were considered naturally inferior to men, their intellectual abilities less capable of development. God had created men and women for different purposes, and therefore with different attributes. Physical and intellectual labour suited men, while women were considered weak in mind and body.[5]

From the start of the new school system, a series of readers for use in the schools was produced by The Commissioners for National Education. With a standardised curriculum as the accepted basis, presentation within the readers reflected accepted societal ideals of the day. John Logan has noted that the readers 'conveyed a world view that emphasised respectful deference to hierarchy, the justness of a divinely sanctioned social structure and the appropriateness of the modest rewards that accrued to honest labour'.[6] Homely tales illustrated on the one hand the honest, hardworking labourer supported by a thrifty and inventive wife, while on the other hand was shown the squalid, complaining cottier with an extravagant, slovenly wife. The separate and subordinate place of woman was made quite clear in a reader published in 1846 which declared that it would teach her 'to know her place and her functions; to make her content with the one and willing to fulfil the other ... to render her most useful, more humble, and more happy'.[7]

A series of manuals produced over the coming decades reinforced the notion of 'separate though complementary spheres'. Needlework was the first subject made compulsory for older girls—and for trainee women teachers. In schools employing only male teachers the regulations allowed for the employment of a female 'work mistress'. Cookery was added to the female curriculum in 1847, and by the 1890s the female manual instruction curriculum, based on the core subjects of needlework and domestic economy included sewing, dressmaking, cookery, poultry and dairy management, laundry work and spinning. Manual instruction programmes initiated for boys included agriculture, drawing, navigation, commercial fishing, and handicraft. Logan notes that while setting out to ensure that their schools would have a central role in the development of the country's resources, the Commissioners' aim also ensured that 'its youth would be systematically initiated into appropriate and consequently separate occupations'.[8]

Regional and economic issues influenced educational involvement. Research has shown that in areas where child labour could still be profitable, education had a low value. This was particularly so in the case of girls, and counties such as Donegal and Derry where female labour was valued had low levels of female schooling.[9] Pre-famine, the number of female pupils was less than half that of male pupils, with the lowest female participation level occurring in the poorer and non-urbanised north and west. Post-famine, changing social and economic considerations caused Irish families to alter this pattern. In Connaught, female school attendance in 1841 was 71 per cent of male attendance; by 1881, the female attendance figure had risen to 106 per cent.[10] In a reversal of earlier patterns, from the 1870s young women were both more literate and likely to be English speaking.[11] Rhodes has noted that from the 1880s, the provinces of Leinster and Ulster—both with significant urban areas—were more likely to favour better male attendance while the educational differential was most advantageous to girls in the rural provinces of Connaught and Munster.[12] Important factors in the latter development were the decreasing need for female labour in family agriculture, allied to changing marriage patterns and increasing female emigration. This shift in female literacy was a rural phenomenon. High female illiteracy levels persisted in the cities of Dublin and Belfast into the early 1900s, 'Cities, unlike rural areas, provid(ing) female employment which occurred at the expense of schooling'.[13] Logan has noted that whereas until the 1880s the illiterates in the population had been among those most likely to emigrate, from then on the reverse was the case:

A period of schooling, now more widespread and cheaply available than ever before, became part of the preparation that an increasing number of girls—particularly in the western counties—made for a life in America, Britain or elsewhere.[14]

Kerby Miller has also drawn attention to the strong positive correlation between literacy and emigration, noting that post-1850 female literacy and emigration rose in tandem, eclipsing male rates in both respects by the century's end.[15]

While rural values allied to family economics combined to permit additional schooling for girls, the same process simultaneously limited schooling for their brothers. Poor school attendance by boys was aggravated by a shortage of manual labour on family holdings during busy seasons, allied to a belief that a limited education was sufficient for those who were destined to farm. Noting that in nineteenth-century

Europe investment in children's education was more likely to favour boys, Rhodes points out that in Ireland:

Family logic dictated that boys receive less schooling because of a greater expectation that they would remain at home on the land where for cultural and economic reasons additional schooling was believed unnecessary. The reverse was true for Irish daughters who were judged more likely than their brothers to live adult lives outside Ireland. The greater educational achievements of Irish daughters might be interpreted as a family tactic that was intended to ease their departure from home. If Ireland was unique in its female literacy and educational practices, that unconventionality might indeed be related to its anomalous position as the only country with a female-dominated emigration pattern.[16]

Until school attendance was made compulsory in 1892, attendance rates nationally were erratic. Many children—particularly girls—attended school only up to the age of nine or ten.[17] From 1892, girls' attendance rates increased to match that of boys. However, the pattern of early school leaving by boys in rural areas continued into the 1920s.

A key factor in female education from the mid-nineteenth century was the growing involvement of nuns in the national school system. The founders of the new Irish orders—in particular Nano Nagle (Presentation Sisters) and Catherine McAuley (Sisters of Mercy) regarded the education of children as the central plank of their philanthropy. Tony Fahey has pointed out that:

By participating (in nineteenth-century mass elementary schooling) nuns strengthened the Catholic Church's hand in education and so helped secure its position in nineteenth-century Ireland; they brought schooling to women and so affected the changing relationships of the sexes. More generally, however, they helped to develop and to extend to all the population the notion of long-term formal schooling as a necessity of childhood and a proper preparation for adult society.[18]

In this way, the nuns linked themselves to the secular project of social organisation, integrating mass populations into orderly, well-disciplined societies. As disseminators of a particular form of social and personal discipline and manners, and as champions of a particular ideal of femininity and women's place in society, they were very much in tune with the trends of their times. Primarily concerned with the education of poor girls, they viewed their teaching duties in religious terms, and were seen as 'paragons of educated bourgeois femininity' by the school inspectorate.[19] In 1853 there were 104 convent schools in the national system; by 1910 this had risen to 345. While still representing a small proportion of all national schools (2.2 per cent in 1853, 4.1 per cent in 1910), they incorporated a substantially larger proportion of the school population (11 per cent of average attendance in 1853, 17 per cent in 1910).[20]

Between 1832 and 1860 there occurred a dual process of change in Irish education. On the one hand 'the ordinary lay National School system took over the primary education of Irish children from the various pay (hedge) schools ... while within the National School system itself, convent national schools were absorbing lay female schools at such a rate that a Special Report on Convent Schools was commissioned by the National Board in 1860.'[21] This showed that convent national schools 'had already acquired an aura of respectability which drew all classes to them, including the middle class'. It was also shown that girls remained longer at convent national schools than at lay schools, often until their late teens. In this way, first- and second-level schooling often overlapped, there being as yet no formalised programme for second-level education for girls. The Commission's report also revealed class distinctions within convent national schools; often there were separate schools or departments for middle-class girls who were taught French and music, while some schools operated a separate school on Sunday for servant girls and those from labouring families, confined to basic reading, writing and religious instruction.

A related and significant development in the area of female education was the system of teacher training. Dominant opinion in the early nineteenth century held that teaching was properly a male domain, an opinion reinforced by the fact that the rural hedge-schools were run almost without exception by men. In 1870 the Powis Commission into Primary Education declared its intention of using female teachers only for 'sewing, or knitting, or platting straw, or other female work'.[22] The national school system involved the use of paid monitors, the lowest grade of teachers, who were examined annually on the books they would teach. Reflecting gender differences that had emerged within the educational system, female monitors were examined on different subjects than their male peers, thus ensuring the continuation of the 'separate spheres' approach. The majority of women teachers were either assistant teachers or paid monitors, with consequent low pay rates. Monitors were picked from among the brightest pupils in each national school district. The wider range of jobs available for boys resulted in less male participation as monitors. Due to the lack of employment opportunities for women, however, there was always a surplus of female monitors during the nineteenth century. This surplus was added to by the growing number of female monitors employed by convent national schools from the 1860s—in many cases due to the Catholic bishops' ban on state training facilities. As a result, convent schools increasingly produced girls trained to work either in national schools or as private governesses. An interesting result of this development was what has been described as 'the feminisation of teaching at national school level'.[23] Reflecting the increasing participation of girls in schooling, the number of female teachers rose from one-third of all teachers in 1840 to just over 50 per cent in the 1870s, a figure which continued to rise during the following decades.

By the end of the century, 49 per cent of national schools were single-sex, where men taught boys and women taught girls or infants. Such schools were almost all in towns with high child populations; in rural areas mixed schools were more common, and in these three-quarters of teachers were women. Many rural schools were two-teacher schools, with husband and wife teaching. Although central to the project of

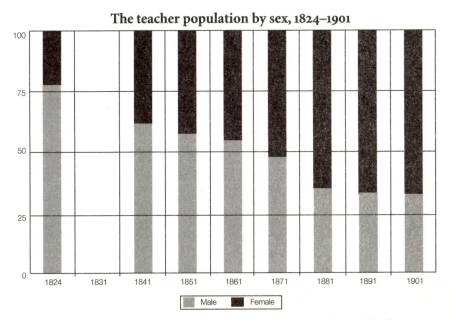

The teacher population by sex, 1824–1901

Taken from John Logan, *The Dimensions of Gender in Nineteenth-Century Schooling*, p. 47.

universal schooling, the female teacher was not rewarded on a similar basis to that of her male counterpart; from the beginning of national education her pay reflected both the lower status of female education and prevailing differences between male and female incomes. Initially paid 75 per cent of male rates rising to 80 per cent by the turn of the century, women teachers also suffered regarding promotion. Acceptance of the unsuitability of a female superior over a male colleague prevailed. While women comprised 55 per cent of all teachers in 1900, they held only 28 per cent of principalships, in each case as a sole teacher.[24] Nonetheless, for many women teaching became an attractive occupation that provided some degree of financial independence. Logan has pointed to two parallel effects of the expansion of female education from the mid-century. While providing occupational opportunity and financial security for many women teachers, it did so under conditions that required an unquestioning acceptance of an authoritarian and patriarchal structure. Regarding the content of education within the school system, he notes that 'it provided equality of access to a curriculum that emphasised and reinforced gender difference.'[25] Similarly Joe Lee has noted as ironic the fact that just when educational opportunities increased for Irish women, the educational system itself began to systematically indoctrinate them into adopting the prevailing male image of women:

> Literacy, for all its ultimate emancipatory potential, became in the short term another instrument for stifling independent thought. Dutiful woman teachers, including many dedicated nuns, taught girls obedience, docility and resignation to the role assigned to them by a male providence.[26]

SECONDARY-LEVEL EDUCATION

While primary-level education was state supported, second-level education was still regarded as a luxury, generally confined to the middle classes and to boys. Boarding schools for girls in nineteenth-century Ireland generally were the preserve of wealthy parents, and were run by branches of European religious orders much influenced by French convent tradition. Based on a hierarchic view of society, with different roles for men and women, the emphasis within these schools was on producing young ladies of refinement, trained in accomplishments and the social graces. The future role of such girls was viewed within the family sphere, as wife and mother. The following extract from an advertisement placed in the *Catholic Directory* in 1880 by one such convent in Wexford run by the Sisters of St Louis of France was typical:

> The deportment and manners of the pupils are scrupulously attended to; no efforts are spared to give the young ladies habits of order and neatness, that they may return to their families not only accomplished but helpful and intelligent in all the duties of woman's sphere.[27]

Clerical support favoured such an approach. Dr Paul Cullen, Roman Catholic archbishop of Dublin, 1852–78, was one such powerful advocate. Commenting on the high school movement then emerging in England (which placed emphasis on public examinations and the inclusion of Mathematics and Latin in all curricula), Cullen argued that a woman's role in society still lay within the family structure, and that the whole emphasis should, therefore, be on the religious and domestic aspects of her education, rather than on the secular and public. In support of his views, Cullen quoted St Paul:

> Teach the young women to be wise, to love their husbands, to love their children; to be discreet, chaste, sober, having a care of the house, gentle, obedient to their husbands, that the word of God be not blasphemed.[28]

Not surprisingly, it was during Cullen's period of office that the majority of French teaching orders of women were introduced into Ireland. By the end of the nineteenth century sixty-two convent boarding schools had been established in Ireland, only six of which were run by Irish religious orders. Thus, girls' secondary education in Ireland was dominated by orders whose traditions and educational ethos originated outside Ireland.[29] With the emergence of an Irish Catholic middle class in the latter half of the nineteenth century, Anne O'Connor has noted that 'in the quest for social prestige through education Irish convent boarding schools supplied a certain status to their pupils which ensured the survival of these traditions until the mid-twentieth century'.[30] Although the French orders did provide day schools for the primary education of the poor, the majority were fee-paying boarding schools, catering for the middle classes. As such, they acquired a status denied to Irish religious orders, whose primary role was seen as catering for the education of the poor. With the growth and development of Irish female religious orders during the nineteenth century, there emerged a system of convent fee-paying day schools aimed at the lower middle classes who could not afford to send their daughters to boarding school. These were started by the Mercy and Presentation sisters. By 1879 there were 46 of these 'pay' or 'pension' schools based in the large towns and cities. The majority of girls who attended these schools were the daughters of prosperous farmers and shopkeepers who could afford to keep them at school until they were fifteen or sixteen years old.[31]

Class distinctions endemic in Irish society at this time were a prime reason for the growth and success of these schools, all of which sought to retain education for girls on class lines. This is confirmed by the views expressed by James Kavanagh, professor in the Catholic University to the Powis Commission on primary education in the late 1860s. Commenting specifically on convent pension schools, Kavanagh noted that they were 'Intermediate or middle class schools, ranked above the primary while being below the regular convent boarding school'.[32] He considered that there was 'no real distinction in principle' between these day pension schools and convent boarding schools, apart from being 'an acknowledgement of the social distinctions that existed in society'. Catherine McAuley's decision to affiliate her primary schools with the National Board while also establishing day pay schools for the middle classes would have far-reaching implications for the future of girls' education in Ireland. Unlike the Christian Brothers who opted out of both these schemes, the decision of female religious orders such as the Mercy and Presentation to run both free and fee-paying schools for girls reinforced existing class distinction within Irish society. Both types of school ran parallel to each other in the same building, catering for the same age range—the difference based on fees or free. The natural development of pension schools into full secondary schools was hindered by the fact that girls stayed on longer at convent national schools, and the pension schools remained as small private schools.

It was not until the introduction of the Intermediate Education Act of 1878 that a clear model of secondary education emerged. Despite this, O'Connor argues, both the convent national school and the convent pay school mark two of the most important developments in the education of Catholic girls in the nineteenth century: 'They were the only schools which gave their pupils the opportunity to move upward in society, catering as they did for both their primary and secondary education.'[33] A third important development was the establishment of a number of non-Catholic schools concerned with a pragmatic and liberal education for girls.

The establishment of the Ladies' Collegiate school in Belfast (1859), the Queen's Institute (1861) and Alexandra College (1866) in Dublin, initiated new directions for second level schooling. Aspiring to the English High School model with emphasis on public examinations and the inclusion of Latin and Mathematics in the curriculum, initially these institutions sought to provide vocational skills to their students and an education comparable to that available to boys at second level. The founders of these institutes—Anne Jellicoe and Margaret Byers—sought reform in the existing education provisions for girls, an extension of the range of subjects currently available, while providing training to middle-class women to enable them to earn their living. Another woman prominent in this movement was Isabella Tod who founded the Ladies' Institute in Belfast in 1867. 'The establishment of these institutions paved the way for demands in legislative reform in girls' secondary education, and also for women's entrance into university.'[34]

Perhaps the most significant breakthrough in the education of girls was the passing of the Intermediate Education Act of 1878. This was followed in 1879 by the Royal University Act of Ireland. Both Acts recognised for the first time the principle that girls and women had the right to sit for public competitive examinations and to take university degrees. Anne O'Connor has pointed out that 'the fact that public opinion in Ireland was at first generally against such examinations for girls, and that many girls did not have either the opportunity or the means to take immediate advantage of either of these Acts, does not alter their crucial importance as a force for changing the role of women in Irish society'.[35] The introduction of the Intermediate examination system forced into the open the diametrically opposed views held on both girls' education and women's role in society. Passed in an attempt to improve school attendance and educational standards, as well as to provide a good basis for university entrance, the Intermediate Education Act was originally aimed only at boys' schools. Cardinal Cullen had made known to the Chief Secretary his opposition to the inclusion of girls' schools in the scheme. Many Irish MPs also were not in favour of extending the Act to include girls, the leader of the Home Rule Party, Isaac Butt, commenting that 'the cry for Intermediate Education in Ireland had no reference whatsoever to girls'.[36] Disagreement among MPs was based on opposition to the idea of equal education for the sexes, allied to the grievance that the inclusion of girls limited prizes available for boys. Speedy and intensive pressure by Isabella Tod and Margaret Byers on government ministers, allied to petitions from Alexandra

College, the Queen's Institute, the Governess Association of Ireland, and a memorial signed by ninety MPs and other supporters, resulted in the Act being extended to girls' schools: 'It was English influence which was the crucial factor in obtaining the inclusion of girls in the Intermediate Education Act, (and) many Irish MPs believed conditions in Ireland were not ripe for complete equality between girls and boys as regards public competitive examinations.'[37] Under the provisions of the Act, secondary schools were funded indirectly by the awarding of prizes to schools based upon annual examination results. National schools were excluded from results fees, and as pointed out by O'Connor, 'these now began to assume their proper role as feeders to convent pension schools.'[38]

Particularly significant for the future development of girls' education was the system of competitive examinations organised by the Intermediate Board of Education. Three different grades were devised, aimed at three different age groups. Insistence on this, in addition to the widening of subject areas, imposed a long-needed structure on secondary schooling. Also significant was the marking system used; while there was a great deal of flexibility in the choice of subjects, it was mandatory that candidates include two of the following—Latin, Greek, English, Mathematics and modern languages. In practice certain subjects were awarded much higher marks than others. English, Greek and Latin were each awarded 1200 marks, while German and French were awarded 700. Consequently there was a strong incentive for schools to teach the former. This secondary system gave a new generation of young women access to the world of competitive examinations, with recognition and reward for academic endeavour.[39] One quarter of those sitting the first public examination in 1879 was female. While girls and boys were examined separately, examinations and rewards were the same for both, and the impressive results of female candidates validated the claims made by campaigners and encouraged curriculum development in girls' schools. Money prizes at each level went direct to the students, with the schools being awarded 'results fees' on each subject passed by a student. While initially public opinion did not favour such examinations for girls, the prestige attached to winning such prizes, emphasised by the publication of school results with details of prizes awarded etc., created a competitive spirit between schools which would soon be played out in academic rivalry between Catholic and Protestant schools.

Participation by convent schools in the Intermediate examination system would be crucial for third level access by Catholic women. While Catholic clergymen continued until the mid-1880s to oppose the

Intermediate system of examination for girls, a small but significant group of middle-class parents began to exercise pressure on them to provide a new type of convent education that would focus on competitive examinations, both under the Intermediate Board and those of the Royal University.[40] In 1887, the *Freeman's Journal,* reporting on the Intermediate results for that year noted that while convent schools had shown their superiority in the teaching of modern languages, they were completely outpaced by their Protestant rivals because of their lack of mathematics. The paper's editorial urged convent schools to adjust their system of teaching to suit the requirements of the Intermediate system.[41]

During the 1890s increasing numbers of convent schools throughout the country became successful participants in the Intermediate system. In 1893, twenty-nine convent schools featured in the results lists; by 1898 this number had risen to forty-five. Increasingly during the 1890s, the emphasis within participating Catholic schools became one of rivalry for results with Protestant schools. Eibhlín Breathnach has noted:

> The capture of convent education by the English values of examination and certification is one of the most interesting developments of this period. The fact that Catholic male education had no difficulty at all in this regard merely highlights the difference in the perceptions of the roles of men and women. The lure of examination fees and the desire to prove that Catholic girls could compete on equal terms with their Protestant peers contributed to the gradual involvement of girls' schools within the Intermediate system.[42]

Referring to a speech by Archbishop Walsh of Dublin in 1894 when he stated that the battle for supremacy in examination results was only starting, O'Connor points out that Walsh was well aware that Alexandra College and School and the Ladies Collegiate School in Belfast—among the most consistent contenders for first place in Intermediate results—benefited greatly from the higher standard of staff and lecturers available due to their university classes. In turn, these high standards attracted particularly able students. Thus 'the first tentative links between girls' higher and Intermediate education was being forged out in the 1890s by this desire to defeat the Protestant girls' schools and colleges in the Intermediate prize lists.'[43] While running a close second on a number of occasions, in 1901 the first convent school succeeded in defeating its Protestant rivals by gaining first place in the overall list with thirty-nine distinctions. Dominican Convent Eccles Street was the school in question; other significant achievements by the Dominicans during this period were the winning of the mathematics medal in both Middle and Junior grades in 1900—both medals long regarded as 'the property of Ulster Protestant schools'.[44]

The nineteenth-century 'university question' and the issue of suitable education for Irish Catholics has been described as 'one of the religio-political questions which Catholic emancipation had left unsolved'.[45] Against this background, the effect of the Intermediate Education Act allied to the Royal University Act of the following year would be immense, preparing a new generation of confident and ambitious leaders. The number of candidates taking the examination increased from 3,945 in 1879 to 11,900 in 1910.[46] Describing the emerging educated youth as 'the nucleus for the later developments of nationalism' one commentator observed in 1918 that 'to understand Irish politics one must ignore the farmer for the moment and look to that epochal event in Irish history, the Intermediate Education Act of 1878'.[47] Noting a confident *Irish Catholic* editorial in 1903 that documented the changes brought to Irish society by the extension of educational opportunity, Paseta has noted:

> Contemporary observers thus understood that education signified more than the acquirement of intellectual capital. It promised opportunity, a rise in confidence and the growth of a powerful, articulate and determined class of Irish men and women.[48]

That increased confidence and articulation would be demonstrated both in the campaign for higher education for women, and in later campaigns for political equality.

1879 ROYAL UNIVERSITY ACT

In 1879 the government established the Royal University of Ireland (RUI). Under this new Act, the existing Queen's Colleges at Belfast, Cork and Galway remained in existence, the Royal University being constituted as an examining body only. Importantly, however, its degrees and scholarships were open equally to men and women, unlike the existing universities which barred women. Public response to the new opportunities for women was muted, the demand for such access having been confined mainly to the pioneering groups of educationalists in Dublin and Belfast. 1882 saw the formation in Dublin of an association entitled The Central Association of Irish Schoolmistresses and other

Ladies Interested in Education (CAISM).[49] This group, with branches in Belfast, Cork, Galway and Derry, aimed to keep a watching brief over the interests of girls within the Intermediate education system and to promote higher education for women in Ireland. A particular problem for aspiring women students was that although they were eligible to sit the examinations of the new body and be awarded its degrees, there were no educational arrangements in place to prepare them for these examinations. Women preparing for such degrees had no choice but to study in private colleges set up specifically for this purpose. The first nine women graduates in 1884 had used a variety of teaching arrangements to prepare for their degrees, in sharp contrast to facilities available to their male peers.[50] Both Victoria College in Belfast and Alexandra College in Dublin had opened separate collegiate departments, employing masters and university lecturers to prepare their students to university level. With no Catholic schools offering similar facilities, Catholic women undergraduates had no option but to attend one of these colleges, and many Dublin women in particular attended Alexandra College. Of the 152 women who graduated from the Royal University between 1884 and 1892, the majority had received their education from Protestant schools and colleges.[51]

The Catholic hierarchy, responding to the growing volume of public opinion on the need for change, and recognising the wisdom of making separate provision for young Catholic women, gave permission for a number of new educational establishments. In Dublin, the Dominican convent in Eccles Street, founded in 1883, was the first convent collegiate school set up specifically to cater for Catholic women. Initially preparing girls for the Intermediate examinations, in 1885 university classes were established at the convent. These continued until 1893 when the college was transferred to Merrion Square in Dublin, and renamed St Mary's University and High School 'for the purpose of affording Catholics ladies complete facilities for higher education in all its branches'.[52] Loreto College, also established in the early 1890s at St Stephen's Green, provided university classes from 1895. In Cork city, a new Ursuline day convent school called St Angela's High School for Girls was established in 1887. Immediately successful in the Intermediate examinations, within three years St Angela's was authorised by the bishop to provide university classes in preparation for RUI examinations. Reflecting Intermediate Examination rivalry between Catholic and Protestant schools, the *Freeman's Journal* reported the awarding of 1st prize in her MA to Katherine Murphy, a student of the Dominican convents in Sion Hill and

Eccles Street. Along with a studentship prize of £300, her achievement was celebrated with a *Te Deum* and was hailed publicly as a Catholic victory over the Protestants.[53]

Allied to the development of women's colleges, many women sought admission to undergraduate classes at the established universities. During the 1880s, the three Queen's colleges gradually conceded on this point. First Belfast, then Cork and Galway admitted women to attend lectures in preparation for RUI examinations. The Catholic bishop of Galway F.J. McCormack was not impressed, issuing a declaration forbidding Catholic girls in the diocese from attending.[54] In Dublin, University College, run by the Jesuit order held fast against permitting women attend lectures, its opposition surpassed in intensity only by the board of Trinity College, the latter arguing its concern for the morals of its male students should women be admitted. Despite the strong performance by women graduates each year, questions over the long-term existence of the RUI cast doubt on the viability of women's colleges. Describing the status of the RUI as a temporary resolution of the vexed university question in Ireland, Breathnach has noted that 'any final solution was expected to include attendance requirements as a prerequisite for the awarding of degrees. At such a stroke the women's colleges, both Catholic and Protestant, would be faced with immediate closure, and Protestant women would be offered the unpalatable choice of a degree in a Catholic university or no degree at all.'[55]

With the gradual admission of women to established colleges from the 1880s, differences began to emerge among women educationalists on the question of full or partial integration by women into university life. By the early 1900s these differences were being articulated within the CAISM and the newly formed Irish Association of Women Graduates and Candidate Graduates (IAWGCG). While seeking full status for women within the formal university structure, many women's colleges sought to retain their separate collegiate organisation rather than embrace full integration. A number of women graduates opposed this stance. Agnes O'Farrelly arguing on behalf of the IAWGCG, declared, 'We don't want women to be shut into women's colleges.'[56] The trend towards full integration continued, with University College admitting second and third year honours students to lectures from 1902. Two years later, in 1904, Trinity College finally agreed to the admission of women students.[57]

It has been argued that both the national school and university systems introduced in nineteenth-century Ireland were essentially post-industrial constructs in a pre-industrial society.[58] Unlike other countries where educational expansion followed industrial growth, the Irish education system expanded in a country virtually untouched by the industrial revolution outside the north-east. Thus, the economic and occupational background of students in Ireland was quite different from their English and Scottish counterparts. Of the two systems, the majority to benefit most from the national school were Catholics, while initially Protestants benefited most from the Queen's colleges. At second and third level, although neither the intermediate system nor the Royal University satisfied all parties, both were remarkably progressive, allowing for the education of all students irrespective of denomination to whom all prizes and examinations were open.[59] In particular, they provided for the education of women on an unprecedented scale; despite ongoing obstacles, women now legally had full educational equality with men. By 1899, women had availed of this opportunity to the extent that the number of girls taking the intermediate examinations had grown by 300 per cent compared to a 190 per cent growth in the number of male candidates.[60]

In 1908 the Royal University was dissolved, the Universities Act of that year establishing two new universities, Queen's University in Belfast and the National University with three constituent colleges in Dublin, Cork and Galway. Trinity College remained as before. Women and men were now accepted equally to all degrees and teaching. With attendance at all lectures and tutorials now compulsory, the need for separate ladies' colleges disappeared. Despite strong attempts by the Loreto and Dominican orders to retain women's colleges for the education of their own nuns, this marked the end of women's colleges. Male and female higher education was now fully integrated—legally at least.

The formation of the IAWGCG in 1902 to represent women from all third-level colleges, irrespective of denomination, was a significant departure from most denominationally-based male organisations. Co-operation between Catholic and Protestant women on common problems faced in advancing women's access to all facets of third-level education was indicative of a high level of net-working between women that would become particularly significant in the suffrage campaign from 1908. Breathneach has commented that through the work of CAISM and the IAWGCG women took charge of their own educational concerns:

> They formulated policies which they represented to government commissions. They acted as watchdogs ensuring that the benefits extended to women by the Royal University Act were not eroded. Their espousal of the principle of integration helped to prevent the

relegation of women's higher education to second-rate status. Less tangible, but of great significance, was their work in winning acceptance of the idea of higher education for women.[61]

From their first admittance to Royal University degrees in the 1880s, up to and including their admission into Trinity College and full integration under the 1908 Universities Act, women students remained under intense scrutiny about their academic achievements, their morality and their appearance. In 1915, the UCD student journal, the *National Student*, published a satiric version of the rules regarding female students:

COLLEGE RULES
For the observance of all students

(a) *Lady Students*
1. No Lady Student is to have hair of the same colour as any male student.
2. No Lady Student is to have feet of the same size as any male student. A register of measurements is taken at entrance, and will be strictly adhered to. No credit will be given for attendance at lectures till these measurements have been taken.
3. Lady Students are debarred, under penalty of rustication, from appearing without at least four chaperons within three miles of St Stephen's Green.
4. No Lady Student is to reside within a radius of ten miles from a male student.
5. Lady Students are not to be seen in Grafton Street or its purlieus after 1 p.m. The DMP have orders from the competent military authority to deport them if seen.
6. No Lady Student is allowed to have more than one inch and three-quarters' length of hair showing beneath her hat.
7. If a Lady Student sees a male student in the College she is to do penance in sackcloth and ashes for the space of one calendar month.
8. Lady Students who read a publication illegally known as the *National Student* are, if discovered, to be publicly decapitated by the Professor of Modern Irish History, of whose duties this shall be one.
9. If a Lady Student is seen speaking to or holding any communication with a student of All Hallows or Clonliffe Colleges, the said student shall be reported to the College of Cardinals, and may incur loss of all

chances of becoming an archbishop.

10. Lady Students may be allowed to walk abroad for fresh air for a maximum period of three minutes per diem. (See Rules 3, 4, 5).

(b) *Male Students*

1. Spitting in the College premises is absolutely forbidden. Permission to be absent from lectures may be obtained in order to allow students to remove themselves to a safe distance while doing so.

2. Smoking is prohibited in all parts of the college except the Students' Room. Students discovered in the practice of this disgusting habit will, after thorough disinfection, be reprimanded over the telephone by the President.

3. No Student is to be discovered in possession of the soi-disant *National Student* (see (a) Rule 8), under pain of fifty strokes on the feet with the bastinado.

4. Any student who wilfully and with malice aforethought sees a Lady Student (except as provided for in these rules) is to be handed over to one of the Deans of residence to undergo spiritual torment for five calendar months. A second offence is to be punished by a year in a reformatory.

5. All meetings, conventicles, or other assemblages of more than two students are bound to submit reports of their proceedings to the President.

6. No student is to be heard mentioning the words 'Kaiser', 'Germany', 'McNeill' or 'Casement' without qualification, and without express permission from the academic council.

6 (b) Students are forbidden to reside in lodgings which have casements. Wherever such are present they must be replaced by French windows. The penalty for infringement of rules 6 and 6 (b) is compulsory enlistment in the OTC.

(c) *General*

1. Lady Students are to be on show for five minutes daily behind barbed wire in the Aula Maxima. All duly registered students of the College, who have paid their fees, will be admitted.

Integration as such did not automatically bring full participation by women at third level. Social constraints and continuing conservative attitudes regarding the role of women were still forces to be reckoned with. The 'modern woman' created by such educational opportunities became a term of derision.[62] In 1900 Bishop O'Dwyer of Limerick had lamented the plight of young men forced to marry 'useless and hopeless women', arguing 'what we want is to make them good housewives. This could be done by educating them in cooking, laundry and needlework.'[63] Writing in 1913 on the true role for women, D.M. O'Kane argued:

> The great Doctors of the Church affirm unanimously the inferiority of women in the intellectual order. This is by no means intended as a reflection of her dignity, as this inferiority arises from the *role* (sic) nature has destined her to fulfil in the drama of life. She eliminates the abstract from her intellectual activity, and seeks triumph in the sensible and the ideal, in which the imagination plays the leading part.[64]

The middle-class nature of demands for higher education did not reflect changed societal attitudes towards women. A frequently used argument in defence of women's demands for access to higher education was that an educated woman would make a better mother: 'Marriage and child-bearing remained the unchallenged goals for women and women graduates who worked automatically gave up on marriage.'[65] Among those graduates who worked, teaching became the main available option, the professions remaining the preserve of men: 'Though Catholic orders took up the challenge with considerable success, Catholic Ireland never fully embraced the goals of higher education ... With the setting up of the new state other forces came into play and the more traditional, Catholic image of women gradually came to dominate.'[66]

TWO NEW STATES

The partition of the country that followed the 1920 Government of Ireland Act resulted in the implementation of differing educational formulae by the two new governments. South of the border, such changes as occurred up to the 1960s were primarily administrative. In 1924, all existing school types were brought under the control of the newly formed Department of Education. Primary, secondary and technical education would be the responsibility of the Minister of Education. In an attempt to impose some control on teaching standards, the Department introduced a voluntary primary certificate examination in 1929. Due to the lack of compulsion only a small number of pupils took this examination. It was not until 1943 that the exam was made mandatory. Concerned with the quality of candidate teachers, the

Department established a number of Preparatory Training Colleges in 1926 for the secondary education of future primary teachers.[67] At second level an important initiative in 1924 was the abolition of the current 'payment-by-examination-results' system of grants to schools. This was replaced by a capitation grant paid for each child following an approved course.[68] Two new examinations at second level were introduced, the Intermediate Certificate Examination to be taken by students after three or four years, followed by the Leaving Certificate Examination after a further two years. The Department also insisted that school managers give teachers security and pay a minimum wage, the state paying a proportion of teachers' salaries. Simultaneously, it insisted on minimum academic qualifications for secondary teachers in the form of a Higher Diploma in Education awarded by universities.[69]

In 1926, an Act was passed to enforce the attendance of children at school between the ages of six and fourteen years. An earlier school attendance Act in 1892—which applied primarily to urban areas—had been largely unsuccessful, and had been opposed by the Catholic bishops as an infringement of parental rights.[70] Under the provisions of the 1892 Act, pupils between the ages of 11 and 14 were allowed to have part-time employment.[71] By 1921 the average school attendance of children less than fourteen years was only about 50 per cent. In the midst of the Anglo-Irish war, the 'First National Programme' on the school curriculum, drafted at a conference held by the Irish National Teachers' Organisation noted that 'the average school leaving age in Ireland was eleven years, much too low'.[72] Poor levels of school attendance were inextricably linked with child labour, particularly on small farms. While the importance of juvenile family labour varied from area to area, a significant number of small farmers were entirely dependent on family labour, particularly along the western seaboard. This issue continued to be debated during the following decades, with reports being presented in the 1930s and 1950s on proposals to raise the school-leaving age. The 1926 Act, however, did result in a perceptible improvement in attendance.[73]

Attempts over the next thirty years to raise the school leaving age all failed, on economic and parental rights grounds. Kennedy has noted that the 1926 Census showed that one quarter of all young persons between the ages of 14 and 15 years were in occupations, 30 per cent of the boys and 17 per cent of the girls. Agricultural occupations were dominant for the boys and non-agricultural occupations for the girls. The school leaving age remained at 14 years until 1972 when it was raised to 15 years.[74]

The Vocational Education Act of 1930 has been described as revolutionising the role of technical schools.[75] The system of technical education inherited by the new government had been of a very basic level. Under the general control of the Minister, the 1930 Act established 38 vocational educational committees throughout the country to be selected by the local rating authorities, and to include representatives from local educational, cultural, commercial and industrial interests.[76] In addition to providing technical instruction, a significant new departure was that such schools would in future provide 'continuation' education in general subjects for pupils who left primary school at the age of 14 years. Vocational schools established under this Act provided an alternative form of post-primary education, less expensive and less academically intensive than fee-paying secondary schools. Seán Ó Catháin has commented:

> By the act of 1930 the Department of Education raised the level of general education for many children who might otherwise have finished their schooling with the primary School, and provided opportunities for a higher degree of technical efficiency so vital in the economic life of the new state.[77]

Ó Catháin also referred to the practical training provided by Vocational Schools to prepare boys and girls for a trade, and to the steady expansion of new apprenticeship training in these schools. Yet, as noted in Lyons, the curriculum followed in the 'continuation' programme was quite different for boys and girls. While Irish and English were taught to all, otherwise the emphasis for boys was on woodwork, metalwork, mechanical drawing and mathematics, and for girls on domestic economy and commercial subjects.[78] With the general exclusion of women from trades, the technical and apprenticeship aspect of the vocational school curriculum was largely irrelevant to women. Rather than marking a new departure for female education, the gender ethos of vocational schools reflected that of second-level education generally. A former vocational teacher, Robert O'Connor, recalled that the official philosophy of such education in rural areas was to keep as many young people as possible on the land, a philosophy rigorously pursued by the Department of Education: 'Boys were to be taught rural science and woodwork to make them better farmers; girls were to be taught domestic economy and some rural science to make them good farmers' wives.'[79]

However, official philosophy was at variance with the ideas of the pupils who attended such schools. Echoing nineteenth-century reaction to schooling as preparation for emigration, O'Connor notes:

> They came for one purpose only, to get an off-farm job. There was no future in being a farmer or a farmer's wife unless you had a very large farm. The boys came to schools specifically to learn woodwork and become carpenters. They tolerated other subjects for the sole purpose of getting the woodwork instruction. The girls gave domestic science a very low rating. They saw no future in it. They wanted to do shorthand, typing and commercial subjects so as to get office jobs.[80]

Despite its aims to provide education for the less well-off, and to retain young people in rural Ireland, the vocational educational system, which was outside church control, was often the object of heavy criticism by some of the hierarchy. In particular Bishop Michael Browne of Galway was very scathing about the system, with the *Irish Independent* describing the schools as 'godless' institutions.

State policy to work for the restoration of Irish as the common language of the country would significantly influence official attitudes towards school curricula and examination results. The establishment of the Department of Education, headed by a cabinet minister, strengthened the hand of the government in applying a policy of language revival. A 'Second National Programme' took effect in 1926, aimed at 'strengthening the national fibre by giving the language, history, music and traditions of Ireland their natural place in the traditions of Irish schools'.[81] Bonus payments were paid to teachers who taught through Irish, all teachers were required to pass an oral examination, and most controversial of all, the use of English was barred from infant classes. In 1928, Irish became an essential subject on the school curriculum, and in 1934, success in it was made a condition of passing the certificate examinations.[82] Akenson has noted that 'from being just one subject of the school curriculum it (Irish) became, overnight, the dominant subject'.[83] Lee has argued that the emphasis on teaching infants in the national schools exclusively through Irish—which resulted in the curtailment of other subjects—provided one further bulwark for the existing social structure in that it inevitably discriminated against already deprived children.[84]

None of the measures introduced in the early decades of the new state promoted an ideal of equality of opportunity in education. Akenson has pointed to the inherent social and educational assumptions of the 1926 School Attendance Act, noting that a primary education was considered sufficient for the bulk of the population, and that it was predicated upon changing the *status quo* as little as possible.[85] Lee too has noted that 'the existing educational system was devoted to the defence of the social structure'. Commenting that the state did little for the poor, he argues that based on the fees system, entry to secondary schools and universities was effectively restricted to the socially comfortable classes: 'As late as 1932, 93 per cent of children did not proceed beyond primary education.'[86]

A number of historians have commented that apart from the administrative changes outlined above, and government policy towards the gaelic revival, there was little change in the structure and control of Irish schools after independence. Seán Ó Catháin has noted: 'Except for the Preparatory Colleges, there was no attempt at State ownership of the schools. The primary and secondary schools remained essentially what they had been: private institutions supported financially in varying degrees by public money and theoretically free to conduct their own affairs.'[87] Terence Brown has commented: 'The general profile of the educational system bequeathed by the departing colonial power remained, even as late as the early 1960s, essentially unchanged.'[88] F.S.L. Lyons has observed that while post-1922 the organisation of education was centralised, neither the primary nor the secondary schools were state-owned, with direct control and appointment of teachers remaining in the hands of the managers, who were overwhelmingly clerical. Lyons does however point out that in addition to the financial pressure it could bring to bear, 'the Department's power to inspect schools and to conduct the public examinations gave it a decisive influence over the development of both the national and secondary programmes.'[89] Brown too has noted that while little educational restructuring had taken place in the first forty years of independence, 'the state, through the Department of Education, had made strenuous efforts over the years to ensure that uniformity of curricula and standards was achieved and maintained.'[90] Akenson concludes that, apart from its propagation of the Irish language, the new government appears not to have been greatly concerned with education. In particular he notes the lack of Dáil time spent discussing education, comparing it particularly with developments in Northern Ireland, where radical reconstruction of the school system was under debate.[91]

Yet, as Kennedy points out, parents were seeking more education for their children, as indicated in the steady rise in school enrolments in the decades before the introduction of free post-primary education. The 1929 figure of 38 per cent of 14–16 year olds in full-time education rose to 42 per cent in 1944 and to 51 per cent in 1962. In 1946, the share of 14–19 year olds in full-time education was 24 per cent; by 1966 that figure had risen to 41 per cent. Of those taking the Intermediate Board examinations before 1922 girls comprised 25–30 per cent of the total; by the early 1950s the numbers of girls sitting the Intermediate Certificate equalled that of boys.[92] In Humpreys' 1951 study of Dublin families, marriage, or the lack of it, is noted among the factors influencing parents regarding second-level education for their daughters. One artisan family stated:

> Most people like ourselves, if it were a question of choosing between a boy or a girl for secondary school, would send the girl, because it would give her a better chance for a good marriage … If a girl dresses well and has the background so that she can meet any type of people and talk with them and hold her own, she has a much better chance of making a good marriage and that is much more necessary for her than for a boy. A boy will get along if he has a good trade and the ability … Education means much more for a girl here than for a boy.[93]

The possibility that a girl might not marry was also a consideration; artisan parents believed that with education 'a good job would stand a girl in good stead throughout her life.'[94] Moving upwards through what Humphreys describes as 'the prism of class', second-level education for girls appears the norm among the various levels of 'clerical and managerial' middle-classes, with the opportunity of university education for girls increasing as one proceeds through those classes. Farmar has highlighted the extent of snobbery in South Dublin in the early 1960s, citing a *Sunday Review* journalist's comment: 'Girls are sent to college not to broaden their education but to meet the right people and to mix with their own class.'[95] He too notes that the 1963 fee-paying system of secondary and third-level education was a speciality of the middle-classes, with only one-third of those who might wish to participate at second level being able to do so. At third level while one in four of the lower professional/managerial/executive class attended, less than one in two hundred children from semi-skilled, unskilled and agricultural labourers did so. Farmar points out that a woman's chance of going to university was even more biased by social origin than a man's, and by the ban on married women working which deeply influenced attitudes to women's education, commenting that 'In the light of the marriage bar it is not surprising that less well-off families decided not to encourage their daughters to go.'[96]

Arensberg and Kimball had noted in the 1930s that parental choices about their children's education had a profound effect on the future careers of their sons and the marriage prospects of their daughters. Again, such decisions were primarily class based, Arensberg and Kimball noting that 'social aspirations for the family are to be won or lost in what happens to their children.'[97] The children of the few wealthy shopkeepers in each Irish town along with the children of professional men were sent to 'fashionable religious schools' in England and Ireland, while those of smaller shopkeepers were sent to the 'genteel atmosphere' of the local Christian Brother or Convent school rather than to the local lay national school. While the training provided by formal education carried many shopkeepers' sons and daughters beyond the confines of their father's occupation, their study notes that the decision of the father was crucial in deciding which occupations their sons would enter. The bigger shopkeepers hoped to hand on the management of their business to one son, and to educate the others for the medical, legal or banking world, while 'His daughters acquire the manners which prepare them to become the wives of professional men or persons of equal status.'[98] The daughters of the smaller shopkeeper might be given additional training to become a nurse or a teacher, or enter the convent, with most however remaining in the shop 'waiting for an opportunity to marry'.[99] Where adult daughters remained unmarried after the marriage of the son inheriting the family business, they are either given 'their portion' at this stage and leave the family home to the new couple, or a small business may be started up for them; 'Many of the spinsters who tend small shops are shopkeepers' daughters for whom provision was made at the time of the marriage of their brothers. Their possession is a contingent one, ending with their death, when the shop reverts to their brother or to his heirs.'[100]

A common theme which emerged from each of the studies cited above was a belief across all classes that woman's place was in the home. Humphreys' study of an artisan family noted that 'For the younger as for the older generation of Dunns, a woman's place is still in the home and a man's prime responsibility is to his family.'[101] The mother as housewife is seen as the primary role model for daughters.

The question of marriage does not enter to any important extent into considerations of the training and education of boys. It has the central place in the training and education of girls, for the role of housewife and mother is the desirable and likely life career for them.[102]

With school instruction in domestic science viewed as supplementary, the Dunn girls 'have learned the domestic skills, the art of management, and the comportment proper to a wife and mother from Joan (their mother) by directly participating with her in the daily routine of domestic duties'.[103] Similarly, 'the managerial mother, both in regard to broad, humanistic matters and in regard to the specific role of housewife, is the major model for her daughters.'[104] Farmar in 1963 also noted that from an early age children would have noticed a sharp difference between the way boys and girls were treated:

Boys were nearly always exempted from household chores, while girls were expected to help with everything ... The marriage bar and other prevailing attitudes reinforced the sense of separate castes: while boys were to be toughened into breadwinners, girls were already undergoing apprenticeships before becoming home-makers.[105]

Humphreys' study noted a significant difference between labouring and artisan families on the issue of education, with labourers' children, male and female, receiving notably less secondary education. Even among the most prosperous labouring families, such education was rare, comprising at most two years of technical education. Partly the decision of parents who needed to supplement the family income, it was also in part due to the wish of the children themselves. A further difference between the two groups emerged when the option of second-level education was available for labouring families, boys usually being chosen instead of girls.[106]

While initial developments in Northern Ireland concentrated on reorganisation of the many existing boards of education into a single department, the North's first Minister of Education went further than his southern counterpart by setting up a departmental committee of investigation into the state of education in the province. The resulting Education Act of 1923 has been described as amounting to 'a revolution in Irish educational practice'.[107] With all schools brought under the control of the Local Education Authorities, appointed by borough and county councils, contributions from local rates would be paid to primary, secondary and vocational schools. Aid would be distributed in proportion to the control which schools accepted from local authorities. The government would be responsible for the payment of teachers' salaries, but local authorities were responsible for providing new schools, and of heating, lighting and other maintenance. Other provisions related to school medical inspections, food for needy children, with enforcement of compulsory attendance for children between 6 and 14 years.[108] Lee has described the Act as being 'among the most ambitious legislative measure ever undertaken in Irish education', noting however that it ultimately failed to achieve its objectives because 'it proceeded on the illusion that Catholic and Protestant clergies were more concerned with education than with power'.[109] Among the provisions that alienated clergy of all denominations were attempts to increase parental control over education through the local authorities, the proposal that schools be open to all children, irrespective of denomination, that religious instruction not be given during hours of compulsory attendance, and that religious tests should not be imposed on teachers.

Ultimately, due to clerical pressure, amendments to the Act ensued during the 1920s and 1930s. In 1947 the school-leaving age was extended to 15 years, and the type of schools children would go to was determined in the Education Act of that year. Under this Act, all children would leave primary school at age 11+, and enter one of three forms of second-level schooling: junior intermediate schools which were free of charge and which provided a non-academic secondary education, grammar schools for academically-talented pupils (fee-charging, with means-tested scholarships available) and day technical schools specialising in purely technical subjects.[110] The type of second-level school a pupil entered depended on the result obtained in the 11+ examination. Initial educational criticism of the proposed 11+ examination was grounded in the belief that the separation of children into two distinct streams of post-primary schooling would involve social class discrimination and would be unfair and undemocratic.[111] Such criticisms would persist during the decades the examination was in operation, accentuated by the experience of many that a decision made at such an early age determined the life and career expectations of a child. As was noted during the House of Commons debates on the new educational proposals, however, most discussion concentrated on the issue of religious instruction.[112] While there were a number of amendments to the Act, primarily relating to financial considerations, in essence the Act was implemented, and significantly extended educational opportunities for northern students. Referring to the effect of the welfare state, and in particular the Education Act, Lee has commented:

> A generation of Catholics weaned on the welfare state, educated to a higher level than ever before, began to emerge from the late fifties. The number of Catholic students at Queen's University rose from 200 to 700 between 1955 and 1959 … Something approaching an independent-minded Catholic middle class was beginning to emerge for the first time.[113]

A notable example of one who benefited from this system is John Hume, who has pointed out that his 11+ examination and subsequent University scholarship made him one of the first generation of Catholics to be given this opportunity.[114]

One historian has stated that 'early in the 1960s the Republic's politicians discovered education'.[115] Following the establishment of a government commission in 1962 to investigate Irish education, a report was published in 1966 entitled *Investment in Education*. Brown has noted that 'The tone, concerns and recommendations of the Commission's report certainly reflect a radical ideological departure in Irish educational thinking.'[116] Lyons too has commented that 'radical rethinking was to be the keynote of the 1960s in almost every field of education.'[117] Among the many reforms introduced in the wake of this report, the most dramatic was the provision of free secondary education. Allied to this was the raising of the school-leaving age from 14 to 15, provision of free transport to children living more than 3 miles from school and free books to children whose families could not afford to buy them. With second-level education mandatory up to 15 years, pupils would now leave primary school at 12 years. The Primary Certificate was abolished in 1967, and a review of the entire curriculum at that level resulted in a radical new Primary School Curriculum in 1971. Another significant innovation of the 1960s was the establishment of state-supported (mostly) co-educational comprehensive schools, followed in the early 1970s by the establishment of community schools which brought together existing vocational and academic secondary schools. Akenson has commented of these changes:

> Undeniably the attempt to reduce the most obvious forms of social class distinction in education marked a change in the way Irish people

thought about the social inequalities in their entire society, just as the large incremental investments in education marked a shift in the position of the child in Irish culture.[118]

Similarly Brown has noted that an article by a 'very crucially placed' assistant secretary in the Department of Education published in 1968 showed a firm commitment to the concept of child-centred education.[119]

As has been shown, there were significant developments throughout the educational field between 1870 and 1970, and within those developments, particular changes relating to girls. In the fifty years prior to partition, the increasing numbers of girls attending school reflected both societal and economic changes. The legislative innovations regarding second- and third-level opportunities for girls during this period generally benefited those of the middle classes, and the vast majority of Irish girls attended only at primary level. Here, increasingly more girls than boys attended school, and for longer periods. Class and gender considerations decided the extent and content of such education. After the Treaty of 1922, the two new governments developed distinct educational objectives. Within Northern Ireland, priority from the start was with a child-centred education. In the South, administrative centralisation was the initial concern, closely followed by restoration of the native language. Both objectives progressed within a framework of compromise regarding clerical ownership of the majority of schools. Northern Ireland policy from 1947 greatly expanded the accessibility of second- and third-level education for all, irrespective of class. During the 1960s in the Republic, a commitment to child-centred education and major innovations at second level transformed the profile of school attendance. Kennedy has pointed to the close association between increased participation in education and rising living standards. Whereas in the 1920s about 80 per cent of the population left school after the primary level, by the late 1990s about 80 per cent left school with the leaving certificate.[120]

The biggest change regarding children occurred as a result of their changing economic status, a change linked to two factors in particular: the move away from agriculture and the extension of formal education.[121] A study published by Combat Poverty Agency in 1994 outlined the main costs associated with children, e.g. food, clothing, education, childcare, etc, and income foregone by parents who care for children. Indicating the degree to which attitudes regarding children had changed, Kennedy notes that unlike reports produced up to the 1950s regarding the raising of the school-leaving age, this study contained no suggestion regarding income foregone *by the child*, or loss to the family budget by the lack of child labour.[122]

In its findings on educational developments during the 1960s, the Report of the First Commission on the Status of Women published in 1972 provides a valuable overview of female education in that decade of change. The Report noted that there were no legal or administrative barriers to the education of girls in Ireland, that equality of access to formal education between the sexes held true, and that participation was equal below the level of university education. It was noted, however, that from the age of 18 years (when third-level education commences) the percentage of boys in full-time education exceeded that of girls.[123]

Persons aged 14–24 receiving full-time education—1996 Census

Age	Males %	Females %
Over 14 years and under 15 years	72.5	75.0
Over 15 years and under 16 years	56.6	61.5
Over 16 years and under 17 years	39.6	47.4
Over 17 years and under 18 years	28.6	33.3
Over 18 years and under 19 years	19.5	19.5
Over 19 years and under 20 years	13.8	11.5
Over 20 years and under 21 years	11.6	7.4
Over 21 years and under 22 years	10.4	5.2
Over 22 years and under 23 years	8.6	3.1
Over 23 years and under 24 years	6.7	1.5
Over 24 years and under 25 years	4.8	1.2

Taken from *Report of the Commission on the Status of Women* (1972), p. 202.

The Report identified a number of key factors affecting the full educational and intellectual development of girls throughout the education system:

- Early conditioning of girls to a domestic role at home accentuated by depictions of girls and women in school textbooks
- Significant differences between the numbers of boys and girls taking science subjects or higher-level mathematics
- Parental attitude towards investment in third-level education for girls, particularly in light of the marriage bar and perceived limited career opportunities.

Accepting that in the 1960s most Irish mothers did not work outside the home, the Report noted that 'accordingly girls are to a large extent conditioned to visualise themselves in a housekeeping role'.[124] Examination of school textbooks had shown that such early attitudes to sex roles were reinforced by the presentation of women and girls in this traditional role. The Report suggested that care be taken to ensure that the profile of the typical girl or woman in such textbooks should show her in active occupations and pursuits as well as in the traditional role.

Regarding second-level education, the Report noted that while a revised curriculum had been introduced in 1969 with, in general, a common syllabus for boys and girls, there were still some compulsory subjects based on sex difference. Girls' schools had to provide singing and home economics; in vocational schools the approved Intermediate Certificate course for boys had to include mechanical drawing or art, and for girls, home economics or commerce.[125] While it was not compulsory to take these subjects in the examination, their retention can be seen as a hangover from previous curricula and values. Accepting that girls had equality of opportunity in access to post-primary education, the Report commented that 'if any discrimination exists it must lie in the quality or emphasis of the education received'.[126] Examination of Intermediate and Leaving Certificate examination results from 1967 assured the Commission that the quality of instruction in girls' schools was if anything higher than in boys'.

Intermediate and Leaving Certificate Examinations, 1967–72: Percentage Pass (Including Pass with honours) of those examined

	1967 %	1968 %	1969 %	1970 %	1971 %	1972 %
Leaving Certificate:						
Boys	87.9	90.6	84.0	78.2	77.4	77.5
Girls	93.9	93.3	86.9	84.5	83.5	85.5
Intermediate Certificate:						
Boys	81.6	83.7	71.7	72.1	72.1	74.6
Girls	88.9	89.8	77.2	74.5	74.2	77.3

Taken from *Report of the Commission on the Status of Women* (1972), p. 209.

Leaving Certificate Examinations, 1967–71: Percentage Pass with honours of those examined in Honours Papers

	1967 %	1968 %	1969 %	1970 %	1971 %
Boys	39.1	43.1	47.2	44.8	50.6
Girls	41.8	41.1	45.1	45.3	49.8

Taken from *Report of the Commission on the Status of Women* (1972), p. 209.

Significant discrepancy was noted however between boys' and girls' schools in the subjects of mathematics and science. Girls were seen to concentrate more on traditional arts subjects to the detriment of the latter. Particularly disturbing to the Commission was the very small numbers of girls taking honours mathematics at Leaving Certificate, with implications for the future supply of female teachers able to teach mathematics at this level.[127]

Leaving Certificate, 1971: Boys and Girls examined in Honours and Pass Papers

Subjects	Number Examined		Numbers who took Honours Papers		Numbers who took Pass Papers	
	Boys	Girls	Boys	Girls	Boys	Girls
Irish, English and other Languages	28,155	32,344	11,201	14,038	16,954	18,306
History and Geography	11,133	12,942	6,072	6,365	5,061	6,577
Mathematics	9,373	8,195	1.803	314	7,570	7,881
Physics	2,447	226	1,345	135	1,102	91
Chemistry	2,937	706	1,813	518	1,124	188
Physics and Chemistry	983	334	527	260	456	74
Agricultural Science	724	26	286	17	438	9
Applied Mathematics	590	12	242	4	348	8
Biology	1,212	2,545	642	1,546	570	999
Home Economics (General)	20	5,928	4	3,274	16	2,564
Accounting and Business Org.	3,343	4,656	1,728	1,676	1,615	2,980
Economics	974	753	575	388	399	365
Technical Drawing	955	2	955	2	—	—
Art	1,340	3,526	548	1,653	792	1,873

Taken from *Report of the Commission on the Status of Women* (1972), p. 210.

The Commission was concerned that the lack of emphasis on these subjects might cut girls off from a number of university faculties and from a wide variety of careers in the fields of engineering, electronics and other specialised employments outside the traditional female areas of employment.

Within the vocational schools, girls were shown to be taking subjects such as shorthand, typing and commerce which would lead to employment in 'traditional' female office jobs whereas a large proportion of boys followed practical courses in science, woodwork and metalwork. Figures for the 1971 Day Vocational Certificate Examination supplied by the Department of Education showed that while 8,587 boys took woodwork and 6,845 took metalwork, no girl took either of these subjects. The Report notes: 'It is hardly surprising, therefore, that very few girls find their way into apprenticeships and technical occupations.'[128] The Report concluded that unless the options for girls were diversified to include technically oriented subjects, 'these schools will continue to stream girls into office jobs with little responsibility and poor prospects'.[129]

Day Vocational Certificate Examination, 1971

Subject	Boys			Girls		
	Sat	Passed	%Passed	Sat	Passed	%Passed
Irish, English and other Languages	18,599	9,413	50.6	12,378	9,220	74.5
Mathematics	8,965	4,334	48.3	3,279	1,449	44.2
Commerce, Book-keeping, Commercial Arithmetic, Business Methods, Retail Practice	735	323	43.9	13,354	8,803	65.9
Rural Science	3,819	2,757	72.2	126	87	69.0
Art	3,344	1,944	59.6	983	467	47.5
Mechanical Drawing	8,864	5,409	61.0	—	—	—
Applied Mathematics	590	12	242	4	348	8
History and Geography	3,822	1,657	43.4	2,845	1,002	35.2
Magnetism/Electricity	129	42	32.6	—	—	—
Science	3,906	2,092	53.6	363	150	41.3

Shorthand-General,					
Shorthand-Secretarial,					
Typewriting-General,					
Typewriting-Secretarial	—	—	—	6,181	2,896	46.9
Domestic Science	—	—	—	2,675	2,080	77.8
Cookery, Needlework,					
Laundry Work and					
Home Management	—	—	—	6,969	6,441	92.4
Woodwork	8,587	5,463	63.6	—	—	—
Metal Work	6,845	5,560	66.6	—	—	—

Taken from *Report of the Commission on the Status of Women* (1972), p. 213.

Regarding third-level education the Report noted that the main disability affecting women was their low participation *vis-à-vis* men. Between 1930 and 1959 the proportion of women to men attending had fluctuated between 25 per cent and 34 per cent. While the Commission hoped that the recent upward trend would continue, the current situation was that for every two boys at university, there was only one girl. Reflecting post-primary trends, women university students tended to concentrate in a narrow range of faculties. In the year 1968/9, 7 out of 10 women were attending Arts or Social Science, 1 per cent of women were in the Engineering Faculty, and in the Science Faculty men outnumbered women by 3 to 1. Regarding the latter two, it was felt that even this level of participation was high given the relatively small numbers of girls taking honours mathematics and science in the Leaving Certificate. Women accounted for one-quarter of students within the Science, Medicine and Commerce faculties.[130]

Number of full-time students in the National University of Ireland and the University of Dublin 1964–65 to 1968–69

Year	Men	Women	% Women
1964–65	8,966	4,040	31.3
1965–66	9,789	4,358	30.8
1966–67	10,646	4,632	30.8
1967–68	10,730	5,108	32.3
1968–69	11,246	5,662	33.5

Taken from *Report of the Commission on the Status of Women* (1972), p. 214.

In its summation on women in university education the Report provides both a current assessment and a forecast on the status of women's education in Ireland. It also, unwittingly, shows the extent of advancement in female education during the previous century:

> The main disability affecting women as a whole in relation to university education is that their participation at this level is much lower than that of men. The reasons for this position are difficult to identify, particularly as girls are participating equally with boys in secondary level education and are obtaining as good results as boys in the Leaving Certificate examination. In addition, there are no formal barriers placed by the universities on the entry of girls. It is probable that decisions by parents in this matter have reflected general attitudes of society and that many parents may have been inclined to invest in university education for boys in preference to girls. As stated above, the extension of the university grants scheme can be expected to bring about an improvement in the position. Also, removal of the marriage bar on a general basis and the growing acceptance of the fact that marriage need not be the end of a woman's career in employment will, we feel, operate very strongly to redress the present imbalance.[131]

FAITH AND PHILANTHROPY—WOMEN AND RELIGION

Religion was certainly the most readily-avowed motive for women's philanthropy. (R. RAUGHTER, *Women & Irish History*)

The nineteenth century was a time of tremendous change in many facets of Irish life. Significant societal changes were reflected on the one hand by the growing strength of the urban middle classes linked to a restructured farming ethos, and on the other hand by a growth in urban poverty allied to mass emigration from the land. In the century prior to the famine Irish population quadrupled; in the following century it was halved.[1] Post-famine Ireland assumed a distinctly male profile, Joe Lee commenting that 'the rise of the strong farmer coincided with the growth of clerical power'.[2] The most significant factor from the mid-nineteenth century was the dramatic increase in the number of religious, male and female. The numbers of male clergy in proportion to the population changed from one Catholic priest to 3,500 people in 1840 to one to every 600 by 1960. While the proportion of priests increased six-fold, the proportion of nuns—as discussed below—rose even faster. Lee has noted that the growing numbers of Catholic clergy were drawn mainly from 'the respectable and fairly comfortable class of the tenant farmers', and inevitably shared the farmers' attitudes.[3] Such attitudes were re-enforced by the curricula and doctrines taught in both Catholic and Protestant seminaries and convents. Evangelicalism was not restricted to Protestant seminaries; rivalry with Protestants for the saving of the souls of an ever-growing poor population sharpened the missionary impulse of middle-class Catholics.[4] The re-organisation and centralisation of the Catholic church in nineteenth-century Ireland was partly dictated by Rome, but would not have happened to such an extent without strong public support. Women religious—or nuns, as they were popularly known—were the spearhead of this initiative.[5]

A number of notable women became involved in philanthropic work during the second half of the eighteenth century. While women had been involved in charitable works prior to this, the extent and structure of such work began to change from this time, and would expand even more during the early years of the nineteenth century. Becoming more organised and professional during the new century, the changing nature of philanthropy has been linked to an emerging middle-class concern with the new industrial proletariat.[6] While Ireland did not have the concentration of industrialised areas becoming common throughout Europe and the US, significant social and humanitarian problems developed throughout the country in the post-famine years. Involvement in such philanthropic work would, in time, lead some women to question their own status and position in society.

Initially the domain of Protestant upper-class women, the emergence of a distinctive wealthy Catholic middle class from the late eighteenth century saw the increasing involvement of Catholic women in such work.[7] In particular, the establishment and growth of many new religious orders reflected this involvement. During the nineteenth century, the participation of both Catholic and Protestant women in such work grew significantly. In many ways, both groups were opposite religious sides of the same coin. Working in various ways to alleviate the conditions of the poor they saw around them, most of these women were from wealthy backgrounds, and did not hesitate to use their money and contacts to further their work. Reflecting their class and position in society, Protestant women and the first generation of Catholic women so involved, were confident, influential and assertive. Other factors common to both were the lack of questioning of the reasons for severe social deprivation, and their acceptance of the existing subservient role of women. In fact the work they became involved in often reflected what was seen as the 'womanly' virtues of charity and humility. Towards the end of the nineteenth century, there would be changes in this regard among a number of Protestant women's groups. It can be argued that these women saw their task primarily as a practical one, not a theoretical or political argument. Religious fervour was a key factor in women's philanthropy, vigorously driving both groups to aid the poor while saving their souls. That same fervour prevented women coming together to work on behalf of the needy, and the issue of proselytism on both sides emerged consistently. While sharing many common objectives—primarily to help the poor, sick and needy—the key different organisational methods between Catholic and Protestant women was based on the fact that Protestant women worked as lay groups, whereas Catholic women's work in this area became the concern of the new religious orders, and with some notable exceptions, generally Catholic lay women were relegated to the margins.

A CAREER IN THE CONVENT—NUNS IN THE NINETEENTH CENTURY

The dramatic change in female religious in Ireland can be starkly illustrated by two simple statistics: In 1800 there were 120 nuns in Ireland; by 1900 there were 8,000.[8] Developments in Ireland reflected trends elsewhere. During the eighteenth and nineteenth centuries, hundreds of new religious congregations of women were formed throughout Catholic Europe, spurred on by the spirit of evangelicalism and the effects of social change. The numbers of female religious rapidly overtook the numbers of priests and male religious.[9] In Ireland in 1851, priests outnumbered nuns by 2,500 to 1,500; by 1901, the number of nuns had more than doubled that of priests and was more than seven times the number of male religious. In the Irish context, the figures are all the more remarkable given the near halving of the population post-famine.

This age of philanthropic zeal saw Protestant women organise to help alleviate need and distress among the poor within a religious framework. Many Catholic women reacted similarly to societal problems among the disadvantaged. Initially starting as voluntary groups of laywomen motivated by a strong religious impulse, over time many developed—not always willingly—into religious communities.

There had been female religious congregations throughout the history of the church. Generally these had been members of religious orders who had taken solemn vows, leading enclosed lives dedicated to prayer and divine adoration. All were responsible to male church authority, be it Abbot, Bishop or Pope. During the seventeenth century the first of the newer orders developed with the formation of Vincent de Paul's French Sisters of Charity. Taking simple rather than solemn vows, this order paved the way for new developments, its sisters going outside the cloister to engage in public works of charity and evangelisation.[10]

Throughout the world the nineteenth century was an age of evangelicalism, with vigorous promotion of religious practice across all

Christian churches and among all social classes. Within the Catholic context, this coincided with the development of a centralised church authority anxious to develop pastoral activity within a changing political and religious environment. In Ireland, these tendencies were reinforced by a catholicism, emerging from the oppressions of the Penal Laws, which identified strongly with political and social reform.[11] Between 1776 and 1875 all the modern religious congregations in Ireland were established, many initially as branches of European congregations. Religious life was attractive to Catholic women for many reasons, not least because the newer orders permitted middle-class women to promote both their philanthropical and missionary instincts. As Clear has noted, 'the sense of collective identity of a disadvantaged majority intensified the crusading zeal of an evangelical age.'[12] Key to this development was the role played by the new female congregations.

In fact, quite a few of the new Irish orders were formed before Catholic Emancipation in 1829. The first of these was formed by Nano Nagle in the 1770s. Like most founders of new orders, Nagle was from a wealthy background. From the 1750s Nagle had run free schools in Cork city on the lines of similar schools she had seen in France—in so doing breaking the Penal code. In 1771, she invited the Ursuline sisters from France to take over the running of these schools, but their strict rule of enclosure did not permit them to go outside the convent to attend these schools. Nagle then set about establishing a non-enclosed sisterhood which would teach in schools for the poor, and also carry out other missionary and charitable work with the old and the sick. The Sisters of the Charitable Instruction formed by her in her native Cork in 1776—recognised by the Vatican in 1805 as the Presentation Nuns—was 'the first female congregation in Ireland to have a specific *social* purpose which found expression in concrete projects, and it was therefore in some demand'.[13] While common on the continent, this kind of sisterhood was unheard of in Ireland at this time. In 1815 the first convent of the Irish Sisters of Charity was formed in Dublin by Mary Aikenhead; some years later, in 1821, Frances Ball set up Loreto Abbey in Rathfarnham as a fee-paying school with a free school attached. The first House of Mercy was established by Catherine McAuley in Baggot Street, Dublin in the 1820s, formally becoming the congregation of the Sisters of Mercy in 1831 (approved by Rome in 1840).

The influence brought to bear by churchmen on the founders of these orders to formalise their organisations is significant. Nagle, Aikenhead, McAuley, Ball and Margaret Aylward (who ultimately formed the Sisters of the Holy Faith) had much in common. All were devout laywomen from wealthy backgrounds, representatives of the strong upper middle class. Each had been involved with or responsible for various charitable undertakings for some years with a group of like-minded laywomen. While their spirituality was intense, Tony Fahey has pointed out that any tendencies towards reclusiveness and otherworldliness were counterbalanced by a dedication to popular philanthropy, a philanthropy which was very much marked by the emerging bourgeois concern, in both Protestant and Catholic circles, for the moral and spiritual degeneracy of the lower orders, particularly in the growing commercial and industrial towns and cities.[14] In this context it is noteworthy that each of the above women's early charitable work was based in their native city or town.

Concern on the part of popes and bishops about how best to control female religious communities had existed throughout the history of the church. Prior to the emergence of these new orders, strict enclosure and the authority vested in superior-generals made this task much easier. With the emergence of new congregations who did not observe enclosure, there was considerable confusion. Ultimately it was left to individual bishops to enforce papal directives on the control of women religious, and they did not always do so in a consistent fashion.[15] Of the women named above, only Nagle had set out to establish a religious community. Ball and Aikenhead were both approached by Dr Murray, later Archbishop of Dublin, to set up congregations based on their charitable work in the city. McAuley quite definitely did not want to establish such a congregation, disliking the ideal of superiors and subjects.[16] Many such groups of women—committed to working for the poor and the sick—were content to live together as lay religious; it was but a matter of time, however, before they would have to accede to the local bishop's insistence that they accept rules and a constitution approved by Rome to ensure their survival. In all cases, the vows taken by such congregations were simple vows, allowing them to work outside the convent walls. Caitríona Clear has commented that:

The change from secular group to religious congregation, from energetic and religious project leader to founder, has been portrayed as a logical sequence of events, but it has been shown that the intervention of bishops was, in all cases, crucial in diverting the socially aware and essentially religious energy of these Catholic Irishwomen into canonically approved channels. In this way these organisations were brought under the control of the church, their leaders subjected to the church's discipline, and their considerable resources of expertise and confidence harnessed by a church which was increasing its political and economic power.[17]

A brief look at the evolution of some such congregations confirms these points. Nagle had worked on her own as a lay woman among the poor of Cork from the 1750s. Some twenty years later, she gathered together a small group of women to take on religious life, while working towards educational and social welfare services devoted entirely to the poor. By 1786 she had opened seven poor schools using inherited money. When her plan for the Ursuline order to take over the running of these schools failed, she set about forming her own religious community to educate the poor. Fahey has noted that it took a further twenty years for the group to obtain ecclesiastical approval and gain a secure footing in Cork: 'Lack of recruits, lack of money and a certain measure of public suspicion had hampered the new organisation in its earlier years and the great difficulties the group experienced in these areas indicate the novelty and pioneering character of their work.'[18] Nagle died in 1784 before her group was formally approved as the Presentation Order in 1805. In its new official mode, the order now had the restrictions of solemn vows and enclosure, quite different to Nagle's original scheme which encouraged sisters to go outside the convent to work among the poor.

Catherine McAuley used her money to establish a free school and a hostel for unemployed women in Dublin in the 1820s. Inspired by strong religious conviction, she lived with a group of like-minded women, all of them working in the community. Despite the good work originating from her House of Mercy in Baggot Street, McAuley's group earned the suspicion of local clergy, hostile to a group of lay women not subject to local ecclesiastical control. McAuley's reservations about forming a religious congregation seem to have been overcome by Archbishop Murray, on the basis that adoption of rules, constitution and a religious identity would ensure the permanency of her endeavours while ensuring the co-operation of local clergy. In 1831 the Sisters of Mercy received papal approbation.[19] By the time the constitution of the order was approved by Rome in 1840, there were already several convents established throughout the country, each taking simple vows, and not being enclosed.

Based on her work among the poor of Dublin, Mary Aikenhead was asked by Dr Daniel Murray in 1810 to consider setting up a religious congregation modelled on the Daughters of Charity. She agreed, and in 1813 the first convent of the Irish Sisters of Charity was established in Dublin, with simple vows and no rule of enclosure.[20] Somewhat unusual—although not unique—among new convents, the Irish Sisters of Charity were centralised in structure, with a mother-house and a superior-general. This system seems to have been favoured by Murray, who encouraged the same for the Loreto convent set up by Frances Ball in Dublin in 1821. Centralised congregations did not meet with the favour of all bishops, however; subsequent Loreto foundations in other dioceses were forced to cut all links with their mother-house in Rathfarnham.[21] Generally, as Clear points out, bishops disapproved of centralised congregations, preferring convents within their diocese to be answerable only to them. Indecision from the papacy throughout the nineteenth century on the proper government of female congregations added to the confusion, and left bishops free to make their own decisions. It was not until 1900 that Pope Leo XIII issued a decree stating 'Let women govern women.'[22] In this he vested primary control of female congregations in their elected superior-generals where they existed. However, this only applied to congregations which already had centralised structures and elected superior-generals, and the majority of the newer groups did not. Not surprisingly, bishops favoured the latter groups, and consequently the Presentation and Mercy orders—from the beginning directly subordinate to the local bishop—became the most numerous throughout the country.

Branches of foreign orders in Ireland were also subjected to episcopal disapproval. In 1861, the St Louis convent in Monaghan was forced to cut all ties with its mother-house in France by Bishop Nally. Similarly, the Good Shepherd order was forced to modify its centralisation structure by the Bishop of Limerick in the same year, while in 1845 the Faithful Companions of Jesus encountered difficulty from the Bishop of Limerick.[23] When Archbishop Cullen tried to force the Dominican nuns in Galway under the authority of the Bishop of Galway in 1851, the nuns stood firm. Wishing to stay under the authority of the Dominican order and its Provincial, the nuns appealed directly to Pope Pius IX, who ruled in their favour.[24] As Clear points out, however, the newly established non-enclosed orders—without such powerful structures behind them—were particularly vulnerable to episcopal interference.

While the founders of new congregations undoubtedly had a strong influence on the type of work subsequently carried out by their successors, none had more than a consultative voice in the framing of the rule and constitutions which would bring their groups under male control within the church.[25] Once established, the lack of a centralised structure among the larger orders such as the Mercy and Presentation prevented a forum for the exchange of ideas or information. It would appear that this was deliberate on the part of some bishops.

The fragmentation of many congregations over various dioceses inhibited expressions of common identity and dissent among religious communities throughout the country. Orders such as the Mercy Sisters, which had spread at an amazing rate, felt the need to centralise in order to maintain cohesiveness and unity. Varying interpretations of the Mercy Order rule from one diocese to another—very often influenced by the local bishop—resulted in differing definitions of what it meant to be a Mercy nun. An example of this was the encouragement by bishops that Mercy nuns in many towns become involved in running day schools for the middle classes, quite outside their original remit of caring and educating poor girls and women.[26] An attempt made by a group of Mercy nuns in 1864 to compile a guidebook of all Mercy convents was thwarted when some bishops refused to allow convents in their dioceses be represented at the inaugural meeting.[27] Mary P. Magray has pointed out that women themselves also played a role in undermining this meeting, particularly the Baggot Street mother-house. Twenty years earlier that congregation had been in a protracted dispute with the Dublin hierarchy over the right to choose its own chaplain. After many years, the convent was ultimately forced to accept the hierarchy's nominee. By 1864, the superior and congregation at Baggot Street were women of quite different mettle to those who had waged a long struggle with the bishops in the 1840s. Their failure to take a leading role in the 1864 meeting resulted in the non-participation of many convents.

From the mid-nineteenth century on, convents were increasingly brought under episcopal control. Noting that 'The outspoken and assertive character of the early leaders stands in stark contrast to the convent leaders of the later decades of the century', Magray has observed that 'a certain slavish mentality crept into the convents, and a qualitative assessment of their records shows a much greater concern with episcopal approval and popularity than had ever existed previously'.[28] The official journal of the Catholic Church, *The Irish Ecclesiastical Record*, contained only occasional fleeting references to nuns, nor was there any similar publication for nuns.

Visible but not vocal, nuns were an Irish Catholic variation on the theme of the ideal Victorian female. Her existence was to be a source of inspiration to her men folk, but she was not allowed to have a voice in matters which directly affected her.[29]

Despite such constraints, women religious were pivotal to the evolution of social and cultural life in nineteenth-century Ireland. Magray has argued that 'the development of women's religious orders should not be seen as a consequence of the transformation of the Catholic church and Irish society, but rather as central to the construction of the new, devout, modern Irish Catholic culture'.[30] Rather than being the product of the 'devotional revolution' of nineteenth-century Ireland, women religious were in fact in the vanguard of religious reform in Ireland. Central to the church's transformation through their close contact with ordinary Irish Catholics, especially young women, the new female orders were particularly successful in fostering new styles of religious devotions and social behaviour. Magray has noted the suggestion that 'the crucial element in the success of the reformed Irish church was its ability to reconcile the magical and the rational elements of religious belief'.[31] In their attempts to win over the laity to ideals of piety and religious practice, the new orders utilised a number of techniques that emphasised religious ritual and ceremony.

The new sisterhood sought to replace old customs and beliefs, particularly common in rural areas by promoting a number of new initiatives that involved pomp and elaborate ceremony. One such initiative which gradually became acceptable was a programme to encourage First Holy Communion for children at age 7 years—introduced to combat an age-old belief that young people under the age of seventeen or eighteen were exempt from attending mass or receiving the sacraments.[32] The introduction of popular devotions such as sodalities and confraternities, each requiring specific religious duties on the part of the laity, frequent church services involving processions and hymn singing were among other new initiatives. Particularly significant in moulding Irish girls into pious and devout Catholics was the 'Children of Mary' sodality, which also served as an important recruiting ground for Irish convents. The emergence of the Christmas crib is credited also to women religious, as are Marian grottos, relics, medals and other sacred items—all used to bind people to the church. Co-operation with male religious in the organisation of 'missions' was another important tool used by nuns to spread devotional practices. Thus by 'employing a multitude of conversion techniques, women religious set out to instil new feelings of piety and to spread a new system of outward symbolism that reflected that piety'.[33]

The wide range of convent-run hospitals and schools during the nineteenth century reinforced the nuns' mission and opportunity to instil new religious practices. In addition, women's formative work in educational and charitable enterprises helped to created the 'caring' path that the church would follow.[34] The Archbishop of Dublin, Paul Cullen, prominent in the centralisation of the post-famine church, was convinced that the female orders were vital agents of religous reform.[35] With the emerging tension between hierarchy and convents as bishops attempted to exert control, women religious were always careful to acknowledge episcopal authority, while also being quick to defend their own. Irish convents placed high value on financial autonomy, a value they frequently resorted to the law to retain. In fact, 'priests and bishops were alarmed at the alacrity with which nuns resorted to courts of law'.[36] Towards the end of the nineteenth century, increasing episcopal control brought an end to this effort at independence.

Generally, however, relationships between the convents and the local clergy and bishops were good. Their work was highly valued in schools, hospitals and poorhouses for a number of reasons: they embodied modern Catholicism; they cost less than lay nurses or teachers; they were not working for personal gain, and they were amazingly versatile.[37] Clear points out that their flexibility and willingness to turn their hand to anything without a formal paid work structure reinforced the low esteem in which such work was held at this time.[38] The somewhat double-edged remark of one cleric in 1899 that 'You can switch a Sister of Charity on to anything' reflected this view, while Cardinal Cullen praised Dublin nuns in 1898 for 'going about their work noiselessly and calmly'. Fahey has commented that 'the position of women in the church echoed the position of women in the home, essential but subordinate'.[39] Indeed there were many parallels. Working with children, the sick and the elderly, the work of nuns in 'the caring professions' was seen as an extension of women's work within the home. In their educational work, nuns sought to ensure the religious upbringing of girls, while preparing them for the accepted female role of wife and mother. The only variation within the latter preparation was class based, middle- and upper-class girls being groomed as accomplished young ladies, working-class girls being taught basic literacy and domestic skills. Radical demands and achievements for educational equality for girls with boys and for career training for middle-class women originated from Protestant women. It was not until certain milestones had been achieved in this area by Protestant schools, following which Catholic middle-class parents began to demand the same standards for their daughters, that convent schools began a somewhat reluctant change in emphasis.

It was not just in the type of education provided to lower- and middle-class girls that convents displayed class distinction; the orders themselves reflected the class divisions of the time. Canon law stipulated that women bring a certain sum of money—or dowry—to the convent when entering. Amounts varied according to the order, and sometimes according to the wealth of the girl's family. The category of religious who entered with a dowry were known as choir nuns, and were employed in the work for which the convent had been founded, be it nursing, teaching, etc. Lay sisters, who could not afford such dowries, worked primarily within the domestic sphere. Distinctions between the two groups were reinforced by detailed differences in religious dress, and by strict demarcation lines of behaviour between the two groups. A guide for the instruction and training of lay sisters in the Mercy Order of 1866 notes that:

> Those admitted should be young, healthy and active: and while on the one hand, too high a degree of refinement would probably render them unfit for the duties of a Lay Sister, on the other hand, any remarkable rudeness, roughness of manner or vulgarity of appearance would be still more objectionable, since the Rule requires that they *should have manners and appearances suited to religious who must be seen in public* .[40]

The reason for distinctions between the two groups is given in the Guide as follows:

> Distinctions like these are prescribed because experience proves their necessity and utility in preserving religious discipline and due subordination in the Lay Sisters, and in checking forwardness, presumption, and disrespect which a footing of complete equality with those whom Providence has placed in a higher rank might often produce in persons of limited education and scanty refinement.[41]

The distinction between the women who became choir nuns and those who became lay sisters was based fundamentally on class, and this division was carefully maintained in the convent. However, it was not only class distinctions which were retained in religious life, but as Clear has pointed out, 'a microcosm of the sex-based division of power and labour which existed in society as a whole prevailed in religious communities of women':

> Domestic work in the larger society was usually performed by women, and was invariably either unpaid or underpaid. By assigning inferior status to the women who cooked, cleaned, scrubbed, gardened, answered doors, washed dishes, fetched and carried, convents were not only preserving class-based divisions of labour, but they were also reinforcing the widespread under-valuation of the work which had been traditionally done by women.[42]

In contrast, the community of the Holy Faith established by Margaret Aylward differed significantly in its organisation. Fired by Aylward's personal convictions, dowries would not be required for admission, there would be no class division between 'choir' and 'lay' sisters; the sisters would be 'walking nuns', visiting the sick poor in their own homes. Jacinta Prunty notes that in 1872, Aylward directed that the sisters 'live in the midst of the poor, looking after their children', residing:

> In an ordinary house attached to the school, and go to Mass like the rest of the faithful ... there will be no need of a chaplain nor of walls of enclosure nor of any ornamentation; and the schools in most localities will be self-supporting.[43]

Analysis of subsequent entrants to the order show that in time, a dowry became increasingly common, but the amount remained modest and allowance was always made for persons with no means who wished to enter. In addition, all Holy Faith sisters, whatever capacity they filled, were expected to contribute to the housework, including 'taking turns at milking cows in Glasnevin before heading off to teach in city schools'.[44] The daughter of a prominent Waterford merchant family, Aylward twice entered and left religious life (the Irish Sisters of Charity and the Ursulines), before moving to Dublin in 1848. She quickly became associated with the Ladies Association of Charity—a lay charity founded five years earlier.[45] Her work with this organisation exposed her to the level of poverty and distress in the city, and in particular she realised that large numbers of Dublin women were the sole support of themselves and their families. Among a series of practical ideas to help working women were plans for a pre-school to allow mothers avail of work. Over the next forty years she remained active in a variety of campaigns to assist women, orphans and the sick poor. Based on her work within such communities, she published graphic reports on the conditions of the poor and challenged Catholic middle-class women to become involved and help the disadvantaged of their parish.

Prunty has observed that Aylward was particularly successful in the latter objective, mobilising Catholic women of standing in the community to become involved in ministering to the poor.[46] Under her guidance, St Brigid's orphanage was founded, through which orphans or children whose parents could not take care of them were boarded out with foster families. Later, in an attempt to counteract Protestant proselytism, she established a series of 'poor schools' in slum areas of the city, deliberately located close to similar Protestant schools. Among the many enterprises with which she was associated, her campaign against child proselytism by Protestant missionaries was the most controversial. Through the family visitation work of the Ladies Association, Aylward became aware of the extent of such proselytism, and took a very public role in exposing various state and voluntary agencies which she accused of engaging in such activities. Of particular concern to her was the care of orphaned Catholic children of mixed religion marriages, an issue described by Prunty as 'a minefield into which charities from both sides of the religious divide were repeatedly drawn'.[47] One such controversial case centring on the abduction of an infant led to Aylward appearing in court in 1860. She was found innocent of kidnapping and complicity, but was sentenced to six months in prison on the lesser charge of contempt of court for not producing the child.[48]

The group of women who with Aylward managed St Brigid's Orphanage (initially drawn from the Ladies of Charity) had just begun to live together under the title of 'Daughters of St Brigid' at the time of Aylward's imprisonment.[49] They now dispersed, while continuing their charitable work. During her time in prison, Aylward decided it was time to take the step to form a congregation. A number of issues influenced her decision; her concern to see continuity in the projects established to date, and her determination to further such work, particularly by establishing more schools in deprived areas. In addition, Archbishop Cullen—a strong supporter of her work—was keen for her to establish an order. Prunty notes that while Cullen was of great assistance in the speedy transformation of this lay community into a religious congregation, Aylward's wish that the order come under the direct control of Rome rather under his Diocese was agreed.[50] By 1862, the Order of the Sisters of the Holy Faith was formed with eight members; by 1869 the number was twenty-seven. In addition to the six schools established between 1861 and 1870, four 'village schools' were established in County Dublin, Kildare and Kilkenny during the 1870s. Aylward remained a singularly opinionated and outspoken woman until her death in 1889, a stance that at times brought her into conflict with the hierarchy.[51] Exchanges between herself (then in her mid-seventies) and Dr Donnelly, coadjutor Bishop of Dublin in 1884 on the issue of church contributions towards the running of St Brigid's (he urged her to trust to charity and relieve the clergy from their contributions) elicited a sharp angry response from Aylward who referred scathingly to the hypocrisy and ingratitude of local clergy, pointing to the amount of money then being spent on church building. Prunty has commented that such exchanges reveal much about the context within which philanthropic Catholic women—lay or religious—operated in Dublin:

It was the assertiveness of the woman manager of St Brigid's in forcing the parish to support the enterprise that led to the hostility of some of the clergy. Women's contribution to the social mission of the Church was to be welcomed and extolled when it was subservient; efforts to place that mission on a business footing smacked of insolence and were considered troublesome'.[52]

The issue of control was raised the following year, Archbishop Walsh expressing concern at the pontifical status of the order, and expressing 'a strong opinion very generally held that the Institute should be under ecclesiastical control and supervision'.[53] As Prunty has observed, however:

The esteem and affection in which Aylward was held by influential churchmen in Dublin, Paris, Armagh and Rome had, on the whole, contributed significantly to her success; her congregation and its ministries were, by the 1880s, sufficiently well established to weather some quite serious clerical opposition.[54]

Despite the growing hierarchical control during the latter half of the nineteenth century, the existence of such convents gave many women the means to engage in socially useful work and a measure of control over their own lives, an opportunity denied to most Irish women during the nineteenth century. Pragmatic compromise with the hierarchy was viewed—albeit reluctantly by some—as necessary to continue with their work. In attracting middle-class women into these congregations the church faced little competition from elsewhere as, 'to be a nun was one of the few acceptable occupational outlets outside marriage and motherhood available to women of respectable background'.[55] In addition to a genuine social and religious commitment to help disadvantaged groups, the lack of alternative careers available for women outside marriage helps explain the huge increase in numbers of women religious during the nineteenth and early twentieth centuries. Evaluations of the role and effectiveness of female religious orders during this period has generally highlighted the positive work of the sisters in the general community, while pointing to an apparent passivity regarding both their own and women's role in society. Noting that the role of women in the church established by the new orders was of missionary importance, Fahey has argued that it was far from shattering the limitations imposed on women in the Catholic tradition. Regarding their influence as role models for Irish women, he notes:

> On the one hand, the determined lowliness with which nuns viewed their lives in the church and their firm subordination to male ecclesiastics paralleled the subordination of women in general. On the other hand, nuns enhanced the lives of women with education and practical social service and provided basic assistance and moral support to mothers in their struggles through childrearing and family life. In this role nuns were hailed and welcomed in their own day.[56]

Despite the widespread expansion of their activities during the nineteenth century into schools, reformatories, industrial schools and workhouses, nuns seem to have made no efforts to question or alter the social conditions which led to poverty. Nor did they question the accepted role of women. From the 1870s onwards, when the political, social and economic role of women was being hotly debated, the silence from such a key segment of Irish women is significant, particularly when one considers their first-hand experience and practical knowledge of women's conditions gained through their work in schools, hospitals and orphanages. Perhaps the answer lies partly in Luddy's comments that 'Nuns, throughout the nineteenth century, had a high social status. Their work in institutions and their own schemes of benevolence gave them a moral and spiritual authority which was unsurpassed by any other group of women in society'.[57] Magray concludes that, ultimately, nuns were victims of their own success. The new generations of women religious that succeeded the independent founders had been inculcated with the virtues of meekness, patience, modesty and piety.

> If depictions of women religious as humble, subservient, and powerless fit at all, they fit the women religious of the years after 1870 or 1880 ... The irony is that as the creators and enforcers of a new, modern, Irish Catholic ideology that idealised meek and docile women, Irish nuns themselves helped to create the very conditions that ultimately robbed them of their autonomy.[58]

PHILANTHROPY AND LAY WOMEN

'Philanthropy is seen as a nurturing ground of feminist consciousness.'[59] Certainly, the veracity of this statement by Mary Cullen is proven by even a cursory glance into the background of many nineteenth-century women who built on early philanthropic endeavours to pursue significant campaigns for women's equality. While not all women philanthropists would become radical feminist campaigners, the extent of their involvement in charitable works was significant. In the period 1800 to 1900 there were at least two hundred societies all over Ireland which were either founded by women or in which women played a significant role.[60] A number of factors led to the upsurge in female philanthropic activity. Chief among these was the huge population increase—doubling in the fifty-year period before the 1841 census—concentrated mainly in the poorest labouring class.[61] Consequent pressure on land, periodic crop failures, declining domestic industries and uncertain seasonable labour, all contributed to increased poverty in the countryside. Unable to survive on the land, increasingly large numbers of the poor moved to urban centres, swelling the ranks of the city poor.

Female philanthropy initially concentrated on attempts to improve the living and working conditions of the poor in their own area. In the period immediately after the famine of 1845/9, such groups focused on setting up schools to teach crafts to Irish girls so that they might earn their living. Anna Fisher (later Haslam) was one such woman, who in the late 1840s set about teaching local girls knitting and crochet. Assisted in the project by her sister, the initiative was very successful. Upward of 100 girls worked in this home-based industry at a time; many used their earnings from this venture to fund their emigration. When Anna left Youghal on her marriage in the mid-1850s, the Presentation nuns in the town took over the project, and under their tutelage it evolved into a well-known embroidery and lace-making industry. Many such schools established throughout the country were similarly handed over in time to the emerging new religious orders. Other groups were more formalised, with close links to English societies. The Ladies Hibernian Society—originally formed in 1823—was one such organisation also active during the famine years. Its report for 1859 noted that 'in 1846–7, there were thirteen thousand female children in the schools of this society, all of whom were fed and clothed and taken care of by its beneficent agencies'.[62]

In the 1860s, a series of articles published in the *English Woman's Journal* on 'The Cultivation of Female Industry in Ireland' indicate the attitudes and aspirations of some middle-class philanthropists of the time. Based largely on experience with pauper women within and outside workhouses, the tone of some parts of these articles makes difficult reading, appearing superior and condescending. The reader is told that:

> The female poor ... are a body of crude material ... There is no parallel whatever between the females of England and Ireland in these ranks. The race predominating amongst the latter requires an entirely different course of treatment from that which suits the former .... The virtues of our female population do not produce spontaneously the same sort of household conveniences and comforts as those indispensable to English family life. This condition cannot be got rid of. It is an idiosyncrasy. There are people in Ireland, as well as in France and Italy, who cannot conform to the habits and manners of their Saxon neighbours; but who, nevertheless attain a civilisation and refinement of their own. Differences are not necessarily inferiorities. Our girls 'don't feel it in their bones' to wash, cook, and polish; and they do not readily yield to the popular urgency to employ them in this species of servitude. For them the work in demand has no ascertained value. No labour is worse paid than this in Ireland, or has done so little for its women.[63]

The author strongly argued that Irish women be trained in the traditional crafts rather than steered towards domestic service, and sought female school inspectors to identify and encourage such crafts among girls. Referring to the 'Family System' by which orphans were placed with suitable families, the author advised a supervisory role for official visitors to check on such families and report to the Board of Guardians. Permission to accept orphans under this scheme should be seen as an incentive for domestic improvement within participating families, in which 'Godliness, cleanliness and industry' would be encouraged.

Lay voluntary societies were most often formed by women of Protestant or Quaker background. With increasing urbanisation, there emerged a wider range of philanthropic endeavours. Following on the establishment of the Magdalen Asylum in 1766 by Lady Arabella Denny to rescue prostitutes from a life on the streets, a number of similar asylums emerged during the nineteenth century.[64] Focusing on poor or abandoned children, women's groups organised numerous orphanages, homes and poor schools. Having established a pattern of visiting female prisons, others set up refuges for ex-prisoners. Charlotte Grace O'Brien was unique in her campaign against conditions endured by women emigrants on board transport ships to America, citing overcrowding, exploitation, sexual harassment and assault.[65]

Religious motivation was the prime force behind the formation of many philanthropic societies from the early nineteenth century:

> Spurred by the ideal of religious duty and the belief that aid to the poor paved a path to personal salvation, Irish women of all religious denominations played a major role in creating, organising and maintaining a range of philanthropic societies which catered for the destitute, orphaned and outcast.[66]

While class and social background were strong factors in membership of such organisations, religion was both a cohesive and divisive force. There was little, if any, interaction between Catholic and Protestant groups, a fact aggravated by strong religious conviction and distrust on each side. Public discussion in the nineteenth century on state involvement in education and health, and the operation of the Poor Law, was dominated by denominational considerations. Prunty has noted that:

> The role of women, both as major providers and recipients of social services, and as committed agents and counter-agents of Church missions, reveals the essential impact that the evangelical movement had on shaping Irish women's involvement in charitable organisations in the nineteenth century.[67]

Missionary zeal operated within both Catholic and Protestant camps. Luddy has made the point that for most philanthropic women, charity work was a spiritual responsibility and theirs was in many cases a grim determination to do God's will. Tensions surfaced particularly between groups caring for poor or orphaned children. One Protestant organisation in particular gained the wrath of Catholic activists. This was the Irish Church Missions (ICM), formed in response to the famine of 1846/47. Organised on the basis of poor or ragged schools and residential homes throughout the country, it was particularly strong in Dublin in the second half of the century. A prominent woman of deep religious conviction—Mrs Ellen Smyly—helped establish six such homes and orphanages in the city from 1852. This work she continued throughout her life, her daughters continuing the work after her death.[68] Smyly's homes, in particular her 'Bird's Nest' orphanage, became the best known of such Protestant foundations. Margaret Aylward, at this time associated with a group of lay Catholic women called the Ladies Association of Charity, was also active in the Dublin slums in a number of endeavours to help poor women and their children.

Prunty has pointed out that the work of the Ladies Association and evangelical groups such as the ICM had much in common in terms of organisation, methods of fundraising, advertising, class involvement and relief provided.[69] It was however, in the care and education of children—viewed essentially as religious and moral tasks, to be carried out along strict denominational lines—that bitter inter-church rivalry occurred.[70] Working in the same areas as the ICM and the Smyly homes, Aylward and the Ladies Association became aware of the extent of proselytising activities of Protestant groups within such communities. Aylward took a very public role in challenging the work of such groups, documenting their activities through fact-finding missions carried on throughout the city, through interviews and by compilation of a register of schools suspected of proselytising:

The fact-finding excursions very rapidly became 'open warfare', with the zealous Ladies of Charity actively involved in physically removing Catholic children from Protestant institutions, and equally zealous Protestant missionaries determined to persevere in their evangelising activity … There are reports of children being dragged away by the schoolmistresses to prevent them being interviewed by the Ladies of Charity; of the Catholic ladies distributing crucifixes among the children, and the Protestant missionaries removing these 'idols' from them; of crowds of Dublin men, women and children assembling to join in the excitement, urging on the disputing parties with cries of 'more power to you'.[71]

Aylward challenged fellow Catholics to emulate the commitment and organisation of groups such as the ICM 'whose zeal outshone that of their Catholic adversaries'.[72] Based on her first-hand experience of the conditions of the poor, and her knowledge of the Protestant missionary movement, Aylward was responsible for the formation of St Brigid's Orphanage in 1857—seen as a rival to Smyly's Bird's Nest. Continuing her anti-proselytising campaign, Aylward also established free Catholic schools in poor areas where Protestant free schools were located, adopting the methods of the latter by providing food and clothing to pupils.

Assessing the broad picture of women's philanthropy in nineteenth-century Ireland Luddy has commented:

> The denominational basis of many charitable societies with similar objectives prevented women from uniting to create large, more extensive and perhaps more efficient organisations. Religious bias not only inhibited women from pooling their financial resources but also from building upon each other's experiences as charity workers. The religious basis of many charitable societies also hindered the development of a critique of the social origins of poverty and destitution.[73]

Research into the development of female philanthropy has revealed a number of common themes. Writing of developments toward the latter half of the eighteenth century, Rosemary Raughter has noted that: 'Charitable women's recognition of poverty as the root cause of the social evils whose effects they were attempting to mitigate … did not find expression in any meaningful critique of the basic structures of a patriarchal and hierarchal society … It might be argued that philanthropic women through their work, their teaching and their example actually reinforced the existing structures of society and stereotypical notions about the female role and nature.'[74] Two main strands developed within philanthropy during the nineteenth century: a benevolent strand which sought to alleviate the symptoms of poverty without questioning the underlying causes, and a reformist strand which attempted to initiate legislative change to improve the lot of the poor.[75] It was from among those active within the latter that early feminist demands would emerge. Richard Evans has pointed to the development of nineteenth-century middle-class liberalism as a key factor in the emergence of nineteenth- and twentieth-century feminism. Citing a series of varying objectives of liberalism across different countries, including national self-determination, parliamentary sovereignty, the ending of slavery, social and moral reform, Evans notes that common to all was a concern with the individual. He argues: 'Individualism provided the ideological links between liberal movements of this kind and the emergence of organised feminism.'[76] With such developments strongest within Protestant communities, Evans declares that 'Feminism, like liberalism itself, was above all a creed of the Protestant middle classes'.[77]

Many, if not most early feminist activists came from families closely involved in liberal movements of this kind; within the Irish context, a similar pattern emerged. The majority of those prominent in reformist campaigns came from a Quaker or Protestant background. Frequently such women—and their families—had been active in the anti-slavery and temperance movements, Anna Haslam and Isabella Tod being perhaps the two best known examples. Catholic women were less likely to become active in campaigns for social change. Allied to the passive role of women within the Catholic church structure, the emergence of new religious orders resulted in most charitable work being left to nuns.[78] As lay women were increasingly restricted to a fund-raising role, the result was the almost complete absence of independent charities organised by Catholic women after 1850 (with the exception of Aylward and the Ladies Association detailed above). Not all Protestant organisations of this time, however, were reformist. In fact, the two largest societies of Protestant women to emerge were the Young Women's Christian Association (YWCA) established in 1866, and the Girls' Friendly Society (GFS) established in 1877—both described by Luddy as socially conservative and inactive in seeking legislation to improve the working and social conditions of the poor.[79] Other more progressive societies to emerge from the 1870s include The Women's Temperance Association (1874), the National Society for the Prevention of Cruelty to Children, the Philanthropic Reform Association, and the Irish Workhouse Association. These latter actively sought legislative change regarding the care of children and the poor, and had mixed-sex executive committees in which women played a key role.[80]

Writing from an international perspective, and in particular against the backdrop of industrialised societies within which socialist and feminist causes interacted to a much greater extent than in Ireland, Evans has noted frequent condescension on the part of radical feminists towards working-class women. Conscious of their social superiority as educated women better placed in life, Evans argues, 'feminists wanted ultimately to re-create working women in their own image'.[81] While Irish social and industrial conditions were quite different from those discussed by Evans, the content of his conclusions can be applied to the objectives of much philanthropic activity. Within an Irish framework, Luddy has observed that:

> The work of philanthropists had much to do with the imposition of values. For most of them a desire to turn poor women into good wives, mothers and housekeepers was the key to the moral and spiritual regeneration of society.[82]

In essence, the majority of women involved in charity work were not consciously feminist. As the century progressed, some of them did come to a realisation of the need to expand their own and other women's areas of employment. In this regard significant societies to emerge included the Belfast Society for Providing Nurses for the Sick Poor (1874)—one of the first societies to train and employ nurses—and the Irish Society for Promoting the Employment of Educated Women (1862), which sought to expand women's work within the commercial field. The latter—later to become the Queen's Institute—aimed to expand the range of women's employment by providing training in a range of subjects including book-keeping, law copying, telegraphy and sewing machine classes. The Queen's Institute continued until 1881, some members later affiliating with the new technical college for artisans. The Girls' Friendly Society (1877) opened an employment registry for domestic servants, and set up hostels in which young girls could stay while seeking employment in Dublin. Increasing emphasis on the extension of employment opportunities for women, allied to educational developments from the 1870s paved the way for a range of demands from women within the social, economic and political spheres.

Despite the social and political limitations of much of their work, the influence of Irish women philanthropists cannot be dismissed as irrelevant. By devoting their time, money and energy to caring for the poor and destitute in nineteenth-century Irish society, the nature of such care was transformed. As Raughter has pointed out, 'Ultimately, it was to force women to engage with social problems and to question the place of women in society.'[83] In addition, through their activities women philanthropists 'created careers for themselves, advanced the position of middle-class women in society, and evolved a complex argument for political rights'.[84]

PART 2

A New Century—Action and Reaction

4

RADICAL SUFFRAGE CAMPAIGN

The argument of the broken window pane is the most valuable argument in modern politics. (EMMELINE PANKHURST 1858–1928)

POLITICAL AND SOCIAL DEVELOPMENTS

From 1900 the Irish Parliamentary Party was reunited under the leadership of John Redmond, MP for Waterford, aided by John Dillon. Following the General Election of 1910 Redmond's party held the balance of power at Westminster and Home Rule for Ireland seemed assured.

While the majority of Irish people supported Redmond's party, there had emerged in the late nineteenth century a new grouping in Irish society with broader objectives than the restoration of a native parliament.[1] The activities of such groups reached a peak in the years leading up to the outbreak of World War I in 1914. Their primary ideology was one of a cultural and national renaissance through a revival of Gaelic language, literature, poetry, drama, folklore and sports. An increased awareness of an historical and cultural tradition was fostered by the development of a literary and dramatic movement by poets such as W.B. Yeats and Æ (George Russell), dramatists Lady Gregory and J.M. Synge, and writers Standish O'Grady and James Stephens. Organisations such as the Gaelic Athletic Association (GAA) and the Gaelic League struck a cord with many young people and developed in them a sense of distinct national identity. The Gaelic League was the most advanced in its attitude to women, being the first to admit women and men on equal terms. Sinn Féin, founded in 1905 by Arthur Griffith, provided a political outlet for many who combined the ideal of an Irish Ireland with that of separation from England. While Griffith advocated a policy of passive resistance—Irish MPs should refuse to sit in Westminster and set up an Irish parliament in Dublin—others saw armed rebellion as the only way to attain the objective of an Irish republic. The various nationalist associations which had developed provided good nurturing ground for recruitment to such an ideal. From 1910 a revitalised Irish Republican Brotherhood (IRB) benefited from the rising militant spirit throughout nationalist Ireland, spurred on by political developments at home and abroad. In 1913 the Ulster Volunteer Force was formed to resist by armed force any attempt to implement Home Rule. By the end of that year it had some 100,000 members, armed with guns and ammunition imported illegally from Europe. The IRB contemplated the establishment of a similar force in the south.

There were however other significant developments in pre-war Ireland. In 1913 Constance de Markievicz (hereafter referred to as Constance Markievicz) told a Dublin audience that there were three great movements going on in Ireland—the national movement, the women's movement, and the industrial movement, 'all fighting the same fight, for the extension of human liberty'. Many young women were involved in one or more of these causes, and the excitement of the time has been articulated by Mary Maguire Colum, a teacher at St Ita's girls school:

> Almost everything significant in the Dublin of that period was run by the young; youth, eagerness, brains, imagination, are what I remember of everybody. There was something else that was in all of them: a desire for self-sacrifice, a devotion to causes; everyone was working for a cause for practically everything was a cause … In addition to other causes I was deep in the women's suffrage movement and had read all the books about the position of women, which corresponded in a way to that of the oppressed races.[2]

NEW SUFFRAGE SOCIETIES FROM 1908

During the early 1900s a new generation of Irishwomen became involved in the suffrage campaign. These younger women had benefited from the educational advances obtained during the late nineteenth century, and many were, like Mary Colum, influenced by contemporary developments in Ireland. One such woman, Hanna Sheehy Skeffington—whose name would become synonymous with the women's movement—wrote of her initiation into that campaign when asked to sign a petition to the House of Commons in 1902:

> I was then an undergraduate, and was amazed and disgusted to learn that I was classed among criminals, infants and lunatics—in fact that my status as a woman was worse than any of these.[3]

A Dublin woman, educated by the Dominican nuns in Eccles Street, Hanna went on to gain an MA from the Royal University, and remained a life-long feminist. From a political family—her father was David Sheehy, a nationalist MP from 1885–1918—she continued active in Irish political life throughout her lifetime. On her marriage to Frank Skeffington in 1903 they adopted the joint name of Sheehy Skeffington. An ardent feminist, Frank resigned his position as Registrar of the Royal University in 1904 over its non-recognition of women graduates.

The emergence of the Women's Social and Political Union (WSPU) in Manchester in 1903, and the militant tactics adopted by its founder Emmeline Pankhurst, marked a significant new phase in the suffrage campaign. Irish influences played a part in the development of the new organisation. Between 1901 and 1904 Christabel Pankhurst (eldest daughter of Emmeline) served what she later described as a 'political apprenticeship of great and lasting value' through her contact with Eva Gore Booth and the latter's work within the North of England Society for Women's Suffrage (NESWS).[4] As Gore Booth's politital protégé, Christabel became an executive member of NESWS and a member of the Manchester and Salford Trade Union Council.[5] (Labour support was very important to the early development of the WSPU, but was not a policy retained for long by Emmeline and Christabel.) Another significant influence on the WSPU leaders would be the strategy of Charles Stewart Parnell and the Irish Parliamentary Party. The WSPU policy of opposing all government candidates at elections was directly derived from Parnellite tactics to 'keep the Government out'—under which the late Dr Pankhurst had been defeated as a Liberal candidate in 1885.[6]

Growing awareness of suffrage demands internationally, and the aggressive tactics of the WSPU in particular, inspired many young Irish women to become involved in the suffrage movement. While some initially joined the long established IWSLGA, others took part in WSPU demonstrations and marches in England, the latter providing what one Irish suffragette called 'a helpful apprenticeship for our campaign in Ireland'.[7] The first in a series of new Irish suffrage societies emerged in 1908 with the formation of the Irish Women's Franchise League (IWFL) in 1908 by Hanna Sheehy Skeffington and Margaret Cousins. Implicit in its formation was recognition of the quite different political scenario facing suffrage campaigners in Ireland. Other factors leading to its formation included impatience with the conservative methods of the IWSLGA, admiration of the militant tactics of the WSPU, and conviction of the need for an independent Irish suffrage society—distinctly separate from English connection.[8] From the outset declaring itself a militant and non-party organisation, the IWFL aimed to obtain votes for women on the same terms as men. Membership was restricted to women, but many men were actively involved as associates. Margaret Cousins later wrote:

> We were as keen as men on the freedom of Ireland, but we saw the men clamouring for amendments which suited their own interests, and made no recognition of the existence of women as fellow citizens. We women were convinced that anything which improved the status of women would improve, not hinder, the coming of real national self-government.[9]

The IWFL decided therefore to work towards having a 'votes for women' clause included in the Home Rule for Ireland Bill then under consideration. Over the next 3–4 years a number of other suffrage societies were formed, militant and non-militant, catering for particular regional, religious or political groups. Among these were the Munster Women's Franchise League, the Belfast-based Irish Women's Suffrage Society and an Irish branch of the Conservative and Unionist Women's Suffrage Association.[10] To co-ordinate the work of the emerging smaller associations, the Irish Women's Suffrage Federation (IWSL) was formed in Dublin in August 1911 with Louie Bennett and Helen Chenevix as joint Honorary Secretaries.[11] By linking together the scattered suffrage groups throughout the country, the IWSF aimed to carry out more effective propaganda and educative work, and form the basis of an organisation to continue after suffrage was attained. Its policy would be non-party and non-militant (although some members were occasionally involved in militancy). The new organisation grew rapidly. By 1913 fifteen groups were affiliated to the IWSF, rising to twenty-four by 1916.[12] Between 1908 and 1912 a campaign of consciousness-raising regarding female suffrage was waged throughout Ireland. Prominent suffrage leaders from England addressed public meetings in Dublin, Cork and Belfast. Corporations, county and district councils were petitioned, and deputations sent to prominent politicians. The pivotal role of the Irish

Parliamentary Party at this time in deciding the fate of suffrage bills before Parliament concentrated the attention of both Irish and English suffragists, although differences in emphasis would emerge.

The diversity of groups within the new Federation can be judged by its inclusion of members from a Unionist background including authors Edith Somerville and Violet Martin (Somerville and Ross) and nationalists such as Mary MacSwiney.

Helen Chenevix later wrote that the suffrage movement 'brought women from sheltered homes face to face with the realities of sweated wages and the wretched conditions imposed on women who had to earn their living'.[13] The formation of the Irish Women's Reform League (IWRL) later in 1911 by Louie Bennett is particularly significant in this context. Formed as the Dublin branch of the IWSF, it was the only women's rights society of the time not to contain suffrage or franchise in its title. Reflecting her personal growing social awareness, Bennett used it to draw attention to the social and economic position of women workers and their families.[14] The IWRL investigated working conditions in Dublin factories, organising public debates and seminars to discuss its findings. In addition to specific industrial disputes and discrepancies in factory wages, health and safety issues were highlighted. Issues ranging from locked factory windows, filthy toilets, 'brutal' language towards employees, and rats in a chocolate factory—all were reported in the *Irish Citizen*, and not surprisingly, led to IWRL campaigns for women factory inspectors. Publication of these findings in the *Irish Citizen* ensured that such information was brought to the attention of a broad spectrum of women's groups.

The IWRL also initiated a committee to watch legislation affecting women, and established a 'watching the courts committee' to observe and report on cases involving injustice to women and girls. Most of the cases reported concerned marital violence, indecent assault on children, and the seduction of young girls—often by employers. Details of such cases were reported quite frankly; lenient sentencing, early release of those convicted and judicial attitudes were all challenged and criticised. Old ideas of propriety remained, however, it being reported that during a divorce case in 1915 the judge requested that 'all ladies' leave court. Another initiative of the IWRL was the establishment of a lending library at its offices in Dublin's Anne Street. Members were encouraged to borrow books from this collection which the IWRL claimed covered all aspects of the Women's movement. Bennett advised a dual approach by IWSF affiliates; in small towns and villages, the personal touch of meetings in private houses she believed did much to dissipate prejudice and embitterment, 'Our people like to see us in their home [rather] than engaged in the doubtful business of "tub-thumping". For work in urban centres, she argued that outdoor meetings were becoming an essential means of spreading the suffrage gospel. Accepting that this was distressful to the ordinary women Bennett insisted: 'most Irishwomen have not faced up to the necessity of making sacrifices for the cause.'[15] Irishwomen from quite disparate backgrounds could now choose between the long-established IWSLGA, the militant IWFL and the middle ground of the IWSF. Activists of the time would probably have agreed with the comment of Margaret Cousins that 'the era of dumb self-effacing women was over'.[16]

Crucial to the dissemination of information on suffrage activities at home and abroad was the establishment in 1912 of the *Irish Citizen*. This suffrage paper provided feminist activists with an important means of communication, education and propaganda. Circulated throughout the thirty-two counties, it acted as an important link between the various societies. Its founders—Frank Sheehy Skeffington and James Cousins—were joint editors until Cousins emigrated in 1913. The paper continued to be published weekly by Sheehy Skeffington until his murder in 1916. Thereafter, it was published monthly until 1920 with Hanna Sheehy Skeffington and Louie Bennett its main editors. Designed to cater for both militant and non-militant societies, its columns kept women throughout the country informed of suffrage developments. Articles were published which were expressly designed to educate Irish public opinion regarding feminist demands. Before the launch of the *Irish Citizen*, Irish women had to rely on British suffrage journals. While these did cover Irish groups, inevitably most attention was given to domestic affairs. There had been an earlier Irish women's paper—*Bean na hÉireann*—published between 1909–1911 by *Inghinidhe na hÉireann* (Daughters of Erin), a nationalist women's group with a strong feminist bias. Many issues covered by *Bean na hÉireann* were similar to those later covered by the *Irish Citizen*. However, disagreement over whether nationalist or feminist demands should take precedence in the contemporary political scenario, plus the strong separatist tone of *Bean na hÉireann*, limited its appeal to a section of Irishwomen.

The *Irish Citizen* made its debut at a peak time of co-operation between women's groups. While its pages reflected a diversity of opinion regarding methods and tactics, they also reflected the vibrancy and commitment of women to their own cause. Its editorials and articles kept readers informed of current national developments regarding women's suffrage, as well as covering broader aspects of feminism and the struggle for women's rights. While the long-established IWSLGA continued its regular indoor meetings the newer groups used a combination of indoor and outdoor events to maximise publicity. A weekly list of such events was published in the paper's *Citizens Diary*. A typical *Diary* in 1913 lists suffrage events to be held that week at up to a dozen venues including Belfast, Ballina, Cahirciveen, Westport and the '9 Acres' in Dublin's Phoenix Park. As a result of such activities, the number of suffrage societies and branches grew from a total of fifteen in November to twenty-nine by May 1913.[17]

POLITICAL DEVELOPMENTS 1910–1914

Due to heightened activity on the suffrage issue, a number of attempts were made from 1910 to introduce a women's suffrage bill in the House of Commons. While many individual MPs favoured the principle of female suffrage, party considerations usually determined their attitude if a bill showed any sign of success. Liberals feared that votes for women on the existing property basis would favour Conservatives; Conservatives similarly feared that any widening of qualifications would favour Liberals. Only Labour consistently supported women's suffrage proposals whilst also working towards its goal of full adult suffrage for all citizens regardless of property qualifications.

After the general election of 1910 the Liberals no longer held a majority, and it was recognised that legislative success would not be achieved with the support of just one party. An all-party 'Conciliation Committee' was established to promote an agreed suffrage bill amenable to all. Six Irish MPs were on the Committee, a number which rose to ten by 1912. The first 'Conciliation Bill' failed in 1910, but by 1911 the second such Bill seemed more likely to succeed. Over 400 MPs had pledged to vote for women's suffrage, and English suffragettes suspended militant activity to await the outcome. Intense propaganda efforts continued by English and Irish suffragettes, however, and in May 1911 the Lord Mayor of Dublin presented a petition in favour of the Bill at the House of Commons. Although the Bill received a majority vote of 167 in May 1911, concern on the part of the Liberal Party on its potential electoral effect resulted in a series of delaying tactics by Asquith, ultimately ensuring that it was, in the words of Lloyd George 'torpedoed'. Militancy was renewed in England at this point. Many Irishwomen took part and were subsequently imprisoned. Division on the issue at cabinet level is confirmed in correspondence between Augustine Birrell, Chief Secretary for Ireland and John Dillon, a senior member of the Irish Parliamentary Party, in which Birrell noted:

> I think this active vocal split in the Cabinet on Women most serious. I don't see how I could remain in a Cabinet which has adopted en bloc Female Suffrage, married and single—and if I couldn't, how could Asquith?[18]

In addition to the known anti-suffrage view of Asquith, the issue of Irish Home Rule then dominant in Irish and English politics was a prime cause in hindering the progress of such a Bill. Some Irish MPs would have agreed with the sentiments of John Dillon to a suffrage deputation that:

> Women's suffrage will I believe, be the ruin of our western civilisation. It will destroy the home, challenging the headship of man, laid down by God. It may come in your time—I hope not in mine.[19]

Yet, other Irish MPs like William Redmond (brother of the Irish party leader) and Tom Kettle (married to a sister of Hanna Sheehy Skeffington, Mary) actively supported the cause in parliament. But, when Home Rule manoeuvrings demanded, they stepped into line under their party leader. The pivotal role of the Irish Parliamentary Party in deciding the fate of suffrage bills (due to its holding the balance of power), concentrated the attention of English suffragists on Ireland—a factor not always helpful to Irish campaigners. Personally hostile to women's suffrage, John Redmond was anxious to avoid any issue which might adversely affect the granting of Home Rule to Ireland. When the Bill came up for a second reading in March 1912, it was defeated by 14 votes. The voting of Irish members was crucial to its defeat. Whereas 10 months earlier thirty-one Irish members had voted for the bill, in 1912 forty-one voted against the Bill with ten abstaining. The Secretary of that Committee, in a letter to the *Manchester Guardian*, confirmed that the most serious single cause of the bill's defeat was the united vote of the Irish members, stating that he had been told that 'it was necessary for the Irish Party in the interests of Home Rule to save the Liberal ministry from the disruptive effects of Women's Suffrage'.[20] Fears of endangering Home Rule, either by precipitating a general election or by triggering the resignation of cabinet ministers were sufficiently strong to ensure that all women's suffrage measures from this point on would be opposed by all Irish MPs.

The action of the Irish Party was to bring upon them the wrath of the English suffragists and suffragettes. Irish suffragists too were perturbed and angry at the course of events. Apart from heckling politicians at public meetings, militant action on English lines had not been implemented in Ireland. Prior to the 1912 vote, Redmond and Churchill had been picketed and heckled during visits to Dublin and Belfast. Three days after the defeat of the Bill, a Home Rule demonstration was held in O'Connell Street in Dublin. The IWFL, taking advantage of the crowds in the city for the occasion, organised a poster parade seeking a measure of women's suffrage within the Home Rule bill. As their march ended there occurred what the *Freeman's Journal*, a Dublin newspaper, described as 'some unpleasant incidents' during which the women were roughly treated by stewards, their posters taken from them and torn up.[21] Some weeks later John Redmond received a deputation from the IWFL, and it became known that he refused to support female suffrage either in the Home Rule bill or after Home Rule was established. Apart from his personal views on the issue, Redmond, like Carson, undoubtedly feared the effect on his party of a vastly increased electorate. At this point the IWFL declared war on the Irish Party. When the Home Rule bill was introduced in the House of Commons in April 1912, it contained no reference to female suffrage, and Irish members were responsible for the subsequent defeat of a number of proposed women's suffrage amendments to the bill. The bill was bitterly opposed by the WSPU which organised a poster parade outside the Houses of Parliament proclaiming 'No votes for women, no Home Rule'.

Later that month, Redmond organised a National Convention in Dublin to consider the Home Rule Bill. Women were excluded. In June 1912 a mass meeting of Irish women was held in Dublin's Mansion House to demand the inclusion of women's suffrage in the Home Rule Bill. At this meeting, chaired by Professor Mary Hayden, trade unionist and nationalist women joined representatives of suffrage societies throughout Ireland. Among those on the platform were Constance Markievicz, Dr Kathleen Lynn, Jennie Wyse Power, Delia Larkin, Mrs Dudley Edwards, Kathleen Cruise O'Brien, Miss Carson and Helen Chenevix.[22] Messages of support were received from many individuals and organisations, including James Connolly, Maud Gonne MacBride, George Russell, Dr Mary Strangman (Town Councillor), Helena Molony and Louie Bennett. The unity of feeling experienced by women from radically different political backgrounds is evident from the speeches given and messages received. On the one hand a Unionist woman argued that 'no democratic government can be considered complete which ignores not only a class but a whole sex', while Jenny Wyse Power argued that 'as an Irish nationalist I cannot see why there should be any antagonism between Irishwomen's demand for citizenship and the demand for a native parliament'. A pithy summary of the political status of Irishwomen was given by Mary Chambers of the Belfast based Irish Women's Suffrage Society (IWSS) when she said that 'whatever may happen in Ireland, suffragists realise that under the Home Rule Bill, as it at present stands, one half of the responsible population of the country will continue to be governed by the other half'.[23] The meeting unanimously adopted a resolution which stated:

> While expressing no opinion on the general question of Home Rule, this Mass Meeting of delegates from the Irish Suffrage Societies and other women's organisations representing all shades of political and religious opinion, profoundly regrets the proposal to establish a new Constitution in Ireland on a purely male franchise, and calls upon the Government to amend the Home Rule Bill in Committee by adopting the Local Government Register (which includes women) as the basis for the new parliament.

Copies of the resolution were sent to each cabinet minister and to all Irish MPs. It was ignored by all. The IWFL decided to initiate militant action in Ireland.[24]

In June 1912 the first militant acts took place when members of the IWFL broke windows in Government buildings in Dublin, including the GPO, the Custom House, and Dublin Castle. Eight members of the League—including Hanna Sheehy Skeffington—were subsequently arrested for the offence. Refusing to pay either fine or bail, all were imprisoned for varying periods of time.[25] From this time up to the outbreak of war in 1914 there would be 35 convictions of women for suffrage militancy in Ireland. Twenty-two of these incidents took place in Dublin, the remainder in Belfast and Lisburn.

Prime Minister Asquith was due to visit Dublin in July 1912 in connection with the Home Rule Bill. He categorically refused to meet with any suffrage deputation during his visit. Some weeks earlier he had declared it would be a calamity if any system of Irish self-government were implemented which excluded from participation any section of Irish opinion or Irish interest. Similarly, when John Dillon rejected the exclusion of Ulster from the Home Rule Bill, stating 'it must be Home

Rule for all, or none at all', the *Irish Citizen* retorted that 'Home Rule for all meant Home Rule for Men'.[26] For days before the Asquith visit inflammatory letters were published in Dublin papers threatening suffragettes if they attempted any demonstrations during his visit. 'Home-Ruler' was the most popular of the many pen-names used. One such letter warned Frank Sheehy Skeffington that 'should he and his suffragist friends begin their dirty tricks, they may expect to receive at the hands of Nationalists more than they had bargained for'.[27] Another writer suggested that police should 'use whips on the shoulders of those unsexed viragoes, slender springy, stingy riding whips'.[28] Newspaper editorials also advised against any suffrage demonstrations during the visit. The *Evening Telegraph* warning Mr Sheehy Skeffington and his supporters to keep their hands off Mr Asquith, stating, 'Any attempt to interfere with the Prime Minister during his visit here will be accepted as a declaration of war on the Home Rule movement.'[29]

A number of demonstrations were staged by Irish suffragettes during the Asquith visit. These included poster parades, breaking windows in a post-office, and heckling by a group of women adjacent to the Premier's boat at Kingstown (Dún Laoghaire)—tactics in line with the rather mild militancy used in Ireland to this point. The focal point of Asquith's visit was a Home Rule gathering in Dublin's Theatre Royal, at which he and John Redmond would speak. Despite strict security for entry to this meeting, Frank Sheehy Skeffington managed to enter disguised as a clergyman, and interrupt Mr Asquith at a relevant point before being unceremoniously ejected. The IWFL had arranged an open-air meeting to be held adjacent to Liberty Hall at the same time as Asquith's meeting a short distance away. Whatever chance there had been of the visit and demonstrations passing off without incident was shattered by the actions of three WSPU members from England who travelled to Dublin for the visit unknown to Irish suffragettes.

Two incidents these women instigated would have implications for Irish suffrage groups. The first of these involved the throwing of a hatchet into the open carriage in which Asquith and Redmond were travelling from Dún Laoghaire into the city centre. The hatchet missed Asquith, grazing Redmond's ear.[30] The second incident was an arson attempt at the Theatre Royal. Curtains in one of the boxes were set alight by one of the women; shortly afterwards an explosion occurred within the Theatre. The Englishwomen were arrested and explosives were found at their lodgings. Newspaper headlines denounced both incidents—'The Virago and the Hatchet', 'Reign of Terror', 'Dastardly Outrage'.[31]

Following their arrest and detention in Mountjoy Prison, the *Evening Telegraph* ran a headline citing one of the women's response to prison officials, 'Ladies who have no religion, only Votes for Women'.[32] In relation to the 'hatchet' attack on Asquith, it is interesting to note that police records show information had been received ten days earlier that an attempt would be made to shoot Asquith during his Dublin visit 'by an advanced section of militant suffragists'.[33]

The IWFL immediately denied all knowledge of the presence of English suffragettes in Dublin, stating that the League had no association with their English counterparts beyond unity of demand. Non-militant groups also dissociated themselves from the militant acts, one group—the Munster Women's Franchise League—expressing 'abhorrence of the wicked actions'.[34] An interesting signatory to this statement was Mary MacSwiney, later to be involved in controversy between suffragists and nationalists. Despite such protests, the immediate effect of these incidents was that all suffrage activity in Dublin became suspect for a time, and subject to mob-violence. The IWFL meeting being held at the same time as the Asquith meeting was attended by a hostile crowd, later augmented by crowds who had been cheering Asquith's arrival across the river. There developed what the *Irish Independent* described as 'trouble of a very serious nature'.[35] The women on the IWFL platform were heckled with shouts of 'we will never forget the hatchet', 'down with the suffragettes', 'burn them', 'throw them in the river'. The crowd became so hostile that police had to form a barrier between it and the speakers' platform. A police inspector later testified in court that after half an hour he advised the women to end the meeting, and some fifty policemen escorted the speakers to O'Connell Street. Along the way, police were forced to draw batons a number of times, particularly in Abbey Street where crowds became particularly menacing, crying 'let us at them and we'll give them what they deserve.' Police finally managed to get the women on a tram out of O'Connell Street, which left with a police escort amid breaking glass as crowds broke its windows.

A number of other incidents occurred about this time. Police rescued one suffragette whom the crowd were on the point of throwing into the Liffey, while other women—including Countess Markievicz—were mobbed by the crowd on Eden Quay. Again, police came to the rescue and escorted the women to safety. Numerous incidents of violence and threats against women occurred that day, not all reserved for known suffragettes. The *Irish Independent* reported that 'Every woman respectably dressed went in danger of being singled out by the mob as a suffragette, and a state of panic prevailed'.[36] The paper reported cases where women's clothing were almost torn from them before the police intervened. Katharine Tynan, Dublin poet and novelist, describing the events of that night wrote that 'women were hunted like rats in the city'.[37] For about two weeks after the Asquith visit, suffrage meetings of all societies were attended by what the *Irish Citizen* described as 'organised hooliganism', with booing, stonethrowing, and verbal abuse.[38] The *Irish Citizen* was not alone in condemning such conduct. The *Irish Independent* editorial of 29 July, championing the right of women to air their views, stated, 'it is certainly not in keeping with our traditional courtesy towards women to find their meetings interrupted and broken up by apparently organised gangs of men and youths.'[39] Even Moran's *Leader* defended women's right to free speech, stating, 'these people, however eccentric they may be, are entitled to advocate votes for women in public … they should not be treated to physical violence.'[40] The *Sinn Féin* journal was also highly critical of the mob, while its national council condemned as 'un-Irish and unmanly the forcible interference with the right of any section of Irishwomen to publicly claim the suffrage'.[41]

At this time, when the popularity of the IWFL was at its lowest, James Connolly showed his support for the women's movement by travelling from Belfast to speak at the weekly public meeting of the League, an action long and greatly appreciated by the women. Members of his union, the Irish Transport & General Workers' Union (ITGWU), often protected suffragettes at such meetings. Ultimately, pressure of public opinion, demonstrated through newspaper editorials and articles, allied to police activity and arrests eventually brought an end to this spate of violence.

The trial of the English suffragettes took place in August 1912. The charge of throwing a hatchet into Asquith's carriage was dropped, the *Irish Citizen* claiming this was due to Redmond's reluctance to appear as a witness. There were precedents for politicians not proceeding with charges against suffragettes. In November 1910 the Chief Secretary for Ireland, Augustine Birrell, after being slightly injured in a fracas with suffragettes in Downing Street, declined to prosecute, but wrote to Winston Churchill, 'let the matter drop but keep your eyes on the hags in question.'[42] For the remaining charge, two of the women—Mary Leigh and Gladys Evans—were sentenced to five years penal servitude; a third—Lizzie Baker—received seven months hard labour. A *Sinn Féin* editorial on the sentences condemned the Englishwomen's actions, warning that Irish suffragists have not yet realised that 'the Englishwoman in politics is as much an exploiter of Irish women as English men had been of Irish men'.[43] Jennie Wyse Power, then vice-president of Sinn Féin, deplored the attitude of this editorial, asking in response 'may one who has suffered suggest to all Irish men to realise that this is a woman's question'.[44] This exchange articulated differences which would emerge again in the relationship between suffragists and nationalists.

The three English suffragettes sought—and were refused—political status. In response they went on hunger strike on 14 August. They were joined in solidarity by Irish suffragettes then in Mountjoy. Hanna later wrote, 'Hunger-strike was then a new weapon—we were the first to try it out in Ireland—had we but known, we were the pioneers in a long line.'[45] The Irish prisoners were not forcibly fed, and remained on hunger-strike for the remaining five days of their sentence. The English prisoners however, were forcibly fed, Mary Leigh for forty-six days, Gladys Evans for fifty-eight days.[46] Forcible feeding had been widely used in England to deal with the large numbers of suffragette prisoners on hunger strike, and was much criticised. Its introduction into Ireland met with much public disapproval, demonstrated in the letters and petitions which poured into the Chief Secretary's office. Birrell in a letter to John Dillon on the subject explained that he was against forcible feeding because it always ended with the release of the prisoner before her time.

> I want to keep these ladies under lock and key for five years and I am quite willing to feed them with Priests champagne and Michaelmas Geese all the time ... but these wretched hags are obstinate to the point of death.[47]

Of the thirty-five Irish women convicted for suffrage militancy between 1912 and 1914, twelve went on hunger-strike. Only the English suffrage prisoners were forcibly fed.

In an attempt to deal with the public outcry in England over forcible feeding, the Government introduced a bill to allow for the temporary discharge of hunger-strikers when their health was endangered, until they were fit enough to be recommitted to continue their sentence. Their period of release would not count as time served. The Prisoners (Temporary Discharge for Ill Health) Bill popularly known as the 'Cat and Mouse Act' became law in April 1913 with the support of the Irish Parliamentary Party.[48]This action was consistent with party action some weeks earlier, when sixty-two Irish MPs had voted confidence in the government's policy of forcible feeding.

As re-imprisoned women usually recommenced their hunger-strike immediately, under the terms of the new bill sentences of a few months could be spread over an indefinite period. Attempts to introduce the Act into Ireland in the summer of 1913 met with widespread protest.[49] The largest of a series of public protest meetings against this development was held in Dublin's Mansion House. Speakers from both militant and non-militant societies addressed the meeting, including Louie Bennett, Professor Mary Hayden and Dr Kathleen Lynn. Constance Markievicz spoke, not as a suffrage society member, but as a separatist and republican who did not want the vote for an English parliament, and who valued the opportunity to 'express her sympathy with those women who were suffering martyrdom for their cause'.[50] A message of support from Pádraic Pearse read to the meeting argued that it was the duty of everyone in Ireland to oppose this measure, whatever their views on women's suffrage. A resolution moved by Tom Kettle, MP, stated that 'this meeting of Dublin citizens regards the Cat and Mouse Act as a dangerous weapon of political oppression (and) condemns in particular the employment of the Act against three Irish women imprisoned for a political protest ... and demands its immediate repeal.'[51] Comments made later by Kettle 'that he was prepared not to sacrifice, but to postpone', any social or franchise reform 'for the sake of seeing Ireland mistress in her own household' were greeted very critically by some of the audience, with cries of 'you're not a woman' and 'that's not the women's view'.[52]

The provisions of the Cat and Mouse Act were not applied, and the three suffrage prisoners were not re-committed as scheduled after two weeks. They did however remain liable for re-arrest at any time until October 1914, when suffrage sentences were remitted under terms of a General Amnesty.[53]

In May that year, a private member's Women's Franchise Bill was introduced in the House of Commons. An official whip was issued to Irish Party members summoning them to be present for 'critical divisions' on this bill.[54] Fifty-five Irish members voted against the bill —seven voted in favour; it was defeated by 266 to 219. John Dillon was not present for this vote; subsequently he wrote to the newspapers regretting he had not been there to vote against the bill. The *Irish Citizen* pointed out that thirty of the fifty-five 'Redmondites' who had voted against the bill were pledged supporters of Women's Suffrage; had they voted in accordance with their pledges the bill could have been carried.

The *Irish Citizen* had claimed that the non-application of the Cat and

Mouse Act in 1913 had been largely due to the support of Irish public opinion. Official records in Dublin Castle indicate a more lenient attitude in the Lord Lieutenant's offices on the issue of forcible feeding than in Great Britain generally. A subsequent unsuccessful attempt to introduce the Act in Belfast re-enforced these claims. Correspondence between the Attorney General and the Assistant Under-Secretary at Dublin Castle notes that:

> I consider it useless to enforce these considerations against either of these two women. The Lord Lieutenant will not allow them to be detained in prison under artificial feeding when they go on hunger strike, and if arrested for breach of the conditions of temporary discharge, they must be discharged again, or allowed to die in prison.[55]

Instructions had been given that no action was to be taken against these women without specific orders of government. Subsequent claims by the Crown Solicitor that 'these dangerous and criminal women' held high influence in Dublin Castle and had been assured that forcible feeding would not be adopted in Ireland earned him a sharp rebuke from the authorities in Dublin.[56]

To what extent this attitude was guided by sensitivity to public opinion, personal disagreement with the policy, or acknowledgement of the fact that militancy in Ireland was on a minute scale compared with Britain is not known. Assessment of Irish public opinion towards the issue of women's suffrage shows a variety of reactions, from amusement to hostility. In 1913 Lloyd George, speaking of suffrage militancy in Ireland, commented that 'militants have gone out of their way to create an anti-suffrage feeling which never existed there before'.[57] As a result of their attempt on the life of Redmond, he claimed, Irish sentiment was now against (women's suffrage), 'whereas before, on the whole it was inclined to be friendly'. Was this an accurate summation? Certainly newspaper letters and articles, and incidents at the time of the Asquith visit would bear out this view. On the other hand, the extent of petitions and memorials on behalf of both English and Irish suffrage prisoners indicates another range of opinion.

By the end of 1912 suffrage societies were more numerous and widespread than ever before. In retrospect, 1912 saw the suffrage movement in Ireland at its strongest. Despite some criticism at the introduction of militancy, sympathy with and respect for the women increased when they proved their earnestness by going to prison for their principles. Hanna Sheehy Skeffington vividly captures the vital spirit driving suffrage campaigners when she wrote:

> We held parades, processions, pageants. We had colours (orange and green), a Votes for Women badge; we made use with feminine ingenuity of many good publicity devices and stunts ... and became a picturesque element in Irish life. Women speakers who could hold their own, meeting heckling on their own ground, being good-humoured and capable of keeping their temper under bombardments of rotten eggs, over-ripe tomatoes, bags of flour, stinking chemicals, gradually earned respect and due attention.[58]

When women were imprisoned, intensive publicity was gained by colleagues through public protest meetings and petitions. The prisoners themselves maintained pressure within the prison by insistence on political prisoner status, threatening and resorting to hunger-strike if necessary. This latter fact undoubtedly won popular approval. Margaret Cousins, writing of her arrival with two other suffrage prisoners at Tullamore railway station en route to that town's jail, noted:

> To our surprise, all the casual visitors at the railway station, all the station porters, car drivers, newsboys, formed a procession of sympathy behind us, and our police guard, and escorted us the short distance on foot from the station to the big feudal-looking Tullamore jail, and gave us a great cheer as we entered its fear-envoking gate.[59]

The women subsequently hunger-struck for six days in support of their demand for political prisoner status. The IWFL engaged in constant activity in the town at this time, and Tullamore urban council passed a unanimous resolution in support of the women's demands. When these demands were met, and the strike called off, the Chairman of the town council came to visit Margaret Cousins, 'bringing a soft down pillow'. Not all their experiences were quite so positive. Hanna Sheehy Skeffington recalled a particularly hostile reception towards IWFL in Roscommon when a crowd in Boyle threatened to throw them into the river, and stoned their hotel, informing a local priest that 'they hadn't had such fun since the Parnell split'.[60]

Public opinion as articulated in the press and journals of the day fluctuated from ridicule to qualified acceptance of some measure of women's suffrage; political considerations coloured the views of many critics, while militancy—particularly that of the English suffragettes in Dublin—aroused downright hostility. The imprisonment of activists and subsequent hunger-striking tactics brought a more favourable attitude. A prominent Dublin journal of the time—*The Leader*—edited by D.P. Moran, generally treated the women's campaign with derision, publishing many topical cartoons. Some of his criticisms, however, were of a more serious nature, and reflected a definite section of public opinion:

> The movement in Ireland smacks rather of imitation of the English, and we do not regard it as a native and spontaneous growth. (It) is a little artificial and there is a suspicion of West Britonism about it. There is a chance that a women's franchise movement suspected of too much connection with the English suffragettes, may create prejudice against it in quarters quite friendly to Women's Suffrage.[61]

In 1912, the *Catholic Bulletin* published a story entitled 'Kitty's fight for freedom'. This told how a young girl, 'enticed into the suffrage movement by a spinster of uncertain age, thin and hatchet-faced', takes part in a suffrage demonstration, meeting a hostile reception and rough treatment by the crowd. Her fiancé, who believed that 'women are made to be cherished and shielded from contact with a rough world', rescues her, the story ending with the blushing heroine telling a suffragette friend that 'it is much more satisfactory to have a man do these disagreeable things for one'.[62] The extent to which this story reflected clerical views on the suffrage issue can be gauged from a number of statements issued over these years. In July 1912, Monsignor Keller of Youghal, speaking to convent-school pupils, attacked the suffragettes as:

> That strange tribe, small in numbers, that has arisen on the horizon in Ireland in quite recent times. They are not men, they are not women. Woman: the idea comprises dignity, self-respect, refinement, reserve. I don't find any of these qualities among the Suffragettes.[63]

Clerical opinion on the suffrage issue had been negative even before the onset of militancy. In 1909, Fr D. Barry wrote in the *Irish Ecclesiastical Record* against giving women the vote on a number of grounds, including the opinion that as the efficient discharge of her duties as a wife rendered it impossible for woman to make her own way in the community, there was no reason why she should have a direct part in the policy of the state. Furthermore, he argued, 'allowing woman the right of suffrage is incompatible with the Catholic ideal of the unity of domestic life'. Fr Barry cited a common objection to the effect on women of party politics and rancorous local factions which would:

> Fare ill with what may be called the passive virtues of humility, patience, meekness, forbearance and self-repression (which are) looked upon by the Church as the special prerogative of the female soul. Catholic principles give no countenance to the movement for extending the franchise to women; not because they are inferior to men, but because the movement is a retrograde one, tending to supplant their position of real superiority by one of nominal equality.[64]

Similar sentiments were expressed by a priest in Ventry when Margaret Cousins of the IWFL spoke to locals on Votes for Women outside the local church after Sunday mass. Taking James Cousins (her husband) to be a visiting worshipper, the priest confided, 'It's a sure sign of the coming break-up of the planet when women take to leaving their homes and coming out in public.'[65] In his 1913 Lenten Pastoral, the Bishop of Ross commented that in an effort to escape from dependence on man, womankind were 'aping his dress, copying his social habits, and displacing him in most callings, except in the trenches and fighting lines', and concluded that,

> many women, bitten by the Higher Education craze, openly and aggressively assert their own superiority, and, reversing God's order, attempt to exercise dominion over men.[66]

The catholic clergy were not unique in denigrating the women's movement. The Dean of St Patrick's Cathedral in Dublin refused permission for a service to be held for suffragette prisoners, and the *Church of Ireland Gazette* advocated deportation for militant suffragettes.[67]

Even the universities were not untouched by the issue. The student magazine of University College Dublin regularly published reports of debates on the subject, editorial support invariably being against its implementation. In the course of a 1914 article discussing what the word 'liberty' meant to intellectuals, the *National Student* stated that, among other things, the word meant votes for women 'with its usual corollary of easily obtained divorce'.[68] The article also argued that nothing had tended to alienate support away from the English Labour Party than its support of secular education and woman suffrage, 'causes which, whatever be their intrinsic merits, have no more to do with democracy or liberty than the man in the moon'.

Hanna Sheehy Skeffington later summed up attitudes to the suffrage campaign:

> The Press, both National and Conservative, official Sinn Féin, the clergy on the whole, were opposed to the militant movement. Some socialists feared that women, if given the vote, would prove clerically-minded. Bishops denounced the new movement in pastorals. Even the Quakers, though usually receptive, were opposed to violence. So from Right and Left wing there were critics.[69]

English suffrage campaigners had become increasingly critical of Irish political manoeuvrings that resulted in suffrage measures being sacrificed for party interests.

Early in 1913, one of the main English suffrage journals, *Votes for Women*, published a highly critical article on John Redmond's role in destroying a series of Conciliation Bills during 1910–192, commenting that:

> We are left with the inevitable conclusion that Mr Redmond will endeavour and will succeed in dealing similarly with any and every attempt to enfranchise women, which is not incorporated in a Government measure.[70]

The article, however, was also highly critical of the role Irishwomen had played to date:

> We have no hesitation in saying that the remedy for this disgraceful state of affairs lies with the Irish women themselves. While English, Scottish and Welsh women have been coming forward and demanding their enfranchisement, the great majority of women in Ireland have placed the claims of their party first and their own citizen rights second.

In explaining why the WSPU decided in 1913 on a policy change regarding activity on the island of Ireland, Christabel Pankhurst noted that 'John

Redmond is to so large an extent the arbiter of the fate of English women (and) Nationalist members hold the fate of the Suffrage Cause for the whole kingdom in their hands'.[71] In September that year, branches of the WSPU were established in Belfast and Dublin, and a campaign was initiated in Ulster to obtain from Sir Edward Carson, leader of the Ulster unionists, the assurance of an equal share for women in his planned provisional government. The *Irish Citizen* voiced the concern of many Irish suffragists in questioning this move. A constant taunt against Irish suffrage groups was that they were 'English societies' and did not represent Irish women. Agreeing that pressure be brought to bear on Carson, its editorial preferred that Irish groups carry out this task, commenting, 'The most successful Irish Suffrage Societies are those which have no affiliation with English organisations, but which are entirely native to Irish soil.'[72] However, the paper conceded that Ulster societies may have left the door open for WSPU intervention by not being sufficiently active in this regard. Up to this time, all Irish suffragette militancy had taken place in Dublin, but from late 1913 the majority of militant acts occurred in Belfast. These differed from the Dublin campaign in targeting private rather than government property, and increased in tempo parallel with the arson campaign of the WSPU in England. Carson's comments to a WSPU delegation in March 1914 that his only responsibility as Party Leader was opposition to Home Rule, and that he had no intention of introducing dissension into his party on the issue of votes for women, resulted in the WSPU declaring war on him and the Unionist Party.

There followed a series of arson attacks on property throughout Ulster, including the destruction by fire of a mansion where Ulster Unionists held military training, and the explosion of a bomb in Lisburn Protestant Cathedral. The WSPU newspaper, *The Suffragette*, was scathing about the contrast in treatment of militant men and women in the North. In April 1914 the WSPU offices in Belfast were raided by police, and the women were arrested on charges of possessing explosives. The *Irish Citizen* described this charge as ludicrous 'in view of the notorious accumulation of explosives and other war-munitions in Belfast by men'. Government records show strong disapproval by sections of the northern public of militant suffragettes. Correspondence from the Crown Solicitor's office regarding the Lisburn bomb noted that:

The news of the explosion awakened the whole town of Lisburn, and knowing the accused, Mrs Metge, to be a militant suffragette, a crowd made an attack upon her house breaking all the windows and bespattering the house with mud. The County Inspector informed me that the rabble had threatened to lynch her if she came back to Lisburn, and he was of the opinion that it would be difficult for him to protect even with a large increase of the police under his control.[73]

Between March and August 1914, thirteen women were arrested for militant acts in the north. Coincidentally, militant activity had almost ceased in Dublin. Why had the IWFL abandoned militancy? With one exception, all militant acts in Dublin were carried out in direct response to parliamentary developments on women's suffrage, and specifically to the role of the Irish Parliamentary Party. From May 1913 no new developments occurred. Interest centred mainly on the attitudes and actions of Ulster unionists *vis-à-vis* impending Home Rule. It is likely that the IWFL deliberately abstained from militant action during this period rather than be associated with the extreme arson campaign of the WSPU in Ulster. In addition, the rising spirit of militarism in 1914, manifested in England by rumblings of war, in Ireland by the activities of the Ulster and the Irish Volunteers, gave pause to some within the Irish suffrage movement. Many of those prominent in the Irish suffrage movement were pacifists, notably members of the IWFL and the IWSF. Despite disagreement over the use of militant tactics, the various Irish suffrage societies had been able to work together under the common goal of votes for women. For Englishwomen, the main objective was to convince government and public alike of the equity of granting female suffrage. Irishwomen faced a more complex political scenario. As committed suffragists began to take sides on the major issues of the day, the initial unity of the movement would become increasingly strained.

Political reaction to and support of the women's campaign within Ireland had varied according to party considerations and current political developments, particularly regarding the possibility of Home Rule. In the pre-1916 period, it was primarily the conservative Irish Parliamentary Party that most resisted women's suffrage. Despite the personal support of some individual members, the majority followed the party line in opposing measures seen as a threat to Home Rule. In articulating his strong opposition to women's suffrage as 'the ruin of western civilisation',[74] John Dillon undoubtedly spoke for his leader and many members of his party. Dillon fervently hoped that no such measure would be introduced during his lifetime. Ironically, the first phase of parliamentary suffrage for women granted in 1918 would help secure his party's defeat.

SUFFRAGE AND LABOUR

Dublin at this time was a city of stark contrasts. On the one hand were the beautiful Georgian homes of the rich at Merrion and Fitzwilliam Squares, and the new affluent suburbs of Rathmines and Rathgar. In contrast, almost one-third of Dublin's population lived in slums where over-crowding, lack of sanitation and poor diet led to disease and a high mortality rate, particularly among infants. Statistically, Dublin's death rate was higher than any other European city. High unemployment with little industrialisation meant that most workers were unskilled, employed on a casual basis, with little union organisation and low wages. It was these conditions that labour leaders such as James Larkin and James Connolly attempted to change. Union activity reached a peak in 1913, and many members would be influential in the Rising of 1916. The Labour movement would also be significant in the women's suffrage campaign of these years.[75]

In September 1913 Constance Markievicz told a meeting of the IWFL that there were three great national movements going on in Ireland at that time—the national movement, the women's movement, and the industrial movement 'all fighting the same fight, for the extension of human liberty'.[76] Initial links between the two groups began with the broadening concerns of the new suffrage groups that emerged in the early 1900s, in particular the IWFL and the IWSF. The latter strengthened the labour connection by its concentration on the social and economic position of women workers. It conducted investigations into Dublin factories, organising public debates and seminars, and publishing details of its findings. The *Irish Citizen* regularly published data on women's employment, highlighting problems within particular regional or sectional industries. One example was their publication of working conditions in Limerick bacon factories, where women workers washing offal were forced to stand in water all day. The *Irish Citizen* and suffrage groups consistently urged the appointment of additional women factory inspectors, as did the trade union movement. At that time there were only two such inspectors in the country, one of whom was based in Belfast. The IWFL wrote to the Independent Labour Party that:

> The woman of the labouring classes today, whether as an industrial worker or as a wife and mother, is the most exploited and overdriven

slave on the face of the earth … She has not only to win labour, but the right to labour.[77]

The *Irish Citizen* maintained its active support of Labour throughout the 1913 strike and lockout in Dublin, suffragists from various societies helping strikers in varying ways. Some like Hanna Sheehy Skeffington and members of the IWFL worked in the soup kitchens in Liberty Hall organised by Constance Markievicz, pointedly wearing their suffrage badges. Bennett, who later cited the events of 1913 as a major influence in determining her future direction, would emerge as a key figure straddling the two movements of women and labour.

Labour journals also increasingly reflected the new alliance, with reports of suffrage meetings and advertisements for suffrage events. That such bonds endured is clear from a note in the *Worker's Republic* in 1915 that 'Several well known and experienced suffragists have kindly consented to undertake organising work in connection with the Union. They are women who showed us their sympathy two years ago'.[78] However, not all trade unionists were over-anxious to enfranchise—or indeed unionise—women of their own class, fearing job losses and wage cuts. Craft unions, in particular, still opposed the admission of women. Rather than admit women and guarantee equal pay, many workers preferred to exclude women altogether. *Bean na hÉireann* (the nationalist/feminist paper) had published regular articles on women's working conditions and the need for their organisation. In 1910, it reported:

> Some leading members of the Dublin Trades Council have been approached regarding the organising of the women workers of Dublin. So far very little encouragement has been offered on this decidedly urgent question. While generally admitting the needs of the unorganised female workers, the male members of the wage earners look with suspicion on their sister slaves and are seemingly loath to offer any practical help.[79]

How did the political wing of the labour movement view feminist ideals and co-operation with the suffrage movement? In 1909 James Larkin (described by the *Westminster Gazette* as a 'kind of labour suffragette'), placed adult suffrage at the head of immediate measures to be advocated by an Irish Labour party. At the 1912 Irish Trade Union Congress (ITUC) a motion demanding adult suffrage, proposed by Larkin and seconded by William O'Brien, exposed the divisions still beneath the surface. One delegate agreed that woman's status as wage-earners should be raised, but feared that granting the vote would 'tend to take away from the peace of the home' resulting in 'the destruction of that nobility of character for which their women were prized'.[80] Hanna Sheehy Skeffington noted that 'organised labour wanted women to help them press for adult suffrage, ridiculing women's suffrage as "votes for ladies"'.[81] There was some justification for that accusation, as the existing franchise was property based and if extended, would only benefit middle-class women. Inevitably, there was within some suffrage groups opposition to a labour alliance solely on class lines. One Belfast suffragist wrote to the *Irish Citizen* in 1914 that 'The Labour movement was very young and its ranks were taken from the lowest. It was not the gentlemen and gentlewomen who sneered at them, but it was the scum, and it would be very dangerous to seek alliance with that party.'[82] At the 1914 ITUC congress, there was disagreement on whether a deputation from the IWRL should be admitted to speak on the issue of women's suffrage. James Larkin objected to such a deputation, arguing that 'the suffrage could be used for or against their class'. James Connolly, while noting his preference for the militant wing of suffragism, argued that 'he was out to give women the vote, even if they used it against him as a human right'.[83] Consistently in the pages of the *Irish Citizen* and at meetings of the IWFL and the IWRL the economic position of women was equated with their voteless condition. Commenting on a letter from Winifred Carney regarding the conditions of Belfast linen workers, the paper stated:

> Without political power to enforce their economic necessities, the women workers of Belfast are virtually powerless to secure the legislative changes which they demand.[84]

James Connolly continued this theme when he told a meeting of the IWFL:

> It was because women workers had no vote that they had not the safeguards even of the laws passed for their protection because these were ignored. They had women working for wages on which a man could not keep a dog. Men's conditions, bad as they were, had been improved because of the vote.[85]

Connolly, described by the *Irish Citizen* as 'the soundest and most thorough going feminist among all the Irish Labour men', was a crucial link between the two movements. A regular speaker at suffrage meetings north and south, Connolly told the 1913 ITUC that until women were made equal politically they could only be half free. At a meeting held in the Albert Hall to generate solidarity for the Dublin strikers and to demand the release of the imprisoned Larkin, Connolly was loudly cheered when he declared that he stood for opposition to the domination of nation over nation, class over class, and sex over sex.[86] In Belfast, later, he stressed that agitation for the vote should be accompanied by the more immediate prospect of better working conditions and pay.

The *Irish Worker* reported on a series of meetings held to discuss Connolly's ideas, noting that 'labour ideas and ideals are entering in and these meetings will make excellent propaganda'.[87] But propaganda for whom? Many Belfast suffragists argued that to follow Connolly's advice would sidetrack the suffrage movement. The question of women's co-operation and involvement with other movements was a vexed one in Ireland as elsewhere. While individuals within the IWFL and the IWSF brought both groups closest to alliance with Labour, this was due to the beliefs of individual members rather than official policy. Based on positive reaction to suffrage support for labour in the Dublin lock-out of 1913, Frank Sheehy Skeffington advised Belfast suffragists to create an alliance with militant labour. Louie Bennett, however, while believing women would find firm allies within Labour, argued that both groups should remain absolutely independent. While she and Connolly had disagreed publicly a number of times, she admired his intellect, noting:

> He was one of the best suffrage speakers I have ever heard and a thorough feminist in every respect: he taught the Transport Union of Dublin to support and respect the women workers' struggle for industrial and political rights.[88]

In *The Re-Conquest of Ireland* Connolly wrote that 'the women's cause is felt by all labour men and women as their cause ... the labour cause has no more earnest and whole hearted supporters than the militant women'.[89] Certainly, the involvement of young, socialist-oriented feminists in the suffrage campaign from 1908 onwards coincided with a recognition by some labour leaders of common disabilities shared by men and women. As the women's movement became organised and

Mother with young children, *c.* 1890. Note that the mother is breastfeeding her baby, while drawing the donkey and cart carrying another child.

Members of the RIC with Excise 'gauger' and an old woman found with an illegal poitín still, Co. Mayo, 1890s. The 'gauger' tested the purity of the poitín, and the term is said to be the origin of the word 'gouger'.

The original company of the Girls' Brigade, Sandymount Presbyterian Church, 1893. Formed to cater for the religious and physical well-being of young girls, it soon spread among other Protestant churches. Its founder, Miss Lyttle, is on the left of the picture.

Five women walking to church, Ahascragh, Co. Galway, *c.* 1890. This is part of the Clonbrock Collection developed by Luke Gerald Dillon, 4th Lord Clonbrock, and his wife Augusta, who were both keen photographers.

'Coming home after shopping', Gorumna Island, Connemara, *c.* 1900. While shopping may appear less stressful than today, it is likely that some distance had to be travelled for basic purchases. Note that the man is wearing shoes while the woman is barefoot.

Women washing clothes, west of Ireland, 1910. As in many societies, washing clothes was traditionally a female activity. Here, women are washing blankets with water heated on site.

Shop girls, the Curragh, Co. Kildare, *c.* 1903. Female employment as shop-assistants greatly expanded towards the end of the nineteenth century and was considered superior to work in factories or domestic service.

Women in Claddagh, Co. Galway, wearing traditional costume, with the fish-catch, 1900–1910.

Women curing fish at Downings Pier, Co. Donegal, 1906–14.

The Congested Districts Board was established by the Chief Secretary for Ireland in the 1890s to alleviate poverty in the west of Ireland. Here, members of the Board receive directions from a local woman.

Miss Crowe and Mr Gildea with their pupils at Kilglass National School, Ahascragh, Co. Galway, *c.* 1902. Some of the small boys on the left are in pinafores, and most children appear barefoot.

Members of the Irish Women Workers Union outside Liberty Hall, Dublin, 1913. A number of these had been imprisoned for activities during the Lockout that year.

During the Civil War period, more than one hundred executions were carried out. Here, on the day of one such execution, Cumann na mBan recite the Rosary in their ranks outside Mountjoy prison, 25 April 1921.

SUFFRAGETTES ORDEAL IN THE PHOENIX PARK.

Miss Bloxham addressing a suffrage meeting in the summer of 1912. Following recent militancy in Dublin, suffragettes had to get police protection for a time due to public hostility.

radicalised, labour leaders saw its potential as an ally. The most positive influence of both groups can be found in the wording of the 1916 Proclamation which was addressed to both Irish men and women, and guaranteed equal rights and opportunities to all citizens. The other main area of influence between the two groups was the movement of women from the suffrage into the labour movement. Through involvement in the former, many hitherto protected and comfortable women were made aware of the problems facing working-class women. Louie Bennett, Helen Chenevix and Helena Molony were among those who would commit their lives to the Irish Women Workers' Union (IWWU).

In contrast the involvement of working-class women in the suffrage campaign in Ireland was minimal. Helena Molony commented in 1930 that the women's movement, 'now unhappily long spent, which aroused such a deep feeling of social consciousness and revolt among women of a more favoured class, passed over the heads of the Irish working woman and left her untouched'.[90] The trade union movement during the years following independence reflected the dominant values, the prevailing ethos of the time, placing emphasis on the family unit, not on individual rights.

FEMINISM AND NATIONALISM

In states struggling for national self-determination ... feminists often subordinated their own aims to those of the parent nationalist movement. (R.J. EVANS, *The Feminists*)

By 1913 there were 18 suffrage societies in Ireland, catering for women of varying political, social and religious backgrounds. Yet, as was pointed out in the *Irish Citizen* that year, there was still no distinct nationalist women's franchise association through which committed nationalists could maintain a watching brief on equality for women.[1] Suffrage groups had been consistently criticised as being mere branches of English societies. While there were some instances where this was the case, generally the newer groups—particularly the Irish Women's Franchise League (IWFL) and the Irish Women's Suffrage Federation (IWSF)—recognised the need to assert their Irishness and independence from English groups. Indeed, the IWFL made clear that one of the reasons for its formation was 'the different political situation of Ireland, as between a subject country seeking freedom from England, and England, a free country'.[2] In fact, many prominent nationalist women were at some stage involved in the suffrage campaign, particularly in the 1908–1914 period. Included in this group were women such as Constance Markievicz, Agnes O'Farrelly, Rosamund Jacob, Dr Kathleen Lynn, Mary MacSwiney and Jennie Wyse Power. Initially two strands of nationalism developed amongst such women: (1) those that supported Home Rule for Ireland and fought for the recognition of women as voters within the Home Rule Bill, and (2) those who sought complete independence for Ireland, believing that the suffrage struggle should wait until this was achieved.

In many cases, women started off supporting constitutional Home Rule, but with the increasing political and cultural tempo during this period, moved towards Sinn Féin and separatism. Hanna Sheehy Skeffington, writing in *Bean na hÉireann* in 1909 on 'Sinn Féin and Irishwomen', addressed both groups when she commented that 'until the Parliamentarian and the Sinn Féin woman alike possess the vote, the keystone of citizenship, she will count but little with either party'.[3] This early distinction between the two differing groups of 'nationalist' women is important for an understanding of opposition to the suffrage campaign. The 'parliamentarian' woman, who supported the Home Rule cause, often deliberately refrained from involvement in the suffrage campaign for fear of damaging the attainment of Home Rule. For a time, it was possible for suffragists within both streams of nationalism to maintain allegiance to both the suffrage and nationalist causes. This became particularly difficult from 1912, with Home Rule negotiations at their height. Comparison can be made with the anti-slavery movement in the United States where women campaigners met with hostility from male abolitionists who claimed that it would damage the cause to connect it with the campaign for women's rights. It was argued that 'to agitate the women's amendment would defeat Negro suffrage'.[4] During the crucial Home Rule years of 1912–1914, a similar argument was made against suffrage agitation by male and female Home Rulers and caused many women to submerge their suffrage views. Mary MacSwiney, a member of the Munster Women's Franchise League (MWFL), and before long to be prominent in the republican cause, argued as late as May 1914 that:

Mr Redmond's one and only business at Westminster is to secure Home rule. He received no mandate for Woman Suffrage, and thoughtful and fair-minded Irishwomen of every political belief recognise that. To maintain that Home Rule is not Home Rule, and should not be accepted unless women are included is puerile. No question but the Home Rule one will turn a single vote at an Irish election until Home Rule is finally attained. The women of Ireland want the vote, but they do not want it, nor would they take it at the expense of Home Rule.[5]

However, with Home Rule apparently assured in 1914, some women felt more confident in airing suffrage views. One such woman—Elizabeth Bloxham—declared herself to be 'one of the very many nationalist women who have refrained from taking any step in connection with the suffrage movement that might in any way jeopardise the passing of the Home Rule bill'. Now, with the bill apparently assured, she appealed to John Redmond to ensure that 'Home Rule would mean freedom for women as well as men'.[6] Mary Hayden also entered the debate in 1914, stating in the *Freeman's Journal* that 'numbers of nationalists have abstained from raising the question (of women's suffrage) merely from fear that they might embarrass the government and delay the passage of the Home Rule bill'.[7] She and other like-minded women now sought an amendment to the bill incorporating women's suffrage on the basis of the local government register. Efforts were made to heal the breach between 'parliamentary' nationalists and suffragists, and to present a united demand for such an amendment. Jennie Wyse Power, reiterating the stance of nationalist women regarding suffrage during the Home Rule years, noted that:

> Now, however, the situation has quite changed, and those of us who are Irish nationalists can only hope that an appeal at this time of the extension of the suffrage to Irishwomen will not fall on unheeding ears (and) that they may be allowed to exercise their right to participate in the government of their own country.[8]

A deputation of militant and non-militant suffragists travelled to London to petition for such an amendment, but neither Redmond nor Asquith would receive them. In March 1914 Sinn Féin held a conference in Dublin to consider the proposed exclusion of Ulster from the impending Home Rule settlement. Jennie Wyse Power, Constance Markievicz and Hanna Sheehy Skeffington were among those who argued that Ulster women must not be excluded without their views being consulted by referendum. Arthur Griffith ruled this notion as out of order. At a larger conference the following month, Griffith put forward an alternative scheme to exclusion, including franchise changes. The alteration of the franchise to include women received much support, but was squashed by Griffith's opposition to it as a 'social question'.[9]

From this point on, it was the growing separatist movement which most threatened the unity of the women's movement in Ireland. While the *Irish Citizen* argued that 'there can be no free nation without free women', the counter argument was made that 'neither can there be free women in an enslaved nation'.[10] This argument had been made over the past five years by the second group of 'nationalist' women—those who sought full independence over Home Rule. Amongst this group, much criticism was directed not against the principle of women's suffrage, but against the propriety of Irish women seeking the vote from an English government. Most advocated equality, but believed it would follow automatically on political independence. The 'suffrage first—before all else' policy of the *Irish Citizen* led to much conflict with those with different priorities. Agnes O'Farrelly, a member of the Gaelic League, articulated this disagreement from the nationalist side:

Are we or are we not fighting for the vote before all other things? Some of us certainly are not. Keenly anxious as we are for the ordinary rights of citizenship for ourselves, we give woman suffrage second place to a charter of freedom—or some measure of freedom—for at all events, the men of our own country.[11]

Pointing out that she was a member of a suffrage organisation, she nonetheless declared:

If the vote comes to women before we get Home Rule we shall gladly accept it, but we cannot agree to 'Votes for Women at all costs'. There is one price we must not pay, and that is the price of nationality.

Similarly, Rosamund Jacob, another suffragist member of the Gaelic League, and later of Cumann na mBan, wrote:

Political rights conferred on Irishwomen by a foreign government would be a miserable substitute for the same rights won, even three years later, from our own legislative assembly. The *Irish Citizen*'s idea of public duty is that we nationalists should abandon for an indefinite time, and even oppose, the cause of national liberty for the chance of getting the vote a few years earlier than we might otherwise get it. The woman who does this is a true suffragist no doubt, but no one can call her a nationalist.[12]

That there was concern about the status of women among some nationalist women had been clear from the pages of *Bean na hÉireann* between 1909–1911. Its editor, Helena Molony, stated of the journal, 'we wanted it to be "a woman's paper, advocating militancy, separatism and feminism"'. The militancy referred to, however, was not that associated with suffragettes. In its pages, the views of nationalist women on the suffrage issue are made quite clear. An editorial in 1909 declared that:

We do not refuse to join the women's Franchise movement, but we decline to join with Parliamentarians and Unionists in trying to force a Bill through Westminster. We prefer to try and organise a woman's movement on Sinn Féin lines, or on lines even broader still. Freedom for our Nation and the complete removal of all disabilities to our sex will be our battlecry.[13]

Correspondence to the journal voiced many similar arguments:

Nobody can deny the right of any woman who believes in sending representatives to the British Parliament, to take part in the English suffragette movement. It is consistent and logical for them to do so. If they do not pretend to speak for the Nationalist women of Ireland we shall have no quarrel with them. The women of Irish Ireland have the franchise, and it would be only humiliating themselves and their country to appeal or even demand the endorsement of a hostile Parliament. They stand on equal footing with the men in the Gaelic League, in Sinn Féin, and the Industrial Movement. They are represented on the executives of all these, and under the present circumstances we should be content to regard these as representing Irish Government. The fact that they have not received the imprimateur of a hostile Government will worry no nationalist woman.[14]

Women in the suffrage movement and those represented by *Bean na hÉireann* shared many basic feminist principles on the role and position of women. *Bean na hÉireann* advocated the unionisation of women workers, discussed the migration of Irish women from the farm, and reported progress on the women's suffrage movement abroad. But it was on the precise issue of agitation for the parliamentary suffrage from 'an alien government' that sharp differences arose.

As our country has had her Freedom and her Nationhood taken from her by England, so also our sex is denied emancipation and citizenship by the same enemy. So therefore the first step on the road to freedom is to realise ourselves as Irishwomen—not only as Irish or merely as women, but as Irishwomen doubly enslaved, and with a double battle to fight.[15]

Relations between 'separatist nationalists' and suffrage groups became more strained from 1914. The Secretary of the Belfast branch of the IWFL reported to Hanna Sheehy Skeffington, 'I had the Connolly girls here last night. They will join but cannot undertake to do any work as they are connected with some Irish association in which they would get into trouble if they took a prominent part in suffrage work.'[16] The formation of Cumann na mBan in April 1914 crystallised the differences between those who sought national freedom first and equal rights second, and those who sought 'suffrage first, before all else'. At the formation of the Irish Volunteers in November 1913, its General Secretary had indicated that there would be work for women to do in the organisation. What would be the nature of this work? When the issue of women's role within the Volunteers had been raised with Pádraic Pearse, he had confessed that they had been so busy organising and drilling the men, they had not had time to consider in any detail what work women might do, but he indicated:

First of all there will be ambulance and Red Cross work for them, and then I think a women's rifle club is desirable. I would not like the idea of women drilling and marching in the ordinary way but there is no reason why they should not learn to shoot.[17]

An article in the *Irish Volunteer* journal early in 1914 suggested that women could do their duty within the movement by forming ambulance corps, learning first aid, making flags and doing any necessary embroidery work on badges and uniforms, the writer asking, 'To a patriotic Irishwoman could there be any work of more intense delight than this?'[18] Shortly afterwards the organisation of women supporters of the Volunteers emerged in Dublin. The first public meeting of The Irish Women's Council, afterwards known as Cumann na mBan, was held in Wynns Hotel in April 1914, presided over by Agnes O'Farrelly. Its constitution stated that:

Cumann na mBan is an independent body of Irishwomen pledged to work for the establishment of an Irish Republic, by organising and training the women of Ireland to take their places by the side of those who are working and fighting for a free Ireland.[19]

The first task they set themselves—the initiation of a Defence of Ireland fund for arming and equipping the Volunteers—unleashed a torrent of criticism from suffrage campaigners. The pages of the *Irish Citizen* became the scene of a bitter war of words between women activists on both sides. Days after the inaugural meeting of Cumann na mBan, an *Irish Citizen* editorial reported on the recent action by two women members of the North Dublin Board of Guardians when rival resolutions on the issue of partition were raised at a meeting of that body. The two women had refused to vote, stating they would take no stand on any political question as long as their right to be members of the State and consulted on such issues was denied. The *Irish Citizen* argued that theirs was 'the correct and dignified position for voteless women to take up', and contrasted forcibly with:

> The slavish attitude of a group of women who have just formed an 'Irishwomen's Council', not to take any forward action themselves, but to help the men of the Irish Volunteers to raise money for their equipment, in generally toady to them as the Ulster Unionist women have done to the Ulster Volunteers.[20]

This latter comment referred to the Ulster Women's Unionist Council (UWUC), which had been formed in 1911 'with the incipient intent of supporting male unionists' opposition to home rule for Ireland'.[21] Regarding Cumann na mBan, the *Irish Citizen* editorial continued that 'such women deserve nothing but contempt, and will assuredly earn it, not only from the freeminded members of their own sex, but also from the very men to whom they "do homage" to quote the cringing words of Miss O'Farrelly'. Such strong criticism engendered counter-criticism. Mary MacSwiney, who had resigned from the suffrage movement in Cork because of the MWFL's involvement in war-work, wrote to the *Irish Citizen* voicing her opposition to the action of the Women Guardians, and her full support of Cumann na mBan. She accused the paper of alienating nationalists from the suffrage cause, an argument agreed with by Helena Molony. In the *Freeman's Journal*, the views of Hanna Sheehy Skeffington are made clear in a report on a recent Cumann na mBan meeting she had attended:

> Any society of women which proposes to act merely as an 'animated collecting box' for men cannot have the sympathy of any self respecting woman. The proposed 'Ladies Auxiliary Committee' has apparently no function beyond that of a conduit pipe to pour a stream of gold into the coffers of the male organisation, and to be turned off automatically as soon as it has served this mean and subordinate purpose.[22]

Not surprisingly, the *Irish Volunteer* report on this same meeting noted that many of Mrs Sheehy Skeffington's remarks 'did not seem to meet with the approval of the majority of the meeting'. In the *Irish Independent*, a reply was made to Sheehy Skeffington's arguments by Máire Ní Chillín, who stated:

> The Volunteers have not sought our help. We give it freely and ungrudgingly. There is a large class of Irishwomen who believe that they are represented at the polls and on the battlefields by their husbands, fathers or sons, who want neither vote, nor rifle, nor stone to help them in asserting their rights, who are willing to act as conduit pipes or collecting boxes or armour polishers, or do any other good thing that would help on the cause.[23]

While many key women involved in establishing Cumann na mBan would not have agreed with this statement in its entirety, the nature of the organisation left it open to charges of passivity. Two of its founders, Mary Colum and Louise Gavan Duffy attempted to clarify this situation in the *Irish Independent*. Pointing out that their organisation was in no sense a ladies auxiliary society, that it was an entirely distinct organisation from the Irish Volunteers with its own committee and constitution, and its own objects of organising women towards the advancement of Irish liberty, they declared:

> We are a nationalist women's political organisation and we propose to engage in any patriotic work that comes within the scope of our objects and constitution. We consider at the moment that helping to equip the Irish Volunteers is the most necessary national work. We may mention that many of the members of our society are keen suffragists, but as an organisation we must confine ourselves within the four walls of our constitution.[24]

Unionist women too sought to focus on their anti-Home Rule campaign, commenting that while on issues such as women's suffrage they might hold differing opinions:

> On the one question of the Union they had no room for differences—the Union was their one rallying point, and held them together with a force that no varying opinion on lesser subjects would interfere with.[25]

In a letter to the *Irish Citizen* in May 1914, Rosamund Jacob had conceded that 'no self-respecting woman will deny that the members of Cumann na mBan will be much to blame if they do not insist on their organisation being represented on the Volunteers executive'.[26] The following month, John Redmond succeeded in having twenty-five of his nominees appointed to the Provisional Committee of the Volunteers. Immediately, the non-party stance of that organisation and of Cumann na mBan was cast in doubt. The *Irish Citizen* pointed to arguments made by apologists for the Volunteers such as MacSwiney, Molony, Jacob, that the organisation was founded on a broad national basis, and that support of them did not imply support of John Redmond. Its editorial asked if suffragist members of Cumann na mBan would continue to support a movement 'which has been captured by the leading anti-suffragist politician in Ireland'.[27] It pointed out that Redmond had already formed a new group—The Irish Volunteer Aid Association—to do precisely the same work as Cumann na mBan had undertaken. This would be staffed and governed by men; women could join and work for it, but no woman had been appointed to its committee. Rosamund Jacob admitted that the position had now materially changed, and deplored the acquiescence of the Cumann na mBan executive.[28] Mary MacSwiney was unrepentant, however, commenting prophetically in the *Irish Citizen*:

> To those who possess a little political insight and a knowledge of the real Ireland, Mr Redmond does not loom so large on the horizon of the New Ireland. Except with people steeped in English tradition there is no opposition to Woman Suffrage in Ireland.[29]

Allied to an earlier criticism made by Rosamund Jacob that the *Irish Citizen* seemed to believe that every nationalist was an obedient follower of Mr Redmond, it would appear that many of those within Cumann na mBan were contemplating a wider political agenda. The core disagreement between suffragists and nationalist women in the pre-1916 scenario would appear to have been summed up in a letter to the *Irish Citizen* by Kathleen Connery of the IWFL which stated:

> If there is ignorance of the suffrage to be overcome in Ireland, it is that type of ignorance which has its roots in a false conception of freedom and nationhood, and which is unable to grasp the simple fact that the freedom of Irish womanhood is a vital and indispensable

factor in true Irish nationhood, not a mere trifling side issue to be settled anyhow or anytime at the convenience of men.[30]

Later political developments would bring the two groups closer together. The cumulative effect of the 1916 rebellion, the murder of Frank Sheehy Skeffington, the execution of republican leaders followed by the mass imprisonment of republican activists, all had a profound effect on women's organisations. Although the 1916 Proclamation had been addressed to Irishmen and Irishwomen, and guaranteed equal rights and opportunities to all citizens, events were to prove that some Irish men needed reminding of these points. Neither the Proclamation nor the imminent passage of a British government Bill giving votes to women over thirty years of age ensured that the way was now clear for women in public life. Following Sinn Féin victories at three bye-elections in 1917, a conference held to unite the various groupings within Sinn Féin appointed a central steering committee of nine, one of whom was a woman, Countess Josephine Plunkett.

Shortly afterwards, at the instigation of Inghinidhe na hÉireann, women delegates to that conference held a meeting of their own. In addition to the Inghinidhe, this meeting was attended by women from Cumann na mBan, the Irish Women Workers' Union (IWWU), and the Citizen Army.[31] It was decided that this group would meet again from time to time when issues of importance to women were under discussion. When the question of suffrage was raised, it was pointed out that Sinn Féin candidates at the recent elections had taken their stand on the 1916 Proclamation which granted equal rights to all citizens; therefore agitation for the vote was not deemed necessary as 'the vote had already been granted to Irishwomen by Irishmen'. However, with the expansion of the original Sinn Féin Committee of nine to include released Sinn Féin prisoners, women delegates met with resistance to their request for increased representation. A letter from the women to the Sinn Féin executive stated:

(our claim) to be represented is based mainly on the Republican Proclamation of Easter week 1916, which of course you are determined to uphold, (and) on the risks women took, equally with the men, to have the Irish Republic established.[32]

Their letter also pointed to the necessity for women's co-operation in the further struggle to free Ireland, and to the advantage of having their ideas on the many social problems likely to arise in the near future. Their request was refused. The group considered sending a deputation to Sinn Féin, but initially decided against this, believing that 'women have applied to them often enough and the matter should be left for Cumann na mBan for the present to see what they could do'.[33] But Cumann na mBan had also been refused representation. Records of the Delegates group indicate that an article written by Dr Kathleen Lynn at this time, urging women to assert their political rights, had been sent to *Nationality*, but not published. Eventually the women did form a deputation to the Sinn Féin executive who agreed to co-opt four women, on condition that none of them represent any organisation and that all be members of a Sinn Féin branch. The four women co-opted were Jenny Wyse Power, Áine Ceannt, Helena Molony and Grace Plunkett. A resolution was prepared by the women for consideration at a national convention of Sinn Féin in October 1917. This strongly worded resolution referred unambiguously to the clauses of the Republican Proclamation which had guaranteed equal rights and opportunities to all citizens, and equality of women with men in all branches and executive bodies, and asked that it be resolved:

> That the equality of men and women in this organisation be emphasised in all speeches, leaflets and pamphlets for the benefit of women hearers and readers who, so far, have had no political training.[34]

Before the convention, the women considered circularising Sinn Féin members already proposed for the new executive regarding their attitudes to that paragraph in the republican proclamation, but decided not to 'for fear that it would weaken our case to appear to think that there could be any doubt on the point'.[35] After some changes, the women's resolution was accepted, the final sentence amended to read 'that the equality of men and women in this organisation be emphasised in all speeches and leaflets'. Four women were elected to the new Sinn Féin executive—Constance Markievicz, Dr Kathleen Lynn, Kathleen Clarke, and Grace Plunkett. The *Irish Citizen* congratulated the Convention for 'embodying in their new constitution, in the most unequivocal terms, the democratic principle of the complete equality of men and women in Ireland'.[36] The paper regretted there was so few women delegates, and hoped to see this inequality rectified at future conventions. Sentiments with which the Women Delegates were in complete agreement. At this stage, they organised themselves formally into a society—Cumann na dTeachtaire—women delegates to all conferences held by Irish republicans. Its constitution noted that the society had been formed 'to watch the political movements in Ireland in the interests of Irishwomen', and its aims were:

- To safeguard the political rights of Irishwomen
- To ensure adequate representation for them in the republican government
- To urge and facilitate the appointment of women to public boards throughout the country
- To educate Irish women in the rights and duties of citizenship[37]

The formation of this society is most significant. Many of its members had been active in some aspect of the suffrage campaign, and in many ways this society appears to have filled a void for committed nationalist feminists. Its formation at this particular time indicates unease amongst such women about their role in the emerging new Ireland. Later events would prove that such unease was not unfounded. Minutes of the Women Delegates meetings between April 1917 and January 1919 give a valuable insight into the thinking of committed nationalist women striving to ensure political equality for all women. Its constitution stated that it would be prepared to confer with other Irish women's societies:

> . . . wherever it can be accomplished without sacrifice of principle because they are convinced that the bringing together of all Irishwomen to discuss matters of common interest on a neutral platform could not but be beneficial to all parties.[38]

This recommendation was indicative of a new co-operative spirit between various women's groups post 1916. A number of factors contributed to this. Links between the suffrage and labour movements were strengthened when Louie Bennett took over the running of both the IWWU and the *Irish Citizen*. The IWFL in particular were close to Cumann na dTeachtaire—in many cases women were members of both—and even the more conservative IWSLGA had links with the new nationalist group, again through some joint membership. Increasingly, the pages of the *Irish Citizen* show a more nationalist bias, supporting the demand for political status for republican prisoners, and condemning forcible feeding. Both Cumann na dTeachtaire and the IWWU adopted St Brigid as their patron, the former declaring that 'such a good suffragist should get recognition'.[39] Shortly afterwards, delegates from Cumann na dTeachtaire attended a conference organised by Dublin suffrage societies in Dublin in the wake of the 1918 Representation of the People Act (which gave the parliamentary vote to some women). The group considered starting a women's paper, but instead decided to concentrate on producing regular leaflets and articles in local papers articulating women's point of view. It also compiled lists of suitable women for appointment to local boards, many of whom were subsequently appointed by the Sinn Féin executive. On a much more mundane level, the scarcity of women's toilets in Dublin was discussed, and Dr Kathleen Lynn (Director of Public Health for Sinn Féin) was directed to submit a plan to Dublin Corporation in this regard.[40]

A number of significant issues emerged in 1918 which led to much co-operation between women's groups. Chief among these was the attempt to introduce conscription into Ireland that year. During the war-years, the issue of conscription had always been in the background, and had been consistently opposed by the *Irish Citizen* and the Labour Party. When the Conscription Act was extended to Ireland in the spring of 1918, women played a major role in the massive revolt of the Irish public against its implementation. Among the many meetings and demonstrations organised against this measure was a mass meeting of women at Dublin's Mansion House, at which women from Cumann na mBan, the IWFL, and other women's organisations pledged resistance.[41]

The other major issue on which women's groups co-operated was the campaign against venereal disease and the related implementation of Regulation 40D under the Defence of the Realm Act (DORA). Concern amongst women's groups about the issue of VD had been evident for some time in the pages of the *Irish Citizen*. In 1907 Arthur Griffith had drawn attention to British Army medical reports which confirmed that there was a higher incidence of VD among soldiers in Dublin than elsewhere in the United Kingdom. In March 1918 Cumann na dTeachtaire organised a conference of women's societies to consider 'this serious menace', which it noted 'was a matter on which women of every shade of political opinion could unite to discuss the best measures to combat this evil'.[42] Indicative of co-operation with suffrage groups was Cumann na dTeachtaire's conferring with the IWSLGA regarding its plans to hold a combined suffrage meeting on the same day. The two groups arranged that their respective meetings be held on consecutive days to facilitate attendance by members at both events. A further sign of co-operation emerged when Cumann na dTeachtaire chose Margaret Connery of the IWFL to chair their conference when Jennie Wyse Power had to cancel due to by-election needs in Waterford. Ten women's groups were represented at the conference, with messages of support being received from eighteen others. Resolutions passed at the conference were sent to the Corporations of Dublin and Belfast.

The implementation of Regulation 40D DORA in August 1918 'to safeguard the health of soldiers' was denounced by the *Irish Citizen* as an attempt to revive the notorious Contagious Diseases Acts which had been repealed in 1886 following strenuous agitation by Irish and English suffragists.[43] Under its terms, any woman could be arrested by the police 'on suspicion' and detained until proven innocent by medical examination. A woman could also be held by police on a verbal charge made by a soldier. Some weeks later, the *Irish Citizen* reported the first case taken in Ireland under the act—that of a Belfast woman given six months hard labour 'for communicating disease' to a Canadian soldier. The paper concluded that the real purpose of the Act was 'to make the practice of vice safe for men by degrading and befouling women'. Again, women's groups came together to protest against what the IWFL described as 'the state regulation of vice'. While determined that every effort be made to prevent the spread of VD, the League deplored the one-sided and discriminatory nature of this regulation.

Despite these two incidences of active co-operation between women activists, old political differences emerged. So, while the IWSLGA took part in the campaign against VD, it did not engage in the anti-recruitment campaign. Nonetheless, during 1918, co-operation between women's groups was at its highest since 1912. In their emphasis on promoting the political education of women, legislation for the benefit of women, the election of women to government, local boards and councils, all these organisations shared similar objectives.

The year 1918 proved a watershed for the women's movement in Ireland on two counts. Firstly, that year women over thirty years of age obtained the parliamentary vote, thereby achieving the primary aim of suffrage groups while removing the one goal common to all. Secondly, the results of that first general election in which women participated confirmed the political incompatibility of the various groups. Reporting on the series of meetings organised by the IWSLGA with a view to future amalgamation, the IWFL noted that 'owing to the disturbed state of the political atmosphere no common basis of agreement could be arrived at'.[44] The bill passed in January 1918 by the British Government granted the parliamentary vote to women over thirty years of age with certain property qualifications, while at the same time the vote was also extended to men of twenty-one years. The age provision avoided the immediate establishment of a female majority in the electorate, particularly significant in a population depleted by huge troop losses during the Great War. That the act was extended to Ireland was not due to a sudden conversion on the part of Irish politicians. On the contrary, attempts were made by both the Irish Parliamentary and Unionist Parties to postpone its extension, both groups fearing the effect of an increased—and unknown—electorate in the next General Election. Despite its limitations, the franchise extension created a demand for more female involvement in national affairs.

With a forthcoming general election, the *Irish Citizen* reported that women were much in demand as speakers on party platforms, noting the disappearance of posters such as formerly published by the Irish Parliamentary Party reading '*Public admitted—ladies excluded*'.[45] The Labour Party was the first to nominate a woman candidate for the election—Louie Bennett—although she did not run.[46] The Trades Union Congress of that year discussed ways in which women could be involved politically as well as industrially. Sinn Féin also sought the support of the new women voters, asking Irish women to 'vote as Mrs Pearse will vote', with the promise that 'as in the past, so in the future the womenfolk of the Gael shall have high place in the Councils of a freed Gaelic nation'.[47] This is not quite the way things worked out! Even before the election, there were signs that all was not well. At the last Sinn Féin convention, two resolutions were proposed asking that no candidate be selected for any by-election 'other than a man who took part in the fight of Easter week'.[48]

Pragmatic politics no doubt, but bearing in mind that the same convention also passed a resolution confirming the equality of men and women in the organisation, one must ask, where did this leave women members who wished to stand for election? When the precise question of women candidates for the general election was raised, Sinn Féin's standing committee vacillated as to whether it would be legal. In the event, the party ran only two woman candidates—Constance Markievicz in Dublin and Winifred Carney in Belfast—leading the *Irish Citizen* to comment caustically that 'it looks as if Irishmen (even Republicans) need teaching in this matter'.[49] Women in fact played a crucial role in this election, both as voters and as party workers, a fact acknowledged by Sinn Féin in the request for 'a woman speaker' at their victory celebrations in Pembroke division. Their request to Hanna Sheehy Skeffington in this regard was made 'in view of the fact that the women voters were the most important factor in our polling district'.[50] In addition to the Sinn Féin landslide victory at that election, there was another particularly sweet victory for Irish women. Although she never took her seat, Constance Markievicz became the first female MP elected to the British House of Commons. Commenting on the 1918 election results, the IWFL noted:

> Under the new dispensation the majority sex in Ireland has secured one representative. This is the measure of our boasted sex equality. The lesson the election teaches us is that reaction has not died out with the Irish Party—and the IWFL which has been so faithful to feminist ideals, must continue to fight and expose reaction in the future as in the past.[51]

Cumann na dTeachtaire argued that women had neglected their opportunities at the election, claiming that had a list of suitable women candidates been presented to all Sinn Féin selection committees, the women of Ireland would have achieved more representation in Dáil Éireann. In hindsight, it would appear that even with such lists, women would have had quite a struggle on hand to convince the Sinn Féin executive. Nonetheless, Cumann na dTeachaire's observations on the role of women in this regard, would unfortunately ring true again in the years to come. A sense of disillusionment continued during 1920 with the numbers of women elected to local councils. Commenting on an *Irish Independent* remark that 'a fair proportion of women' had been elected under the local government election of that year, the *Irish Citizen* retorted angrily that five out of eighty in Dublin City, or forty-two in the whole country, scarcely resembled a fair proportion.[52]

Another cause of unease to the paper was the increasing incidence of women being appointed to public boards and positions primarily because of their republican connections. This factor was not surprising, given the *volte face* in Irish political life. What was of concern to feminists, however, was the fact that unlike the women of Cumann na dTeachaire, so few republican women post 1916 held or articulated feminist ideals. In 1917, an article in the *Irish Citizen* highlighted a key weakness in the attitude of many Irish women:

> Many of you stand aloof from feminism because of the political movement. But you have not justified your abstention from the women's struggle by becoming a force within the new movement. You are in revolt against a subjection imposed from without, but you are tacitly acquiescing in a position of inferiority within.

It went on to warn that:

> If in the course of time the new national movement becomes wholly masculine and stereotyped ... you cannot escape your share of responsibility for such a disastrous state of things. If you leave men alone to carry out the task of national creative endeavour, you will have no right to complain later that there are flaws in construction; and there will be flaws, grave and serious flaws, if the women of Ireland fail to demand and take their full women's share in the national heritage.[53]

In the aftermath of 1916, with large-scale imprisonment of male republicans, Cumann na mBan took on a more active and aggressive role. Its work on behalf of prisoners' dependants, and its determined and focused propaganda campaign to keep the memory and ideals of the executed leaders constantly before the public eye, led Brian Farrell to note that in the year after the rising 'it was the women who *were* the national movement'.[54] He and other writers have pointed out the similarity between the Ladies Land League and the post-rising role of Cumann na mBan when 'again it was left to the women of Irish-Ireland to keep the movement going'.[55] Although young women now flocked in their thousands to join the organisation, few articulated feminist concerns. Both Rosamund Jacob and Hanna Sheehy Skeffington were concerned at the 'lack of feminism among Sinn Féin women in the provinces'.[56] Cumann na dTeachtaire can be seen as an attempt by some nationalist women to bring feminism within their political remit. As late as 1919, however, the *Irish Citizen* was still critical of Cumann na mBan's status within the republican movement:

> The women are emphatically not a force in the popular movement —they have no status and no influence in its local councils ... and are looked upon rather in the light of an ornamental trimming—useful to give a picturesque touch on occasion and, of course, to carry on the traditional role of auxiliaries which so many generations of slave women have been content to accept.[57]

Margaret Ward has pointed out that while Hanna Sheehy Skeffington joined Sinn Féin in 1918, she did not join Cumann na mBan, believing that 'it had not shaken off its auxiliary to the men's status'.[58]

Suffragists had always maintained that possession of the

parliamentary vote would give women the power to influence government. That influence—or perhaps fear of that influence—was very real in the early days of the new state. Adult suffrage had been included in the 1916 proclamation and, in the spirit of that proclamation, was included in the Irish Free State constitution of 1922, under whose provisions all citizens of twenty-one years were enfranchised. This last phase of franchise extension to women however was not attained without a final struggle. During the acrimonious treaty debates of the 2nd Dáil in 1922, the issue of women's suffrage received heated discussion. Until the provisions of the proposed constitution became law, only women of thirty years could vote. Both pro- and anti-treaty sides claimed the support of the majority of Irish women, yet it would appear that as in 1918 when John Redmond's party had feared the effect of a new female electorate, now the pro-treaty side feared the effect of granting adult suffrage to all citizens over twenty-one years. The vociferous anti-treaty reactions of many women within the nationalist movement, including the majority of Cumann na mBan, did little to reassure them in this regard. Ward has pointed out that 'for feminists, women's issues were firmly back on the agenda'.[59]

As part of a revival of suffrage methods a deputation led by Hanna Sheehy Skeffington met with Arthur Griffith and de Valera to stress the need for women's inclusion. One of the deputation, Marie Johnson, recorded that 'Griffith was most ungracious, de Valera more suave, more inclined to placate, seized the chance to agree, realising that it meant well to have intelligent women on his side agreed to all our requests for full citizenship'.[60] When the precise issue of extending the franchise to women over twenty-one years took place in March 1922, the furious reaction of the six women Dáil deputies to proposals that such an extension could not legally be done until after the forthcoming elections led to bitter and often nasty exchanges. Those who supported the women's stance were accused of attempting to defeat the treaty, Arthur Griffith declaring that many suffrage campaigners acted 'not in enthusiasm for woman's suffrage, but in enthusiasm to destroy the Treaty'.[61] The scenario facing women was similar to that of the Home Rule era—the British monarchy would still have a role in the Irish constitution, and the partition of the country would be institutionalised. It was 'a proposal devised by men, to be voted upon by an electorate dominated by men'.[62]

In March 1922, pro-treaty women formed an organisation—Cumann na Saoirse (League of Freedom)—to publicise their position. Keen to play a role in the establishment of the new state, the group included many wives and relatives of Free State government members.[63] The forceful commitment of women on both sides of the treaty issue left a bitter legacy for many years. In particular, the role of republican women during the civil war was viewed by Free State supporters as unwomanly, turning them into 'unlovely, destructive minded, arid begetters of violence'.[64] In 1924 P.S. O'Hegarty declared that during the civil war 'Dublin was full of hysterical women (who) became practically unsexed, their mother's milk blackened to make gunpowder, their minds working on nothing save hate and blood'. On the other hand, he argued:

> Left to himself, man is comparatively harmless. He will always exchange smokes and drinks and jokes with his enemy, and he will always pity the 'poor devil' and wish that the whole business was over … It is woman … with her implacability, her bitterness, her hysteria, that makes a devil of him. The suffragettes used to tell us that with women in political power there would be no more war. We know that with women in political power there would be no more peace.[65]

Were women in political power? From the perspective of one writing of a newly born state in which equality of citizenship was included in the Constitution, it may indeed have appeared so. It was not long before the issue was put to the test.

PACIFISM, MILITARISM AND REPUBLICANISM

Militarism in the most subtly dangerous form has its hold upon Ireland. Those women who take up the crusade against militarism must not tolerate the 'fight for freedom' and 'defence of rights' excuses for militarism. (LOUIE BENNETT 1915)

The outbreak of war in 1914 had serious repercussions for the women's suffrage movement worldwide. That movement had become increasingly international in outlook from 1904 with the formation of the International Woman Suffrage Alliance (IWSA) by women from the United States, Australia and Europe.[1] Described by Richard Evans as representing the dynamic side of feminism, the IWSA voiced radical feminism on to an international level, giving members a sense of belonging to a great and irresistible current of world opinion.[2]

During the first ten years of the IWSA a series of international congresses were held, with ever-increasing representation from member countries. Irish activists were kept informed of developments through the suffrage press. In 1913 the seventh—and largest such conference—was held in Budapest. Among the 300 official delegates from twenty-two countries were three Irishwomen—Hanna Sheehy Skeffington from the Irish Women's Franchise League (IWFL), Louie Bennett from the Irish Women's Suffrage Federation (IWSF), and Lady Margaret Dockrell from the Irish Women's Suffrage and Local Government Association (IWSLGA).[3] Charlotte Despard's biographer has noted that the 'international stance of so many suffragists during the First World War owed something to the contacts made at Budapest'.[4] Within a year, however, political developments placed the unity of the

IWSA under severe strain. In fact, from the beginning of the war a significant section of the international suffrage movement adopted a pacifist stance, thus causing division within most national women's organisations. A Women's Peace Party was formed in the United States in January 1915 by Carrie Chapman Catt (President of the IWSA) and Jane Addams.[5] These developments were followed with close interest in Ireland. Unlike many suffrage organisations worldwide, the three Irish associations which had been represented at Budapest continued throughout and after the war of 1914–1918. This was a testament to the commitment of such groups to the cause of suffrage rather than a reflection of a unified stance regarding the war. In fact, there was a wide variety of opinions as to the correct stance for women in Ireland at this time, particularly in the early war period. Generally societies with close English connections abandoned or postponed all suffrage work and became involved in war relief works. The IWSLGA was most involved in such works which ranged from the making of bandages for veterinary hospitals in France to the endowment of a hospital bed in Dublin Castle Red Cross Hospital for wounded soldiers. Jingoistic references in their annual reports to 'our brave soldiers and sailors' and to the fact that 'women are helping to save our empire' offended both nationalist women and feminists, the latter considering that such activities were inconsistent with the aims of suffrage societies.

The IWSF and its Dublin branch, the Irish Women's Reform League (IWRL), also became embroiled in controversy. An emergency executive meeting of the IWSF in August 1914 proposed the suspension of active suffrage propaganda and the organisation of constructive relief work. Accordingly it was decided to support the newly formed Emergency Council of Suffragists—through which suffragists could engage in remedial work without abandoning suffrage ambitions. Among the projects engaged in was the establishment of workshops in Dublin employing 100 girls. The IWRL was particularly committed to involving women in temperance work, and to the protection of young girls on the streets. Statistics were compiled on intemperance in Dublin and the League was responsible for the temporary closure by the military of 'two obnoxious public houses'. The IWRL also opened a café and recreation centre for women, and voiced its concern at the opening of a munitions factory in Dublin. It demanded minimum wages for the women employees and the appointment of at least one woman on the Munitions Tribunal.

The *Irish Citizen* had made its anti-war stance clear from the beginning of the war, causing offence to groups such as the IWSLGA. Publication of its poster 'Votes for Women Now! Damn your War' was also objected to by some members of the IWRL as being outside the remit of a non-party suffrage organ. Further controversy ensued within the IWSF when their Cork branch—the Munster Women's Franchise League (MWFL)—presented an ambulance to the military authorities. This action forced the resignation of Mary MacSwiney who declared that the majority of members were 'Britons first, suffragists second, and Irishwomen perhaps a bad third'.[6] Bennett wrote to Sheehy Skeffington at this time expressing her feeling of despair that women's groups were 'like sheep astray and I suppose when the necessity of knitting socks is over—the order will be—Bear sons, and those of us who can't will feel we had better get out of the way as quickly as we can'.[7] Early in 1915 the IWSF reversed its policy regarding the suspension of suffrage activities. Pointing out that its objective was the enfranchisement of Irish women and that all philanthropic activities were of secondary importance, it urged members to work for attainment of this objective before the end of the war. Louie Bennett would have been influential in this decision, writing in the *Irish Citizen* that 'Women should never have abandoned their struggle for justice, war or no war'.[8] Asked by Sheehy Skeffington to write a piece on women's war-time work, Bennett's initially responded, 'I'm afraid I would have nothing to say about occupations open to women through the war, whatever I might have to say about occupations closed.' She did later write such an article for the *Irish Citizen*, commenting:

Since the war began, with one notable exception, I do not think any position demanding the use of brains has been entrusted to a woman. Women have been asked to knit, to nurse, to collect tickets, to deliver letters, to make munitions, to do clerical work of every kind, but from any work in which they could utilise their intellectual gifts or show any powers of initiative, they have been and are rigorously excluded. Women ought to protest and rebel against this criminally stupid disregard of a rich fund of intellectual energy. There is no patriotism in passive submission to such blundering dominance.

Referring to trade union fears of problems to be faced at the end of the war regarding the low pay of women workers who had taken men's jobs, she declared:

At a moment when it was futile to demand enfranchisement

[women's suffrage societies] could have maintained the demand for 'equal pay for equal work', and the struggle to raise the social status of woman so that she might not be treated as a pawn in a game.[9]

Soon after the formation of the Women's Peace Party in the US early in 1915, the IWRL suggested to the IWSF executive that a campaign be initiated to educate public opinion against the prevailing militarist spirit. Bennett—the proposer of that motion—asked in *Jus Suffragii* (Journal of the IWSA):

Are we right to tolerate in silence this modern warfare, with all its cruelty and waste? More and more the conviction grows that it is full time that women rose up and demanded with no uncertain voice a truce for reflection, for debate upon the questions.[10]

In the *Irish Citizen* she urged all suffrage societies to organise meetings and study groups on the issue. The IWFL strongly supported these developments. Weekly articles and editorials in the *Irish Citizen* kept women informed of progress.

Following the German withdrawal of its invitation to host the 1915 congress, the IWSA president, Carrie Chapman Catt, cancelled the conference entirely. Many members vigorously disagreed with this decision. In response a group of Dutch suffragists met with women from Belgium, Britain and Germany, and planned an international women's peace conference in the Hague on 28 April 1915.[11] The *Irish Citizen* monitored these developments in Ireland. However, at a conference held to discuss possible Irish participation fears were expressed by some that such activity might imply disloyalty to those fighting at the front. Recording 'hot debates on the Peace Congress Scheme' at committee meetings of the IWRL, Lucy Kingston concluded that Ireland would not be represented 'simply because of ultra Loyalists' objections'.[12] Similar sentiments were being expressed throughout Europe. In the British press, intending participants were derided as 'pro-Hun peacettes' going to 'pow-wow with the fraus', and their desire for a negotiated peace was denounced as treachery.[13] Almost all governments tried to prevent their women attending the Hague conference. German delegates were stopped at the Dutch border, but twenty-eight managed to get through. No French or Russian woman was able to attend. The American delegation of forty-one was delayed on government orders in the British channel for three days and delegates arrived just after the Congress started. From a total of 180 British delegates only twenty-four were—very reluctantly—granted travel permits by the Home Secretary, an action almost immediately negated by the announcement that all cross-channel travel was suspended indefinitely. Only three British women actually reached the Hague—two of whom had crossed some days earlier and another who had travelled with the US contingent.

While feminist groups in belligerent countries adopted varying degrees of nationalist rhetoric, the situation of Ireland posed particular difficulties. Initial differences within Irish suffrage societies reflected pro- and anti-war positions, either on loyalist or feminist grounds. Despite these divisions some Irish women planned to attend the Hague conference and an Irish committee was formed from the various suffrage societies to promote the event. It was decided to send seven delegates.[14] Of these, only Louie Bennett was granted a travel permit, and in the event was prevented from travelling due to the Admiralty embargo. A public protest meeting was called in Dublin on 11 May by the IWFL to protest against the government's action. James Connolly and Thomas MacDonagh were among the speakers. In a letter of support Pádraic Pearse declared the incident another example of British policy to exclude Ireland from international debate, adding that much good would be done if the incident ranged more of the women definitely with the national forces. Echoing unease with nationalist attitudes towards suffragists, Margaret Connery of the IWFL, chairing the meeting, asked why it would not range more of the national forces definitely with the women.

Particularly significant for Irish pacifists was the development of strong nationalist and separatist feeling and a desire to make England's difficulty Ireland's opportunity. In an environment where both nationalists and loyalists prepared for military confrontation, pacifism became an increasingly unpopular notion. This reflected worldwide reaction to feminist peace campaigners during the war years, with the overwhelming majority of women's groups in all countries supporting the war effort.[15] Louie Bennett and Frank Sheehy Skeffington were among the leading Irish proponents of pacifism during this period. From the outbreak of war the latter had continuously published anti-war articles in the *Irish Citizen*. Arguing that war was one of the social evils arising from the subordination of women, he declared that:

War is necessarily bound up with the destruction of feminism … feminism is necessarily bound up with the abolition of war. If we want to stop wars, we must begin by stopping this war.[16]

Bennett, echoing current debate on feminism and militarism, wrote in the *Irish Citizen*:

> Suffragists of every country must face the fact that militarism is now the most dangerous foe of woman's suffrage, and of all that woman's suffrage stands for. The campaign for enfranchisement involves now a campaign against militarism. And if we are to conquer militarism we cannot postpone doing so for any 'whens' or 'untils'.[17]

Debate during and after the Dublin protest meeting regarding the Hague conference shows that these issues were now clearly set in an Irish context. Thomas MacDonagh's address to this meeting laid bare the thorny dilemma with which Irish suffragists would have to grapple within the year. Declaring openly that as one of the founders of the Irish Volunteers he had taught men to kill other men, and had helped to arm thousands of Irishmen, he nonetheless described himself an advocate of peace 'because everyone was being exploited by the dominant militarism'. Acknowledging his anomalous position, his one apology for helping to articulate a different kind of militarism in Ireland was his belief that 'it would never be used against fellow countrymen'.[18] Louie Bennett voiced her concern at the tone of this meeting in the *Irish Citizen*:

> Militarism in the most subtly dangerous form has its hold upon Ireland. Those women who take up the crusade against militarism must not tolerate the 'fight for freedom' and 'defence of rights' excuses for militarism. To use barbarous methods for attainment even of such an ideal as freedom is but to impose a different form of bondage upon a nation.

Stating her considerable dissatisfaction with the ideal of pacifism reflected by the meeting, and disappointment at the obvious lack of any sense of internationalism as a world force, she argued:

> If (Ireland's) nationalism is real and vital, it will suffer no loss from a generous attitude of mind towards the country to which she is for the moment subject. The nation which cherishes wrongs and old hatreds becomes bound up spiritually as well as politically.

She hoped to see Irishwomen rising to the task of developing such a spirit of internationalism, pointing out however that:

They cannot do so unless like those Belgian, German, and Englishwomen who attended the Hague Congress, they are willing to surrender certain national prejudices and inherited enmities.[19]

Writing privately to Hanna Sheehy Skeffington, Bennett noted that the tone of the meeting was far more anti-English than anti-militarist, and that while the present war was reckoned barbarous and immoral, it would appear that a war for Ireland would find many supporters.

That seems to me a thoroughly superficial form of pacifism—hardly worthy of the name. I do not care for a pacifism which is not truly international, which is not tolerant towards *all* nations. I shall in future take no part in peace meetings which put Irish nationalism above international tolerance, and which are embittered by anti-English feuds.[20]

While Louie and Hanna would ultimately differ on the issue of justifiable warfare, the following extract from Hanna's letter to Thomas Haslam early in 1915 shows her still close to Louie's viewpoint:

Mr Haslam must remember that every war is regarded by each country engaged in it as a sacred and holy war. It is always the other side that is the aggressor. We are always fighting for religion and freedom; the enemy (the ally of yesterday, the friend of tomorrow) is always the foul foe of civilisation and progress. Women must rid their minds of such cant by cultivating a necessary detachment which will regard war in itself as a crime and a horror unspeakable.[21]

The debate was widened by the publication of an *Open Letter to Thomas MacDonagh* by Frank Sheehy Skeffington in response to the public protest meeting. In this Skeffington enunciated clearly the views of pacifist feminism towards militarism and in particular towards Irish militarism. Commenting on MacDonagh's speech, Skeffington noted:

You spoke vehemently and with unmistakable sincerity in advocacy of peace. You traced war, with perfect accuracy, to its roots in exploitation. You commended every effort made by the women to combat militarism and establish a permanent peace. And in the same speech you boasted of being one of the creators of a new militarism in Ireland; High ideals undoubtedly animate you. But has not nearly every militarist system started with the same high ideals?

Skeffington considered it highly significant that women were excluded from the Volunteer organisation, indicating a reactionary element in that movement. While agreeing with the fundamental objectives of the Irish Volunteers, and acknowledging its merits, Skeffington commented:

> As your infant movement grows, towards the stature of a full-grown militarism, its essence—preparation to kill—grows more repellent to me ... European militarism has drenched Europe in blood; Irish militarism may only crimson the fields of Ireland. For us that would be disaster enough.[22]

Shortly before the Easter Rising Louie Bennett and Frank Sheehy Skeffington took part in a public debate with Constance Markievicz on the motion 'Do We Want Peace Now?' From the attendance of five to six hundred, only a handful supported Skeffington. Bennett was appalled that Markievicz and her supporters preferred to see the war continue if it meant defeat for England and subsequent freedom for Ireland. She intervened, strongly disagreeing with what she saw as cowardice. James Connolly spoke after her, promoting the idea that now was the time to strike against England. Bennett later wrote how this meeting had depressed her, describing its spirit as 'bad, sinister, lacking in any idealism to redeem its bitterness'.[23] While admiring Connolly intellectually and praising him as a thorough feminist, his commitment to military action prevented Bennett from working with him in the labour movement (see chapter 8).

While fully committed to the internationalist ideal, Bennett was nevertheless convinced of the need for separate Irish representation at international feminist gatherings. She had first raised this issue in the spring of 1915 with the IWSA.[24] The Hague peace congress of that year saw the formation of an International Committee of Women for Permanent Peace (ICWPP). After the war this became the Women's International League for Peace and Freedom (WILPF) Subsequently a series of national committees were formed in Europe and the US. Initially Ireland was part of the British branch and Bennett was the Irish representative on its executive. From the beginning she sought a separate Irish branch. A formal resolution to the ICWPP in October 1915 asked for independent representation for any nation feeling itself a distinct entity and enjoying or aspiring to enjoy self-government.[25] Expressing the discontent of Irish members, Bennett demanded that the principle of nationality should be clearly established in the constitution of the ICWPP, and that 'the

Committee shall act in accordance with their own resolution that autonomy shall not be refused to any people'. She pointed out that 'a branch of an English organisation is rarely, if ever, successful in Ireland. And in the matter of peace, the difficulties are intensified'.[26]

In January 1916 the Irish branch took matters into their own hands, renaming their section the Irishwomen's International League (IIL). Prolonged and often bureaucratic correspondence with Head Office in Amsterdam on the issue continued through 1916. Bennett continued to make the point that it was not the number of representatives Ireland would be allowed on the International Committee that was at issue, but rather the principle of independent representation of Ireland. She emphasised that 'the peace movement in Ireland must be indigenous and independent to be in any sense successful'.[27] The status of small and subject nations was discussed in depth by the ICWPP, and raised by Bennett at every international executive meeting. Strong support was given by the British branch, named the Women's International League (WIL), which late in 1916 stated:

> Unrest in Ireland we believe to be the result of tyranny and wrong, and the only way to peace is that of freedom and justice. So long as we deny these to Ireland we cannot expect that the rest of Europe will have much confidence in our desire to safeguard the rights of 'small nationalities'. We are proud to know that the Irishwomen's International League is standing bravely for *all* the ideals for which we are banded together—feminism, nationalism and inter-nationalism, peace and freedom.[28]

Confident that full national status would soon be granted, the IIL in October 1916 argued that their insistence on the practical recognition of the principle of nationality within the International Committee had:

> . . . done some service to the cause of Irish nationalism, and of nationalism all the world over. For we are helping to give Ireland international importance and responsibility by basing her claim for independence on a moral principle. The small and subject nations have world duties and world responsibilities, and at this time it ought to be the duty of a nation placed as Ireland is, to make her contribution to the cause of permanent international peace, by a clear and uncompromising advocacy of the principle of nationality.[29]

Finally in December 1916 the IIL was formally accepted as an independent national organisation.[30] A similar campaign had been waged by the IWSF within the international suffrage movement. Writing in 1917 to *Jus Suffragii*, its executive asked why Ireland was consistently omitted from the list of member countries published each month, commenting:

> Readers of your valued paper are thus given to suppose that Ireland is either a part of Great Britain or that she is non-existent. I hope that by publishing this letter you will allow me the opportunity of assuring them that neither of these suppositions is correct.[31]

This was to prove a more protracted campaign as the constitution of the IWSA only granted separate representation to countries with independent powers of enfranchisement. National recognition was finally granted to Ireland within the IWSA in 1922.

During the early months of 1916 the IIL continued to work for the complete enfranchisement of women, and to foster co-operation with women of other countries in attaining permanent international peace. On the home front it pledged to work for 'a just and reasonable settlement of the Irish question by helping to promote goodwill and a better understanding between different sections of people in Ireland and by steadfastly opposing the use of destructive force by any section'.[32] Regular meetings were held to discuss the Hague resolutions and other topical issues arising from the war. Conscription was condemned, the right of small nationalities to independence was stressed, and support was given to the establishment of a conference of neutral nations to facilitate a mediated settlement to the war. The formation of a League of Nations as proposed by President Wilson was strongly supported and the re-organisation of Europe on the principle of nationality welcomed. Concepts of independence and nationality were to dominate Irish political life over the coming years, and groups such as the IIL would not be immune from friction over these issues.

The Easter Rising of 1916—and the murder of Frank Sheehy Skeffington—placed immense strain on women's groups generally, and on pacifist groups in particular. Bennett—who took over Skeffington's mantle as *Irish Citizen* editor and pacifist voice—notified ICWPP Headquarters that Irish members now had to concentrate on encouraging a more conciliatory spirit among the various sections of Irish life. Her personal views on independence for Ireland were stated quite clearly when she asked 'How far is it immoral, even criminal, to postpone practical recognition of the "sacred right of freedom" to this particular small nation of Ireland?'[33] The abandonment of an active suffrage campaign in Britain in favour of various war-works prompted Bennett to describe English suffragists as 'a servile sex'. Noting that Irishwomen were more independent so far, she urged caution 'for our political women hang on blindly to their particular political half-good fetishes, whether Sinn Féin or Redmondites'. Documenting various committees with little representation of women, where male members made decisions regarding women's issues, Bennett wrote to Hanna Sheehy Skeffington in despair—'There is no getting away from it, women in general are a poor crowd, willing to be under the thumb of men.'[34] In a letter to Lloyd George, John Redmond and other Irish politicians on behalf of the IIL, Bennett argued that:

We hope presently to find Ireland playing a helpful part in a common effort of all civilised nations to set up such political machinery as will ensure permanent peace; and we therefore appeal to you to support now the claim of Irishwomen to representation in any system of Government which may be established as testimony that safe and constructive government must rest on right rather than might, on reason rather than on physical force.[35]

ICWPP records indicate that censorship fears prevented publication of this letter in their newsletter *Internationaal*. Following the IIL's first annual general meeting in January 1917, Bennett forwarded a statement to head-office in Amsterdam regarding recent declarations for a proposed League of Nations. Welcoming President Wilson's proposals to the Allies in this regard, the statement noted:

Such a re-organisation based upon the principle of nationality (by which we understand the recognition of an articulate demand on the part of any people for independence) can be brought about only by free discussion among the nations and requires for its realisation the co-operation and consent of all. As members of a small nation we have a special interest in this pronouncement of the Allies, and we trust that when the re-organisation of Europe is effected, the right of our own country to full and free development on the basis of nationality will be fully acknowledged.[36]

Despite the turbulent events of the previous year, this oblique reference was the only mention of political developments in Ireland in this first anniversary message. Some months later Bennett forwarded to the ICWPP executive in Amsterdam a number of resolutions passed at an IIL conference in Dublin for consideration in the post-war situation. These included proposals regarding women in public life, the rights and responsibilities of small nations, and a League of Nations. Their assertion of the rights of small nations declared that 'every people united by a conscious sense of nationality shall have the right to choose the government under which they shall live and to determine their own way of development'.[37] Significantly, during 1918 the IIL's letter heading was changed to Gaelic with the English title in smaller print underneath.[38] Irish and English branches of ICWPP worked very closely during this period, particularly on the treatment of Irish political prisoners and on opposition to conscription in Ireland. In the autumn of 1918 Bennett was invited by the Women's International League (WIL) executive to address a series of meetings throughout England. During this trip she managed to obtain a brief interview with David Lloyd George, the British Prime Minister, seeking the release of Irish prisoners. A report on her visit commented:

A few more visitors like Miss Louie Bennett would do a power of good. Those who had the opportunity of hearing her speak at the 1917 Club and for the WIL will never again wonder at Ireland's intense nationality. She has shown too, that in Ireland the Trade Union Movement is far more than the mere demand for better wages and fairer hours, important as these are. The enthusiasm which blazes in the Labour Movement in Ireland is a revelation to people whose causes are for their spare moments.[39]

Charlotte Despard commented, after hearing Bennett, that Irish people 'would not now be satisfied with Home Rule. They desire to have their Nationality recognised.'[40] A special executive meeting of the WIL held the morning after Bennett's London appearance declared its shame that British statesmanship had left Ireland in the hands of an arbitrary, repressive, militarist government, and called for the withdrawal of the military occupation of Ireland.[41]

During 1918 a number of war-related issues saw suffrage and other women's groups in Ireland organise in unison. Chief among these was the campaign against the proposed implementation of the Conscription Act to Ireland. The Irish parliamentary party voted against the measure and returned to Ireland in protest. Among the many meetings and conferences organised in protest against this proposal was a mass meeting of women at Dublin's Mansion House, at which all present pledged to resist conscription. A national women's day was organised during which women throughout the country pledged not to take jobs vacated by men who were conscripted. In Dublin, along with representatives of various women's societies, Bennett led her union members in procession to the City Hall to sign this pledge.[42] The Conscription Act was not enforced in Ireland. Informing Amsterdam of the IIL's work in this successful campaign, Bennett wrote: 'We hope that the fact that Ireland has remained free from Conscription may help in securing freedom from it for all countries.' Pointing out that the IIL was now pre-occupied with the problem of self-determination for Ireland, she noted: 'We desire to see President Wilson's principle in regard to government by consent fully applied in the case of the Irish nation.'[43]

In May 1919 the ICWPP held its second congress in Zurich. Plans to hold this post-war congress side by side with the official peace congress at Versailles had to be abandoned as delegates from the defeated powers were refused permission to enter France. Among the smaller countries represented for the first time was Ireland with Louie Bennett as its delegate.[44] At this congress the ICWPP was renamed the WILPF and its headquarters moved to Geneva.[45] An 'Appeal On Behalf Of Ireland' issued to the congress by the Irish branch sought support for Ireland 'in her legitimate struggle for rights of self-determination'. This appeal asked delegates:

> Help us to regain our birthright, the right to meet and work with other Nations on an equal plane. We want, all of us, to regain it by honourable means. We can say of Dáil Éireann that it is on fire for justice, that it bears ill will to none, if only the alien government which crushes and oppresses the people could be ousted.[46]

An IIL post-congress document addressed 'To The Smaller Nations' pointed out that following the Versailles peace treaty smaller nations were now in greater peril than ever before, commenting that 'imperialism seems to have entrenched itself behind a travesty of the original conception of a League of Nations'. Signed by Louie Bennett, this document described nationality as 'a strong and indestructible human instinct, necessary as an incentive to progress, [but one which must be] closely allied with internationalism, as no nation may live for itself alone'. Calling on all smaller nations to make common cause with Ireland in an alliance of non-imperialistic peoples committed to self-determination, whose object would be a true League of Nations, Bennett wrote:

> We declare our belief that the fate of many other nations is involved in the fate of Ireland: her continued subjection will inevitably encourage further violations of fundamental principles of international morality; but her liberation would make a definite advance towards such a World Commonwealth as alone can promise equal security for all peoples. Therefore the liberation of Ireland is the concern of all who seek peace and freedom.[47]

These were tempestuous times for a pacifist organisation. Bennett wrote to Emily Blach in October 1920: 'Things are very difficult here and we are hard put to it to keep our little group together. We are really living in a "war-zone" in Ireland, and our minds and hearts are racked daily.'[48] During 1920 Bennett and Balch corresponded regularly on the issue of passive resistance, to which both were committed. Bennett had been active in promoting the ideal of passive resistance from the time of the anti-conscription campaign, and had presented an outline for such a scheme to the Labour Party in December 1919. In March 1920, however, she informed Balch that passive resistance in Ireland had been engulfed in the terrible cyclone of force on all sides, pointing out: 'It is practically impossible to do more than have a few conferences on the subject, as it seems a mockery to sit down and discuss it in cold blood in these days in Ireland.' Referring to the Irish experience of hunger strike, she stated:

> I do not think any nation would carry out a scheme of passive resistance unless they are inspired by an intense *spiritual* (sic) passion, a religious fervour that lifts the soul of the people. I believe that if the Irish Catholic Church had joined whole heartedly in this national struggle and come forward with a scheme of passive resistance, that it would have been done, and done successfully. I think and hope Ghandi is great enough to achieve something of this sort in India.[49]

Despite often radically different political loyalties, women's groups in Ireland joined together to campaign on a number of controversial issues from 1918. In addition to the anti-conscription campaign, women's groups also protested against the implementation of Regulation 40D under the Defence of the Realm Act (DORA), seen as an attempt to revive the notorious Contagious Diseases Acts which had been repealed in 1886. A further remarkable example of joint action occurred in 1919 with an 'Appeal on Behalf of the Principal Women's Associations of Ireland' to their sisters in other countries to demand the establishment of an international committee of inquiry into the conditions of Irish political prisoners. In sending a draft of this petition to Geneva in November 1919 Bennett explained that it was be signed on behalf of four women's organisations 'who realised that the subject of political and war prisoners is one that is striking the hearts of many women in many countries'.[50]

The following month, however, she asked Geneva not to publish the petition for the moment as 'there had been a little difficulty about signatures'. That there were some initial differences among signatories is not surprising when one notes that they included Constance Markievicz, Hanna Sheehy Skeffington, Maud Gonne MacBride and Bennett herself. By January 1920 these difficulties were sorted out, and the petition was forwarded. It was argued that should England refuse to allow what France, Germany, Austria and Italy had willingly accepted, her government would stand self-condemned. Outlining the loss of free speech and press under English military rule, it concluded with an appeal to the civilised world to 'break down the wall of silence with which England seeks to surround Ireland'.[51]

In the autumn of 1920 the Manchester branch of the WIL organised a fact-finding trip to Ireland to investigate conditions. A report of their findings was published, and discussed at a series of public meetings held throughout England.[52] At all of these meetings resolutions were passed and forwarded to the government demanding the liberation of prisoners and a truce during which Irish people might determine their own form of government. This report formed the basis for extensive propaganda by the British and Irish WILPF in conjunction with other national sections. In the United States Jane Addams and Emily Balch were among those who responded. Prior to the British WIL trip, Bennett had sent a cable to Addams in Chicago asking that 'Irish Woman Workers and International League beg American women urge Presidents intervention on behalf Irish prisoners dying for their political faith'.[53]

As a result of such pressure a lobby of Congress and a commission of inquiry into Irish affairs were established. A wide cross-section of all interests was included on this Commission—senators, congressmen, mayors, governors, trade unionists, and WILPF president Jane Addams. In January 1921 Bennett and Caroline Townshend (an officer of the Gaelic

League) travelled to Washington as IIL delegates.[54] Introducing her testimony on behalf of the IIL, Bennett explained:

> There are going on at the present time two lines of conflict: there is the conflict between the Irish Government, the Dáil, and the British Government, along what one might call civil lines; and there is also the physical conflict, the conflict between the two armies. We thought it would be interesting to lay before your Commission facts in regard to the way in which the British Government have tried to block all the efforts of the Irish to establish or carry on industry, and to carry on their own local councils (and) their own courts of law as established by the Dáil.[55]

In the course of her evidence and questioning, Bennett's personal views on many of these issues emerge. Some members of the Commission were puzzled by the fact that a Protestant woman could be acceptable as organiser of a trade union whose membership was primarily Catholic. Bennett assured them that she had found no antagonism whatsoever in this regard, although she confessed that when she first became involved she feared there might be some opposition.[56] With members of the IWWU numbering six thousand workers, she noted that only about six of these were Protestant. Questioned about her personal political affiliations, Bennett replied that she was not involved in any political work. When asked if she were Republican in sympathy, she replied 'Yes, I am.'[57] Her evidence shows her to be most supportive of the Republican court system established by the Dáil, pointing out however that these courts have been driven underground by the British Government. The opening paragraph of a formal statement prepared by the IIL for the Commission read by Bennett stated:

> The Irishwomen's International League affirms that the responsibility for the bloodshed and violence in Ireland rests upon the British Government, which refused to allow her the indefeasible right of all nations to freedom, outlaws her duly elected Parliament, and persistently attempts to rule the people by force.

In conclusion, the statement declared:

> The Irish people have proved how unconquerable is the spirit of nationality. The peace and happiness of the world depend upon the

measure of freedom given to that spirit. If Ireland wins her freedom now, the world will see a triumph of spiritual over material forces, and may look forward to the future with a diminished dread of devastating wars.[58]

From a somewhat different perspective Mary and Muriel MacSwiney also gave evidence to the Washington commission. Cogniscent of the importance of the women's role in the Irish national movement, Cumann na mBan instructed MacSwiney in her subsequent tour of the US to assure Americans that 'the women of Ireland are standing with the soldiers and that "no surrender" is the watchword'. MacSwiney's biographer notes that 'the organisation did not want women represented as a pacifist group urging the men to lay down their arms'.[59] A broadsheet published about this time entitled *Irishwomen and the Irish Republican Army* emphasised that Irishwomen were as proud of their national army as were women of other countries of theirs and ranked them with the world's bravest. The document concluded:

The women of Ireland consider it a crime for any young Irishman of military age *not* to carry arms in the defence of his country, and that it is an even greater crime for any person of Irish blood to refuse to harbour and assist our brave soldiers.[60]

Writing privately to Emily Balch, Bennett commented, 'I urged any groups of women I met in America to make this question of Ireland a moral rather than a political issue, so that it may be in some sense released from the entanglement of the anti-British movement in the States.'[61] That the Irish government was aware of WILPF activities is clear from a study of Irish foreign policy between 1919 and 1922. Writing to Éamon de Valera in 1919, representatives of Dáil Éireann who were in Paris for the Allied peace conference—ever mindful of Ireland's need for international support—expressed the hope that Bennett would call to them on her way back from Zurich.[62] In 1921, Harry Boland pointed out to de Valera that WILPF's president, Jane Addams, likely to be a member of an American delegation on disarmament, was also a member of the committee investigating conditions in Ireland.[63]

Acceptance of the Treaty by Dáil Éireann and the ensuing civil war had profound effects both on the IIL organisation and on individual members attempting to ally pacifist convictions with political commitment. In her diaries Rosamund Jacob recorded discussions with

Bennett about the Treaty and Document NO. 2 which, she observed, Bennett despised.[64] With the lack of insight of one observing events from a distance, WILPF head-office believed that acceptance of the Treaty meant that Ireland could put the nightmare of violence and outrage behind it.[65] Explaining that in fact the Treaty was not popular and was reluctantly accepted, Bennett stated that there was much grief and shame about it amongst a very large 'minority'. She asked Emily Balch:

Can you be surprised? We are asked to accept Common Citizenship with an Empire whose deeds we loathe—an Empire which today holds down Egypt and India as it has till now held down Ireland. There are men and women who could not take the oath of allegiance without sacrificing every instinct of honour in their nature.

She hoped that de Valera would be strong enough to lead his followers away from political division and concentrate on education and economic reconstruction, but she was unsure, noting that:

The women here are a dangerous element—fierce, vindictive, without any constructive ability but with immense ability for obstruction and destructive tactics. A healthy opposition to the Free State would be excellent, without it Ireland may become as materialistic as England.

Bennett explained to Balch that she did not fear injustice to religious or political minorities but hatred of England could not disappear overnight. Pointing out repeated instances of degradation of Irish men and women over the previous two years by English armed forces, she commented that:

Nothing is so hard to forgive as degradation, and in these past two years the English armed forces have very literally forced Irish men and women to lick the dust. Men and boys who have been cruelly beaten, held up to the mockery and torment of a mob, tortured to betray their own people or forswear their own convictions—will never forgive or forget.[66]

In June 1922 Bennett wrote to Sir James Craig appealing against the use of force and coercion in Belfast. Declaring the futility of using a partisan police force as a means of securing order, and asserting that lasting peace could never be secured by violence, her letter stated:

We believe that a solution of the present tragic problem can only be found through negotiations with the Government of southern Ireland, and we therefore earnestly appeal to you, in the interests of civilisation, to enter into such negotiations, and to arrange for a truce while they continue. Sooner or later, negotiations must begin. We beg you to let them begin now.[67]

When simmering post-treaty tensions finally escalated into civil war in June 1922, Bennett with Mary O'Connor of the IWWU set about trying to evacuate families living in the vicinity of the Four Courts. The Minister for Defence was petitioned to allow women and children in the danger zone be re-housed in empty houses, and to be supplied with foodstuffs. A group of concerned women representing labour, nationalists and former suffragists met in Dublin's Mansion House to co-ordinate peace efforts. Two delegations were picked to present peace proposals to leaders on both sides. The first delegation, received in Government Buildings by Michael Collins, Arthur Griffith and William T. Cosgrave, was told that there could be no truce until anti-government forces surrendered their arms. The second delegation to the republican side was informed of the latter's refusal to negotiate on any terms.[68] Following these attempts to secure a cessation of hostilities, a Manifesto of Condemnation was issued by the IIL which was refused publication by the press and consequently was posted up in Dublin by the women themselves.[69] Later in the year the IWWU issued a manifesto asking leaders on both sides to state publicly their willingness to accept an unconditional truce, declaring: 'We are sick of battles, and bloodshed and terror. We want peace: we want work: we want security of life and home.'[70]

The IIL was experiencing its own civil war at this time. Bennett informed Geneva of its impending dissolution, explaining that its existence over the previous two years had been precarious and unsatisfactory for those who tried to be consistently pacifist.

The civil strife in Ireland in the last few months has driven the larger majority of people into one or other political camp: both sides have raised objections to the attitude of the IIL.[71]

The success of the IIL in raising public awareness in England and the US on the issue of Irish political affairs, may in fact have contributed to this crisis. Women like Hanna Sheehy Skeffington and Rosamund Jacob—long associated with the League—had become increasingly republican in attitude. Lucy Kingston noted that its 1920 packed annual general meeting showed 'great attendance of SFs [Sinn Féiners] including Gonne MacBride, Capt. W. Mrs S.S. [Sheehy Skeffington] etc.'[72] Describing one of the Mansion House conference peace meetings chaired by Bennett in the summer of 1922, Jacob noted that it was attended by 'great crowds of women but none of them apparently really keen on peace'.[73] As a result of political differences this Peace Conference of Women ultimately collapsed. Bennett informed Geneva:

> The Republican section of this conference drifted into party propaganda, especially in regard to the prisoners ... the Free State element in the IIL have, almost to a woman, resigned on account of our association with the Mansion House Conference.[74]

Bennett still felt that they were right to have tried. She also felt, however, that the time had come for radical changes within the IIL. She suggested a new Irish section of WILPF be started under new influence, commenting: 'Miss Jacob is too Republican, I am too actively connected with Labour, to be anything but a danger to the sort of organisation that is needed.' Arguing the necessity of maintaining an all-Ireland society, 'to maintain social links and to obliterate the ugly antagonism now existing', she disagreed with Geneva's proposal for a separate northern section, stating this would make the process of reconciliation even more difficult. Two weeks later at its annual general meeting Bennett formally resigned as secretary, warning the group against allowing on its committee 'women who take prominent place in contemporary politics'.[75] However, the new committee for 1922/3 did include many high-profile political women. Charlotte Despard was its chair, at the same time being chair of the Women's Prisoners Defence Association (formed in 1922 with Maud Gonne MacBride). Rosamund Jacob, Hanna Sheehy Skeffington and Maud Gonne MacBride were also much involved.

Not surprisingly such a volatile committee led to numerous incidents of disagreement. One such incident occurred in January 1923 when Rosamund Jacob was arrested and imprisoned for allowing republicans the use of Hanna Sheehy Skeffington's house. Lucy Kingston commented tartly that, while Sheehy Skeffington would undoubtedly have agreed with Jacob's action, it was somewhat rash of Jacob considering her role within the IIL, noting 'we are not benefitted in any way by having our Secretary in prison.'[76] Kingston's diary also reveals that the issue of Charlotte Despard's resignation was raised more than once, each time

Despard declaring herself a pacifist and neutral regarding government. Kingston was relieved that Mrs Dix was joint secretary: 'she is sane and thoroughly pacifist and does not stink in the eyes of government like Mrs D(espard) and Mme G.MacB.' Early in 1923 a special meeting was called to consider the following resolution by Louie Bennett:

> That membership of the Irish Section is open to all who hold that in resisting tyranny or striving for freedom only such methods may be used as will not involve the taking of life.[77]

In a country in the midst of civil war this resolution stripped the *raison d'être* from a group such as the IIL. After heated discussion it was rejected by just one vote. The issue of the legitimate use of force remained a thorny one and would continue to dog the IIL during its remaining years. For the moment the League survived, noting in its annual report that 'taking into account the terrible crisis through which the country is passing, we have not done too badly'.[78] Lucy Kingston and Rosamund Jacob represented Ireland at the Third International Congress in Vienna in June 1921, while Marie Johnson filled that role in Washington in 1924. Johnson was happy to tell the Congress that Ireland now had full adult suffrage.[79]

In 1925 the IIL invited the international executive of WILPF to hold its Fifth International Congress in Dublin the following year. The invitation was enthusiastically accepted. It was seen by Jane Addams and her executive as an 'extended peace mission'. Its official history notes that:

> The choice owed something to the courageous stand for non-violence of Louie Bennett and her co-workers, as well as to the tragic situation of Ireland itself.[80]

Bennett had always been highly regarded by the WILPF executive, and from early 1926 she features regularly in correspondence regarding the forthcoming congress. In the work of organisation she was assisted by a committee of eleven, with Rosamund Jacob, Lucy Kingston and Helen Chenevix playing key roles.[81] And it was quite a mammoth task for a small national section to undertake. Interesting details emerge from correspondence between Dublin and Geneva over these months, with the Irish section advising on sensitive political issues, protocol and customs. Lucy Kingston informed Geneva that the government had at last realised the importance of bringing so many visitors to Dublin, although she cautioned—'we are careful ... not to put our Branch too greatly under the Government "wing". This would incriminate our League with a certain section of the public.'[82] Bennett further warned Geneva to exercise caution in press notices regarding conditions under which the National University was obtained for the congress, pointing out that the university president alone had authority to allow the use of college buildings, and emphasising:

The Government have nothing whatever to do with it. See to it that in all public notices he is given credit for lending it, and that no whisper of Government aid is made. This is very important.[83]

The Congress which took place between 8–15 July 1926 was attended by 150 delegates representing twenty countries. This was the first gathering of an international organisation to be held in the Irish Free State since its recognition by Britain in 1921. A reception to mark its opening was attended by both Éamon de Valera and W.T. Cosgrave. This first public function attended by both leaders since the civil war naturally attracted much comment. R.M. Fox recounts that when Bennett concluded her opening address to the conference by inviting the 'president' to say a few words,

The two rival groups in front of the platform, stiffened and glared defiantly at each other. Everyone waited breathlessly to see which of the two Presidents would step up and speak in the name of the country. But as Louie Bennett disappeared from view, there mounted in her place, a third President, a small grey-haired, determined looking woman—Jane Addams, the President of the International League for Peace and Freedom. So the moment of tension passed.[84]

However apocryphal this account may be, records show that there had been a series of meetings between de Valera and Rosamund Jacob of the IIL in the previous months. De Valera had indicated that he would not meet members of the Free State government socially, but he would meet them in business assemblies. It would appear that he thought it strange that Dr Coffey and he were not asked to speak and welcome the delegates. Jacob pointed out to him that this would not fit in with the non-political ideals of the committee. Consistently during her interviews with de Valera, Jacob pointed out that if republicans did not participate in the conference, the government side would gain sole access to foreign delegates. That her strategy worked was confirmed when de Valera promised to publish any pre-conference material in *An Phoblacht,* and to attend the conference opening. Subsequently he attended a post conference party, at which Jacob noted he was surrounded by a circle of delegates who were listening to him and arguing with him.[85]

But the work of the congress was very serious. Within an overall theme of 'Next Steps towards Peace', plenary sessions included speakers and discussion on colonial and economic imperialism, women and world peace, relation of majorities and minorities, conciliation, arbitration and disarmament. Addressing the congress, R.J. Mortished, assistant secretary of the Irish Labour Party, admitted that Ireland could scarcely claim to have either an international or pacifist outlook. He noted however that the WIL 'has come to us with a magnificent defiance of the destructive power of hate and a magnificent faith in the power of love informed by intelligence'.[86]

A public meeting was held in the Mansion House under the auspices of the conference on the theme 'Next Steps towards World Peace'. The title had been amended on the advice of Bennett to Geneva because 'we think the word world essential in view of our faction fights here'. Some two thousand people are reported to have attended this event which was chaired by Bennett. At this meeting Jane Addams spoke of the great Irish pacifist of international repute, Frank Sheehy Skeffington. Quoting a phrase of Skeffington's—'I advocate no mere slavish acceptance of injustice. I am, and always will be, a fighter'—Addams highlighted WILPF's agreement with his appeal for new methods free from physical violence for ending struggle[87] (Jacob claimed that all the papers deliberately left out this quote). In reply Hanna Sheehy Skeffington, representing the Republican group, thanked Addams for her tribute to her late husband, and urged the WILPF to continue its stress on peace and freedom, quoting Pearse, 'Ireland unfree can never be at peace.' She felt it most appropriate that the congress met in Ireland 'because Ireland is the country that knows most what foreign violence and militarism mean'. Her speech aroused great enthusiasm. Jacob noted in her diary that:

> When Hanna rose to second the vote of thanks, a roar of applause broke out for all the world as if it was de Valera, and went on and on and on (with cries of up the Republic) till Louie got quite annoyed with the enthusiasm and demanded 'Will you let Mrs Skeffington speak!'[88]

Jacob commented that she had seldom enjoyed an occasion more, noting that Sheehy Skeffington had got in some good punches—praising Jane

Addams as chairman of the 1920–21 commission 'whose evidence was and I believe still is seditious literature in Ireland'. Sheehy Skeffington went on to state how easy it was to be a pacifist in time of peace in comparison with wartime conditions. Interestingly, neither Sheehy Skeffington's reception nor the latter two quotations from her speech were printed in the official report of the Congress. Writing of Bennett's life thirty years later R.M. Fox commented of the incident, 'one could sense the emotional pull between the pacifist and militant Republicans, who were still unreconciled to peaceful methods.'[89]

One of the British speakers at the congress, Helena Swanwick, related how dissident members of Irish WILPF ('The Black women') remained outside the conference because they had taken part in the civil war and were still involved with revolutionary republicans. She noted that in several European countries, including Ireland, 'The necessity for catastrophic revolution is maintained by those who are united in their opposition to international wars. They seem to me to be opportunists, because they drop their principle when it inconveniences them.'[90] And there was criticism from other quarters for such action. The *International Woman Suffrage News*, complimenting the Irish committee for a successful congress, noted that the 'only regrettable feature was the use made of the Congress as a platform for intense nationalist propaganda. We feel [this is] a misuse of what should be purely international and pacifist.'[91]

It is clear from correspondence between Geneva headquarters and Louie Bennett that there was unease at such incidents. Neither the official WILPF report of the Congress nor its Journal—*Pax International* —mentioned these issues, but praised the Irish section for its efficiency and hospitality, and its tact in getting all parties together. In particular they complimented Bennett for her poise, tolerance and quiet strength. Bennett was elected to the executive committee of WILPF at this congress.

The reverberations of republican actions during the Dublin congress were remembered in the lead-up to WILPF's 1929 Congress in Prague. Mary Sheepshanks confessed to Bennett:

The prospect of having those Republicans at Prague fills me with dismay. They did their best to spoil the Dublin Congress and did succeed in doing a certain amount of mischief ... I thought they were so bitter and unscrupulous and unfair.[92]

From this correspondence it can be deduced that there were some lively meetings of the IIL in the months before Prague. Irish delegates to

Prague were to be Bennett, Hanna Sheehy Skeffington and Rosamund Jacob. At the last minute Bennett could not travel (due to her mother's ill-health), but she forwarded a copy of a paper she had been asked to present on 'The Machinery of Internal Peace'. Bennett had informed Geneva that she would prefer not to speak on the political aspects of the subject, but rather, on the industrial aspects. A copy of this paper came to the attention of Sinn Féin, whose publication of extracts and hostile editorial comments plunged the IIL once more into fierce controversy. Sinn Féin wrote to WILPF in Geneva taking issue with Bennett's 'misleading and prejudicial comments regarding the state of government in Ireland'. It was claimed that she had accused Sinn Féin of attracting young people of an adventurous spirit as well as cranks, vagabonds and villains, commenting that 'an irregular minority of this sort inspires fear in Government and constitutional circles'. Outlining a resulting vicious circle of arrests, victimisation, terrorism and reprisals, Bennett had stated that while Sinn Féin were not in sympathy with the ideals of Labour, they would not hesitate to use it to secure the complete independence of Ireland. She commented:

> In Ireland, as elsewhere, the Communist is endeavouring to exploit nationalism (in its Republican cloak) for his own economic ends. It is unlikely that Communism will ever gain any real economic hold on Ireland; but it can add zest and money to the Republican forces. Working class discontent is a peculiarly dangerous element in a country where there is a political minority which refuses constitutional representation and looks to revolution as the means of emancipation.[93]

Angrily refuting Bennett's implications regarding funding, Sinn Féin declared that it had more genuine sympathy with the ideals of Labour than all the time-servers who exploited the working-class cause. Criticising official Labour for succumbing to temptation, accepting senatorial sinecures, and climbing on the shoulders of the workers to positions of emolument, their letter noted that:

> Miss Bennett's assumption of an inherent right to voice the ideals of Labour is only less farcical than the posturings of the titled personages who pollute the English Labour movement.

Despite Bennett's somewhat haughty response to Geneva that she had disregarded Sinn Féin's letter as unworthy of notice, the Irish section was thrown into turmoil as a result of this controversy. At its next committee meeting Lucy Kingston noted: 'L.B. is attacked for her paper by (1) S. Féin (2) Fianna Fáil (3) Republ. members of our Committee. Find myself on her side for once, and certainly Mrs S.S.[Sheehy Skeffington] and the rest shew no mercy ... An implacable crew where "The Rock of the Republic" is concerned'.[94] Bennett further informed Geneva that Hanna Sheehy Skeffington was particularly enraged:

> All through the past year there has been considerable dissatisfaction amongst the really pacifist group, owing to the presence on the Committee of people who openly state that they consider the use of force essential to achieve a social revolution, or to achieve national freedom. They lay emphasis on the WIL object of *freedom* rather than peace ... Things have now reached a climax ... and I think a split is inevitable.[95]

The situation outlined by Bennett had been complicated further by the recent election of Maud Gonne MacBride to the IIL committee. Its then Secretary—Una M'Clintock Dix—had explained to Geneva:

> Realising that a peace committee with Mme MacBride on it was farce I wrote to her privately asking her to resign. She refused after consulting Mrs Sheehy Skeffington saying it would not be fair to those who elected her.[96]

A series of stormy committee meetings ensued with debate centering on acceptance or rejection of the Washington Object which excluded from membership those who justified defensive warfare and armed revolution. A majority decision in favour of the Object was subsequently amended by a smaller gathering. Bennett and Chenevix were among those who then resigned from the committee, with Bennett informing Geneva that both felt it essential that the Irish branch be purged of political opportunists. Kingston noted this was 'the saddest WIL Cte. I ever attended'.[97] Although Dix disliked this show of sharp practice she acknowledged that it provided a way out of their dilemma and enabled the group to remain in existence—however precariously.

Another significant factor in the impasse which was noted by Dix was the clash between the strong personalities of Bennett and Sheehy Skeffington.[98] WILPF's Geneva office viewed the matter most seriously, placing it on its executive agenda and pointing out that any serious dissension within a national branch was a source of concern for the whole league. However, by spring 1930 the group appeared to have weathered the storm. Its AGM voted to return to the Washington Object, and many former members rejoined, including Bennett. Within a few months, however, a further controversy would prove fatal. From October 1930 IIL members had been collecting signatures for a disarmament declaration initiated by WILPF. In the spring of 1931 the IIL, in association with the League of Nations Society, organised a public meeting to debate the issue. It was decided to invite as guest speaker Patrick McGilligan who was Minister for External Affairs in the Free State government. This choice of speaker caused uproar among a section of the committee—partly because of McGilligan's political identity, and partly because he had been a member of the government which had executed republican leaders. Others felt that such objections were politically sectarian, and that McGilligan should be heard. On losing a subsequent vote to rescind the invitation, a number of members announced their intention to disrupt the meeting. The proposed meeting was subsequently cancelled, with both the president and secretary resigning in protest. Rosamund Jacob wrote to Geneva desperately trying to retain some WILPF presence in Ireland, asking if there was a precedent for two groups to operate within one section where controversial matters arose. Explaining this specific incident she informed Geneva:

> The upshot of the affair is that the cleavage which has always existed in our Section has become so definite that we are in danger of a break-up, unless some new method of organisation can be devised. I think the clearest way to describe the cleavage is to say that some of us would put peace before freedom, and others would put freedom before peace.[99]

Despite Jacob's efforts the groups did disintegrate at this point. Many former members had become active in the disarmament movement and were not anxious—and one gathers had neither the heart nor energy—to continue reeling from one destructive split to another. Involvement in the disarmament campaign provided many women with a means to remain involved in the peace movement without engaging in divisive political arguments. The issue of 'justifiable warfare' caused dissension in many national sections of WILPF—up to and after World War II. Ireland in the 1920s was a country recently emerged from insurrection and civil war, where political division was still a fresh wound, and in which many women still believed the struggle for national independence was not yet complete. While condemning militarism in its imperialistic mode, some justified the need for further military action to attain national objectives. Others within the Irish WILPF could not accept such views. While some Irishwomen remained involved with WILPF as individual members, it would be almost sixty years before a WILPF branch was re-established in Ireland.[100]

In his examination of European feminist and socialist women's opposition to the First World War, Richard Evans details the overwhelming support of the war by feminists throughout Europe, commenting that 'Feminist pacifism (became) the creed of a minority, of a tiny band of courageous and principled women on the far-left fringes of bourgeois-liberal feminism'. Arguing that the 'first-wave' European feminism of the late nineteenth century was closely connected with the ideology of bourgeois nationalism, Evans notes that in some countries 'feminists identified with the movement for national self-determination to such an extent that nationalist aims almost took precedence over feminist ones'. By the early 1900s however, he notes, the connection between nationalism and feminism was being challenged by a minority of pacifists within the feminist movement, while an even larger group of socialist women rejected accepted notions of the female character and mission, arguing for the primacy of class consciousness and proletarian solidarity. Evans argues that any connection between pacifism and feminism was political and ideological, not 'natural' or inevitable. Noting that pacifists tended to come from a limited but distinct strand of feminist ideology on the democratic left of the movement, he concludes that 'the views of the feminist pacifists were limited in their appeal because the historical links between nationalism and feminism were still strong in the late nineteenth and early twentieth centuries'.[101] Developments in Ireland appear to reflect his thesis.

PART 3
Marriage, Motherhood and Work

THE SOCIAL AND ECONOMIC ROLE OF WOMEN IN POST-FAMINE IRELAND

Economic circumstances conspired to make Ireland an increasingly male-dominated society after the Famine. (J.J. LEE, *Women in Irish Society*)

MARRIAGE, FAMILY AND MOTHERHOOD

At the beginning of the twentieth century family life in Ireland was determined by class and economic factors. These factors were reflected quite differently within urban and rural areas. In urban centres families ranged from slum dwellers through the working class, to the professional and growing middle-classes. The range in rural areas spanned farm labourers, tenant farmers, owners of large farms, and a significant number of landed gentry.[1] Within both areas, the lack of money, employment or property was crucial in determining life style. At this time, less than one in three men in the prime age group 25–34 had married.[2] When marriages occurred, children were numerous, although widespread poverty and the lack of any meaningful health services were reflected in a high rate of infant mortality. Low marriage rates were closely related to widely varying economic opportunities between rural and urban areas, and were closely interlinked with patterns of emigration.

In the first year that marriage registration was made compulsory in Ireland in 1864, just over 20,000 marriages were registered.[3] The marriage rate varied from a low of 3.6 in 1880, rising to 7.4 in 1973, falling to 4.5 in 1998. Concealed within such national figures are distinct regional variations, one notable concealment being the extent to which the low marriage rate was a rural phenomenon. Of those born about

1900, the lowest marriage rates were among farm labourers (half were still unmarried fifty years later); next lowest were small farmers and unskilled urban workers, while the highest proportions of marriages were among large farmers, professional and other skilled workers. In fact, 'the proportion of male labourers (agricultural and non-agricultural) who never married was about *four times* the corresponding proportion among professionals and employers.'[4] In 1954 the Commission on Emigration noted that 'As Ireland's population has been predominantly agricultural, the deterioration of the marriage pattern, which the famine set in motion with a severe initial impetus, has been largely a rural phenomenon'.[5]

Never-married men and women 1901–71 (%)

	Men			Women		
Year	25–34	35–44	15 & over	25–34	35–44	15 & over
1901	28	62	43	47	72	51
1926	28	55	42	47	70	57
1951	33	60	47	54	72	57
1961	42	64	52	63	77	61
1971	58	71	54	74	82	64

Taken from Finola Kennedy, *Cottage to Crèche* (Dublin 2001), p. 24.

The lowest recorded number of marriages occurred in 1932, being 13,029, while the highest number was 22,833 in 1974. With Irish marriages rates generally responding to changes in economic activity, it is not surprising that the lowest rates occurred during the 1930s at a time of widespread depression, aggravated by the Economic War with Britain. Post World War II the rate improved, particularly in Dublin aided by the development of large housing estates on the outskirts of the city. However, the effects of post-famine marriage patterns involving late and low rates of marriage, allied to high celibacy and female emigration rates were still being felt in rural Ireland into the 1960s.

Average annual number of marriages and marriage rate per decade since 1871

Decade	Average annual number per 1,000	Average annual rate
1871–80	18,014	4.5
1881–90	14,692	4.0
1891–1900	14,805	4.5
1901–10	15,325	4.8
1911–20	15,785	5.1
1921–30	14,245	4.8
1931–40	14,359	4.9
1941–50	16,585	5.6
1951–60	15,742	5.4
1961–70	17,430	6.0

Taken from Finola Kennedy, *Cottage to Crèche* (Dublin 2001), p. 49.

MOTHERHOOD

Maternal mortality rates remained high in Ireland up to the 1950s, and were higher in rural than in urban areas. Investigations carried out by Dr James Deeny (chief Medical Adviser in the Department of Local Government and Public Health from 1944) into the causes of high maternal mortality rates had revealed a pattern of few and late marriages, high birth rates, with a large number of older women raising large families and at risk because of late pregnancies. While those who attended any of the three Dublin lying-in hospitals received excellent care, 'with the vast majority of births in the country care was inadequate and (in consequence) too many women died in childbirth'.[6] One example cited by Deeny was a maternity and child clinic in Bedford Row, Limerick, which he discovered to be dirty and seldom used with the 'dried slime of snail-tracks on the examination couches'.[7] A comparative table among eight countries in 1950–54 showed Ireland marginally in second place to Italy for maternal deaths.[8] It has been pointed out that the apparent dismissal by the Emigration Commission in 1954 of maternal death numbers as 'small from a population perspective'—being 'only' 139 per annum during the 1940s, reflected a culture wherein maternal mortality was a fact of everyday life.[9] A variety of causes contributed to maternal deaths, including haemorrhage at childbirth, toxaemia, and puerperal infection. From the 1950s the use of penicillin and other drugs dramatically reduced such deaths.

Maternal mortality rates, 1921–71 (per 100,000 births)

Year	Rate	Number of deaths
1921	481.0	293
1931	431.0	246
1941	321.0	182
1951	164.0	103
1961	45.0	27
1971	22.5	15

Taken from Finola Kennedy, *Cottage to Crèche* (Dublin 2001), p. 51.

Trends in maternal mortality, selected countries, 1950–54 to 1990–94 (average annual deaths per 100,000 births)

Country	1950–54	1985–89	1990–94
UK	81.7	6.9	7.2
Denmark	72.7	5.3	4.8
France	78.6	10.1	11.2
Ireland	141.1	4.2	4.1
Italy	142.4	6.1	5.8
Netherlands	82.9	7.0	5.0
Spain	102.3	4.7	4.1
Switzerland	122.8	6.4	4.2
USA	67.5	7.6	7.9

Taken from Finola Kennedy, *Cottage to Crèche* (Dublin 2001), p. 50.

INFANT MORTALITY

Between 1900 and 1995 the infant mortality rate fell from 99 to 6 per 1,000 live births. Examination of the table on page 162 for the period 1864–1970 reveals the stark reality and magnitude of this problem during the late nineteenth and early decades of the twentieth centuries. Citing the absolute number of deaths which occurred, Finola Kennedy points out that 'in the first decade of the (twentieth) century, 6,500 children under one year died on average each year, compared with 550 in the 1980s'.[10] Tod Andrews, born in 1901, noted in his memoirs that 'when I was a child, every mother of young children lived in constant dread and sometimes real terror of illness … There was every reason for parental terror, because the mortality rate for children in the city was very high.'[11]

Between 1935 and 1941 enteritis in infants became endemic. By 1941, 1,000 such infant deaths occurred annually, 600 of these in Dublin.[12] The Schools Medical Service examinations of children revealed 8,000 children with heart defects, and another 8,000 with chest disorders. In addition, there were a great number of generally unhealthy children, the vast majority of which could have been prevented.[13] Noting that 'the most important determinant of children's health was social class', Mary Daly has pointed to a dramatic differential in mortality statistics:

> For children aged between one and five years, mortality among the professional classes in 1905 was 0.9 per thousand. In the middle classes the figure was 2.7; for artisans and petty shopkeepers it rose to 4.8, reaching 12.7 in the case of hawkers, labourers and porters.[14]

Citing the results of a study he had conducted in Belfast during the early 1940s which was reflected in Dublin, Deeny noted that 'it was the children of the poor, of large families in poor areas, who died'.[15] In contrast to maternal mortality—which was highest in rural areas—infant mortality was highest in cities. The highest rates were to be found among poor tenement dwellers.[16] Kevin Kearns has pointed out that about 20 per cent of all deaths in Dublin's inner city in the 1920s occurred among children less than one year old, nearly all of whom were among the poorer classes.[17] While infant deaths steadily declined during the twentieth century, Kennedy has noted that in 1951 such deaths exceeded deaths from tuberculosis—which were 2,107—by almost 800. Furthermore, whereas TB deaths declined rapidly, by 1955 infant deaths exceeded TB deaths by nearly 1,400.[18] Significantly, infant mortality rates varied markedly according to whether the child was legitimate or illegitimate, one out of every four illegitimate children born in 1930 dying in the first year of life. While the infant mortality rate generally declined during the 1930s, particularly in urban areas, the rate for illegitimate children rose in the same period.[19]

An insight into one aspect of this problem has been provided by Deeny's records of his early Custom House days. While checking returns for infant deaths he noticed something unusual in Cork. Having traced the matter to a home for unmarried mothers on the outskirts of the city at Bessborough, he found that from a total of 180 children born there during the previous year, more than 100 had since died. He subsequently visited the home, and while all appeared fine at first glance, his detailed examination of each infant revealed that all suffered severe skin infection and green diarrhoea 'carefully covered up'. With this evidence of a staphylococcus infection, Deeny immediately closed down the home, sacking the matron (a nun) and the medical officer, noting, 'The deaths had been going on for years. They had done nothing about it, had accepted the situation and were quite complacent about it.'[20]

Average annual deaths of infants under 1 year and infant mortality rate by decade since 1864 (per 1000 births)

Period	Average annual number	Rate per 1,000
1864–70	10,222	96
1871–80	10,104	97
1881–90	7,795	93
1891–1900	7,357	99
1901–10	6,522	91
1911–20	5,591	84
1921–30	4,222	70
1931–40	3,907	68
1941–50	4,278	66
1951–60	2,258	37
1961–70	1,553	25

Taken from Finola Kennedy, *Cottage to Crèche* (Dublin 2001), p. 51.

RURAL MARRIAGE AND FAMILY

Describing marriage as a microcosm of the society which developed in Ireland after the famine, David Fitzpatrick has argued that in its rigidity, restrictiveness and ultimate inefficiency, the marriage institution embodied broader economic and social relationships.[21] An important element for examination within this study is the effect of marriage patterns post-famine on the role and status of Irish women, both married and unmarried—effects which would last into the mid-twentieth century.

A number of historians have debated the extent to which the Famine of 1846 can be held responsible for the changes in Irish society during the latter half of the nineteenth century. Daly has pointed out that while traditional interpretations have generally regarded the Famine as *the* critical factor precipitating such change, more recent scholarship has questioned certain aspects of this 'watershed' theory.[22] Rita Rhodes has noted that evidence from recent studies reveals a more complex Ireland than a purely 'watershed' perspective allows.[23] Characteristics of post-

Famine Ireland that were supposedly brought into existence by the Famine have been identified as having an existence in a pre-Famine context, while the kind of society supposedly destroyed by the Famine was found to be in existence in the west several decades after the Famine.[24] Rhodes identifies three areas of research necessary for an understanding of the complexities of nineteenth-century social history—demography, economics and social structure. All three areas impacted on women's lives. Crucial to a determination of the status of women in Ireland is an examination of the choices available to them regarding work, marriage, and in many cases, emigration. What has emerged from research findings to increase our knowledge of life for women in Ireland during this period?

One fact on which historians agree is the dramatic change in the Irish population pre- and post-Famine. In the century before the Famine, Ireland's population quadrupled; in the following century it was halved.[25] Population decline, once begun, was not consciously reversed until the 1960s. Despite the significant drop in the years immediately after the Famine, the Irish population of 6.6 million was still among the highest ever recorded.[26] However, whereas Ireland had usually recovered rapidly from earlier famines, quite the opposite occurred this time, the population falling to 4.4 million by 1911. Joe Lee argues that the peculiar cause of this development was not the Famine, but the long-term response of Irish society to this short-term calamity. Similarly, Daly agrees that while there is little doubt that conditions and attitudes in Ireland changed during the course of the nineteenth century, what is at issue is the extent to which the Famine can be held responsible for these changes. In the crucial area of population decline, she argues that 'the catastrophe of the Famine would seem to have only accelerated trends which were already in train'.[27]

Lee has cited six main factors as influencing post-Famine demographic development: the changing rural class structure, rising age at marriage, declining marriage and birth rates, a static death rate and emigration. While the combination of these six factors was unique to Ireland, they did not combine within the country in precisely the same manner from decade to decade or from province to province, resulting in marked regional fluctuations in the pace of population decline.[28] Overall, however, as indicated in the following table, the Famine initiated a transformation in the rural social structure. Within that community, the class balance swung sharply in favour of farmers, and within the farming community it swung even more sharply in favour of bigger and against smaller farmers: 'These striking shifts in rural social structure may help explain ... the apparently abrupt reversal of demographic direction involved in converting the Irish from one of the earliest marrying to the latest and most rarely marrying people in Europe.'[29]

Rate of population decline (%) 1841–1911

	Leinster	Munster	Ulster	Connacht	Ireland
1841–51	15.3	22.5	15.7	28.8	19.9
1851–61	12.9	18.5	4.8	9.6	11.5
1861–71	8.1	7.9	4.2	7.3	6.7
1871–81	4.5	4.5	4.9	2.9	4.4
1881–91	7.1	11.9	7.1	11.8	9.1
1891–1901	3.3	8.3	2.3	10.1	5.2
1901–11	+0.8	3.8	0.1	5.6	1.4
1841–1911	41.2	56.8	33.8	57.0	46.4

Taken from J. Lee, *The Modernisation of Irish Society 1848–1918* (1989), p. 2.

Within pre-Famine Ireland, although the majority population had exercised little control over resources to be inherited by children, a minority of strong tenant farmers had viewed familial control as a necessary prerequisite for the preservation of family land and status: 'The post-Famine majority of father-farmers also shared this concern for the land and exercised authority as family guardians of the holding. These farmers, moreover, now were the dominant class and their values would shape the demographic anomaly that Ireland was to become for the first five decades of the twentieth century.'[30] Lee has confirmed that outside the West of Ireland there existed a pre-Famine pattern of higher marriage age, insistence on dowries and low sub-division rates, noting that a disproportionate number of Famine survivors belonged to this class. Those who survived from the labouring and cottier classes were forced to adopt such attitudes. Whereas pre-Famine there had been more labourers and cottiers than farmers in the country, by 1900 cottiers had virtually disappeared and there were twice as many farmers as labourers.[31]

The Famine therefore can be seen to have dramatically universalised trends that were already in operation, with 'the late- and non-marriers of "higher" social status in Irish society provid(ing) the link between the pre-and post-Famine eras of Irish history'.[32] In addition, the experience of the Famine can be seen as 'the great convincer', demonstrating to all the folly of previous agrarian and marriage practices. Irish men and women became convinced that early marriage was reckless marriage, and that non-marriage was an option too: 'As the Irish changed their marriage patterns, they basically adapted the behaviour of the more economically stable elements in the society, convinced that the devastation and destruction of the late 1840s had in part been caused by irrational, carefree marriage and family practices that failed to treat conjugal life as a fundamentally economic enterprise.'[33] Studies by both Art Cosgrove and Caoimhín Ó Danachair have confirmed that class distinction was rife in rural Ireland. Cosgrave has noted that 'The widest social gap in rural Ireland was that between the farmer and the landless labourer, and marriage rarely, if ever, bridged that gap',[34] while Ó Danachair has stated that 'the landless labourer was the untouchable of Irish rural society'.[35] The effects of post-Famine marriage patterns involving late and low rates of marriage, allied to high celibacy and female emigration rates, were still being felt in rural Ireland into the 1960s.[36]

Once married, the female became a reproducer rather than a producer: 'Failure to bear children was generally blamed on female rather than male incapacity, and cast "a great shadow" upon a marriage.'[37] Arensberg and Kimball noted in their 1930s study of family and community life in Ireland that evaluation of the 'new woman' by her parents-in-law centred on her fertility. 'Pregnancy is her major duty. She must have children.'[38] While farmers might express their desire for children in terms of the need for more helping hands around the farm, Arensberg and Kimball argue that it was primarily 'the continuity of the human nexus which is the true goal'.[39] A Limerick report to University College Dublin (UCD) Department of Irish Folklore in 1951 noted that a childless wife 'often had to suffer bitter reproaches from her people-in-law until such time as she'd prove fruitful'.[40] Infertility was considered to be the 'fault' of the woman, an informant to the Irish Folklore Commission noting, 'The old people considered a childless marriage to be due to some inferior quality in the girl, which, in their opinion, rendered her unworthy of their son.'[41]

Noting that the lack of children was a source of shame to a husband, Arensberg and Kimball quoted one woman: 'The man wants children because he is afraid others will tell him he is no good if he hasn't any. Children are the curse of the country, especially if you haven't any.'[42] Their study notes that in country districts a man may beat his wife for this reason; he may 'bounce a boot off her now and then for it'. They also describe the workings of the 'Country Divorce' which allowed a man send a barren wife back to her parents (though Catholic law forbade him to remarry). While said to be rapidly dying out at the time of their research, they refer to the custom surviving in altered form.[43] Generally, the continuity of succession would be arranged by making the land over to a brother, on condition that he marry and produce an heir. Arensberg and Kimball note that such cases 'are particularly revealing in our analysis of the desire to preserve the family unity and its identification with farm and household through the generations'.[44] On occasion the bride's father would withhold part of the dowry until she survived the birth of her first child, presumably on the assumption that she would be thrown out by her husband, without her fortune, in case of 'functional failure'.[45] Such provision was often included in the terms of the 'match' reflecting the identifying continuity and the importance to all parties of the girl's bearing children for the family into which she marries: 'Most often the second instalment of the fortune is not paid until the first child is born, or, with more legal formality, until a year after the marriage contract is completed'.[46]

A woman without children or only daughters could also be required to leave her husband's land if her husband died. Describing this practice to the Irish Folklore Commission, a Galway man explained, 'If the husband of a woman who had married into a place died childless within a year or a few years of marriage, the widow was often sent home to her parents, in which case the dowry was returned with something added to it.'[47] Rural Irish society considered that the childless widow had no bond with her husband's family, and being 'hardly regarded as having moved out of her own kindred; she is buried when she dies, not with her husband but with her father'.[48] There were instances of families without male children nominating a daughter as heir; in such cases it was the incoming son-in-law that had to bring a fortune, usually much larger than the girl's. In such marriages it was common that the farm married into continued to be known by the girl's patrilineal name for at least a generation.[49] As in many other rural societies, children were regarded as economic assets, and 'reproduction continued to serve as a form of social insurance by generating potential emigrants whose remittances would provide parental pensions and the means for further emigration'.[50] As late as 1965, in a Dáil Debate regarding the *Succession Act*, 1965, John A. Costello gave an example of the very different treatment afforded daughters and sons. He told the story of a man with seven daughters who finally had a son, the son becoming the apple of the father's eye.

Outlining all his plans for his son—the best school, university, etc.—the man's attitude was summed up in his comment 'You would like to do the best you can for the one child you have.'[51]

A PATRIARCHAL SOCIETY

Joe Lee has argued that economic circumstances conspired to make Ireland an increasingly male-dominated society after the Famine.[52] He has pointed to three key post-Famine developments that drastically weakened the position of women in Irish society—the virtual collapse of domestic industry, a shift from tillage to livestock (pastoral) farming, and a significant drop in the number of agricultural labourers and small farmers. The first of these developments removed a substantial source of independent income for women, while the second resulted in women being physically needed less around the farm.[53] The third removed the pre-Famine trend for early marriages based on sub-division of land; the system of impartible inheritance which became dominant after the Famine ensured that the land could not be sub-divided, but would be inherited by a single (usually) male heir.

The patriarchal society that emerged post-Famine was distinguished by an increasing emphasis on larger farms, land becoming the principal criterion for status. Within the context of property, lineage and inheritance becoming important concerns for the family, the position of women deteriorated and the authority of fathers and the position of sons within the family grew stronger.[54] Another factor that promoted patriarchalism was the strong desire to preserve the identification of the family name with the land. Arensberg and Kimball's research confirmed that 'the desire for continuity further enhanced the position of the father (who) comes ... to stand for the group which he heads; the farm is known by his name, and wife and children bear his name likewise'.[55] All of these factors made Irish society more exclusively male-centred. The power of this strong farming class lasted many decades, its values permeating Irish society into the mid-twentieth century. The spread of such values into urban areas from the late nineteenth century was facilitated by the growth in clerical power and the expansion in education. Both areas were dominated by farmers' attitudes, as 'the rise of the strong farmer coincided with the growth of clerical power'.[56]

Control over landholding increased the authority of father-farmers over their children, particularly in relation to marriage. Social status associated with landholding provided another patriarchal tool, as fathers determined to a large extent when and whom their children would marry. As a result of changing marriage patterns, women became increasingly subservient to the male authoritarian figures of father and husband. A great emphasis developed on the amount of dowry a girl could bring with her to a marriage. Girls now became more dependent on their father for a dowry. Daughters, particularly those of strong farmers, had few economic opportunities to earn the cash necessary for the dowries demanded by farm families.[57] As a father would usually only dower one daughter, girls became more submissive to their father's wishes, losing the relative independence possessed pre-Famine in the choice of a partner.[58] Elizabeth Malcolm has confirmed this pattern, noting that 'marriages in post-Famine Ireland were few and late and were usually arranged by the parents, especially the father, in order to form economic alliances with local farming and shop-keeping families'.[59] The payment of a dowry by the bride's family to her father-in-law rather than to her husband or to a common household purse can be viewed as 'a fine for the transfer of a redundant female from one family to another'.[60] Arensberg and Kimball observed that in line with the farm being identified with the patrilineal and patronymic family line of the land-owner, 'the girl is an outsider brought into that group, the money appears as a payment for (her) inclusion. There is significantly no corresponding recompense or payment to the girl's father. He loses both daughter and dowry.'[61] Marriages between farming and labouring families were not encouraged, Lee noting that such marriages 'were considered unnatural', farmers' children preferring celibacy to labourers.[62]

Change in percentage of holdings 1841 and 1901

Province	Above 1 and Under 5	Above 5 and Under 15	Above 15 and Under 30	Above 30
Leinster	-64.6	-44.0	+6.1	+119.4
Munster	-78.8	-68.3	-12.2	+245.3
Ulster	-80.2	-36.6	+113.3	+361.5
Connaught	-87.5	+2.1	+486.0	+427.7
Ireland	-79.8	-39.0	+69.0	+238.3

Taken from R. Rhodes, *Women and the Family in Post-Famine Ireland* (New York and London, 1992), p. 43.

Changes in marriage practices had a number of effects. Increasing life expectancy meant that sons had to wait longer to inherit the family farm.

Until the parents died or retired the son was usually treated as an unpaid labourer, expected to obey his parents and unable to marry without their consent.[63] In turn, this led to a later marrying age for males and a widening age gap between husband and wife. Whereas before the Famine about 20 per cent of husbands were ten years older than their wives, by the early twentieth century this figure stood at 50 per cent. As a result Irish farmers were often middle aged before they married, with many never marrying at all. After marriage, the increased number of younger wives and older husbands reinforced male authority.[64] Despite later and less frequent marriages post-Famine, and the predominant 'stem-family' system which allowed only one child to inherit the farm, marry, and produce the next generation, family size remained large, five or six being the norm.[65] As noted in the work of Arensberg and Kimball in County Clare in the 1930s, dispersal of the other members of the family following the marriage of the heir formed a crucial part of the rural Irish household system. With usually only the heir and one daughter married and dowered, all the rest 'must travel'.[66] High fertility could exist because 'surplus' children would emigrate and through remittances provide for younger children and the maintenance of parents. While some siblings chose to continue working on the family farm, or found employment elsewhere within the country, for many the only option was emigration.

By the end of the nineteenth century, Ireland had achieved a distinctive pattern of late marriage allied to a high rate of permanent celibacy. Within this society it was increasingly difficult to achieve independent adult status; rather dependency became a long and often permanent condition.[67] One study has shown that the proportion of unmarried fifty-year-old women rose from an eighth in 1841 to a quarter by 1911, indicating that 'non-marriage was a far more important factor than marriage postponement in causing the depopulation of post-Famine Ireland'.[68] The values associated with a patriarchal society had a significant effect on Irish daughters, Rhodes noting: 'In the name of family and land, Irish daughters would be noted for distinctive behaviours that identified them as among the least-likely to marry and most-likely to emigrate.'[69] By the turn of the century, 'modernisation' for Irishwomen came to mean 'departure'.[70]

As a further result of this pattern of young brides and older husbands, many farms fell into the hands of widows who continued to exercise authority over their sons and daughters. In particular such widows often resisted the marriage of the inheriting son, unwilling to compromise their power as farmers or to welcome a daughter-in-law.[71] Households headed by widows were a particular feature of rural life that contributed to both late marriage age and permanent bachelorhood of sons.[72] By 1911 Census returns indicated that over three-quarters of all women in agriculture were female farmers, mostly middle-aged or elderly widows or single women. With the introduction of the old-age pension in 1911, qualification for which required the handing over of the family farm, the number of such female farmers fell.[73]

Percentage unmarried at ages 20–24, 25–29 and 25–34

Year	20-24		25-29		25-34	
	Male	Female	Male	Female	Male	Female
1841*	91.9	80.7	Not available	Not available	42.6	28.9
1861	90.5	76.3	66.2	48.5	55.1	40.4
1881	92.8	82.1	70.8	53.2	60.0	43.1
1901	94.8	86.4	Not available	Not available	68.0	52.3
1911	95.1	86.5	Not available	Not available	70.1	53.7
1926**	96.0	87.0	79.8	61.8	71.7	52.6

Taken from R. Rhodes, *Women and the Family in Post-Famine Ireland* (New York and London, 1992), p. 111.

*Ages 17–25 and 26–35   ** 26 Counties

EMIGRATION

Between 1801 and 1921 approximately eight million people left Ireland.[74] While the number of emigrants rose sharply post-Famine, this to some measure was a continuation of pre-Famine trends.[75] Arensberg and Kimball's research showed that 'far from the Famine's having started the emigration from the present Free State … the thirty years before 1845 spread the emigrating spirit through all but the highest class until it became the favourite remedy for hard times'.[76] Examining the reasons for the decline in rural population, they pointed out that restricted employment opportunities due to changed farming methods cannot be considered the sole cause. With population decline the most marked among small farmers, their numbers falling from 6,548,000 in 1841 to 2,963,000 in 1926, Arensberg and Kimball argued that other demographic statistics, particularly marriage, must be considered. Their study showed that 'No other occupational class, not even the professional class, delays marriage so long or has so many celibate members'.[77]

What was significantly different post-Famine, however, was the type of emigrant. Approximately half of pre-Famine emigrants had been family groups, this phenomenon reaching its peak in the mid-1840s. Emigration at this time took place in the context of a growing population; post-Famine it would become associated with a declining population.[78] As noted earlier, despite a pattern of late and few marriages, Irish family size at the turn of the century was still large, five or six children being the norm. A result of this was an extremely youthful population, 62 per cent being under the age of thirty-five years in 1911.[79] Younger sons without a farm or inheritance prospects and younger daughters unlikely to receive a dowry had little hope of marrying or of finding reasonably paid, long-term employment. Thus it was the younger children of labouring and small farming families who formed the largest groups among the waves of emigrants leaving Ireland in the decades between 1850 and 1920, most of whom left in their late teens or early twenties.[80] Noting that 'Irish-style marriage was a minority experience for the Irish people after the Famine', David Fitzpatrick has argued that effectively by getting rid of the majority of each generation through emigration, the residual population managed to preserve far more of its previous way of life than most observers of the Famine catastrophe had expected.[81]

Faced with poor marriage prospects and virtually no employment opportunities, increasingly large numbers of women left rural Ireland. Between 1891 and 1911 young women would form the majority emigrant group, leaving Ireland with a predominantly male population. Kerby Miller has noted that 'It was the women whom the dowry system could not accommodate who poured overseas into American cities in the late nineteenth and early twentieth centuries'.[82] This dominance of female emigration would remain a constant in Irish life up to the 1960s.

It has been argued that the late nineteenth century was 'a dismal period for women in Ireland'.[83] There is no doubt that Ireland's unique marriage pattern—and survival method—was harsh on both daughters and sons. While it is true that the bargaining position of women deteriorated in the employment and the marriage markets alike, it has also been argued that as Ireland increasingly became a place that women left 'because they could not find a meaningful role for themselves in its social order and because American opportunities for young women beckoned ... These young women ... saw themselves not as passive pawns in life, but as active, enterprising creatures who could take their destiny in their own hands.'[84] In his study of 'female escapology' Fitzpatrick has observed that 'The independent movement of millions of unattached girls ... bears witness to the fortitude as well as the deprivation of the Irish female ... Acceptance of subordination to Irishmen was by no means general among Irishwomen.'[85] Unlike other ethnic groups, the Irish achieved this through the emigration of individual single women rather than women in family groups.[86] For those women who left Ireland, the nineteenth century was often a period of triumph rather than subjection. Rhodes too has noted: 'For Irish daughters, emigration could operate as a vehicle that would permit both the fulfilment of traditional familial values as well as the satisfaction of individual needs that could not be met within rural Ireland.'[87]

Education and emigration were the two principal strategies adopted by Irishwomen and their families in search of higher status, one sometimes feeding the other. Significant educational developments took place between the Famine and World War I. Whereas prior to the Famine most Irish men were illiterate, the census of 1911 shows that virtually every young Irish adult could write.[88] In particular, literacy rates for women improved most dramatically during the late nineteenth century. The superior performance of girls in primary education at this time reflected not only their desire to improve themselves, but also their declining importance in the labour market. As girls were needed less around the family farm, they could be released more for education.[89] Did female education encourage emigration or vice versa? Citing contemporary sources which believed that education fostered emigration, and noting unsuccessful attempts by the Education Board to train cooks and laundresses for the home only, Fitzpatrick argues that 'the amenities provided in National schools were ruthlessly exploited by children and parents aware that the possession of common household skills would enhance the emigrant's attraction to foreign employers'. Noting that evening schools were crowded with 'migratory crammers', with crash courses for emigrants being tolerated by certain state agencies, Fitzpatrick concludes that 'in general, enthusiasm for education and emigration were found to coincide'.[90] With female emigration more prevalent amongst the literate, both factors converged, 'becoming complementary rather than alternative routes of escape for Irishwomen'.[91]

Another interesting differential between male and female emigrants has been posited in studies by Hasia Diner and Elizabeth Malcolm. Malcolm has noted that the profile of those who emigrated overseas and those committed to asylums in Ireland contain a number of striking similarities but also some interesting differences. Both groups were overwhelmingly young, single, Catholic, unskilled men and women from labouring and small farming families. Finding that 'while the majority of emigrants at the turn of the century were female, the majority of asylum inmates were male', Malcolm asks, 'Were asylum inmates in fact those who, for whatever reason, did not emigrate?'[92] Pointing to the age differential between emigrants (mostly under twenty-five years) and asylum inmates (generally in their thirties or forties), Malcolm argues that on reaching middle age with no prospect of marriage or of economic independence, the discontent of those who had not emigrated could have become unmanageable within the confines of the family. As women either found it easier or were more highly motivated to leave than men, she notes that more young male Catholic rural labourers stayed behind and more of these men in early middle age were committed to asylums. Malcolm points out that the asylum was never feared by the Irish in the way they feared the workhouse; committal to the former was often used as a tool to discipline unruly members while committal to the latter was seen as a disgrace.[93]

Pointing to parental preference for sons in many cultures, with maternal dominance characterising the family structure of a wide range of ethnic groups, Diner has noted that research into the ethnic dimensions of psychiatric disorders in the US and in Europe point to 'staggering statistics of Irish male schizophrenia'. She further notes that 'Many psychocultural studies have asserted that Irish men never could overcome the emotionally debilitating effects of being overwhelmed by their mothers'.[94] Daughters however, less valued and less manipulated by their mothers, left Ireland more willingly and with little emotional pining.

ILLEGITIMACY

Some daughters who left Ireland, did so most unwillingly. These were the unmarried mothers, driven out by desperation and shame. Dympna McLoughlin has challenged the myth of nineteenth-century Ireland as some 'idealised asexual age' in which there was no pre-marital sex, no prostitution, infanticide or child abandonment, pointing out that in fact these issues long pre-date the nineteenth century.[95] Unmarried mothers coped with their pregnancy in varying ways depending on their circumstances. The workhouse was sometimes the only refuge for many single pauper women with children. Utilising paid emigration schemes, pauper women often left their children in the workhouse, many later sending money for their children to join them.[96] Within the farming community, the plight of an unmarried girl who became pregnant was critical. With the emphasis on agreed or 'matched' marriages amongst those with land in post-Famine Ireland, the increased importance of female virtue was stressed, as 'an unvirtuous daughter could be the ruination of an otherwise thrifty and farseeing man'.[97] McLoughlin has noted that 'sexual prudery in nineteenth-century Ireland had little to do with the church and all to do with the economics of the emerging middle class'.[98] Frequently girls were cast out by their families, and forced to become vagrants, many resorting to the workhouse or prostitution. Women for whom a marriage partner could be found never fully redeemed the disgrace caused to themselves or their family.

Such attitudes continued into the new Irish state, Arensberg and Kimball noting that the country people's attitude toward illegitimacy and pre-marital sex were one and the same, being viewed as a disgrace on both the girl and her family. The only options offered by a girl's 'disgraced' family when pregnancy occurred outside of wedlock was either to make a match for the girl, or her expulsion, emigration being the norm.[99] Even where a marriage was arranged for such 'poor, unfortunate girls', the stain remained on their character.[100] Based on a girl's full status within the family system, wherein sexual and economic activity was integrated, it was noted that 'her sexual conduct is no concern of hers alone'.[101]

During the first decades of the Irish Free State, the issue of illegitimacy was the subject of much consideration by both church and state. Unmarried mothers were represented as either 'innocent victims or corrupting agents ... poor girls or potential blackmailers (who) brought shame to their nation and their families'.[102] The average illegitimate birth rate per annum between 1920–1930 was 1,707, rising each year from 1926. Concern at these increases, allied to a strong belief that there were many more unregistered births, was noted by the Committee on the Criminal Law Amendment Act (CCLAA) in the early 1930s.[103] Most significant too is the fact that the death rate for registered illegitimate babies was five times greater than for legitimate babies, many such deaths occurring in institutions.[104] A 1920s report on the extent of illegitimacy in Dublin workhouses had shown that almost all maternity cases admitted were 'illegitimates', the majority from rural areas.[105] A number of other agencies also catered for unmarried mothers, most of which had been formed as refuges for 'fallen women' or prostitutes.[106]

From the early 1920s a series of homes specifically targeted at unmarried mothers were established by orders of nuns, sometimes in co-operation with local authorities. 'Repeat offenders', often deemed to be 'feeble minded', were particularly harshly treated, with many of these 'intractable' unmarried mothers being admitted to Magdalen asylums, which proved difficult to leave.[107] The severe regime operated in these homes, reflecting the official outlook of the day towards both first time and repeat 'offenders', resulted in increasing numbers of women opting to travel to England to give birth and have their babies adopted.[108]

From the formation of the state, particular concern had been expressed about the migration of unmarried mothers. The numbers of such emigrants increased significantly from the early 1930s, continuing up to the 1960s. The focus of Catholic clergy and lay agencies such as the Child Protection and Rescue Society of Ireland (CPRSI) was to prevent the children of such mothers being adopted by non-Catholic families in England, a problem which by the 1960s was described by the CPRSI as 'assuming proportions far greater' than the worst years of proselytism in Ireland.[109] No legal adoption existed in the Republic of Ireland until 1952, and even then there was opposition to its introduction based on religious, constitutional and inheritance grounds. Paul M. Garrett has pointed out however that there were *de facto* adoptions, particularly during the 1950s when many Irish-born illegitimate children were handed over to childless Catholic American couples, with the seeming complicity of the Catholic Church.[110] Through its 'Crusade of Rescue', the CPRSI in co-operation with English agencies, who were concerned at the number of unmarried mothers from Ireland arriving at its doors, assisted in the repatriation of over 2,600 unmarried mothers between 1948–1971.[111] Until the late 1960s there was little support or tolerance towards unmarried mothers in Ireland, their fate being one of shame and disgrace. Luddy has noted the irony that 'in a state that applauded motherhood, (they had) no rights as mothers'.[112]

In her study of illegitimacy, abortion and infanticide based on Irish folklore and documentary sources, Anne O'Connor has noted that Irish religious legends and folk ballads on these themes were common, with two opposing images of women emerging—the unrepentant child murderess and a 'sinner-saint' Mary Magdalene figure.[113] From the early nineteenth century government controls became more stringent in dealing with such 'social problems'. Public opinion seems to have taken a more lenient attitude towards these offences, with few prosecutions actually occurring.[114] With 'significant rates of infanticide' noted by McLoughlin among nineteenth-century pauper women, within the confines of the workhouse such an act was hard to conceal, the workhouse being the first port of call by police when a dead infant was found.[115] Court records in the early years of the twentieth century show a number of convictions for infanticide.[116]

Rarely the subject of official public debate, the issue of infanticide was raised during Dáil and Senate debates on the 1934 Criminal Law Amendment Bill by Deputy Rowlette and Senator Oliver St John Gogarty (both medical doctors). In discussion on the proposed ban on the sale or importation of contraceptives contained in the bill, Gogarty described infanticide as 'the dreadful alternative facing the unfortunate poor'.[117] With emigration to Britain restricted during World War II, it was probable that more pregnant women had to remain in Ireland. In 1949 the Infanticide Act was passed, allowing special grounds of temporary insanity as a means of reducing a charge of murder to that of manslaughter. That same year there were five recorded cases of infanticide.[118] The Commission on Emigration in 1954 while highlighting the high rate of illegitimate infant death also referred to infanticide. It dismissed its importance, however, on the grounds that 'its incidence is not sufficiently significant to require comment from us'.[119] Kennedy has pointed out that 'infanticide was a reality regardless of the absence of comprehensive statistics'.[120] Its very nature involved concealment.

It has been argued that the extent of Irish mothers travelling to Britain to give birth and have their children adopted was 'not wholly displeasing to the Irish authorities since it served to distort the nation's illegitimacy rate and artificially push it downwards'.[121] The similarities between the 'secretiveness' and 'silence' associated with illegitimate birth and adoption in Ireland up to the 1960s, and a similar 'silence' surrounding Irishwomen's journeys to British abortion clinics since that time has been noted. Garrett points out that a similar argument might be applied in the current situation, whereby 'once again, unresolved tensions and problems centred on the denial of women's reproductive rights are being *exported*'.[122]

DOMESTIC VIOLENCE

Another area directly affecting women—an area that has also been 'silenced' over many generations—is that of domestic violence. During the 1870s, *The Irish Times* and *The Cork Examiner* reported weekly court cases of wife-beating that were before the local Magistrate's Court. National Archive records for the period 1853–1920 contain over one thousand appeals by men convicted of beating their wives, mothers or sisters. With these sources indicating that wife-beating in Ireland was widespread and brutal, Elizabeth Steiner-Scott points out that 'Women in Ireland had to endure daily beatings, verbal abuse, psychological torture, and grinding poverty which made it often impossible for them to escape their tormenters'.[123] There was, however, virtually no public outcry on this issue, nor was there a demand to extend English legislation on this matter to Ireland. Sentences imposed for such offences were less than for offences against property.[124] Frances Power Cobbe, an Irish-born woman active in the early women's movement in England, and particularly prominent in highlighting domestic violence, wrote in 1878: 'In the worst districts of London … four-fifths of the wife-beating cases are among the lowest class of Irish labourers.'[125] Her further comment that 'in their own country Irishmen of all classes are proverbially kind and even chivalrous towards women' is contradicted by the facts as reported by courts and newspapers. Joanna Bourke has noted that in the early 1900s in rural Ireland most cases of domestic violence 'centred increasingly on accusations of poor housework', a defence for which there was support in some quarters.[126]

Between 1912 and 1920, the suffrage/feminist paper, the *Irish Citizen*, regularly published articles on the abuse of women, but from the foundation of the new state 'silence surrounding domestic violence returned until well into the 1970s'.[127] Was this a reflection of hierarchal concerns that the privacy of the family be maintained, or a continuation of earlier nationalist reluctance to expose—or admit—the existence of such a problem? Kevin Kearns has noted that in tenement society wife-beating was widely recognised but seldom discussed publicly. One woman told Kearns that 'the men at that time were very hard on their wives. They'd drink a lot and come home and beat some of them up. I saw men not only hitting but kicking their wives.'[128] Despite habitual abuse from her husband, a wife was expected to remain married, one woman recalling that, 'He was your husband and when you married him you had to do what he *told* you. Like it or lump it! Or you'd get a few punches.'[129] Outsiders rarely became involved in a row between husband and wife, the one exception being the 'granny' who was the 'matriarch'. Reflecting Steiner-Scott's findings that where a husband was charged for such abuse, their wives commonly sought mitigation or cancellation of any penalty, Kearns has also noted that a wife rarely testified against a violent husband.

URBAN FAMILY AND MARRIAGE

Lee has pointed to the gradual infiltration of rural values to towns post-

Famine through the twin agencies of a clergy predominantly from a farming background, and an expanding educational system mainly staffed by teachers from a similar background and increasingly under clerical influence.[130] Brendan Walsh has noted that significant differences in marriage patterns existed between different population groups, commenting that while the characteristic Irish marriage pattern was more pronounced in the poorer rural communities, 'The urban population displayed a better marriage pattern, but there were interesting differentials between socio-economic groups'.[131] While professional and managerial groups tended to have the lowest level of 'definitive celibacy', they tended to marry relatively late; 'Manual workers, on the other hand, tended to marry early, but relatively high proportions in these groups remained unmarried.' Walsh associates these differentials with the educational and career paths of people in these groups.

Internal migration within Ireland primarily affected the Eastern provinces, Dublin and Belfast being the main cities chosen. The Census Commissioners in 1841 noted that most immigration to Dublin came from Wicklow, Meath, Wexford and Kildare. Women outnumbered men in such internal migration, leading the Commissioners to comment: 'The number of females coming from Wicklow and Kildare will especially attract attention. Indeed, the excess is so considerable, that it appears to have even affected the proportion of sexes remaining in those counties.'[132] This pattern continued into the twentieth century, women tending to migrate from counties neighbouring Dublin and Belfast, or from the same province. Noting that the vast majority of Irish servants were children of small farmers, estate workers, the semi-skilled and the unskilled, Mona Hearn has pointed out that domestic service was in particular the cause of considerable migration of young girls: 'The lack of alternative employment was a crucial factor in limiting career choice for these girls; in fact the usual choice facing them was domestic service or emigration.'[133]

Domestic service became a traditional haven for women from rural Ireland. Putting a daughter 'in service' was considered a safe option by parents in tune with the ideology of Victorian Ireland. Hearn points to the striking difference between the birthplace of most servants and the population of Dublin city and county. Census returns for 1911 reveal that only 28 per cent of servants working in Dublin houses were born in Dublin city or county; 42 per cent came from neighbouring counties and the rest of Leinster, 30 per cent from the other three provinces and

Britain. On the other hand, 70 per cent of the general population of Dublin city and 65 per cent of the population of Dublin county were born in Dublin city and county.[134] Daly has confirmed this pattern, noting that 'migrants in Dublin, in marked contrast to emigrants, tended to come from the more prosperous parts of Ireland, the counties adjoining Dublin, with a substantial number coming from England'.[135] Domestic service reflected a particularly young profile; in 1911 47 per cent of indoor female servants were under 25 years of age—only 18 per cent were over 45. The majority of these were single; they either married late in life and left service or did not marry at all. While approximately half of the female population of Dublin married between the ages of 25 and 34, only 3 per cent of servants did likewise.[136]

The employment of young country girls as servants in urban areas became an essential element in the creation of the new bourgeoisie. Ability to afford servants reflected living standards; the higher the social class, the more servants were employed. While professional and wealthy families often employed six or seven servants, most middle-class families employed at least one. So accepted was this practice that it formed part of an argument by the Civil Service Federation in the 1930s in seeking an examination of their pay. Outlining the differences between a civil servant's household and a working-class household, it was argued that 'At least one maidservant was normally employed in the former and the period of dependence of the children was more extended than in a working-class family'.[137] In his autobiography, Tod Andrews drew a vivid picture of the four main divisions of class in Dublin in 1907, moving from the Catholic upper middle class, through the 'middle middle' class and lower middle class, to the working class:

> The top of the Catholic heap—in terms of worldly goods and social status—were the medical specialists, fashionable dentists, solicitors, wholesale tea and wine merchants, owners of large drapery stores and a very few owners or directors of large business firms … At the bottom of the heap were the have-nots of the city, consisting of labourers, dockers, coal heavers, messenger boys and domestic servants.[138]

It was estimated that an income of £150 p.a. was needed in 1911 to afford a domestic servant.[139] Tony Farmar noted that 'full-blown middle-class respectability was difficult to maintain on much below £250 a year'.[140] Middle-class men rarely earned enough to marry before their thirties.

Only the rich could afford to buy homes, the majority of middle-class renting their homes. In 1907, the wages of unskilled Dublin labourers was generally less than £1 a week, and often as low as 15s. Commenting that on such pay, ' a working man, even though sober and with a small family, found it was virtually impossible to provide adequately for his family', Farmar notes that 'As a result the family diet was usually poor and insufficient … the constant items (being) bread, usually without butter, and well stewed tea with sugar'.[141]

HOUSING—RURAL

Both Joanna Bourke and Mary Daly have pointed to census data collated on inhabited houses in urban and rural areas between 1841 and 1911. Houses were divided into four classes according to the number of rooms, the number of windows, and the materials from which the house was built. In Dublin city fourth class houses were those with one room and one window; third class 2–4 rooms and windows; second class 5–9 rooms plus windows; first class was any larger house, including institutions.[142]

Houses in Dublin City 1841–1911

	First Class	Second	Third	Fourth
1841	10,171	8,289	1,494	155
1851	10,827	9,693	1,680	44
1861	10,688	10,486	1,740	21
1871	10,459	11,455	1,891	91
1881	9,067	13,061	2,064	14
1891	8,720	14,638	2,391	7
1901	8,673	18,855*	—	11
1911	8,688	26,785*	—	4

* Includes third class houses

Taken from M. Daly, *Dublin—The Deposed Capital* (Cork, 1985), p. 278.

Within rural areas, fourth class houses were small mud huts, third class had windows and between one and four rooms, and were built of sturdier material, second class houses were often good farmhouses having five to nine rooms and windows, first class houses were generally 'gentlemen's houses'.[143]

Rural houses and housing 'classes' 1861–1911 (%)

Year	'Class' of house			
	First	Second	Third	Fourth
1861	3.1	32.7	54.0	10.3
1871	3.6	35.2	42.2	19.0
1881	4.8	41.7	48.1	5.3
1891	5.8	49.3	42.4	2.9
1901	6.4	55.8	36.3	1.5
1911	7.2	64.2	27.8	0.8

Taken from Joanna Bourke, *Husbandry to Housewifery* (1993), p. 207.

In both urban and rural areas, problems existed for those living in the poorer form of housing, in certain cases with extreme overcrowding. Anne O'Dowd's study of women in rural Ireland, shows that dwellings for small to medium sized holdings in the nineteenth century were small, providing shelter not only for the family, but often also for cows, goats, and poultry. One account cited by O'Dowd is that of Brigid Ó Maolfhabhaill, recorded by the Irish Folklore Collection (IFC). Referring to her home in County Mayo in the 1870s, Brigid recounted:

> At that time people had everything in the house between cows and cattle and pigs and calves, and perhaps a donkey. (Well alright then) they had the cows tethered down at the end of the house and another small place made for a couple of pigs. There was a bed beside the fire and the horse was tied to the front of the bed … In the winter when there was bad weather it was usual for the cows to be in the house from morning until evening. When there was weather like this the people had to sweep out and clean out after the animal many times in the day.[144]

Similarly, O'Dowd cites Peig Sayers recalling the houses in Kerry in the 1880s and 1890s:

> Long ago the floors got very little brushing when a horse was tethered at one end of the kitchen and perhaps two calves tethered to the side walls of the house … When the animals were put out in the summer, the houses were cleaned and lime was put on the floor and the housewife was in better charge.[145]

By the early 1890s, the Congested Districts Board had begun to spend money on the improvement of farmers' holdings, including the construction of outbuildings as well as the construction of new houses. David Smith has commented that 'These home improvements were partially designed to discourage inhabitants from housing their livestock in the main family dwelling, a convention that had appalled English travellers in Ireland for years'.[146] A further effect of moving livestock out of the main dwelling house was to take them out of reach of those who traditionally tended them, i.e. women. Census returns reflected improvements in rural housing; whereas in 1891 almost half of all rural houses were third or fourth class, twenty years later in 1911, nearly three-quarters were first or second class. A series of Acts from the 1880s providing for the building of labourers' houses resulted in a quarter of a million people being rehoused by 1914.[147] Arensberg and Kimball's survey in the 1930s shows a striking uniformity of design among houses for small farmers, noting that 'the variations in house types and forms are more associable with differences of class than of locality'.[148] Referring to the work of the Congested Districts Board (1893–1923) and subsequent developments by government agencies, they note that 36 per cent of Clare's population lived in three-room dwellings, 24 per cent in four-room dwellings, and 12 per cent in two-room dwellings.

When they turned their attention to the town of Ennis, Arensberg and Kimball noted that Ennis housed its citizens in much the same way as all urban areas, 'in general, the larger and poorer the family, the smaller its space. On the farm in general, the small farm means a small house, and many human beings in it. In town, space is at a premium, and only the well-to-do learn privacy or divide a dwelling into many parts.'[149] Commenting that 'Ennis is only an instance of the general conditions of the nation', and that the work one does very much determines the type of house one lives in, and its location in the town, they pointed out that 'If one works with one's hands at manual labour, one has little chance for more space than one or two rooms shared with three or four other persons. If one's work is skilled, one's chances are considerably better.'[150] Their work also noted that while the back streets of Ennis are no urban slum, they have the role of slum in the town.

From the 1890s, local councils began seriously to invest in housing for labourers, and as noted above, by 1914 a quarter of a million had been rehoused.[151] Referring to the view of reformers, who saw better housing as both a moral and social question, being one of the most effective instruments of social change, Bourke has pointed out that reformers hoped improved housing would mean improved housework. Contemporary sources believed that human surroundings either 'elevate or degrade', and that if Ireland was to contain a 'moral, sober, intelligent, healthy and industrious people' they must have improved homes. She cites the idealisation of the new labourers' cottages as illustrated in the Lenten pastoral of the Bishop of Cloyne in 1911:

I have seen many of these new cottages, outside and inside. It is a pleasure to visit them. The outside walls fresh with whitest limewash, the windows kept regularly painted, the woodbine and the clematis winding around the door, an indication of the development of taste; inside … the floor is brushed and unspotted, the simple household furniture is neatly kept and arranged, and the mother of the home, the proud queen in her own little realm, is surrounded by healthy, happy children.[152]

Improved houses would (and were expected to) increase female workloads.[153] The extent of such workloads has been vividly documented by Arensberg and Kimball in their description of a typical working day in the life of a farm wife. First in the family to rise to start the fire, her work continues throughout the day preparing meals, baking bread, housecleaning and washing, caring for the children, feeding and milking cows, being the last to bed, having settled the fire in the hearth. Notable too is their observation that farm women and children did not eat with their menfolk, waiting until the latter had finished.[154]

To the modern mind, reform of housing without a piped water supply is somewhat unthinkable. In addition to health concerns, the issue of domestic water supply was one that directly affected women and their work within the home—in both rural and urban settings. Daly has noted that fetching water for domestic use appears to have been regarded as women's work, both in Ireland and in most traditional societies.[155] In 1911, Mrs Harold Lett, president of the United Irishwomen, protested about the number of labourers' cottages in county Wexford that had been built over half a mile from water supplies, pointing out the difficulties posed for labourers' wives, 'trudging half a mile up a hill carrying in one hand a can of water and with an infant tucked under the other arm, while one or two mites hang on to your skirts'.[156] Dublin tenement dwellers and many women living in small towns and villages were also forced to fetch water from a distance and the available water was often polluted.

Most of the problems in urban centres had been resolved by the 1950s, with considerable improvements in rural areas during the 1960s, yet by 1971 over 42 per cent of rural homes continued to lack any supply of running water—'not even an outdoor tap'.[157] Post World War II, with high priority being given by government to the preservation of rural Ireland, a nationwide scheme for rural electrification was carried out. Welcomed ostensibly as an aid to modern farming, it has been noted by Daly that electrification was viewed primarily as a means of improving leisure and social facilities: 'The fact that leisure products were used by men, while household appliances were primarily of benefit to women, is an important consideration in this argument.'[158] Lack of commitment—and indeed interest—on the issue of water supply by politicians and civil servants has been interpreted as being both gender and class based. Whereas both male and female organisations were involved in the campaign to promote electricity, the supply of rural water appears from the beginning to have been viewed as a matter of concern only to women:

> Most of the benefits of running water would accrue to women: women (and children) carried water from the well; women were solely responsible for laundry, washing-up and other domestic cleaning. The major farm task which would benefit most from running water, dairy hygiene, such as cleaning milk utensils, also appears to have been primarily a woman's chore.[159]

To a government concerned with emigration and the depopulation of rural areas, the lack of interest in providing a facility that might have produced an environment more attractive to young Irish women is surprising. Despite the commitment of Seán MacEntee, Minister for Local Government and Public Health in 1947, to the necessity for a nationwide piped water supply, succeeding governments did not share this priority. In fact, while subsequent ministers devoted considerable energy to improving housing standards, the matter of piped water was not seen as a related issue.[160]

As detailed in Chapter 11, in 1960 the government sought the assistance of the Irish Countrywomen's Association (ICA) in promoting piped water. Strong opposition from farming groups reduced significantly the effectiveness of this campaign, and severe budgetary cutbacks in the mid-1960s resulted in water schemes suffering significantly.[161]

HOUSING—URBAN

By the early 1900s, Dublin had the worst slums in Europe.[162] Slums had existed in Dublin well before the nineteenth century, but the tenement process was greatly accelerated after the Act of Union in 1801. With the dissolution of the Irish Parliament, there followed an exodus of prominent citizens and government officials from the capital, leaving numerous terraces and squares of large Georgian mansions. Another key factor in changing the social structure of Dublin in the late nineteenth century was the movement of significant numbers from the city centre to the outskirts with the development of new suburbs. Reflecting the expansion of the middle classes, this move to the suburbs 'was initiated by the professional and upper middle classes seeking new residences which were physically removed from the dirt, smells and congestion of the city centre'.[163] Reflecting a quite different social pattern from eighteenth-century Dublin where both rich and poor tended to live in close proximity, 'in the nineteenth century the gulf between the classes undoubtedly widened'.[164] During the course of the century, as property values plummeted, many such properties were bought up by investors.[165] Daly has detailed the often complicated ownership of these houses, most averaging three levels of ownership. Commonly, a head-landlord let a property on a long lease to a lessee who in turn let it on a yearly lease; this second lessee in turn re-let rooms as weekly tenancies, and it was not uncommon for weekly tenants in turn to sublet a room or part of a room to a lodger.[166] In this way, the former homes of the nobility 'were crudely converted into multiple single-room dwellings and crammed full with poor families'.[167] Under this system, a typical Georgian house could accommodate between fifty to eighty people.

By the close of the nineteenth century Dublin's tenement districts had deteriorated into what were known as 'slumlands', with certain areas especially noted for their squalor. Other categories of tenement included inner-city homes built for tradesmen during the eighteenth century, which due to structural conditions, overcrowding and lack of sanitation needed replacement, plus many smaller, more recently built properties erected in lanes and alley-ways at the rear of streets and houses which were also overcrowded and insanitary, lacking air and light.[168] Even within the limited house-building programme undertaken by Dublin Corporation in the city from the 1880s, conditions were extremely overcrowded; 'families of ten in two-roomed flats were not uncommon'.[169] Kearns has pointed out that by 1900 'one-third of Dublin's population, some 21,747 families, lived in single-room dwellings in 6,196 tenements, many condemned by Dublin Corporation as "unfit for human habitation".[170] The effect of overcrowding, unsanitary conditions, allied to an employment pattern of casual and seasonal labour, had profound implications for the health and well-being of children and families generally.

Accommodation of families Dublin City 1871–1911 [171]

	First Class	Second	Third	Fourth
1871	5,033	10,523	16,819	25,952
1881	4,692	11,013	16,660	23,360
1891	4,694	13,279	14,536	19,347
1901	4,635	33,199	—	21,429
1911	4,599	37,202	—	20,564

Taken from M. Daly, *Dublin—The Deposed Capital* (Cork, 1985), p. 278.

The majority of such dwellings were in extremely poor repair, damp, infested with dry rot and woodworm, with no running water and, at best, one primitive toilet and water tap in the yard for the use of the whole house. While some were beyond repair, others though structurally sound were filthy, overcrowded and in need of capital spending to provide sanitary facilities.[172] Tenements were dangerous places to live. With multiple families cooking and heating on an open fire, it was acknowledged that 'practically all slum dwellings are fire-traps'.[173] In addition, many were structurally unsound, and several such houses collapsed during the early 1900s, killing many inhabitants.[174] Despite such hazards within these buildings, the greatest threat to health and life came from sickness and disease which was rampant throughout the tenements.

Sanitation and diet were two significant factors in the spread of disease. Kearns has described graphically the problem of dark, disgusting, evil-smelling privies which, allied to each family's 'slop-bucket', created immense hazards to health. He notes that 'it was common to find human excreta scattered about the yards and hallway passages. Privies and ashpits sometimes became infested with typhoid germs and yards were regularly flooded with stagnant water and waste creating an environment in which flies, insects, and vermin thrived'.[175] Basement tenants were in particular danger, seepage from sewer pipes often emitting poisonous gases. Doctors visiting such dwellings often could not see across the room even at noon, children often developing an eye condition similar to that of miners. Kearns notes that 'inspectors and newspaper reporters confronted with the filth, foul air, human stench and vermin sometimes became physically ill'.[176]

Daly has noted that between 1860 and 1914 'Dublin's public health administration emerges as singularly ineffective'.[177] Partly caused by financial difficulties, there were suspicions of lax administration, particularly concerning the vested interests of tenement landlords. The latter were to be found in every stratum of society, with no lack of social stigma. At an inquiry held in 1900 the Liverpool medical officer criticised the enforcement of health regulations in Dublin. Whereas a detailed register of all tenement property existed in Liverpool and all were regularly inspected by the authorities, Daly has commented that in Dublin 'such inspection and enforcements might have interfered with allies and friends of councillors'.[178] Widespread ownership of tenement property among the shopkeeper and publican class, described as 'the back-bone of Dublin Corporation', made control of such property more difficult.[179] Although responsibility for controlling the cleanliness, overcrowding and sanitary facilities of tenement property rested with the Corporation, lack of definition and implementation of relevant bye-laws resulted in little improvement. Unwillingness on the part of politicians to curb tenement landlords and to enforce improvement was a major factor in lax enforcement. A Housing inquiry held in 1914 revealed that sixteen members of the Corporation were owners of tenement properties, virtually all of which were held to be in poor repair, and all of which had received rates rebates, ostensibly for improvements carried out.[180]

The strength of tenement landlords undoubtedly weakened legal enforcement; one of the tenements which collapsed in 1902 (killing one person) was the property of Alderman Gerald O'Reilly, who was subsequently elected Lord Mayor in 1908. Daly has observed that 'many cases of neglect seem to have been motivated by concern for landlords' rather than tenants' interests'.[181] Kearns has pointed out that in the 1930s there were only thirty Sanitary Officers to visit the homes of 32,000 families in the city. During the latter decades of the nineteenth century another source of disease was the proliferation of slaughter houses and dairy yards, many of which were located in the most densely populated and disease-ridden areas of the city. Again, corporation action was belated and ineffective. By the turn of the century the number of slaughter houses had declined by 50 per cent, due to natural wastage rather than to corporation policy, but 'In 1906 the overwhelming majority of the city's meat was still slaughtered in private establishments.'[182]

A similar unwillingness to interfere with powerful vested interests is apparent in official attitudes towards dairy yards, many corporation inspectors apparently turning a blind eye to insanitary conditions. The city's dairy yards were implicated in several outbreaks of typhoid, and with cases of scarlatina and tuberculosis.[183] In addition, many sellers of milk lived in tenements where they stored milk, resulting in frequent contamination. The implications of such conditions for the health of children and mothers continued into the 1940s, and will be examined in Chapter 11.

Studies of the diet of Dublin's working class from the early 1900s show a heavy dependence on bread and tea, very limited consumption of meat—primarily bacon, occasional herrings, and vegetables limited to potatoes, onions and cabbage. This diet compared very unfavourably with that of the peasantry in rural Ireland. The latter ate home-baked brown bread while Dubliners ate white shop loaves. Rural diets relied more on potatoes, with a higher milk and meat content.[184] Dubliners differed from their English counterparts in eating virtually no cheese or pulse vegetables. The limitations of the Dubliner's diet was in part related to poor cooking facilities, 'Tenement houses were generally equipped only with open fires; coal was costly and many of the poor relied on cinders rejected by the rich for their fuel.'[185] The role of inadequate diet was critical in both tuberculosis and other diseases, with malnutrition being a major factor in the high mortality resulting from a measles epidemic in 1897–99. Census returns for 1911 reveal that tenement families were more likely to be headed by women, with fewer working men per household.[186]

Dublin comparative household structure 1911

	Corporation	Tenement	Artisans Dwelling
N	337	402	399
% Female Head	15.13%	30.84%	13.78%
Mean Age Female Head	53.71 years	52.4 years	54.7 years
Occupied Female per Household	0.53	0.46	0.3

Taken from M. Daly, *Dublin—The Deposed Capital* (Cork, 1985), p. 307.

Next to keeping a roof over her family's head, a mother's chief concern was securing food and clothing. Most families had barely enough food for physical survival but an insufficient diet for full heath, most being seriously malnourished.[187] By the 1930s it was determined that over the generations there had developed within the general tenement populations a form of congenital debility which weakened their natural resistance to sickness. Kearns notes that 'it was always the rule that the father and eldest sons, particularly if they were employed, received the lion's share of whatever food was available. Mothers, because they wanted to make sure their children were decently fed, often got the least nourishment by choice.'[188] Noting that 'absolute poverty persisted for decades after Independence', Kennedy has cited two examples of such poverty in Dublin:

At a meeting of the Welfare Section of the St John's Ambulance Brigade in November 1941, Sir John Lumsden described how two poor Dublin mothers owned one pair of shoes between them, and wore them in turn to attend the welfare dining room of the Brigade to avail themselves of dinners, at a time when the *Herald Boot Fund* was providing boots for poor children. During the previous year over 70,000 dinners had been served to an average of 235 mothers. At the same meeting, Dr Ninian Falkiner, Master of the Rotunda Hospital, said that in his hospital and its district they had attended 5,000 mothers in the previous year, 1,000 of whom were suffering from malnutrition. He said, 'Malnutrition was an unpleasant word, and was sometimes a substitute for a more unpleasant one, semi-starvation.'[189]

A series of articles published in *The Bell* in the early 1940s entitled 'Other People's Incomes' noted that at an income of £100 per annum a family was in severe poverty 'with no fruit, no vegetables, no cheese, no eggs', and must rely on the charity of the St Vincent de Paul Society.[190] The outbreak of war in 1939 aggravated an already desperate situation for many families. Chapter 11 will consider attempts by governments, trade unionists and women's groups to alleviate such conditions.

TRADE UNIONS AND IRISH WOMEN

The labour history of Irish women ... is an example of repeated effort and commitment to trades union organisation among workers who were seen as difficult to organise, who posed insurmountable problems within the industrial framework or were seen as a threat to the traditions or customs of the organised workforce of those times. (THERESA MORIARTY, *Work in Progress*)

The trade unionisation of women workers between 1870–1970 evolved through a number of key stages. Up to World War I, any advances made were primarily within women-only unions, reflecting both the categorisation of women's work and hostility from male trade unionists. From the 1920s to the late 1960s most growth took place within mixed unions, reflecting changing work patterns for women, but not necessarily equality with their male colleagues.

Between 1880 and 1920 there were a number of attempts to unionise women workers.[1] This would prove a most difficult task, partly due to the reasons cited by Moriarty above, but due also in large measure to Ireland's predominantly agricultural profile. Irish society post-Famine provided few opportunities for women's employment outside domestic service or agriculture. While towns presented some additional work for women, mainly in shops, offices, or in low-grade industrial employment, in the countryside virtually the only options available were poorly paid—often seasonal—agricultural work, or work on family farms. Ulster provided more opportunities for women workers in the linen and shirt-making industries. Although Belfast women were involved in the linen strikes of the 1870s, their trade union organisation was not systematically undertaken until the 1890s.[2] With the exception of the Irish National Teachers Organisation (INTO) which admitted women from 1868, there was therefore virtually no trade union organisation among women, a factor not helped by the generally negative attitude of male craft unions which excluded women from their trades and apprenticeships. Allied to a belief that a woman's place was in the home, unorganised women workers were resented by many male trade unionists as a source of cheap labour and a threat to wage stability.

A number of key factors occurred during the nineteenth century to change the nature of women's work. Increasing mechanisation allied to the collapse of domestic textile industries from the mid-century resulted in much work that had been home-based being transferred to a factory setting. Unlike Britain, however, where the decline of domestic textile employment was compensated by the emergence of large-scale factory employment, in Ireland such development only occurred in the North-East of Ulster, primarily in the linen mills and factories. Outside of Ulster, factory work for women was also to be found in the clothing and textile industries, notably in cotton and woollen mills, albeit on a much smaller scale. Other factory-based employment for women at the turn of century included laundries, biscuits and baking manufacture, Dublin's Jacobs biscuit factory being one of the largest with approximately 2,000 women employees.[3]

New technological developments such as steam-powered looms, and in particular the sewing machine, combined with the development of department stores or 'monster houses', encouraged the mass production of low-cost ready-made clothes. As a result, during the 1860s much imported English-made clothing was being sold in Dublin department stores. In response, Dublin tailors opposed mechanisation of their trade, largely on the grounds of the reduction of skills but also because this opened the possibility of employing more women and children.[4] Their fears were realised, with the new style clothing industry that emerged concentrating on a combination of large workshops (many of which were attached to the new monster stores) employing between 50–200 women, and a system of outworking whereby garments were finished by hand in the women's homes.[5] A report on factory conditions for women presented by Anne Jellicoe to the Social Science Association Congress in Dublin in 1861 had noted that while the numbers employed were much less than in England, there was 'large room for improvement and reform'.[6] Jellicoe highlighted that the majority of such women were to be found in the ranks of 'toilers and spinsters'.[7]

In addition to various sections of textile production, other areas of women's employment noted by Jellicoe included paper mills, bookbinding, pin factories and the picking and sorting of rags in marine stores. Jellicoe also pointed to the advent of the sewing machine, commenting that 'its busy whirr will soon be heard in every street'.[8]

One of the earliest documented accounts of women's action against their working conditions occurred between 1869 and 1872, when Dublin seamstresses embarked on a campaign for better conditions and higher pay.[9] Unlike their male colleagues in the tailoring trade who took strike action during these years, the seamstresses decided on an alternate form of action carried out through a letter-writing campaign in the *Freeman's Journal*. By detailing their working conditions and demands in such a public forum, the seamstresses hoped to appeal to the compassion of their readers and to raise the issue of implementation of factory regulations. Fear of losing their jobs, lack of industrial muscle, and their wish not to become involved in militant action that might endanger 'much that is homely, much that is beautiful ...' in Irish womanhood were among the reasons chosen for this form of action.[10]

The census of 1871 showed 2,604 women employed as seamstresses and shirt-makers in Dublin. Working more than ten hours a day over six days, seamstresses worked either in small workshops or in their employer's home. Factory Inspector reports noted that many worked in over-crowded workrooms and unsanitary conditions for very little money. It was also noted that employers were adept at evading existing legislation, e.g. on the occasions when employees were allowed a half-day holiday on Saturday, they were given work to complete at home instead. Nor could the women expect support from the tailors, whose jobs were being lost to the sewing machine, and further threatened by the increasing number of women in the clothing trade. Advocating customer power, the paper suggested that when buying clothes, ladies should enquire into the working conditions of seamstresses, a tactic supported by the workers. While supporting the women's campaign for better hours and conditions, the paper was more reticent regarding pay, advocating 'if possible, better wages'.

A further issue brought forward by both the women and the Public Health Committee of Dublin Corporation was the possible moral danger posed to seamstresses if conditions were not improved. On the one hand it was argued that many seamstresses were forced into prostitution as a result of poor pay. The Public Health Committee, on the other hand, questioned whether giving women a half-day on Saturdays would be 'dangerous morally to these classes'. While a number of letters were published demanding that such remarks be withdrawn, as

Christine Hynes points out, the damage was done, this latter argument giving employers another pretext for denying women a half-day.

The women's campaign resulted in some short-term improvements, with the *Freeman's Journal* in 1872 noting that after raids by sanitary inspectors 'seamstresses got, for the first time, a taste of the luxury of light and air at their employment'. Such benefits were not to last, however, as many of the workshops closed following the recession of the late 1870s. Where workshops continued to exist, without the glare of publicity conditions reverted to previous patterns. In the early 1890s reporting on conditions in a number of Dublin clothing workshops, the Royal Commission on Labour noted, 'There is no ventilation except through the windows, and these can seldom be opened because dust blows in upon the linen. The girls suffer severe headaches.'[11] The seamstresses' unwillingness to unionise can be viewed as a result of their conditioning and vulnerability regarding their status as workers, allied to a lack of support from craft workers.

Following the first Trade Union Congress (TUC) held in Dublin in 1880 a number of attempts were made to organise women workers in the city. None of the eight female delegates attending this congress were from an Irish union. Their contributions to Congress debates were widely reported in the press, and were followed by meetings with women workers in the city. At one such meeting, the President of the TUC, John Murphy, a Dublin ironfounder declared:

> It might seem strange to many of the Dublin people to see ladies on platforms, but [his] experience at the Trades Union Congress showed him that it was most important that women should take care of their own interests. Men were apt to lose sight of those interests in the struggle for what appeared to them to be of more momentous import. [He] hoped the Dublin ladies would not be kept back by feelings of mistaken modesty for helping forward this movement.[12]

Two women's unions developed from this meeting, the Dublin Tailoresses' Society and the Bookfolders and Sewers Union. Neither union lasted long, both closing the following year.[13] Further attempts at women's organisation took place in the 1890s in Belfast and Derry. This developed as a result of a drive for the unionisation of non-craft general workers during the 1880s, and the formation of local councils of trades unions in Belfast, Dublin and Derry. In 1891 the National Union of Gasworkers and General Labourers invited Eleanor Marx to organise the female workers of Derry.[14] During her visit she spoke of the low pay and severe work practices in shirt-making factories in the city, including the wide range of fines. Among the latter were fines for laughing and looking out of windows; in addition women workers were charged for the steam they used in order to work the machines, and were also made pay for anything that went wrong with a machine.

In Belfast there were an estimated 70,000 women working in the linen industry in the 1890s. Unlike other industries, both married and single women were employed on a large scale. They worked as spinners, weavers and stitchers, and as outworkers who sewed, embroidered, hemmed and drew threads in their homes.[15] Industrialisation of the linen trade produced appalling working conditions:

> Wet steam spinning threw off airborne lint and showers of spray, which clung to the mill workers and drenched their clothes. Unventilated workplaces incubated infectious diseases. Poorly guarded machinery caused injuries, with little right to compensation.[16]

The industry was highly stratified, with each section of the workforce being accorded a subtly different status, determined by their gender, type of employment or skill, custom and even dress. The latter was illustrated in contemporary reports of a meeting held to organise the women during the TUC congress in Belfast in 1893:

> All round the hall were the neater girls in smart hats and jackets, probably the girls from the wareroom of the city, but all down the center tables ... were the mill-girls themselves. Ragged and tattered, with pinched wan faces, aged before their time, holding round them the shawls that barely hid the slovenly vest beneath.[17]

The Textile Operatives' Society of Ireland (TOSI) was formed during this TUC congress. By 1897 it was reported to have 1,600 members.[18] This would survive to become a permanent member of the Irish Trade Union movement, and the only women's union for over a decade.

In 1897 Mary Galway, a hem-stitcher, was appointed its organising secretary, and was subsequently elected onto the executive of the Belfast Trades Council. At the time of her appointment, there were nine other unions in the linen industry, all of which excluded women. In addition to seeking better wages and working conditions for her members,

Galway consistently fought for removal of the fines system, the implementation of safety procedures, and the appointment of a woman factory inspector because 'the men inspectors seem to have too much to do to pay any attention to the women workers'. In 1897 she led 8,000 workers, 'mostly women and girls', in a successful strike against the enforcement of strict discipline and penalties in the linen factories and workshops. Negotiations between Belfast Trades Council—represented by Mary Galway—and the employers resulted in considerable modification of the rules. As Miriam Daly has pointed out, 'this is the first instance in Ireland of a woman negotiating directly with the employers in a major trade dispute.'[19]

The Irish Trade Union Congress (ITUC) had been formed in Dublin in 1894, and Galway would dominate its formative years, notable for being 'the only woman delegate consistently in attendance (and) the only woman recorded as addressing the Congress between 1901–1913'.[20] At the 1907 ITUC she was voted onto its executive body, the parliamentary committee, and was re-elected every subsequent year until 1913. Therese Moriarty has pointed out that Galway 'was not only the first woman in Ireland to be elected to the national congress executive, but a pioneer of trade union women elsewhere', the first woman member of the British Trades Union Congress not being elected until 1917.[21] Galway created another 'first' in 1909 when she became the first woman vice-president of the ITUC—the first of only five women to hold this office up to 1999. She was not afraid to criticise male trade union complacency towards working women's conditions. The ITUC annual report for 1901 noted her complaint that:

> The Trades Council of Belfast made no serious effort to organise women in that city. After eight years work, she regretted to say that out of sixty thousand female workers in Belfast, only twelve hundred were members of the Textile Operatives' Society of Ireland. If the Trades Council of Belfast was really in earnest, they should begin at home.[22]

Another issue of great concern to Galway was the sweated condition of Belfast outworkers. Thousands of women and children worked in their homes on the produce of mill and factory, carrying out hemming, stitching, embroidery, handkerchief and shirt-making. In 1910 a storm of controversy erupted after the Belfast medical officer of health published a report castigating the pay and conditions of the city's home workers. Other reports, such as that of Ireland's first woman factory inspector,

Hilda Martindale, backed up these findings. As Moriarty notes, 'thousands of home workers made up a highly exploited and almost invisible, inaccessible workforce, beyond the view of workplace inspection.'[23] Economic necessity, domestic obligations and the lack of child-care facilities forced many women into this work. Galway took a very public role on this issue, both within and outside the ITUC, calling for the inclusion of all sweated labour in factory and home to be brought under the new trades' board. The extent of public outcry, and widespread press coverage, resulted in a parliamentary inquiry in 1912, followed by the establishment of a trade board in 1915 to regulate the workers' rate of pay and length of hours. Despite this, however, home workers remained outside the ranks of trade unions and therefore beyond the powers of regulation of pay rates and conditions. Sadie Patterson, who became active in the linen trade union in the 1930s, and who at the age of 12 had worked at home with her mother, has movingly recounted her mother's last day before she died in childbirth in 1918:

> It was my job to go to the warehouse to collect the bundles of work and then the following day to return the finished goods. Mother was paid a pittance. I have her last pay packet: 'Wages 16s 3d for 50 dozen sheets and overalls, less 1 sh(hilling) for thread'. On her last day on earth she worked to 6 p.m. and died four hours later.[24]

It was not just in homework that children were involved. One mill-worker outlined graphically to James Connolly the regime in factories for women and children:

> ... it's over forty-five years since I started work in the mills. I was just turned eight when I began. When you were eight you were old enough to work. Worked in steam, making your rags all wet, and sometimes up to your ankles in water. The older you got the more work you got. If you got married you kept on working. Your man didn't get enough for a family. You worked till your baby came, and went back as soon as you could, and then, God forgive you, you counted the years till your child could be a half-timer and started the same hell of a life again.[25]

From the early 1900s there would be a number of significant developments regarding the organisation of women workers. The Drapers' Assistants' Association (DAA), formed in 1901 by Michael

O'Lehane, admitted both men and women, the first union to do so since the INTO. Dermot Keogh has observed that by recruiting female members, 'O'Lehane showed himself to be most clearly liberated from the prejudices of his trade union colleagues'.[26] By 1914, 1,400 of the union's 4,000 members were women.[27] Drapers' assistants served a seven-year apprenticeship, following which they had no job security, often working over 80 hours per week with only Sunday off.[28] Key objectives for the organisation were a minimum wage, fixed hours and payment for overtime, sick benefits and a weekly half-holiday. In addition, the DAA sought the abolition of the living-in system, the fines system imposed by employers, and the arbitrary system of instant dismissal that then prevailed. The living-in system was a particular source of grievance, drapers' assistants being forced to live 'over the shop' or boarded out in specially rented accommodation. Under constant supervision and subjected to the discipline of the employer for practically 24 hours a day, staff were often housed in overcrowded unhealthy dormitories, sometimes being locked in at night. A number of department stores suffered serious fires between 1891 and 1913. In two of these, eight employees lost their lives. The inquest following one of these fires—in Dublin's Camden Street—discovered that staff had been locked securely into the building, and as the DAA journal noted 'were trapped like rats in a cage'.[29]

The formation of the Irish Women Workers Union (IWWU) in 1911 was a particularly significant development, both for the role it would play in improving pay and working conditions for women, and for the high profile attained by its women leaders. Its foundation followed a successful strike for better pay by 3,000 women at Jacob's biscuit factory in Dublin in 1911. Delia Larkin was its first Secretary, and Jim Larkin its President. During the subsequent Dublin Lock-Out of 1913, the entire membership of the IWWU came out on strike in support, remaining out for six months. Many were dismissed subsequently for their action. The formation of this Dublin-based women's union had reverberations in Belfast, where there were still some 18,000 unorganised mill-workers outside the TOSI and the many male unions. Based in Belfast at this time as District Secretary of the Irish Transport & General Workers' Union (ITGWU), Connolly was only too aware of their working conditions, commenting in 1912 that 'many Belfast Mills are slaughter-houses for the women and penitentiaries for the children'.[30] Attempts by Connolly to organise these workers into a newly formed women's branch of the ITGWU—the Irish Textile Workers Union—led him into conflict with

Mary Galway who saw the new union as a rival, and it has been suggested with Jim Larkin also, who objected to this development and ordered that the women be transferred into the newly formed IWWU.[31] Marie Johnson, Nelly Gordon and Winifred Carney were key activists who joined Connolly in organising the textile workers.

In 1915, Helena Molony took over Delia Larkin's role in the IWWU, following the latter's departure for Liverpool. Molony, feminist, separatist and officer in the Irish Citizen Army, worked closely with Connolly (now back in Dublin) in promoting the IWWU, and in organising a women's co-op run from Liberty Hall. Shortly before the 1916 Rising Molony sought the help of suffragist Louie Bennett in re-organising the IWWU.[32] Bennett later wondered why Molony had approached her, commenting, 'I knew nothing about Trade Unionism, but I was drawn to Liberty Hall by the prickings of conscience so many of us felt after the 1913 strike.' Later in her life she recalled her clandestine visits to Liberty Hall during that dispute:

> At that time I belonged to the respectable middle class and I did not dare admit to my home circle that I had run with the crowd to hear Jim Larkin, and crept like a culprit into Liberty Hall to see Madame Markievicz in a big overall, with sleeves rolled up, presiding over a cauldron of stew, surrounded by a crowd of gaunt women and children carrying bowls and cans.[33]

Following Molony's request, Bennett had a 'warm discussion' with Connolly during which she argued against his mixing of nationalist and labour ideals. Although anxious to help, Bennett made it clear she could not support any organisation threatening force.[34] Imprisoned after the Rising of 1916, Molony made a further appeal to Bennett for help with the IWWU. This time Bennett responded positively, and in August 1916 she and Helen Chenevix attended the Trade Union Congress in Sligo. From that time she became identified with the work of the IWWU, an association which would continue for the next forty years. Molony rejoined the Union executive following her release from prison. Together Bennett, Chenevix and Molony would form a formidable triumvirate on behalf of women workers. Gains achieved by the IWWU over the coming decades in many ways were disproportionate to its membership, and were to a large extent the result of the commitment of these women to the rights of women workers and women generally.

Bennett viewed her attendance at that 1916 Congress as a first step in her trade union education. Through the pages of the *Irish Citizen* she expressed views similar to those of Connolly:

> The rapid development of organisation in the Irishwomen's world of labour is the best possible contribution to the whole cause of feminism. There can be no real freedom and independence of women until they are economically free.[35]

Invited in January 1917 to organise the women printers, she later recalled:

> I had absolutely no idea how to go about it. But I was burning with enthusiasm. I had no money. No office. No furniture. Nothing. But I went out and I got one member to start me off. I put her name down in a twopenny jotter and hoped fervently for more.[36]

So began what she described as a 'timid campaign' of waiting outside printers' workshops at six o'clock in the evening thrusting handbills upon disinterested women workers. Initially there was little reaction, but eventually:

> Then suddenly there came a stir and a rush: Mondays evenings saw the long room packed with girls and women eager to pay their pennies and to pour their grievances into my confused ear.[37]

Soon women from other industries came to join, and a bigger office was opened in Dame Street. Within months, membership was over 2,000 and growing, and included women in the printing, box-making, laundry and textile industries. In the spring of 1918 the IWWU was officially registered as a trade union with Bennett and Chenevix as its honorary secretaries. By this time membership exceeded 5,000. From the outset Bennett insisted that the women's union operate independently from Liberty Hall and remain solely a women's union, a point of much debate over the years. The union's first industrial action soon occurred. When the Dublin Master Printers' Association refused to recognise the IWWU and its pay claim on behalf of women printers, a six-week strike and lockout ensued. Financial support from the Dublin Trades Council during the strike, and the subsequent successful outcome to the dispute gave a further boost to the union.

The IWWU next sought to organise laundry workers, and in September 1917 Bennett wrote to the owner of the Court Laundry, Cecil Watson, requesting a meeting in this regard. Watson indicated his support for unionisation and improved wages, provided his competitors did likewise. Subsequently a meeting to organise his workers was held in the Court canteen.[38] Although they would have differences over the years, Watson would be one of Bennett's most supportive employers. In her study of the IWWU Mary Jones has pointed out that from this time the union actively sought the co-operation of employers in favouring trade union labour.[39] In negotiations with employers, Bennett's policy would be conciliatory rather than confrontational. Preference for conciliation, however, did not mean a lack of commitment to strong action by the union on behalf of its members, as subsequent strike action would demonstrate.

From the beginning union policy concentrated as much on improving working conditions as on wage increases. Bennett maintained that whereas wages were the primary concern of male workers, for women workers conditions were equally important, declaring, 'Holidays, shorter hours, and a little latitude as to spells of leisure during working hours, are concessions dear to women in factories or workshops.'[40] Recalling the laughter and wild exultation which had greeted union assertions in 1917 of a worker's right to one week's paid summer holiday—an unheard of proposition then—she noted that this gain was far more appreciated by women than a wage increase. Her concern with working conditions concentrated much on health and safety in the workplace. In particular she argued for more women factory inspectors, pointing out that the Free State government had appointed a total of four factory inspectors for the whole country, only one of whom was female.

Under the aegis of the IWWU, the Irish Nurses' Union (INU) was established in 1919, one of the first of its kind in Europe. The Irish Times' sense of horror at this development showed the depth of opposition existing toward women's organisation. Nurses were asked 'not to dethrone and degrade the profession by dallying with the promises of Trade Unionism. A strike of nurses would be hardly less painful and disconcerting than a strike of wives in favour of, say, a forty-hour week of domestic activity.'[41] Helena Molony proceeded to shock that paper even further by establishing a Domestic Workers' Union. This, and further attempts to unionise domestic workers, met with little success. Bennett's close identification with Labour did not inhibit criticism where she felt it necessary. During the Irish Convention of 1917, the *Irish Citizen* reported:

When Labour Sunday was celebrated in Dublin a few weeks ago, no woman was invited to stand on the platform by the Labour Party. The women of Ireland might have all been free to enjoy the comforts of a home, a fireside, and a cradle to rock for all the interest the Labour Party of Ireland manifested in their affairs.[42]

In the post-war—and (limited) post-suffrage—situation, was the continuation of women in a separate union still the best method of organisation for women workers or was the 'one big union' a better idea? Late in 1919, a lively debate took place on this issue between Bennett and Cissie Cahalan (DAA) in the pages of the *Irish Citizen*. Advocating separate organisation, Bennett argued that it was futile to deny latent antagonism between the sexes in industry:

> There is a disposition amongst men workers not only to keep women in inferior and subordinate positions, but to drive them out of industry altogether. Moreover, men have not the same aspirations for women as women have for themselves, and in a mixed organisation much time and trouble would have to be wasted in securing the co-operation of men in a demand for reforms of which women may feel urgent need. So long as women occupy a subordinate position within the Trade Union movement they will need the safeguard of an independent organisation.[43]

In addition she noted that pay increases demanded and accepted for women workers within mixed unions were almost always considerably less than those obtained for men. The question of women's working hours, allied to night work, and work before and after child-birth, she pointed out, were other issues under consideration at present for which women needed an independent organisation. Cissie Cahalan, one of the few examples of working-class involvement in the Irish suffrage movement, defended the concept of mixed trade unions. She laid the blame for the under-involvement of women on their own shoulders, arguing that women's reluctance to go forward as candidates for branch or executive committees left the management of trade unions in male hands. Women's position in the labour movement, she argued, while weak was not subordinate, and could become stronger if women ceased to be apathetic and took up their responsibilities. She claimed further that gender-segregated unions might prove an effective weapon for bosses in times of dispute, arguing:

> If women in the industrial world want a place in the labour

movement, they must seek it in the Labour Parliament, shoulder to shoulder with the men and not in any separate organisation apart and isolated.[44]

The arguments raised in this debate continued for many years, Bennett's involvement within the trade union movement reinforcing her beliefs. In 1930 she noted that but for the IWWU, woman's voice was rarely heard at trades union congress or trades council. Pointing to large areas of women's employment—teachers, clerical workers, shop assistants— which were almost always represented by men, she commented wryly, 'What a touching and flattering confidence in the male sex.'[45] Interestingly her critic from 1919, Cissie Cahalan, writing in the same journal observed that it was 'deplorable to find men who still think of woman as the enemy—and shut their eyes to the real barrier to a full and complete life for all—the capitalist class'.[46] Helena Molony likewise concluded that working women had made little progress since Connolly's time, pointing out that women were still excluded from certain industries because of their gender, and that a woman's wage was still only twenty to thirty per cent of a man's average wage.[47]

While disagreement with Bennett's views concentrated mainly on the issue of single-sex unions, little criticism was voiced towards her views regarding women's right to work. Bennett did not believe the time was right for women to 'invade' men's industrial preserves, claiming that 'the class war must be fought out before women could fight for equality of opportunity'. Referring, in 1919, to the controversial question of women's admittance to skilled trades, she explained:

> The fact that the majority of working men are the supporters of a wife and children and only a minority of working women have similar responsibilities, makes the most progressive of us hesitate to urge women industrial workers to invade men's trades and it would be madness for women workers to attempt to disturb fundamentally the present distribution of industrial work.[48]

Bennett's views were reinforced over the following years when deteriorating employment opportunities in Ireland became allied to an increased perception of the woman worker as a threat. Trade union and labour acceptance of church, state and societal convergence on the ideal of a family wage, removing the need for married women to work outside the home, would be reinforced by legislative restrictions during the 1930s.

Bennett's intense involvement in the IWWU was reflected in the pages of the *Irish Citizen* during her periods of its editorship in 1917 and 1920. Increasingly articles and editorials focused on pay and conditions, with calls to women workers to 'organise, organise'.[49] Eventually the IWWU and the INU decided to use the paper as their official journal and source of communication with members throughout the country. Not all within the suffrage movement approved of the changing ethos of the *Irish Citizen* from being a feminist suffrage paper to a feminist trade-union paper. Most objections derived from a perceived need for an independent feminist paper without any party affiliations, Hanna Sheehy Skeffington pointing out that 'no party, unhappily, is yet quite free from sin where women are concerned'.[50] Bennett's determination to publish the *Irish Citizen* as a feminist labour paper ultimately caused Sheehy Skeffington to cancel their agreement, the latter arguing the need for an independent, non-party, feminist editorial policy for the paper. Many suffragists were uneasy also at the tone of some Bennett articles, firmly based as they were on acceptance of prevailing attitudes towards women and the home. Unease with IWWU dominance within the paper did not always rest on feminist principles, however, one correspondent to Hanna noting, 'we want moral and temperance points raised, not anti-(Liberty) hall squabbles ... I fear women workers are likely to be no use re morality and temperance.'[51]

Following the passing of the Representation of the People Act in 1918, which granted the parliamentary vote to women over thirty, Bennett was nominated to stand for the 1918 general election. The *Irish Citizen* congratulated the Irish Labour Party on being the first political party to choose a woman candidate. Bennett subsequently declined the invitation due, no doubt, to the intense machinations between Labour and Sinn Féin as to whether or not Labour should contest the election. The ITUC congress of that year discussed the implications of the new women voters, William O'Brien commenting that 'means must now be found to associate them with us in our political as well as in our industrial work.'[52] However, reporting on the local elections of the following year, Hanna Sheehy Skeffington noted that 'official labour has the unenviable distinction of entirely ignoring women on their ticket'.[53] The question of direct political involvement by the IWWU was to be a source of disagreement within the union over the next two decades. Rank and file members consistently opposed the establishment of a political fund or affiliation to any political party. Divisive political views, particularly on the issue of Free State recognition, added to a belief that the IWWU should focus on industrial matters alone, were among possible reasons for such opposition. The attitude of the Labour Party did little to encourage change. Describing overtures made to the party from the IWWU in 1923, Jones has noted that 'articulate women trade unionists found only a measured welcome'.[54]

Rising unemployment during the 1920s, exacerbated by increased mechanisation and work measurement schemes, prompted IWWU initiatives on behalf of the unemployed. A campaign was launched in 1925 seeking the extension of unemployment benefits, deputations being sent to the Dáil, Senate, poor law and civic commissioners. The Government response to such demands was harsh. Joe Lee has noted that during the 1920s the Cabinet waged a coherent campaign against the weaker elements in the community, taking the view that the poor were responsible for their poverty. Unemployment was deemed to be the result of either laziness on the part of the unemployed or the restrictive practices of trade unions. Announcing the cessation of certain unemployment payments in 1924 the minister for industry and finance, Patrick McGilligan, stated that the government had no responsibility to provide work.[55] This was the background against which Bennett and the IWWU operated. In 1926 Bennett wrote to President Cosgrave protesting against government action to relieve distress in Dublin by distributing food tickets from the Dublin union rather than from unemployment exchanges. Over the years Bennett insisted that due regard be made for the dignity of those in receipt of any such relief.

A committee for the relief of unemployment, established in 1927, included representation from all political parties, but President Cosgrave refused to appoint a woman member. Its subsequent report in 1928 contained no reference to women. The IWWU was particularly critical of labour members on this committee who had, in effect, ignored women workers and would doubtless have agreed with Jones's comment that 'quite clearly, the question of the employment of women had no place on the political agenda'.[56] Nor would it appear that outside the IWWU executive were political concerns very high on the agenda of ordinary union members. Allied to the continued rejection of its attempts to establish a political wing, the frustration and impatience of the executive can be judged in its criticism of poor member participation in the May Day celebrations of 1929:

So far as women are concerned, the May Day demonstration organised by the Dublin Trade Union Council last year demonstrated only that Dublin women are too shy, too proud, too indolent or too stupid to support the men trade unionists in a triumphant display of solidarity.[57]

Writing in the *Dublin Labour Year Book of 1930*, Bennett, Molony and Cahalan each addressed the issue of women in the political wing of labour. All were unhappy with that role. Molony, referring to the 'sorry travesty of emancipation', advised women and the labour movement to reflect on Connolly's writings and beliefs. Bennett noted that despite the fact that women made up 50 per cent of the electorate political parties still treated them as a side issue and women themselves made little use of their political power. She commented that politically the labour movement was completely in the hands of men, and it was evident that working-class women did not desire to be so involved. In a similar vein, Cahalan noted that there was not one woman labour representative in the Dáil or Senate. She observed that this reflected the situation of women within the labour movement itself, pointing to the few women delegates appointed to the male-dominated Irish Labour Party and Trade Union Congress (ILPTUC).

In 1932 Bennett became the first woman president of the Irish Trades Union Congress. Her address to that congress reflected her international and trade union concerns, particularly in relation to the growing threat of fascism. She also insisted that trade unions adopt the same pay scale for men and women in industry, claim, for all workers, a wage adequate to support dependants, and oppose the concept that simplified mechanical processes necessarily involved the use of cheap labour. With the voluntary separation of the political and industrial branches of labour in 1930, Bennett had again urged women to enter the political arena. Cautioning members that old prejudices still existed, and that women should be wary of accepting a powerless role within the Party, she urged women to remember that 'the movement is bigger than any of us, bigger than any section of us. We women have our part to play in it, and if the men fail to open the doors for our entry, then we must open them for ourselves.'[58] The way to open doors, she argued, was to form a political wing.

Towards the end of 1933 members finally agreed to the formation of a political wing of the IWWU, prompted no doubt by legislative moves that had been developing since the late 1920s to restrict women's employment. The trade union movement generally supported such restrictions, believing that women were supplanting men in industrial and service employment. In fact, there was no evidence to support such beliefs, rather there were many more instances of men and boys taking over jobs previously done by women in laundries and factories.[59]

From 1934 attention focused on Seán Lemass's forthcoming Conditions of Employment bill. The IWWU sought and were refused consultative status in the framing of this Bill.[60] Lemass agreed to receive their deputation only when the final draft was ready. At their 1935 annual convention, IWWU delegates voted in favour of affiliation to the Irish Labour Party and indicated their intention to resist all attempts to restrict women's employment. Bennett took a high-profile stance in this campaign. Declaring that women were necessary and not superfluous workers, she argued that their inferior political status had until recently contributed to their exploitation as workers. Regarding government attempts to cope with unemployment by replacing women workers with men, she asked if hunger and want were more tolerable to women than men. She did not accept that Lemass's proposals to restrict women's employment addressed the fundamental problem of unemployment, arguing that they in fact posed a threat to all workers. For Bennett the only sound policy was one of equal status for all workers, a wage scale based on the value of work without sex discrimination, and shorter working hours. This trenchant defence of women's right to work was modified somewhat by her concession that women were more suited to certain industries than men, for example, the textile, sugar, confectionery and tobacco industries. Mechanical processes within such industries found intolerable by men could, she argued, be endured by women 'with less evil effect on their nervous system'.[61]

Over the summer of 1935 the battle over the Conditions of Employment Act was at its height. While assuring the IWWU that the status of women workers would not be affected, Lemass refused to delete section twelve of the bill which gave the government power to restrict or prohibit the employment of women in industry. In the Dáil he argued against the objections put forward by Bennett and the IWWU. Following his announcement that deputations would be received from interested parties regarding amendments to the bill, the IWWU looked to the Labour Party for support, but to no avail. Earlier that year, the IWWU executive had expressed its concern that some male trade unionists shared the government's point of view. Subsequently, at a meeting with the party leader, William Norton, it became clear that no support would be forthcoming for the women's stance. In fact Norton told a Labour Party conference that congress welcomed the bill as a safeguard against exploiting employers.[62] In protest, Bennett was authorised by her executive to withhold affiliation fees to the party until further notice. The long argued-for alliance with Labour had lasted less than two years. The IWWU initiated a campaign outlining the implications of section twelve and seeking the support of male trade unionists.

Debate on the issue at the ITUC in August 1935 showed the extent of trade union hostility to any amendment. Pointing out to Congress that the restrictive powers of the proposed act were merely a prelude to other legislative developments which could impose a dangerous form of control on all workers, Bennett proposed a motion on 'equal rights and equal pay', arguing that the question was not one of sex but of wages, and should be dealt with as such.[63] William O'Brien of the ITGWU, while seconding her resolution, revealed that section twelve had been framed in response to a request of his union's national executive.

In the ensuing debate, most speakers argued that the replacement of male workers by lower paid female workers provided justification that men should benefit under the act.[64] Generally it was felt to be 'a very wrong thing that young girls should be sent into factories and young men kept out'. Some women trade unionists from mixed unions supported this stance, commenting that 'too many women inside the factory were a menace to the industrial classes'. The congress secretary argued that while the Labour movement generally was in favour of equality, increasing mechanisation which facilitated the replacement of male workers with cheaper female workers posed a dilemma. He, along with the majority of members, believed that the needs of male workers should be paramount to preserve the greater good of working people generally. Defending the right of man as breadwinner, one speaker enthusiastically declared, 'Woman is the queen of our hearts and of our homes, and for God's sake let us try to keep her there.'[65] Helena Molony in a scathing reply deplored 'such reactionary opinions expressed … by responsible leaders of Labour in support of a capitalist Minister'.[66] The Labour leader, William Norton, was adamant in his opposition to the IWWU, citing Molony's assertion of women's right to be carpenters and blacksmiths as proof of a wish by women workers to displace men. In addition he ordered a public reading of the memorandum presented to Lemass by congress which, he claimed, committed congress in principle to the restriction of women in the workplace. The final insult to the IWWU was the passing by congress of its resolution on equality of rights and pay.

The IWWU stance was supported by women's groups at home and abroad. During the 1930s there was intense debate in women's journals worldwide on the issues of women's right to work, to retain their nationality after marriage, and their relegation to the domestic sphere under fascist regimes. At a meeting in Dublin's Mansion House in November 1935 held in opposition to the Conditions of Employment Bill, speakers included Professor Mary Hayden, Hanna Sheehy Skeffington and Dorothy McArdle (a staunch supporter of de Valera). At this meeting, Bennett restated her view that Lemass's concern was not for the welfare of women but for their control. She further stated that the Labour Party had not faced the question of arbitrary limitation of female employment squarely, commenting 'The Conditions of Employment Bill was a sugar-coated pill for the workers.'[67] In the Senate the bill was strongly attacked by Kathleen Clarke and Jennie Wyse Power.[68] Arguing that the bill contradicted the equality of citizens declared in the 1916 Proclamation, Clarke noted that some justification might have been acceptable if certain industries were deemed injurious to women's health rather than the apparent blatant attempt to exclude women from the workforce. Jennie Wyse Power, another Fianna Fáil senator, pointed out the importance of women's wages for family support, stating angrily that women did not want groups of men deciding these issues. In effect, however, that is precisely what happened. Despite an intense campaign of lobbying and publicity, Lemass dismissed the women's protests as completely unrepresentative of the vast majority of women. The bill became law in 1936 with majority support in both houses of the Oireachteas, including all labour representatives.

While it has been argued that the practical effects of the 1936 Bill on women's employment was negligible,[69] the psychological effects cannot be underestimated, effects which were further embellished by the constitution of 1937. Bennett and the IWWU joined other women's groups in protest against certain articles relating to women within the proposed constitution. The IWWU executive formed one of the many women's deputations to de Valera seeking amendments. Following one such deputation by the IWWU in May 1937, de Valera subsequently conceded amendments to articles 16 and 45, eliminating what the IWWU referred to as 'the obnoxious phrase "inadequate strength of women"', and substituting the word 'citizen' in place of 'women and children'.[70] At this point the IWWU ceased its involvement in the women's campaign against the constitution. Bennett defended this action by pointing out that the first loyalty of a woman's union was to the trade union movement as a whole, and that the IWWU was of the opinion that 'we can best protect ourselves against any dangers inherent in the Constitution by enlisting as our allies in the women's cause those who are already our allies in the great cause of Labour'.[71] It was now the task of the IWWU, she argued, to make male trade unionists realise that it was in the interests of the whole labour movement to establish the principle of equal pay and equal opportunities for women and men. Two main considerations appear to have prompted this decision. The IWWU annual report for 1937 stated that the union was not prepared to engage in a campaign of opposition on the grounds of sex discrimination, pointing out that there were other articles in the constitution which posed more serious threats to the interests of both male and female workers. The other main consideration was the status of women within the wider trade union movement. Memories of male trade unionist and Labour Party hostility during the 1936 controversy were still alive in the minds of the IWWU executive. An alliance with what was disparagingly dismissed as an elite of intellectual middle-class women campaigning for sex equality would not have helped the union's efforts to improve women's status within labour. Crucial too, was the acceptance by Bennett and her executive of contemporary church and state attitudes regarding the role of women in the home.

Public reaction during this controversy reflected popular attitudes to women at work which accepted that after marriage women's place was in the home. Of particular significance was the fact that many women trade unionists accepted restrictions on the employment of married women, and the often ambivalent attitude of Bennett and the IWWU executive reinforced such acceptance. Throughout her life Bennett argued trenchantly for equal rights for women in political, social, educational and professional spheres. However, her 1919 stance that under the then existing industrial system women workers could not fight for equality without regard for wives and mothers, alongside her assurance that women would not invade men's industrial preserves, displayed a personal attitude consistent with conservative popular opinion. In her presidential address to the ITUC in 1932 Bennett had outlined concerns about the growing numbers of women and girls employed in industry as a result of increased mechanisation. Again her argument was double-edged:

This modern tendency to draw women into industry in increasing numbers is of no real advantage to them. It has not raised their status as workers nor their wage standard. It is a menace to family life, and in so far as it has blocked the employment of men it has intensified poverty amongst the working class.[72]

Mary Daly has pointed to the mental confusion which persisted in this regard within the IWWU into the 1950s. Its 1953 congress, for example, supported an equal pay proposal but sought to debar from its benefits the young married woman and the single girl. Jim Larkin reacted to this contradictory action by commenting that before any success could be achieved 'women would have to propagate the idea of the principle among their own sex and get acceptance for it'.[73] Similarly, Larkin's motion to Dáil Éireann promoting equal pay did not receive the vote of any woman TD even though, as he pointed out, they received equal pay with their male colleagues. Undoubtedly the attitude of Louie Bennett and the IWWU regarding full economic equality was short-sighted and in the long term damaging to the position of women in Irish society.

Other issues which absorbed the time and energy of the IWWU were the campaign against the trade union bill of 1941, and the wages standstill order which enforced a stay on wages from May of that year. Viewing the Trade Union bill as 'an attack on the right of workers to form and join unions of their choice without undue interference from the State', the Dublin trades council formed a council of action to campaign against both initiatives.[74] Bennett told the AGM of the IWWU that the bill was 'the thin edge of fascism, and a very serious threat to the independence of workers'. She joined other trade unionists in an open-air protest meeting at College Green against the bill in June 1941. In its opposition to the wages standstill order, the IWWU pointed to the hardship imposed on large sections of poorly paid workers at a time of soaring prices. Despite strong opposition from the council of action and the IWWU, the new bill was passed. Following the TUC in July 1941, Bennett launched a scathing attack on William O'Brien. In particular she criticised the lack of attention at the TUC to the problems of unemployment, food prices and fuel shortages, which 'for us women hit right home to our closest interests'. As a result of O'Brien's 'hustling through' these issues, Bennett reported, 'we walked out of the Congress as a protest against this contemptuous treatment of matters acutely affecting trade union interests'.[75]

While Bennett's preference for negotiation rather than confrontation was well known, when necessary, strikes there were, and none more noteworthy than the Laundry workers strike. In 1945 laundry worker members of the IWWU voted for strike action to obtain a fortnight's paid holiday. Laundresses had sought increased holidays, reduction in overtime, and regular working hours from 1934. Their claims had been shelved during the war years, employers refusing to negotiate. An exception to this was the Court Laundry which, in 1944, unofficially agreed to a second week's paid holiday. As a result the Court was the only laundry to function during the strike. Now the claim for two weeks' holiday became a political issue. Working conditions in laundries were particularly bad. Eleanor Butler (later Lady Wicklow) recounted Bennett taking her on a tour of Dublin laundries:

> She made me wade into the steamy laundries, with floors flooded. The women wore overalls and nothing underneath because they couldn't stand the heat and the steam. They sometimes wore wellingtons if they were lucky, if not battered old shoes. Their conditions were appalling, so much that a very high proportion of these women got TB and suffered from rheumatism.[76]

The IWWU placed much emphasis on the health risks involved in laundry work, arguing that shorter hours and extra holidays were necessary to minimise such risks. In rejecting the IWWU demand, the Federated Union of Employers (FUE) intimated that no increased holidays would be granted until the government declared a statutory fortnight's paid holiday. The minister for industry and commerce refused any such concession. Despite discussions between the ITUC and the FUE, no resolution was reached. On 21 July 1945, 1,500 women commenced strike action that would last fourteen weeks. Bennett laid the blame for the strike directly on the shoulders of the employers. Writing to the press she made it quite clear that the FUE, and not the IWWU, were responsible for the deadlock.[77] Before the advent of the home washing machine, laundry customers were both domestic and commercial.

Despite the great inconvenience caused it soon became clear that the striking women had public opinion on their side. No opportunity for publicity was missed. Four of the striking laundresses wrote a letter of complaint to *The Irish Times* about its lack of cover of the dispute. Commenting that the pages of the paper pasted up in its Fleet Street windows were full of news of foreign people and events, with only two lines being given to the strike of 1,500 Dublin women, and nothing at all about their conditions of work, the women declared that '*The Irish Times* is too grand for dirty linen'. Following this criticism, the paper's well-known columnist Patrick Campbell—'Quidnunc'—visited the IWWU offices. Subsequently, in his column, he detailed the women's demands, reporting a number of times humorously, but scathingly, on the labour-intensive daily routine of a laundry worker.[78]

Despite the fact that at this time the trade union movement was torn by dissent, and had in fact split into rival congresses, support for the strikers came from all sides. The strikers themselves kept morale going with regular meetings, parades, media coverage, and the sale of a strike song, sung to the air of the war-time song 'Lily Marlene', sold at 1d a sheet. Mai Clifford, a participant in the strike, later recounted that 'efforts to dampen such enthusiasm were pressed by the employers through various media campaigns waged against the general secretary, Louie Bennett'.[79] Ultimately the women were successful in their claim, and as in the case of official tea-breaks introduced some years earlier, set an example quickly followed by male workers. Clifford noted that the successful outcome to the strike 'gave an enormous boost to the union and heightened the profile of the IWWU as a militant and progressive union'.

Membership of the IWWU appears to have peaked in the early 1950s.[80] Despite the Conditions of Employment Act, the number of women employed in new industries grew steadily during the 1930s, although this had not been the objective of either government or most trade unions. This fact was not ignored for too long by mainstream unions, and from this point on most growth in female trade union membership took place in mixed unions and in clerical and white-collar unions.[81] Despite a continuing fall in number, the IWWU remained in existence until 1984 when it amalgamated with the Federated Workers Union of Ireland (FWUI). A number of factors contributed to its decline: the virtual disappearance of commercial laundries, increasing mechanisation, and increasingly, women's membership of mixed unions.

Without doubt, the IWWU had played a leading role in advancing the cause of women, not solely within the workplace, but also within the labour movement. At its peak of activity from the 1920s to the 1940s, it operated against a backdrop of economic hardship, emigration and war. In addition it had to fight not just employers, but perhaps more significantly, other groups within the trade union and labour movement who resisted an expansion of women's role. Its leaders were the only trade unionists consistently articulating the concerns of women workers. In retrospect, it can be seen as both the victor and victim during the years of its existence. Reflecting on the achievements of women workers to a teachers' group in 1947, Bennett recounted the horrific conditions of women workers in 1917, underpaid and exploited, working a fifty-four hour week, sixty in laundries, with no paid holidays. She credited women for the considerable reforms achieved in working conditions over the previous thirty years, pointing out that:

It was the women who inflamed the campaign which won shorter working hours, the extension of the annual holiday, the break in the five-hour shift. And it is the women workers who are leading the drive for amended factory laws, a higher standard of health services and of hygienic environment. Women's influence has in fact proved a humanising factor in industry.[82]

Similarly Sylvia Meehan has noted:

Women's contribution has been a more generous one. They could have argued simply for equal pay and women's rights. They did more than this, bringing with them a humane concern for all of society's underprivileged and handicapped sections.[83]

A notable example of the increased female participation in mixed unions was the Irish Transport and General Workers Union (ITGWU) which had less than 1,000 female members in 1930; ten years later this had risen to over 6,000. By 1950—just as the IWWU numbers began to decline—a total of 55,000 women were unionised, a figure that would increase to 100,000 by 1970.[84] Some old principles proved just too embedded to shake, however. Despite comprising most of the growth in union membership during the 1960s, mainly concentrated in the larger general unions, it was pointed out in 1975 that 'women are still notably absent from virtually all craft unions'.[85] Echoing IWWU arguments from earlier years, Daly has noted that while mixed unions sought improvements in women's pay and working conditions, 'until the second half of the twentieth century, they rarely articulated the point of view of women workers, nor did they do anything to redress inequalities in pay and career prospects for women'.[86] Despite its high proportion of women members, prior to the 1970s the ITGWU had only one woman on its national executive—Sheila Conroy—first elected to the executive in 1955, a feat she repeated in 1958.

Conroy has pointed to indifference on the part of both male officials and female members on the issue of women's role in the movement. Noting that the main emphasis of male officials was seen to be the negotiating of increased pay and conditions for male workers, Conroy has commented, 'They hardly considered (women) to be members of the same union.'[87] An example she gives relates to Labour Court negotiations in the early 1950s for a five shilling pay increase for catering workers. When the talks finally ended at 2.00 a.m., Conroy recalls someone asking 'what about the women workers?' The response was, 'We'll give them two and sixpence.'[88] Ironically, despite her impressive track record in the trade union movement, Conroy herself was a victim of the marriage bar, having to resign her trade union post on marrying John Conroy, ITGWU General President in 1959.

Intimations of change in women's role in society from the 1960s were reflected in trade unionism, with increased discussion on equality of pay and opportunity for women. The formation of a Women's Advisory Council (WAC) by ICTU in 1959 provided a useful forum for articulation of such issues. Increased public and media debate on differing male and female wage rates, particularly in relation to national pay awards, heightened awareness among women members, culminating in the establishment by ICTU of a Committee on Equal Pay in 1965. Another related factor at this time of strong economic growth was the rise in marriage rates, with earlier marriages. Increasingly as more Irish women left the workforce on marriage, either because of the marriage bar or because of the economic climate, a skills shortage of experienced women workers emerged. Daly has noted that this combination of factors 'resulted in a small number of women being promoted into positions hitherto regarded as male preserves'.[89] Ultimately such pressure resulted in the virtual erosion of the marriage ban in private industry from the early 1970s, although it was not formally eliminated in the public service until 1973.

The Commission on the Status of Women, established in 1970, remarked in its Report of 1972 that while women made up one-quarter of all trade union membership in the country, there were only seven full-time female officials out of a total of 230. It was noted that generally active participation by women in trade union matters was extremely low, with very few female shop stewards. The WAC had informed the Commission that a major barrier to the participation of women was the attitude of many male trade unionists, stating that 'if women are to build up confidence to seek opportunities in the work environment, the attitudes of men would have to undergo radical changes (becoming) more receptive and supportive of women's needs and demands'. The Commission concluded that trade unions must re-examine the role of women in their organisations, and face up to the challenge of adapting themselves to facilitate constructive participation by their women members. Had the wheel come full circle?

WOMEN AND WORK

The story of Irish women's employment from the Famine until at least the 1960s must (also) be placed in the context of falling total employment, late marriages, high marital fertility, a high level of permanent celibacy and a significant level of emigration. (MARY E. DALY, *Women and Work in Ireland*)

PAID AND UNPAID WORK

Between 1870 and 1970, the issue of women's work was treated in a variety of ways by statisticians, government agencies, politicians, the churches, and women themselves. Attitudes varied according to the type of work performed, the location where it was carried out, and whether it conformed to stereotypes of femininity. Early eighteenth-century reports were positive regarding women spinning or engaged in crafts in their own homes, acknowledging the importance of women's contribution to the family income. As the nature of women's paid work changed during the nineteenth century—whether they went to the factory or engaged in 'piece' work for factories in their homes—a more negative attitude emerges towards women's work. It has been noted that 'Women's work has rarely been viewed merely as a source of income; it has tended to be evaluated in the context of women's wider roles as mother and carer for the family'.[1] Generally, the 'unpaid' aspect of women's work within the home was either taken for granted, or exalted as the 'proper place' for women. Into the early decades of the twentieth century 'paid' work was accepted as necessary only for certain categories of women, mainly those from poor labouring and small farming backgrounds. The work available was generally domestic service, low-paid factory work or seasonal agricultural labour. Following the expansion of female education, a small but significant number of middle-class women began to enter the workforce from the 1890s, concentrated in newly emerging white-collar clerical jobs, teaching and nursing.

Daly has pointed to the difficulties encountered in determining the level of women's work based on census returns, partly due to confusion among officials in defining the concept of 'work'. As a result, 'Irish occupational data has seriously underestimated the contribution made by women who were engaged in the family economy'.[2] While productive labour carried out by women within the factory or office was counted by census takers, the contribution of women within the family economy was generally ignored—although the contribution of men in a similar setting was invariably included. So we find that although post-Famine agriculture increasingly relied on family members rather than hired labour, census takers generally excluded farmers' wives and other female relatives from the agricultural workforce, while including male relatives, 'The sons of farmers were regarded by nineteenth-century census officials as productive workers, farmers' daughters were not.'[3] A notable exception to this practice was the census of 1871, the only occasion when the number of wives working in family businesses was counted. It showed that over 30 per cent of agricultural workers were women, of whom two-thirds were farmers' wives. This census also showed other categories of wives working in family businesses—11,020 shoemakers' wives, 2,899 butchers' wives and 3,829 wives of innkeepers.[4] Further details of working wives included the following:

Wives of specified occupations 1871

Civil Service:	Author:	Teachers:	Gen. Domestic Servants:
55	1	1,146	5,883
Midwives:	Actress:	Pawnbrokers:	Unspecified Dealers:
205	29	31	3,174
Shopkeepers:	Seamstresses:	Agriculturalists:	
5,858	13,000+	250,000+	

Taken from Finola Kennedy, *Cottage to Crèche* (Dublin, 2001), p. 75.

Census enumerators became increasingly reluctant to record female relatives as productive workers, Luddy citing one instance in Co. Leitrim in 1901 where Kate Carr was included as a farmer along with her husband. Ten years later her husband again put her name down as a farmer, but the census enumerator crossed this out and placed her in the unoccupied category.[5] As a result of changing official interpretation of what constituted productive labour after 1871, wives who did not have a separate occupation other than that associated with their husband were classified as being in an unpaid domestic occupation; thus more and more women were to be found in the 'non-productive' category of census documentation. While Census returns between 1841 and 1911 show the number of men with designated occupations remaining steady at 64 per cent, the number of women with designated occupations declines rapidly from 27 per cent to 19 per cent during the same period.[6]

Number of men and women with designated occupations, 1841–1911 (000s)

Year	Women	Men	Total
1841	1,169.6	2,342.2	3,511.8
1851	938.2	1,903.4	2,841.6
1861	845.7	1,827.4	2,673.1
1871	817.3	1,655.4	2,482.7
1881	814.6	1,571.9	2,386.5
1891	641.1	1,504.3	2,145.7
1901	549.9	1,413.9	1,963.8
1911	430.1	1,387.2	1,817.3

Taken from Joanna Bourke, *Husbandry to Housewifery* (Oxford, 1993), p. 27.

The Irish Free State (IFS) in its 1926 Census went some way in remedying the under-recording of women's work by including farmers' daughters and other female relatives, *but not their wives*, in the agricultural labour force. That same census also created what Daly calls a 'nebulous category of women' defined as those 'engaged in home duties'.[7] These were not included in the occupied labour force, and were limited to one woman per household of six and under. Had farmers' wives been counted as part of the occupied workforce the proportion of Irish women in the labour force would have been very similar to the proportion in Britain. While the 1926 population census returns showed a figure of 109,000 women in agriculture, a 1927 IFS Census of Agriculture (which included part-time workers) indicated there were over 263,000 women engaged in agriculture.[8]

RURAL WOMEN

Nineteenth-century Ireland was predominantly rural in character; in

1841 only 20 per cent of the population lived in towns—by 1971 this had risen to 59 per cent.[9] There were only three towns with more than 50,000 inhabitants—Dublin, Belfast and Cork. While the Famine of 1845–48 had dramatic effects on population figures, marriage rates, and the nature of farming, Ireland retained its rural character into the twentieth century. This character was reflected in the type and amount of work available to its women.

The modern distinction between paid and unpaid work was not always so clear-cut, Daly noting that 'for most Irishwomen in the past, work, whether paid or unpaid, was a matter of survival. Family need rather than individual choice determined whether women worked within the family economy or outside the home.'[10] Mary Cullen's examination of the 1835 Commission of Inquiry into the Condition of the Poor noted that 'the labouring family operated as an interdependent economic unit where husband and wife—and children when they were old enough—contributed to family survival by paid and unpaid work'.[11] When a family could no longer survive by independent labour, the wife regularly became the sole family breadwinner, primarily through begging, which was viewed solely as women's work. Anne O'Dowd has noted that from the mid-nineteenth century, women begged less, tending more to become seasonal labourers or to stay at home minding the family holding while their husbands travelled for work.[12] In its exposition of the number of women working in agriculture, the 1871 Census revealed that the majority of paid female workers were young single workers recruited for six-month periods at hiring fairs, many the daughters of farm labourers or small farmers who subsequently emigrated.[13] Research by the Department of Irish Folklore in UCD shows that as late as the 1950s women were still making a considerable contribution to work on the land, work that was both arduous and back-breaking:

> They carried loads on their backs and on their heads, they bound oats, saved hay, weeded, thinned, cut seed potatoes, planted and picked potatoes, pitched sheaves, stacked corn, footed and drew out turf, drew seaweed and kelp from the shore to dry land, pounded furze for feed for animals, shaped mud turf, spread and tied flax, picked mussels, baited lines and gutted fish.[14]

This finding reflects the comment of an early nineteenth-century English observer that 'women in Ireland are treated more like beasts of burden than rational beings (and are) degraded in a manner disgraceful to the other sex and shocking to humanity'.[15]

Historians are agreed on a number of reasons for the decline in women's employment from the mid-nineteenth century. In addition to the huge population loss post-Famine through death and emigration, the on-going collapse of the domestic spinning industry from the early 1840s accelerated the downward spiral of female employment. Apart from the north-eastern section of the country, where the impact of decline was cushioned to an extent by the growth of factory employment and new forms of domestic industry, elsewhere throughout the country there were few alternative sources of employment. Both Luddy and Daly have noted that, coupled with declining employment for male agricultural workers, the loss of women's earnings from domestic industry ended the prospect of early marriage for landless or near landless couples, and pointed increasing numbers towards emigration.[16] Changes in agricultural methods after the Famine—the decline of tillage and increasing mechanisation—also reduced demand for female labour. By the end of the century women's field work appears to have been restricted to those areas where tillage was still important, mainly in remote parts of the west, and where seasonal migration had reduced the numbers of male workers. In these poor areas, women were still used as beasts of burden, carrying turf and stones. Another source of female earnings noted by Luddy was the work of wet nurse and the boarding out of children from charitable institutions or workhouses.[17]

Daly has commented on the fact that some historical accounts deplore the loss of women's employment post-1850, while suggesting that women's status was higher earlier in the century. Many of the women recorded as working in the 1841 census were engaged, however, in a struggle for survival through begging, casual dealing, or back-breaking agricultural work at a fraction of the male rate. While acknowledging that some of the post-Famine decline in female employment was led by changes in the structure of agriculture and industry, Daly argues that the fall in the supply side of the market cannot be ignored. In particular the virtual disappearance of the cottier or labourer class in the second half of the century, allied to the sharp drop in the number of small holdings, greatly reduced the two groups closest to subsistence level existence: 'The falling proportion of such families and the increasing flow of emigrants' remittances meant that many women were under less pressure to seek poorly paid employment.'[18] In addition, increasingly women themselves chose the option of emigration.

For those who remained on the farm, women's duties were increasingly concentrated around the farmyard and house. Milking, butter-making, rearing hens, pigs and calves were deemed to be strictly female tasks. In particular, 'egg-money' was an important source of income for rural women—often the only source of discretionary income. So established were these tasks as 'women's work', in many areas men would not milk cows, hiring arrangements often including a clause to this effect. Nor would men handle the sale of eggs or hens, becoming the butt of communal jokes and derogatory nicknames if they did so.[19] Caomhín Ó Danachair has confirmed the division of labour on the farm; the production and marketing of cattle and of crops was the man's business, while that of the farmyard—milk and butter, and fowl, eggs and feathers—was the woman's business: 'The farmer's wife took her produce to market, sold it to the best advantage and controlled the money thus gained. A common sight on market day was the stream of horse and donkey carts being driven by women to the town and returning in the evening with goods purchased in the town.'[20] He also points out that young girls were initiated into this custom, often being given a clutch of eggs and a hatching hen, while older daughters might have a flock of hens, geese, ducks or turkeys. In his study of the Congested Districts Board established by Arthur Balfour in 1891 to improve the conditions of the people of the west of Ireland, David Smith argues that this 'first regional development agency in the British Isles' recognised women as an integral and traditional part of the rural economy. By breaking with bourgeois Victorian paradigms, particularly in relation to women's labour, Smith notes that:

> Rather than viewing women as peripheral to the earning power of the male head of the household, the board saw women as an integral contributor in cash terms to the budgeting strategy of the family ... It can be argued that the board's policies targeted women as income earners as much, if not more, as it did men.[21]

Board inspectors noted the contribution of women and girls to the family income, through money for eggs, butter, and piece-work hand-knitting.

To the board, women were integral to the economies of these families, whether they fulfilled this role in the domestic setting of their own homes, in the fields, or in the homes of those for whom they worked as domestic servants. These women brought cash into the home.[22]

Strategies developed by the Board sought to use the traditional roles of women to increase cash into the household economies of the region. Among the schemes initiated in this regard was the establishment of poultry farms to raise the standard of eggs and poultry. With the establishment of fish-curing stations, instructors were appointed for women and children in this and in net-mending, again adding to women's employment and income. Domestic classes conducted by the Board aimed to give girls migrating to hiring fairs skills and certification that would help them obtain higher wages.

In implementing these schemes, the Congested Districts Board conceived of rural women's labour in a unique way. It took the traditional roles of women and made them into more efficient cash-earning positions.[23]

In addition the Board sought placements for such students as domestic servants in Dublin, Belfast and Cork. Domestic-economy training also proved useful for girls wishing to emigrate, an outcome the Board did not seem particularly happy with.[24] The Board strongly encouraged domestic industries, organising classes for women and girls to learn lace work, crocheting, embroidery, knitting, spinning and weaving. Students were paid cash during their training, and in addition, many became paid instructors. Grants were given to factories employing women such as the woollen factory at Foxford and a knitting factory at Ballaghadereen, both run by the Sisters of Charity, and to individual women to purchase power looms. By 1903 there were 45 such classes in existence, training having been given to some 3,200 pupils. Ultimately, however, due to economic pressures and competition, these efforts were not commercial successes, but as Smith points out they did mark an attempt by the Congested Districts Board to train women and girls in a remunerative field that would allow them to remain in the home.[25] Despite the availability of some work in domestic industries, changing employment strategies, particularly among families in the west of Ireland resulted in 'young women (being) increasingly likely to accept the training in a cottage industry and use the first earnings on a ticket to America'.[26]

The sharp decline of women in the labour force from 1891 to 1911 has been attributed to a number of factors, generally agreed on by historians of the period. Domestic service had expanded significantly in post-

Famine years, reaching a peak in 1881 of 48 per cent of employed women.[27] From this point the number so employed steadily decreased, the 1911 census showing that manufacturing industry had bypassed domestic service, although the latter remained as the second highest employer of women until the 1950s.[28] In towns and cities, another growing area of employment during these years was that of shop assistant. Considered to be more respectable than domestic service, this had the advantage of providing live-in accommodation, but the disadvantage of very long hours and low pay. Emigration continued to remove large numbers of women from Ireland; by the 1870s women accounted for half of all emigrants, and would remain a majority until the outbreak of World War II.

Developments within agriculture towards the end of the nineteenth century had a significant effect on women's earning potential. In particular, the emergence of co-operative creameries brought about 'the most dramatic change in women's farm employment'.[29] O'Dowd has commented that 'the introduction of creameries to the Irish countryside at the end of the 1880s effectively and swiftly removed milking and buttermaking from the female environment of the home, to a factory milieu run and managed by men'.[30] This move resulted in substantial loss of female employment both through loss of earnings from buttermaking by women on the farm, and through loss of jobs for girls traditionally employed as dairy-maids. Bourke has calculated that whereas in 1881, women formed 43 per cent of workers employed in the broad range of milk and dairy products, this figure had reduced by 10 per cent by 1891, and continued to decline into the 1920s.[31] From being an area in which women could earn cash directly through sales at markets, now their role was reduced to deliverers, payments for butter going to men in the shape of milk cheques from creameries. As time went by, hired male labourers would combine milking with other general farm work. When attempts were made to organise poultry and egg production on a co-operative basis in the 1890s, women resisted tenaciously. Experience of earnings lost when dairying was removed from the home to the co-operative a decade earlier had not been forgotten.

Anxious to retain control over their 'egg-money', women also preferred their traditional method of selling eggs directly to 'higglers' or local shopkeepers, the latter often in exchange for groceries. This method was easier for farm women to combine with their home duties, and as Bourke has noted, 'The houseworker who sold or exchanged her eggs with the local shopkeeper or higgler was acknowledging the economic value of her time and energies within the home.'[32] O'Dowd has commented that 'Women fought to hold on to the profits from the sale of eggs and would not allow them and their business to become swallowed in the male affairs of the creamery'.[33] Generally, egg co-operatives were not a success, and farm-women managed to hold on to their monopoly up to the 1950s.

There are, however, differing interpretations regarding other reasons for the continuing drop in female employment figures in rural Ireland between 1881 and 1911. Bourke suggests that 'In the generation prior to 1914 Irish women transformed their position within society: bidding farewell to labour in the fields and in other men's homes, they enlisted for full-time work in the unpaid domestic sphere'.[34] Arguing that a boom in the rural economy from 1890 allowed women to opt out of paid employment, she notes that in 1901 only 430,000 women in Ireland were employed, compared with 641,000 twenty years earlier:

> Scorning paid domestic service, young women thronged to classes in rural housewifery ... Single women performed housework, free of charge, for fathers, brothers, and uncles. Or they emigrated. Married women nursed their children and strove to improve the standard of services that they provided to their family, while widowed women competed with their children's spouses in the production of domestic goods. Female labour came to be dominated by housework.

Daly, however, has commented that the scale of decline—more than one female job in five lost between 1881 and 1891—is puzzling and contrasts sharply with the trend in the previous two decades. Pointing out that four-fifths of all job 'losses' occurred in the vague category 'others engaged in service', which included female family members such as sisters and aunts who helped with household chores, she argues that these women did not 'opt' out of paid employment; most would only have received board and keep within a household. Rather, she suggests that the apparent scale of decline is possibly the result of differing practices by census enumerators.[35] Kennedy too queries the reasons for the 'astonishing change' between the 1871 census which gave a figure of 362,000 'Wives of Specified Occupations' for the 32 counties, and the 1926 census in the 26 counties which returned just 23,895 married women as 'gainfully employed'. The Irish census collectors had been instructed in 1871 by the authorities in London to transfer wives, until then included in the domestic class as engaged in home duties, into the 'indefinite and non-productive' class and to transfer wives *with* specified occupations out of the occupational categories in which they were included, into the domestic class. Kennedy records the objections of the Irish Commissioners to this imposition. Pointing to the implications of transferring all wives of specified occupations to the Domestic class under the English system, the Commissioners argued that:

> nothing, as it occurred to our judgement, could be more erroneous in principle than such a classification. A wife of specified occupation may be a milliner or dressmaker, a draper, a governess or schoolmistress, bookbinder, or a seamstress ...
>
> The Domestic class, under the scheme in hand, abstracts at a clean sweep, every wife of a professional or industrial calling from the class to which she is naturally referable, and transfers her to a class which represents in great part not so much a calling as a relation.[36]

Forced to accept London's instructions, the obliteration of wives of specified occupations from an occupational classification was copper-fastened in the 1881 census which stipulated that wives of specified occupations should not be separately tabulated, but referred to 'the particular headings under which their calling naturally ranged'. Increasingly over the next two decades, large numbers of women were gradually transferred from classes in which they had previously been included. The 1891 census report noted that 140,000 wives, formerly included as 'Others engaged in Service' had been transferred into the 'Indefinite and Non-productive class'. Notwithstanding the high unrecorded occupational involvement of women, Kennedy has pointed out that the gradual disappearance of wives from recorded occupations should be borne in mind when considering the very low level of recorded workforce participation by married women in Ireland. A similar situation emerged in England in 1881 when women's household work was excluded from the category of productive work, and from that time housewives were classified as unoccupied. Whereas prior to this change the economic activity rate for both men and women had been recorded as close to 100 per cent, following these changes only 42 per cent of women were classified as economically productive.[37]

URBAN WOMEN
The first population census taken in the IFS in 1926 confirmed the employment profile of Irish women which had been developing over the

previous thirty years or so—a low participation rate for both married and single women, a concentration of workers in agriculture and domestic service, and a high proportion of working women employed within the family economy.[38] Sixty per cent of women at work were in either farming or domestic service; less than 10 per cent worked in industry. By that year also, about 25 per cent of women aged 45+ were unmarried, compared with a figure of 10 per cent pre-Famine.[39]

Changing work-patterns, resulting either from mechanisation of existing trades, or the development of new employment opportunities, created demands for goods and services. It was primarily in Ulster that women benefited from such developments. The increasing numbers of clerical workers during the latter half of the nineteenth century created a demand for a ready supply of shirts with detachable collars and cuffs. In this regard, the shirt-making industry of Derry was a most successful source of women's employment. Adapting through increasing mechanisation from the 1850s, by 1902 the industry in counties Derry and Donegal employed approximately 18,000 factory employees and 80,000 outworkers, 80 per cent of whom were women. Belfast too had an important making-up industry, while in Dublin smaller numbers of women and men worked from home as suppliers of shirts and suits to city department stores.[40] Daly suggests that the discrepancy between census figures for 1891 which recorded 13,691 female dressmakers in Dublin compared with less than 5,000 such workers given in the 1895 Factory Returns, indicates that many women worked from home as self-employed workers doing repairs and making clothes for personal customers.[41] Employment opportunities for women in mills and factories predominated in Ulster; elsewhere, Irish towns and cities provided limited and poorly paid industrial employment for women.

The census of 1907 showed that outside Ulster, there were 1,700 women employed in woollen mills—most plants were small and the majority were situated in Cork. This census also shows that the only other factory-based industries to employ more than 1,000 women were biscuits, baking and laundries. Jacob's biscuit factory in Dublin, with 2,000 women workers, emerged as the largest employer of women outside the textile and clothing industries.[42] Despite a decline in numbers entering domestic service from the 1880s, the 1911 census shows that one-third of all occupied women were servants, and service remained a significant source of employment until after World War II. The numerical significance of domestic service is reflected in the fact that a separate occupational class in the census was devoted to it.

Workhouses, orphanages, industrial schools and reformatories were an important source of servants for middle- and lower middle-class people, and for local farmers. Many such homes employed only one 'general' servant, and with virtually nothing in the line of labour-saving devices available, a vast amount of daily menial labour was expected of such a servant.[43]

In his book *Ordinary Lives: Three Generations of Irish Middle Class Experience*, Tony Farmar outlines a typical day in the life of a servant in a small household with only one servant:

6.30	Open house: see to kitchen
6.50	Sweep and dust diningroom; lay breakfast
7.20	Brush boots
7.30	Brush stairs
7.40	Clean front door and hall
8.00	Make breakfast
8.15	Serve breakfast
8.45	Take pail upstairs, empty slops (from the utensils in the bedrooms); strip and make beds, tidy bedrooms
9.30	Wash breakfast things
10.00	Allocated work for that day—e.g. washing, clean kitchen, ironing etc.
12.00	Prepare vegetables for dinner—the mistress will actually cook the meal
12.30	Change into more formal wear
1.00	Serve dinner
1.45	Wash dinner things
2.30	Afternoon walk (with children)
4.45	Prepare and serve nursery tea
6.30	Bath children
7.00	Wash tea things
7.30–9.00	own time, except on Monday and Thursday
9.15	Serve supper
9.45	Bedtime

Demand for servants was fed by the expanding middle-class suburbs of Dublin and Cork, and by the fact that there was little alternative employment available. Numbers of servants were less in Belfast where manufacturing jobs existed for women.[44] Generally therefore, at the beginning of the twentieth century, the majority of women worked in poorly paid, low status, often specifically female jobs. Outside the officially recognised workforce, many women, married and unmarried, contributed substantially to family income, helping to run pubs, grocery shops and other retail businesses with husbands or fathers. In his autobiography, Tod Andrews pointed out that mothers were often involved in earning the family living, even though this may not be recorded in official statistics. His own mother ran a dairy and provision shop in an era when a proliferation of small local grocery shops existed. Kennedy has pointed out that most of these shops (except those run by widows) would have been registered in the name of the man of the house.[45] Another common source of income was keeping lodgers, although this did not bring any increased status. In their study of shop-keepers in Ennis, Arensberg and Kimball noted that while wives often helped their husbands in the running of the family business, 'the kitchen is the province of the woman as she discharges her never ceasing domestic duties'.[46]

Because prosperous middle- and upper-class women very consciously neither contributed to family income, nor to household chores, the role of those who did so tended to be downgraded, and the woman of leisure, devoting herself to accomplishments or a full-time home maker, became the ideal. With such ideals gradually permeating all Irish society by the turn of the century 'an income-earning wife was probably only acceptable among the lower reaches of the working classes and among farm labourers'.[47]

Class and social status were dominant in Victorian and Edwardian Ireland. The low status accorded to women's work had far-reaching implications, with the majority of women working out of necessity rather than as a means of self-fulfilment. Noting that most were transitory rather than permanent members of the labour force, working in their youth, or in times of need and returning to home life if circumstances improved, Daly has pointed to the twin factors of a vulnerable, predominantly young female work-force allied to a rapid turn-over, factors which made these workers difficult to organise. As a result, women's work was generally classified as unskilled or semi-skilled, even though many of the tasks they carried out in linen mills or with the sewing machine required considerable expertise. Often forced through family circumstances to work for extremely low wages, women were open to exploitation by employers. As a result of low pay becoming synonymous with low status, women workers increasingly became the object of resistance by male workers, particularly craft workers, who became convinced that the proper place for women was in the home.[48]

Yet many women were forced to supplement—or provide—the family income, particularly in areas where male employment was seasonal or casual. This was the situation for the majority of the urban poor. Writing from a Dublin perspective, Kearns has noted that with secure work for men scarce, women often worked in small factories (making shoes, shirts, sacks, rosary beads), or as domestics, charwomen or washerwomen. Street trading was a traditional female occupation, particularly fish, fruit, vegetables, flowers and second-hand clothing. Many women walked miles into the countryside for a day's work picking potatoes, cabbage or fruit.[49] Mary Waldron, born in 1913 in Gloucester Street, a street of packed tenements—'there were eleven families in our house'—recalled that women fish dealers walked out to Howth at four in the morning with their barrows.[50] Generally, the responsibility of rearing a family and maintaining a household fell upon the woman:

> A mother was expected to care for the children, prepare meals, do the shopping, wash, clean, iron, budget the money, go to the pawn, deal with the relieving officer and St Vincent de Paul Society men, and settle family disputes.[51]

Many had to manage all this in addition to working outside the home at menial jobs or by taking in washing or sewing. Kearns's book vividly relates personal histories of men and women who lived in the tenements. In detailing the struggle for survival in overcrowded rooms with little or no sanitation, families struggling to cope with large families of twelve or more on a meagre diet, the stories resound with the positive aspect of communal living, Elizabeth 'Bluebell' Murphy recounting, 'It was a hard life (but) we were all one family, all close. We all helped one another.' Murphy also recalled her work in Keogh's sack factory on the Quays:

> You started at fourteen for ten shillings a week. We used to wear smocks and worked from nine to six. We were doing both the making and the repairing. We made jute and cotton bags and we used second hand sacks, we took them in and had to examine them and take out all the dirt and grain out of them. Turned them inside out and clean them and darned them on sewing machines. I don't know how I'm alive with the dirt and dust. Had to scrape everything off the bags to be darned and the husks of the grain would get all over you and we'd

be *sweating* doing the darning. And we went to Tara Street baths (once a week). Oh, that felt *great* after a week in the factory.[52]

Many women kept small 'huckster' shops to supplement the family income. Nancy Cullen told Kearns of her mother's shop:

She used to sell cabbage, onions, potatoes and cigarettes and coal and turf and sticks for the fire. And she sold a lot of paraffin oil cause most people only had oil lamps. Me mother'd give food on credit. She might get it back, or get half of it back.[53]

Prostitution was another significant female occupation during the nineteenth century and into the early twentieth century. Present in all cities and many towns, it was particularly in towns that housed army garrisons that prostitutes were likely to be highest in number.[54] In Dublin, the famous 'Monto' district thrived as a red light district until the 1920s when Frank Duff and the Legion of Mary caused its demise.[55] Prostitution had its own social hierarchy, ranging from women who catered to very wealthy clients, to those who managed their own brothels, to the lowly street walker. Women camp followers and those who went with soldiers and sailors were considered to be on an even lower scale than street walkers.[56] In addition to 'Monto', there were numerous brothels or 'kip houses' throughout tenement Dublin, and many prostitutes who lived in the tenements plied their trade on O'Connell Street, Grafton Street and St Stephen's Green.[57] A number of contributors to Kearns's book refer to prostitution as an accepted part of life in city centre areas. Mary Corbally, one of fifteen children living in one room—who later married at 15 and gave birth to twenty-one children, of whom fourteen survived—commented:

I don't feel any shame in coming from the Monto. The reputation was there because of the girls. In them years they was called 'the girls' and in later years they'd say they were 'unfortunate girls', but never 'prostitutes'. We never heard the word 'whores', never heard 'prostitute'. The girls hung around on the streets and the men used to come mostly off the boats. Most of the girls that I can remember was from the country. Very rarely you'd hear of a 'brothel', it was a 'kip' and the madams we called them 'kip-keepers'. The girls were good and generous. If you went for a message for them you'd get thrupence or sixpence. And if they seen a kid running in his bare feet they'd bring him into Brett's and buy him a pair of runners.[58]

Similarly, Timmy 'Duckegg' Kirwan recalled the 'unfortunates' as being mostly country girls, in their early twenties, very kind and good natured, buying shoes and boots for barefooted children, and clothes for babies. Both Kirwan and Corbally infer that the madams were from Dublin, Kirwan stating that local people didn't mind the madams; 'they were the best in the world for helping the poor ... and they had the old people in the neighbourhood working for them, cleaning the delph and collecting the glasses ... giving them a few bob.'[59] Similar to Corbally, Kirwan's mother worked for the madams, cleaning up and scrubbing and washing the house to make a few bob for the family; 'the poor people worked for them, they *had* to.' The landlords (and their relatives) of the tenement houses lived in by both Corbally and Kirwan also owned 'kip houses'.[60]

In her extensive research on prostitution in Ireland, Luddy has highlighted one particular groups of camp followers—the 'wrens of the Curragh', so called because the women 'live(d) in holes in the banks (ditches)' around the Curragh army camp in County Kildare. Numbering up to sixty women at any one time, the women actually lived in makeshift huts along the perimeter of the army camp.[61] While many were prostitutes, not all were; as Luddy points out, some of these women were involved in long-standing common-law relationships with soldiers (it was the practice of the army authorities at this time not to recognise soldiers' marriages unless they were living in married quarters in the camp).[62]

Before World War I, the overwhelming majority of women with recorded occupations were poor, the only exceptions being a small number of female professionals and commercial clerks.[63] Although small in number, these professional and commercial jobs represented a significant new element of choice for some women. By the end of the nineteenth century trades such as millinery, drapery and retail services offered important occupational opportunities for women who previously might have entered domestic service. Working as a shop assistant carried a similar advantage to that of domestic service, i.e. staff usually lived-in, but it was held to be more respectable than service. However, shop work entailed long working hours and harsh living-in conditions combined with strict discipline. Female shop assistants faced the additional problem of trade bias against them.[64] The expansion of professional and white-collar employment in the early twentieth century provided new job opportunities to middle-class women. While women were often only reluctantly 'allowed' into employments that were deemed suitable, the growth of opportunities in the teaching, nursing and growing white-collar employment areas gave many single women a choice between emigration and an uncertain spinster future.

With expansion in the field of education, increasing numbers of middle-class girls were being educated in schools, and by the end of the nineteenth century the profession of private governess was gradually replaced by women teachers in schools. Competition between schools had forced curriculum changes which prepared girls for state examinations on an equal status with boys. Teaching quickly became the main employment of women graduates, and by 1911, 63 per cent of teachers were women.[65] Bourke has pointed to the number of promotional opportunities available for female teachers, noting that over half of all school principals were women, primarily due to the large number of single sex schools. She also points out that for rural educated women with some familial or local support, teaching was one of the few expanding possibilities.[66]

The introduction of the typewriter in the 1870s and its widespread adoption by business fuelled the expansion of the clerical support sector as an almost exclusively female preserve. By World War 1 an increasing number of the young and unmarried female population worked as clerks, typists, book-keepers and secretaries.[67] The first 'lady typewriter' in the civil service in Ireland was appointed in 1901 in the Department of Agriculture and Technical Instruction, and by the beginning of the twentieth century 'a permanent pensionable career was becoming an acceptable role for a Catholic woman'.[68] Factors which helped acceptance of this process included the opening up of post office examinations to girls on a competitive basis, the desire of employers to gain cheap clerical labour, the high percentage of unmarried women in Ireland—all allied to improved educational standards for girls.

Anne O'Connor has noted that the post office was the official pioneer of women's employment in both England and Ireland during the last two decades of the nineteenth century, being the only government department employing female clerical labour on a large scale. Doubtless, a large part of the attraction for the government was the fact that the rate of pay for women civil servants was considerably lower than the male rate. The competitive aspects of the civil service examinations were particularly important at a time when the class distinctions of society tended to limit middle-class women to narrow occupational spheres. O'Connor has noted, 'respectability more than anything else often determined the choice of future career for many middle-class women.'[69] The new clerical opportunities opening up during the early decades of the twentieth century, while widening job opportunities for girls benefited mainly those living in the larger urban areas of Dublin, Cork and Belfast. These were the centres for civil service examinations, and as a result, special coaching schools were set up to prepare girls for the examinations. Similarly, the spread of secretarial and commercial colleges training girls in these cities reflected the growing demand for such workers. In 1906 twenty-three pupils of Skerry's School of Shorthand and Typewriting obtained posts in various Dublin offices; that same year the first examinations were held for four lady clerkships by Guinness's brewery. Census returns reflected the upsurge in women's clerical employment. Numbering 907 in 1892, women clerks increased to 3,437 by 1901 and to 7,849 in 1911.[70]

Allied to a public acceptance of the need to fill certain positions was a strong belief in the 'separate spheres' outlook that designated certain jobs to be carried out by women only. Nursing was a prime example of an area where women were accepted as part of a 'caring profession'. During the latter half of the nineteenth century, nursing gradually emerged from being an untrained branch of domestic service to a career involving apprenticeship and training, considered a suitable occupation for ladies.[71] In 1917, Canon Sheehan declared that the eagerness and zeal with which so many women had entered nursing during the previous few years was 'proof' that nursing was the 'natural duty and calling of young girls'.[72] Margaret Ó hÓgartaigh points out that Sheehan overlooked the fact that so many other occupations were closed to women, and that males could not train as nurses in Ireland.

In addition to voluntary hospitals established by Protestant philanthropists, female religious orders became predominant in hospital work during the nineteenth century. Orders of nuns both founded and largely staffed new hospitals.[73] Tensions between religious and lay nurses on the question of training and professional status continued into the 1930s. Trained lay nurses working in religious-run hospitals were often supervised by nuns who had not received formal nurse training. Also, lay nurses were obliged to do all night duty as most nuns refused to do so. With nuns providing essential health services to the state at a low cost, at times when nursing nuns came under pressure to professionalise, the local bishop and community often supported them. A Kilkenny bishop was told by one such nun in 1921 that 'nuns require no special preparation except the instructions they receive from their Reverend Mother on nursing'. A writer in the *Freeman's Journal* in 1895 asked: 'what is a trained nurse? A chit of a girl with a paper certificate from some Dublin hospitals

... or, a devoted nun.'[74] As Ó hÓgartaigh concludes, 'nuns were seen as superior to lay nurses, regardless of qualifications.' Furthermore, many of the characteristics associated with nuns such as piety, obedience and self-discipline became part of nurse training programmes.

Lay nursing reformers often held similar views to religious regarding the profession. Dr Anna Hamilton suggested that nurses should lead 'a life of celibacy, sacrificing marriage and family to devote themselves body and soul to caring for the sick and poor'. Her examinations for nurses stressed the importance of 'punctuality, calmness, docility, reflection, (the state of one's) uniform, cleanliness, patience, kindness, coiffure, discipline, conscience, manners, and voice'.[75] Often working for half the salary of a lay nurse, nuns were particularly welcomed by Catholic Poor Law guardians on economic grounds allied to their perceived embodiment of modern Catholicism. First admitted to nurse in the workhouse hospital by the Limerick board of guardians in 1861, by 1895 sixty-three boards of guardians had placed their workhouse infirmaries in the care of nuns; by 1903 that number had increased to eighty-four. At this point just over half of all workhouse hospitals were staffed by nuns.[76] Their willingness to provide inexpensive care established a tradition of poor pay and long hours for nurses. Working for a low salary was in many cases a deliberate strategy used by the nuns to make themselves more acceptable to boards of guardians, a strategy that may inadvertently have damaged the monetary value of women's work in nursing.[77] Lay women found it difficult to 'compete with the resources, commitment, sense of authority and religious spirit shown by the nuns'.[78] It has been argued that the legacy of nuns in nursing was similar to that of Nightingale's, with vocational commitment, not professional preparation, being emphasised.

Following the 1898 Local Government Act, the local government board laid down criteria for trained nurses including two years placement in a clinical or other hospital and examination; over the next number of years their practice not to appoint any untrained or uncertified person gradually was implemented as trained nurses came on stream. Formal training for lay nurses was provided by the Sisters of Charity in their St Vincent's Hospital in 1892, while the Mercy congregation began training programmes in Jervis Street Hospital and the Mater in 1891. Nuns themselves did not acquire formal training until 1897. Yet arguments for placing nuns in workhouses continued as before, a Dr Ryan of Baileborough writing in 1907:

For the modern craze that would exalt the girls who devote a couple of years to learning nursing as a trade above those ladies who devote their lives to the service of God's poor, I have nothing but contempt. The manual and technical knowledge is easily acquired by any person of education, but the sympathy with suffering, the self-sacrifice, the devotion to duty, all of which are so necessary to the nurse, are only fully acquired by those who look for their reward to their Heavenly Master.[79]

Luddy notes that through the effort of nuns, nursing had been transformed from the most menial of women's work to the most exalted. Nuns consolidated their power by extending their services into nurse training, a power they rarely shared with lay-women. Through their insistence on control of those under them, despite any professional qualifications their subordinates might hold, they created separate spheres within the world of nursing, and divided it along religious lines. 'Status came from the wearing of a nun's habit rather than from the possession of qualifications.'[80]

Religious life for women had undergone phenomenal growth during the nineteenth century. By 1901 their number had increased to 8,000 dispersed across 368 convents. Nuns worked in the full range of social and welfare services required by the state including schools, hospitals, orphanages, reformatories, laundries. Fahey has noted that 'To be a nun was one of the few acceptable occupational outlets outside marriage and motherhood available to women of respectable background'.[81] Examination of census returns for 1911 show that nuns emerge as the largest single women's group within the professional field. Even more than teaching, the religious life offered an alternative to marriage, emigration or spinsterhood to rural and urban women alike.

Female occupations 1911

Occupation	Number Employed
Nuns	8,887
Catholic women teachers	8,500
Catholic midwives	790
Certified Catholic nurses	621
Catholic women in subordinate medical services	2,513
Women civil servants	1,858
Women clerks and typists	7,849

Taken from M. Cullen, *Girls Don't Do Honours* (Dublin, 1987), pp 15 and 54.

Women working in Gaeltacht industries, Belmullet, Co. Mayo, July 1938.

Women graduates, Trinity College Dublin, mid-1930s.

A machinist at work in Cahill & Hearn's Boot Factory, Waterford, 1941.

Ironing class at Presentation Convent, Dundrum, Co. Tipperary, 1944.

Factory workers at Smith's Hosiery, Balbriggan, 1946.

Five women hand-sorting unprocessed tobacco leaves, Dundalk, Co. Louth, *c.* 1930–40s.

Women queuing for food during 'The Emergency' (World War Two) at The Demesne, Dundalk, Co. Louth.

Women plucking turkeys, Cork, December 1945.

An emigrant family leaves Cóbh, Co. Cork, on a Cunard Liner for Canada, 1953. While the children look somewhat apprehensive, their mother seems more relaxed. Among the family's possessions packed for the trip is the young girl's doll.

Sack-making in Guinness Brewery, St James's Gate, Dublin, 1948–52.

Pedestrians in O'Connell Street, Dublin, 1973. Within a few years, very few nuns would be wearing the formal habit pictured here.

Daly has highlighted some of the limitations on career opportunities for professional women during the early 1900s, noting that both teaching and nursing were poorly paid, and were to a large extent controlled by religious communities.[82] Women were accepted into these professions on the basis of the 'separate spheres' principle, whereby certain areas of work were identified as an extension of women's 'caring' role in society. This could sometimes work in favour of women, particularly in primary teaching where it was considered that 'men were unfit to teach children less than 7 years of age'. Yet, as Bourke points out, the 'idea that women made "better" teachers because of an "innate" relationship between women and child-rearing was not seen to conflict with the view that *mothers* should not be teachers'.[83]

Many teachers and nurses were forced to resign on marriage. Unease and sometimes resentment towards pregnant and/or married teachers was an issue that would recur again in the 1930s (see Chapter 10). Female teachers were paid less than their male counterparts, the pay of a female secondary teacher in 1905 being approximately the same as that of an unskilled labourer.[84] Both male and female teachers lacked security of employment, often being replaced by cheaper, unqualified ex-pupils, both lay and religious. Trainee nurses were required to live-in under regulations as draconian as those suffered by many domestic servants. Gender, while vital at this time in obtaining a nursing position, was not the only factor taken into consideration, e.g. Public health nurses had to be female, unmarried, or widowed.[85] Men could not train as nurses in the IFS, and although there were less than ten male nurses in the state in the 1920s, they were paid more than their female colleagues.[86] The fact that in Ireland nursing was almost entirely a female occupation was seen as an opportunity for advancement. However, many senior positions such as secondary school principals and hospital matrons were monopolised by nuns.

Ó hÓgartaigh has pointed out that despite state registration of midwives and nurses in 1918 and 1919, the persistent presence of the unregistered in the profession militated against full professional development, the tradition of religious nursing orders posing particular barriers to professionalisation. Similarly, Daly has noted that although a system of teacher registration was introduced in 1918, unregistered teachers continued to outnumber registered women teachers during the 1930s. While the Irish Royal College of Physicians was the first college to admit women to its examinations in 1877, with the first women graduating from the Irish College of Surgeons in 1890, there were only 33 qualified female medical doctors in Ireland in 1911 (although the census of that year recorded 68 female medical students). There were as yet no female lawyers; not until 1919 did the Sex Disqualification Act give women access to careers as solicitors or barristers. Daly relates the horror of the Institute of Chartered Accountants when a woman applied for admission as a student in 1901; the first woman was not admitted until 1925.[87] In fact, wherever women were thought to be encroaching on traditional male areas of employment, there was strong resistance from both trade unions and professional bodies.

Occupational profile of female labour-force 1911, %

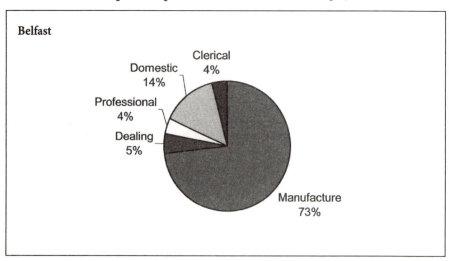

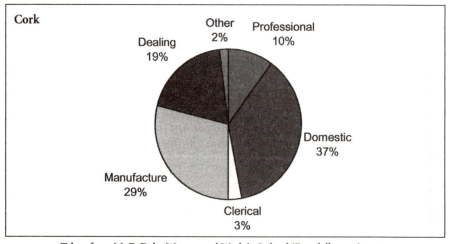

Taken from M. E. Daly, *Women and Work in Ireland* (Dundalk, 1997), p. 34.

Occupational profile of female labour-force 1911, %

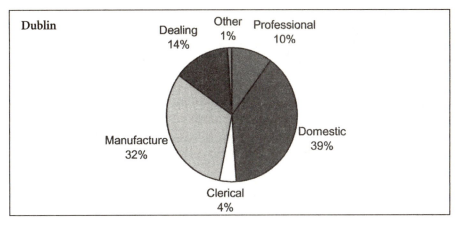

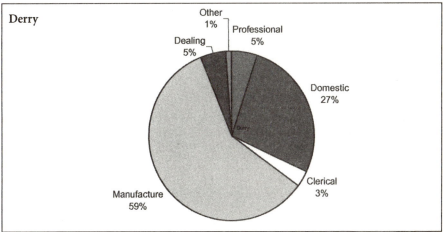

Taken from M. E. Daly, *Women and Work in Ireland* (Dundalk, 1997), p. 35.

POST-1922

Employment figures for Irish women during the first sixty years of independence remained at a low level in comparison to other European countries. In particular, there was a significant disparity between the numbers of women in the work-force north and south of the border in the early years, and in the profile of women workers. The IFS census of 1926 sheds much light on this disparity. South of the border two areas of employment predominate for women at this time—agriculture and domestic service—comprising over 60 per cent of women. In comparison, less than one-quarter of women in Northern Ireland worked in agriculture or domestic service. More than one-third of women in the South were engaged in agriculture, a higher figure than before as this census included all female relatives working on farms, with the exception of farmers' wives.[88] Inclusion of the latter would have increased the agricultural dominance.

Significant differences also appear in the number of married women workers on either side of the border. While 14.5 per cent of married women held occupations in Northern Ireland in 1926, only 5.6 per cent of married women in the Irish Free State (IFS) did so. There were only 8,000 married women employees in the IFS that year, most of whom were either self-employed or worked in the family economy.[89] The 1926 census also indicated that less than half of single women aged 14 and over in the IFS were in employment, compared with more than 87 per cent of men. Comparable figures in other countries in Western Europe were in excess of 60 per cent. With an accepted substantial degree of unrecorded and unacknowledged unemployment among single women, many of whom would have been engaged in unpaid domestic duties, the significance of such a figure as a constraint on Irish women's lives has been noted. The high proportion of women not in paid employment 'held considerable implications for their welfare, status, and security, particularly in light of their poor marriage prospects'.[90] In 1926, 24 per cent of women aged between 45–54 were single and likely to remain so; their younger sisters faced a similar scenario.

Women's labour market participation by status (percent)

	Single*	Married	Widowed
1926	48.6	5.6	40.6
1936	53.3	5.6	39.3

*percentage of single women aged 14 and over

Labour-force participation by age

	1926		1936	
	Male	Female	Male	Female
14–15	29.6	17.1	34.2	21.1
16–17	72.2	44.6	69.6	48.3
18–19	90.5	59.9	87.6	63.7
20–24	96.2	59.1	95.5	61.3
25–34	96.6	35.0	97.1	37.7

Taken from M. Daly 'Women in the Irish Free State 1922–39' in *Journal of Women's History* (1995), p. 103.

The high rate of female participation in second and third level education—apparent from the turn of the century—continued to rise during the 1920s and 1930s. In a society where one-quarter of women did not marry, increasingly families came to see that education provided a means for employment and financial independence. The extent of new white-collar posts opening up for women increased that awareness. Within the IFS, the establishment of a civil service based on the British model saw the emergence of low-grade clerical positions restricted to women. During the first ten years of the new state, the number of such civil servants increased from 940 to 2,260.[91] Despite the low pay, there were protests against male exclusion on the grounds that preference should be given to male veterans of the war of independence, and that these were the only civil service posts open to applicants with primary education. Women representatives argued that such was the keen competition for these jobs that most were filled by women with several years' secondary education. Daly notes that but for the pressure on the government to find work for veterans by restricting several competitions to ex-service men, including at least one of 'a particularly easy standard', women's employment in the civil service would have risen even more rapidly.[92] As it was mainly middle-class families who could afford secondary education at this time, the resulting predominance of middle-class women in such jobs led to some criticism. With an ever-increasing emphasis on providing jobs for men, the emergence of what were deemed 'pin-money' girls was resented in some quarters.[93]

An interesting development during the 1930s that benefited both women workers and the fledgling Irish health service, was the establishment of the Hospitals Trust Sweepstake in 1930. The success of this venture soon led to the necessity for large numbers of clerical staff (by 1932 it employed over four thousand permanent staff), providing a welcome addition to Dublin life where female employment was hard to come by.[94] The significance of this new employment opportunity for women in an era of economic depression with very little job security for women workers was highlighted by the decision of Arnott's department store to sack two women employees with twenty-five years' service because they were 'too old' at forty years of age.[95]

Within industry, there were generally clear demarcation lines between male and female jobs. In certain areas this was based on the physical demands of a given task, but very often women were automatically allocated the lower skilled and therefore lower paid jobs. Hill and Pollock have noted that bias in terms of pay was part of the much lower status accorded to jobs deemed to be the provenance of women. 'This was such that employment once associated with one sex often changed in prestige and reward when it became the property of the other.'[96] Generally, when men took over a traditional female task, the value and status of that task was raised; the contrary was the case when women were allocated jobs formerly held by men. While male workers often accused women of encroaching into their field of employment, the reverse was often more likely to have happened.[97]

With some 40 per cent of Irish-born people emigrating in search of labour, competition between the sexes for those jobs that did exist in Ireland was intense. Employment opportunities for both sexes were poor. Like their sisters, many men who would not inherit a farm or business saw education as the only means of obtaining meaningful employment. Among those who did not emigrate, secure employment—particularly in the public sector—was much prized. Generally across the occupation spectrum, men had a higher participation rate, access to many low-paid labouring jobs closed to women, and male-dominated skilled trades and apprenticeships. They were also more likely to control farms or family businesses by middle age. However, 'their greatest asset was the general acceptance within Irish society, irrespective of gender, that men were the primary breadwinners'.[98]

Within the IFS 62 per cent of female industrial workers in 1926 were employed in the clothing and textile sectors, with a further 23 per cent employed in food, drink and tobacco.[99] During the 1920s population declined, emigration increased and employment rates fell. By 1932, when Fianna Fáil took office, international recession had sharply reduced emigration to the US. Great Britain now became the most popular destination for emigrants, followed by the USA, Canada, and Australia.[100] While female emigrants to Britain slightly exceeded male, Pauric Travers notes that between 1924 and 1952 the proportion of female emigrants to the US remained very high, exceeding male figures. The Fianna Fáil Government of 1932 sought to halt population decline by reducing emigration; the latter, it hoped, would be achieved by increasing employment, which in turn would boost Ireland's low marriage rate.

Although priority was given to creating new jobs for men, it was young single women who benefited most from the industrialisation programme of the 1930s. Despite evidence of additional tariff protection being granted to firms on condition that they hire men rather than women, the 1936 census showed that women filled 59 per cent of the new jobs created in manufacturing industry (primarily between 1932 and 1936).[101] By 1936 women comprised almost one-third of the manufacturing workforce compared to just over a quarter in 1926. Primarily centred on light manufacturing industries such as pharmaceuticals and electrical appliances, the new industries created involved assembly, low-grade processing and packaging—jobs carried out by women in other western economies.[102]

With male unemployment increasing during the 1930s, exacerbated by restrictions on emigration, the level of disquiet and resentment among politicians and male trade unionists at the rising numbers of women in industry continued to grow, despite women's low pay and status. Such attitudes had been increasing from the formation of the new Irish state, particularly in regard to married women at work, and reflected general public opinion. The latter was in part a result of Catholic social teaching, allied to the acute shortage of jobs and high emigration levels. During the 1920s the first legislative moves were introduced to curb female employment in the civil service. A ban on the employment of married women as primary teachers was implemented during the 1930s, followed by a complete marriage bar on women in the civil service. O'Dowd has argued that despite the early granting of women's franchise, subsequent Free State legislation seemed aimed at limiting the public role of women. The resulting barrier to the advancement of women in the civil services— and their mere token role at a higher educational level—greatly restricted the influence of women in shaping state intervention in the economy, health, welfare and the social services:

> Women were channelled instead into less powerful professions such as nursing, typing, clerical-secretarial work and shop-keeping. These were either ideologically reconcilable with their roles as wives and mothers, or else they replicated in the wages economy the caring and servicing functions they already undertook within the home.[103]

During the course of a Commission of Inquiry into the Civil Service held during 1932–35, a submission was made by a committee representing all grades of women civil servants. This submission provides an all too rare inside view of the issues concerning working women at this time. The committee made clear at the outset that the areas of dissatisfaction they would list were 'not altogether the result of conscious arrangement, but of tradition and custom ... much of it unconscious, some of it arising ... from men's feeling of chivalry towards our sex'.[104] While this may be seen as an attempt at appeasement in introducing their memorandum, the tone of their document leaves one in no doubt as to the strength of their feelings. In particular, they argued against differential scales, for equality of promotional opportunity, for the payment of widows on a par with married men, and suggested that women be retained in the service after marriage 'in cases where it would be obviously in the public interest to do so'. Arguing strongly on the issue of equal pay for equal work, they commented:

> The employment of women in the Service has increased enormously since the Treaty, but we cannot object too strongly to an extension which has no other object than the exploitation of our sex as cheap labour ... We bitterly resent the inferiority of status which lower pay for equal work creates.[105]

They also remarked caustically that:

> In An Saorstat equal pay for equal work among members of the Oireachtas has not meant the reduction of the allowance of unmarried men and women members. The *servants* of the Oireachtas are not so fortunate.[106]

Regarding equal opportunity, they pointed out that women comprised 37 per cent of general service grades, but only 3.5 per cent of posts higher than Clerical Officer. Noting the success rate of women when competing with men in examinations where sex is not known, they observed that it was hardly fortuitous that they are so rarely successful when they compete with men for promotion where sex is known:

> Since women are always allotted the lower scale of pay in each grade any additional differentiation against them, such as in this matter of promotion ... forces us to the conclusion that the price our sex must pay for freedom to choose the Service as a career has to be paid more than once.[107]

Commenting on the marriage bar they pointed out its implications for the employment of all women, not least the prospects of those unmarried women who remained in the service. While those forced to retire on marriage appear the most obvious victims of this rule, in fact all female civil servants suffered disadvantage regarding promotional opportunities on the basis that they *might* marry. The committee further argued that while the importance of the family is such that no one would dare to suggest that there is a disadvantage in the employment of married men, 'yet there is no hesitation in levelling against women the charge that their retirement on marriage is a loss to the State'.[108] With retirement on marriage being compulsory, they argued that widows should be reinstated if they so desire. In conclusion they emphasised that they asked for no special treatment, stating pointedly, 'We ask that the equality of treatment which has been granted to us in theory by the Constitution should be yielded in practice.'[109]

Mary Kettle, a member of the Commission, in an addendum to the Report, noted her disagreement with a number of the Report's findings. In regard to equal pay she dissented from paragraph no. 180 which argued that as it was 'the common practice of the community' to pay women less than men, it was beyond the scope of the Commission to investigate this beyond accepting that the average man, unlike the average women, was usually the head of a dependent household. Kettle argued that 'the fact that the general community acts in an unfair manner towards women is no justification for the Civil Service also doing so'.[110] Viewed against the backdrop of resistance to the employment of women, and the pending 1936 Conditions of Employment Act and the 1937 Constitution, the articulation of such strong arguments from female civil servants is particularly significant. Even more significant is the official ignoring of such views.

Diarmaid Ferriter has commented that 'the 1950s was the decade in which an ethos which tolerated, if not encouraged, the sanctification of deprivation was to be challenged', citing economist Liam Kennedy's view that:

The 1950s are etched in the popular imagination as the decade of crisis and stagnation in the Republic. Yet ... it was during the 1950s that the foundations for a decisive break with a mediocre past were laid. Investment in infrastructure and even more importantly, a variety of institutional innovations, helped lay the basis for future development.[111]

From the First Programme for Economic Expansion in 1958, through to Ireland's entry into the European Economic Community (EEC) in 1973, a series of radical measures were introduced in the fields of economics, trade, education, industrial relations, housing and communications with knock-on effects for unemployment and emigration. In his study of Ireland in the 1960s, Fergal Tobin has pointed to the vital *psychological* impact of that First Programme on a demoralised country, noting the real sense that, at last, a corner had been turned:

> The new economic policies of Seán Lemass and T.K. Whitaker were working, and for the first time since independence the prospect existed of a sustained improvement in the material prosperity of Irish people in Ireland.[112]

What was the impact of the resulting changes during the 1960s on the rights and opportunities for Irish women? Comparison with Northern Ireland again provides a remarkable contrast. The rising participation of women in the workforce in the North from 1960 contrasted with a corresponding decline in such participation by women in the Republic. A number of factors contributed to this. The economic success of the 1960s in the Republic and resulting prosperity led to a younger and higher marriage rate. The baby boom that followed saw more women leaving work to raise families. In addition, there was also a high discrepancy between the availability of part-time work in Northern Ireland and Britain and the Republic. The significant rise in Northern female participation was in large part due to the availability of such work for married women. In contrast, the level of part-time work for women in the Irish Republic was one of the lowest in the European Union; by 1984 only one employed woman in nine worked part-time.[113] Women comprised 25.5 per cent of women in the Irish workforce in 1966,[114] an almost identical figure to that of fifty years earlier. There were, however, some changes in the type of work available to women, and in the profile of working women. The most dramatic fall in women's work occurred in agriculture and domestic service, although it should be noted that the latter accounted for over 9 per cent of working women in 1961.[115]

Margaret MacCurtain has pointed out that the 1950s marked a high point in female religious vocations in Ireland, peaking around 1960 until 1972, and then declining decisively.[116] The high number of female religious up to mid-century—and their key role in social services—reduced career options available for lay women.[117] The number of women in manufacturing in 1961 remained at the 1951 level of 35 per cent, falling to 27 per cent by 1981. Areas of increased female employment included industrial employment, shop and clerical work, teaching and nursing. In a retrospective look at 1960s Ireland, Mary

Maher noted that with the exception of hairdressing, skilled trade apprenticeships were open only to boys, resulting in the average female school leaver without the Leaving Certificate entering that 43 per cent of the workforce employed as factory operatives, shop assistants, waitresses or servants. Of those whose families could afford second-level education, some 20 per cent of daughters worked in offices, 12 per cent entered the 'lower professions' of nursing and teaching, while less than 1 per cent entered the 'higher professions'.

Two key issues impacted on women's employment—education and the marriage bar. Maher has commented that 'career' was not in the vocabulary of girls in the early 1960s.[118] Nor does it appear to have been in the vocabulary of government, employers or trade unions in regard to women. Ferriter has suggested that up to the late 1950s 'There was still an ethos predicated on the idea that a woman working was acceptable in terms of economic necessity, but intolerable in the context of them having independent career ambitions'.[119] A sharp rise in female trade union membership during the 1960s—from 60,000 to 100,000—was mainly concentrated in white-collar employment. Often working alongside male colleagues performing the same work, these women were more conscious of unequal pay and lack of opportunities than women traditionally working in jobs exclusive to women.[120] The emergence of centralised pay bargaining during this decade emphasised such inequality, women receiving less than men in early national wage agreements. As a result of a more militant stance on the part of female trade unionists, allied to increased awareness within trade unions and government of impending equality concerns, from 1969 women in the public sector received equal increases with men. While equal pay was granted to a number of clerical workers in the semi-state sector, this did not apply across the board until later in the 1970s. Whereas in 1960 women workers received 53 per cent of the male rate, this increased to 54 per cent in 1969 and to 59 per cent in 1971, Daly noting that while a large gap still remained, gains in the latter two years had been greater than in the previous thirty.[121]

The marriage bar on women in the public service, reflected in a general acceptance within industry and society that women should not be employed after marriage, was a particularly significant factor in limiting opportunities for all women. As was noted within the Civil Service, the enforcement of a ban on married women had the effect of restricting women to the lower grades of work, and inhibited promotional opportunities on the basis that women *might* marry and

therefore could not be relied upon. At the time of Ireland's entry into the
EEC, only 7 per cent of married women were in the workforce.[122] The first
break-through in relation to the marriage bar occurred in the 1950s
partly due to a shortage of women national teachers and partly due to
the findings of the Commission on Emigration. At first allowed to work
on a temporary basis, in 1958 the marriage bar for married national
women teachers was repealed in 1958.[123] At second level, while the
marriage bar did not officially apply, in effect few schools employed
married women. During the 1960s, due to the loss of women through
early marriage, a shortage of women workers occurred in some areas,
and employers who had previously operated a formal or informal
marriage bar began to hire married women, often on a temporary basis.
Maher has pointed to the familiar classification of 'temporary married'
in many organisations at this time.[124] Even where such arrangements
applied, the lack of statutory maternity leave ensured their temporary
nature. Another disincentive to remaining at work was the high rate of
income tax applied to working wives, a factor noted in the 1972 Report of
the Commission on the Status of Women. The absence of equal pay for
equal work in addition to the above factors contributed to the low
participation rate by married women in the workforce. On entering the
EEC in 1973 Ireland had the lowest percentage of women working out of
eighteen countries. While the number of married women at work
increased from the late 1960s, reaching 20.4 per cent by 1981, this was still
only half the number of married women workers in Northern Ireland
and the UK.

There is no doubt that the many societal changes occurring during
the 1960s and 1970s profoundly altered the outlook and lifestyle of many
Irish people. The advent of television allied to the opening up of debate
on many social issues not previously discussed in a public arena, the
influence of the 1965 Investment in Education report followed by the
introduction of free education in 1967, the rise of a more consumer-
driven society, expansion in house building, increased opportunities for
foreign travel, growing exposure to the culture and ideas of Europe and
the US—including the impact of social unrest in these areas—all added
to the melting pot that was Ireland in the 1960s and 1970s—'after the
inertia of the fifties, here at last was life.'[125] Women too would be affected
by these factors, and Ireland's membership of the EEC from 1973, allied to
the 1972 Report of the Commission on the Status of Women and the
emergence of a radical women's liberation movement, would in time see
the articulation of significant demands by Irish women regarding their

role and participation in the work force.

Government appeared a reluctant partner in regard to women workers, attempting to postpone equal pay implementation in the 1970s, and backing an Industrial Development Authority campaign in the 1960s and 1970s for male-only industrial jobs.[126] On both issues the Government was unsuccessful, primarily due to EEC influence and growing demands for gender equality. Initially, Irish women themselves provided a paradox, using the improved economic situation of the 1960s to leave the labour force. A comparison can be made to Bourke's thesis that following a boom in the rural economy from the 1890s, Irishwomen abandoned farm-work to concentrate on home duties. The differing circumstances in 1960s Ireland, however, were hugely significant. Despite the scale of discriminatory practices against them, particularly in regard to pay and marriage, women were on the cusp of significant changes, changes in their working conditions and opportunities due to equality directives en route from Brussels, in the control of their fertility, in their educational opportunities, and above all in their self-image.

PART 4

Women in the New Irish State

THE QUEST FOR EQUAL CITIZENSHIP 1922–1938

Women have very little to hope for from political revolutions. Social revolutions offered an opportunity for reforms which go nearer to the heart of things and affect the lives of women more closely than mere political revolutions. (MARGARET CONNERY, *Irish Citizen* 1919)

WOMEN, WORK AND THE IDEOLOGY OF THE IRISH FREE STATE

During the decade before the establishment of the new state, a significant minority of Irish women had become increasingly articulate and active in feminist, nationalist and labour concerns. To the number of nationalist women involved before and during the Rising of 1916, many thousands more were added in the wake of the Rising. From this point up to the bitter political divisions caused by the Treaty in 1922, such women played a significant role in the development of the emerging state. Whereas many nationalist women active before 1916 held feminist beliefs, opting to put equality demands 'on hold' until independence was attained, most of those who joined post-1916 did so primarily on nationalist grounds. In the final issue of the suffrage paper the *Irish Citizen* in 1920, Hanna Sheehy Skeffington commented: 'There can be no woman's paper without a woman's movement, without earnest and serious-minded women readers and thinkers—and these in Ireland have dwindled perceptibly of late.'[1] State legislation regarding women's employment and public role during the opening decades of the fledgling state would instigate reaction from women activists of the suffrage era, and from a younger generation of women increasingly concerned at injustices in the new Ireland.

Following the extension of the parliamentary vote to women over 30 years in 1918, and the general election of that year in which women voted and stood as candidates for the first time, the *Irish Citizen* editorial declared:

> We want equal pay for equal work, equal marriage laws, the abolition of legal disabilities, the right of women to enter the hitherto banned learned professions, women jurors and justices, in short, the complete abolition of various taboos and barriers—social, economic and political—that still impede women's progress.[2]

Ten years on these objectives were still far from being attained. In 1930, Helena Molony advised women and the Labour movement to review their objectives and policy in the light of Connolly's writings, pointing out that:

> Women since his day, have got that once-coveted right to vote, but they still have their inferior status, their lower pay for equal work, their exclusion from juries and certain branches of the civil service, their slum dwellings, and crowded, cold and unsanitary schools for their children, as well as the lowered standard of life for workers, which in their capacity as home-makers, hits the woman with full force.[3]

It has been argued that as far as the political rights and constitutional status of women were concerned, the new Irish state of 1922 was all that might be desired.[4] The equality of rights and opportunities of all citizens guaranteed in the 1916 proclamation had been endorsed in the Free State constitution. Yet, early hopes that women would play a significant role in the new Ireland were soon quashed as a series of restrictive measures were introduced by government.

The first occasion that an intimation was given of such intent came in 1924 when, in a departure from legislation of 1919 (that had granted women the right to sit on juries) a Juries Bill was introduced providing for the exemption of women from jury service on application. The Cumann na nGaedheal Minister for Justice, Kevin O'Higgins, argued that the purpose of the 1924 Act was 'to get rid of the unwilling woman juror'.[5] Later he would claim that such equality had not been demanded by the Irish electorate, the 1919 Bill having been implemented only because Ireland was then still part of Great Britain.[6] Women's groups were alarmed at the proposal to exempt women purely on the grounds of sex, arguing that to allow women to evade the duties and responsibilities of citizenship was 'unfair to the men citizens and derogatory to the women'. They denounced this 'retrograde step' which they feared 'would open the door a little wider to the forces of reaction'.[7] Their fears were justified; 1925 saw the introduction of the Civil Service Regulation (Amendment) Act, and in 1927 a further Juries Bill, both designed to curtail the role of women. The former was an attempt to restrict women from entering higher-ranking civil service posts solely on the grounds of sex.

Under the terms of the 'Civil Service Regulation Act' passed in 1924, all competitive examinations were open equally to all persons born in Ireland or who were citizens of Ireland 'who possess the qualifications as to age'.[8] The Irish Women's Citizens' Association (IWCA) noted that all three Civil Service Commissioners appointed under the provisions of this Act were men. The Act gave the Minister for Finance power to confine any competitive examination 'to persons belonging to a specified class', but not, as the IWCA pointed out, to persons of one sex. However, in the autumn of 1925/6, advertisements were placed confining examinations for certain higher Civil Service posts to persons of one sex, but on legal advice this was found to be illegal, and the examinations were thrown open to women and men. The Civil Service Regulation (Amendment) Act was then proposed 'to do legally what was attempted to do illegally'.[9] (As with the 1924 Juries Bill, the government again disregarded existing legislation, in this case the 1919 Sex Disqualification Act and Article 3 of the 1922 Constitution, both of which guaranteed equality of opportunity regardless of sex). The Minister for Finance, Mr Blythe, explained that it was necessary to amend existing legislation because 'the Civil Service Commission had not power to confine examinations to members of one particular sex' and that 'in certain situations in the Civil Service you must discriminate with regard to sex'.[10]

A number of women's groups joined in protest against the proposed Bill, arguing that civil servants should be chosen for their competency, not their gender. The IWCA report noted that the comment of the Minister of Posts and Telegraphs regarding the efficiency of women in his department—'I wish I had none of them'—made women even more suspicious of the agenda behind this Amendment. In the Dáil, the Bill was supported by the only sitting female deputy, Margaret Collins-O'Driscoll, despite the fact that she was 'not enamoured of the Bill' and her recognition that it 'limited to a certain extent the appointments for which women were eligible'.[11] Although she was canvassed by 'very influential' women to vote against the bill, the Deputy justified her support for the measure by stating that she 'failed to see how it infringed upon women's rights under the Constitution'.[12] In the Seanad, however, both Eileen Costello and Jennie Wyse Power (Cumann na nGaedheal) strongly opposed the Bill, Costello describing it as both morally wrong and monstrously unfair. In her trenchant opposition to the Bill Wyse Power pointed to the unjustness of this 'sex discrimination (being) made by a male Executive Council and by practically a male Dáil' without any consultation with any women.[13] Drawing on her long involvement in nationalist politics, she noted the changing response to women's participation in public affairs, regretting that such a Bill had come 'from the men who were associated in the fight (for freedom) with women when sex and money were not considerations'. The forceful opposition of both Costello and Wyse Power were largely instrumental in the Bill being defeated by 20 votes to 9.[14]

The Juries Bill of 1927 provides a keen insight into the attitude of the Free State government towards the participation of women in public life. The Bill proposed to exempt women completely from jury service. This time, women's groups protested even more forcefully. The IWCA and the Irish Women's Equality League (IWEL) argued that on the one hand as women were equal under the law, they had a right to sit on juries, while on the other hand women's perspective would benefit the legal system.[15] Again, women's groups charged the government with violating its own Constitution, pointing to the equality of citizenship guaranteed under Article 3. The issue of mixed juries as a necessary factor in the interests of justice was raised by many, the Irish Women Workers' Union (IWWU) arguing that as both sexes were likely to stand in the dock as offenders, 'it is just and right that the question of their guilt should be submitted to juries consisting of both men and women'.[16] The advisability of women jurors on cases involving children and young girls was also stressed. For the government, Justice Minister Kevin O'Higgins argued that:

> The vast majority of the women citizens of this country, as of most countries, dislike this work, dislike it intensely, and would be grateful to the Government that would relieve them from it. We can afford to relieve them from it .... The machine will work without compelling the woman juror to come forward.[17]

In Dáil debate on the issue, O'Higgins's personal views were made quite clear. Asking if women who sought to participate in public life were the exception or the norm, he argued that 'it is the normal and natural function of women to have children ... (and) to have charge of households'. He dismissed those who objected to the proposed legislation as 'self-appointed spokesmen ... not representative of the vast majority of women in the state'. In fact, he argued, such groups were trying to force unwilling women into jury service because they saw the bill as a slight on their sex; rather, the Minister claimed, the government were relieving women of an unwanted and unnecessary obligation by, '(conferring) on women citizens all the privileges of citizenship and such of the duties of citizenship as *we* thought it reasonable to impose upon them'[18] (author's italics). O'Higgins informed the Seanad that frequently government had to prevent people getting something which they think they want and which would not be good for them, noting, 'In this matter I am really the champion of the women in the State, but I never expect to get any gratitude for that.'[19] In the latter regard he was correct, his arguments serving only to fuel women's opposition to his proposal. One area focused upon by women's groups was the government's justification of the new legislation based on the low number of women who actually served on juries. In a forceful letter to the *Voice of Labour*, Hanna Sheehy Skeffington challenged O'Higgins's assertion that few women had shown interest in jury service:

> For over three years practically no woman has been chosen by the State to serve on criminal cases, women being ordered en masse ... to 'stand aside' when they answered their name in court ... There is no record available, in fact, no note being taken of the numbers of women challenged by either State or prisoners, and Mr O'Higgins's statement, therefore, is based on a deliberate misrepresentation.[20]

Valiulis has pointed out that underlying the political controversy were two key questions, (1) whether women could claim a direct relationship to the state or should familial commitments take precedence; and (2) whether women had a right to participate in the public and political life of the state. O'Higgins's view was quite clear in articulating separate spheres for men and women. In the Dáil debate he argued that 'a few words in a Constitution do not wipe out the difference between the sexes, either physical or mental or temperamental or emotional'.[21] In the Seanad he described women's reproductive capacity as 'women performing the normal functions of womanhood in the State's economy'.[22] Consistently in both Dáil and Seanad the government saw no contradiction in taking away from women rights which they already enjoyed under the Constitution. Inside and outside parliament, women who demanded the right to jury service became increasingly categorised as 'abnormal', with 'normal' women being defined as those who accepted that their primary role was within the home. Newspapers of the day asserted that 'real women' or 'ladies' had no desire to serve on juries, to be wrenched from 'the bosoms of their families, from their cherished household duties, from the preparation of their husband's dinners'.[23] Those activists who fought against the Bill were described as 'nothing more than feminists who wanted women to imitate men', one paper declaring that 'The women of the Free State are not to be judged by their loud-voiced, self-constituted advocates, who are eternally spouting and writing to the newspapers and marching in processions'. It was argued in the Dáil that:

> Between the ages of twenty and forty the majority of women ... (have) a much more important duty to perform to the State than service on juries, that their functions were motherhood and looking after their families, and they objected to these other women, who have missed these functions, and who wanted to drive to serve on juries those who have something else to do.[24]

As a result of the women's campaign and strong opposition within the Seanad, the government accepted an amendment to the Bill, which although exempting women as a class from jury service, allowed individual women to have their names included on jury lists on application. Male ratepayers would be automatically called for jury service, women ratepayers would be eligible but had to volunteer. In this form the Bill became law, and remained in force until 1976.

The 1924 and 1927 Juries Bills and the 1925 Civil Service Act did not take place in isolation. Rather, they were introduced against a backdrop of social restrictions implemented during the first fifteen years of the IFS focusing on censorship and control. The Censorship of Films Act (1923), one of the first acts passed by the new government, allowed a male censor to cut and/or refuse a licence to films considered 'subversive of public morality'.[25] Divorce, which (in a law inherited by the IFS from the British) had been available by private parliamentary Bill, was banned in 1925. Margaret O'Callaghan has drawn attention to 'the shocking elections of the 1920s' during which 'vicious campaigns' by Catholic bishops, clergy and lay zealots 'attempted to destroy politically any Senate candidates believed to be at all sympathetic to divorce'.[26] A Committee of Enquiry on Evil Literature set up by the Minister for Justice in 1926 paved the way for The Censorship of Publications Act of 1929. This Act empowered a board of five men to prohibit the sale of any book or periodical it considered 'indecent or obscene', as well as all literature advocating birth control. On this latter issue directly affecting women, both clergy and politicians were adamant that birth control literature be excluded and that the issue should not even be open to discussion, 'public ignorance (being) seen as the best basis for maintaining public morality'.[27] This was made quite clear in a Dáil debate on the Bill in 1928 when the Minister for Justice declared, 'We have decided, call it dogmatically if you like, that this question shall not be freely and openly discussed.'[28] That some women were aware of the Bill's implications and were attempting to have amendments introduced is noted in the memoirs of Lucy Kingston, who wrote to other Quakers and political figures about what she described as 'an insidious move against birth control'.[29] Whyte has pointed out, however, that while the 1929 Bill made it illegal to advocate the use of contraceptives, their sale or importation was not banned for another six years.[30]

What role did the churches play in the development of a conservative and increasingly coercive society in the infant years of the new state? As early as 1925, at their meeting in Maynooth the Irish Catholic Bishops warned of a threat to traditional societal values of faith and purity, purity being considered particularly under threat.[31] Easier availability of imported books, magazines and films portraying more liberal lifestyles added to the concern of the clergy for the effect on young people, particularly young women. Evil, viewed by the bishops as intrinsically foreign, could, they believed, be banned and erased by strong censorship. Harder to contend with, however, was what Margaret O'Callaghan has described as the evil that came from within. In this latter regard, woman was considered the seat of temptation, a potential 'occasion of sin' at all times.[32] During the years following independence 'sexuality was increasingly seen as the site in which morality resided'. In 1927 the Catholic hierarchy issued a joint pastoral on 'The Evils of Modern Dancing' which listed the dance-hall, the bad book, the film and immodest fashions in female dress as contributing to the general decline of public morals.[33] 'Jazz-dancing' and unlicensed and unsupervised dance-halls were seen as a threat to sexual morality, and in particular female morality. The clergy, magistrates and newspapers continually blamed dancing and dance-halls for rape, illegitimacy and infanticide and a host of related evils.[34] In 1924, the Bishop of Galway, deploring the dance-craze, advised fathers, 'If your girls do not obey you, if they are not in at the hours appointed, lay the lash on their backs. That was the good old system, and that should be the system today.'[35]

Both North and South of the border accepted standards of female decorum and modesty were seen to be threatened by post-war fashion trends, the impact of Hollywood in this regard being viewed as a particularly baneful influence. In Belfast, Winifred Campbell recalled, the preachers' reaction to the fashion for bobbed hair, shorter skirts and low necklines resulted in the Churches stressing the need for religious revival and mission campaigns sprang up everywhere; 'We were preached to in the factory, at open-air meetings, lunch-time services.'[36] In the South, pastorals from the bishops and letters and articles in the press during the 1920s and 1930s continuously warned of the dangers to traditional Irish life. A contributor to the *Irish Independent* in 1926 bewailed: 'The cult of sex is everywhere. Sex is blazoned on our fashion plates, palpitates in our novels, revels in our ball-rooms.'[37] The Catholic Truth Society pointed the finger of responsibility directly at women:

> The women of Ireland, heretofore, renowned for their virtue and honour, go about furnished with the paint-pot, the lip-stick ... and many of them have acquired the habit of intemperance, perhaps one of the sequels to their lately adopted vogue of smoking. A so-called dress performance or dance today showed some of our Irish girls in such scanty drapery as could only be exceeded in the slave markets of pagan countries.[38]

The bishops admonished mothers 'who preferred talking on a platform or in a council chamber ... who shirked or neglected their duty to their children', to remember that 'you are Irish mothers: do not forget your glorious traditions ... Appear seldom on the promenade, and sit oftener by the cradles; come down from the platform and attend to the cot.' Some objections to modern fashions were class-based as 'modern dress defied hierarchy and did not signify one's place in the class structure.'[39] A significant controversy emerged in 1934 over the decision of the National Athletic and Cycling Association to allow women participate in the same meetings (but not the same events) as men. John Charles McQuaid, then president of Blackrock, wrote in protest to the Athletic Association decrying their 'unCatholic and un-Irish decision', later describing mixed athletics as a social and a moral abuse. McQuaid cited the Pope's view that the Christian modesty of girls must be safeguarded, 'it is supremely unbecoming that they should flaunt themselves and display themselves before the eyes of all.'[40]

Traditionally hostile to state interference on issues of family morality and welfare, nonetheless the Church now sought state legislation in these areas. Through Episcopal statements and lay campaigns, public debate on issues affecting women's private lives increasingly became male dominated. A particularly notable example of female exclusion in the 1920s was the unpublished Inter-Departmental Inquiry regarding Venereal Disease, under which a male committee heard only male witnesses.[41] That women were not involved was all the more noteworthy considering that as recently as 1918 Cumann na dTeachtaire had organised a conference of women's societies to consider 'the serious menace of venereal disease in Dublin', and the issue had received much coverage in the pages of the *Irish Citizen*.[42]

Was the conservatism of the new state as reflected in these Acts unique to a small, predominantly Catholic country recently emerged from civil war? On the contrary, it has been noted that similar conservative attitudes emerged worldwide following the 1914–18 war.[43] In the immediate post-war situation, emphasis hinged on population issues and on the need to reverse the fall in birth rates. Pro-family campaigns were initiated in almost all European countries, emphasis being placed on women's reproductive role. The dominant political ideologies of the decades following the Great War agreed that the role of women was within the family, developing 'the cult of the cradle'.[44] Suffrage activity had ceased in many countries during the war years, with voting rights being granted to most women post-war. The absence of a focused women's movement in the post-war years allied to national governments' emphasis on retrenchment and rebuilding helped the promotion of women's family role. The pre-dominance of conservative values during these years was strengthened by Catholic social thought and emergent fascism, all of which had fixed views regarding the role of women. Pro-family campaigns were mounted in almost all European countries in an effort to reverse the slide in birth rates.[45]

Within an Irish context, Margaret O'Callaghan has argued, the Irish hierarchy's revulsion against the anarchy and breakdown of social and familial bonds during the civil war was a strong element in determining the shape and ethos of the Irish Free State (IFS); in the years following the civil war the Catholic hierarchy asserted the immense authority of the Church of the majority in the IFS in the field of faith and morals.[46]

Both new Irish governments, North and South, were conservative and authoritarian. Within both states, the dominant church soon adapted to the new regime, each in time flexing their doctrinal and authoritarian muscle. Substantial theological differences between Catholics and Protestants over the role of women resulted in differing emphases on moral reform within the new states.[47] To this were added different attitudes on the role of the clergy. The unmarried Catholic clergy saw its role as an outside agency enforcing Catholic social thinking on the family and the role of women. Protestant clergymen—usually married—took a different perspective, directing the role of moral guardian to fathers and husbands within the family unit. The Presbyterian Church in Ireland was unique in debating the issue of female ministers during the 1920s, its General Assembly in 1930 agreeing the eligibility of women, although none was appointed for some fifty years.[48] Predominantly during these decades, a male voice—clerical or political—laid down the guidelines and rules to be followed by women. The steady exclusion of women from (already limited) areas of public life emphasised the male monopoly.

The 1930s saw the introduction of significant social and employment legislation which would impinge on Irish women for some forty years. The Criminal Law (Amendment) Act of 1934 dealt with the age of consent, contraception and prostitution. In 1930 a Committee under the chairmanship of William Carrigan, KC, had been appointed by the Cumann na nGaedheal government to consider if legislation in operation since the 1880s was in need of modification, and if new legislation was needed to deal with juvenile prostitution.[49] While amendments had taken place in England, Scotland and Northern Ireland during the 1920s, in the Free State the law was seen to be relatively more lenient with regard to sexual offences, particularly against young persons. An example of this was in the case of indecent assault where the age of consent had remained at 13 years. The report of the Carrigan committee presented to government in 1931, painted 'a bleak picture of "social conduct" in the country (which) was never released to the public'.[50] The Commissioner of the Civic Guard informed the Committee that:

> There was an alarming amount of sexual crime increasing yearly, a feature of which was the large number of cases of criminal interference with girls and children from 16 years downwards, including many cases of children under 10 years.[51]

The police estimated that less than 15 per cent of such cases were prosecuted due primarily to the difficulties of the prevailing judicial system which sometimes led to children 'being treated as accomplices in a crime rather than victims of an outrage'.[52] With Fianna Fáil in power from 1932 the new Minister for Justice, James Geoghegan, delivered a severely critical opinion on the Carrigan report to the Executive Council, recommending that it should not be published; 'that it contained sweeping statements against the state of morality in the Saorstát which, even if true, should not be given currency by publication'.[53] The *Irish Press* in 1932 subsequently published some of the committee's recommendations, principally that the age of consent (in the case of carnal knowledge) be raised from 16 years to 18 years, and that a female police force be established in Dublin. The latter had been long sought by women's groups.

An all-party Committee of Deputies was established by the Executive Council to consider what action should be taken in light of Carrigan's recommendations. This committee, chaired by Geoghegan, was more lenient than Carrigan regarding the age of consent, recommending it be raised to 17, not 18, but was less severe regarding contraceptives, not recommending a complete ban. Incorporating and amending the findings of the Carrigan report, the work of this committee formed the basis for the Criminal Law Amendment Bill of 1934. Some differences did arise between the Committee and the government drafters of the bill on the issue of contraception, articulated by the Minister for Local Government and Public Health, Seán T. Ó Ceallaigh. The latter disagreed with the proposal to allow qualified medical practitioners prescribe and supply contraceptive appliances to their patients, views which were also reflected in correspondence to the Department of Justice.[54] Under this Act it was proposed that:

- the age of consent be raised from 16 to 17 in respect of carnal knowledge or attempted carnal knowledge
- the age of consent be raised from 13 to 15 in respect of indecent assault
- prostitution be controlled through heavier fines and greater powers for the police
- the importation and sale of contraceptives be banned.[55]

The sections of the Bill regarding the age of consent and prostitution received particular attention from women's societies, social workers and women Senators, all acutely aware of the need for increased protection of women and children. While the broad thrust of the bill was generally welcomed by such groups, controversy ensued on particular sections. A Senate committee formed to examine the Bill (which unlike the Government Committee did have women members) suggested a number of amendments. One such amendment proposed that the age of consent in the case of indecent assault be raised from 15 years to 18 years, it being pointed out by Senator Kathleen Browne that 'we are giving less protection to our young girls than the governments of Great Britain and Northern Ireland'.[56] The amendment was ultimately defeated in the Dáil, the Minister describing it as 'absurd'. Regarding prostitution, women's groups sought equality of treatment in law for a woman found soliciting and her client.[57] While the proposed bill referred to 'Every common prostitute who is found loitering', the Senate special committee proposed as an alternate wording, 'every person who in a street or public place solicits or importunes any person of the opposite sex for an immoral purpose'.[58] In aiming to penalise men as well as women, the Senate proposal marked a departure from accepted double standards of morality.

Clancy has noted that the Minister could not accept these recommendations, finding them 'unworkable', commenting that men who solicited women could be dealt with under existing law 'for insulting behaviour'. Women found guilty of soliciting under the new Government Bill, however, could be penalised by a possible six month prison sentence.[59] The spirit of the Contagious Diseases Acts of the nineteenth century and 1918 in which responsibility for sexual morality was held to rest solely with women can be seen to live on in this section of the Bill.

It has been noted that less debate took place among women's groups on the proposed ban on the sale of contraceptives and contraceptive devices. Whereas feminists were in broad agreement on the other areas of the Bill, there were mixed opinions on this subject.[60] The fact that the country was 90 per cent Catholic, while significant, was not the only contributing factor as differences of opinion occurred across religious divides. Debate on the issue did take place in the Senate, however, with Kathleen Clarke being successful in the deletion of the relevant section in the Special Committee. In his support of contraception, Senator Oliver St John Gogarty referred to the 'dreadful alternative' of infanticide.[61] This issue had been raised earlier in the Dáil by Deputy Rowlette who had concluded that Section 17 of the Act 'would be likely to lead to an increase in crimes such as criminal abortion and infanticide'.[62] Awareness of the extent of this problem has been noted by O'Callaghan, citing an infanticide trial in Cork in the late 1920s, when the presiding judge commented that 'infanticide has become a national industry in parts of this country. The numbers of newly-born illegitimate children murdered is very great'.[63] Notwithstanding Senate attempts, the ban on contraception was retained in the government bill. The Criminal Law (Amendment) Bill became law in February 1935.

A significant consequence of the debate on the issues contained in the Bill—and of unease at the resulting legislation amongst women's groups—was the formation in March 1935 of the Joint Committee of Women's Societies and Social Workers (JCWSSW).[64] In its 50-year commemoration report, the JCWSSW pointed to both the 1931 Carrigan Report and the 1934 Criminal Law Amendment Bill as deciding factors in its formation. Not surprisingly, therefore, the Joint Committee sought the raising of the age of consent, similar laws regarding prostitution for both men and women, the establishment of a female police force, an increase in the number of Probation Officers, and the restoration of the right of jury service to women. An interview with the Minister for Justice was at first refused, but eventually granted. The Minister, while promising to consider the issue of women police, appeared more interested in the idea of additional Probation Officers, of which there were then only two in Dublin. As the IWRL had done twenty years earlier, committee members arranged to attend the Courts regularly to monitor sentencing of women charged with soliciting, a practice which revealed that almost automatically such women were sentenced to six months on the testimony of one policeman. Other issues the Committee campaigned for were the right to visit women prisoners (a campaign which took seven years), legal adoption (attained in 1952/3), and better representation of women in the newly formed Senate.[65]

The response of succeeding governments to the question of women police, however, is intriguing. Extending from the years of suffragist activity while Ireland was still under British rule through the Free State and into the new Irish Republic, a series of government ministers baulked at the idea of a female police force. The only exception in more than forty years occurred during World War I, when through the influence of Anna Haslam and the IWSLGA a number of women's patrols received the approval of the Dublin Metropolitan Police Force to help in its fight against immorality on the Dublin streets. Limited in scope and authority (they had no powers of arrest) the patrols were viewed by the IWSLGA as 'merely a preliminary step to greater things'.[66] After independence, however, far from expanding, the existing members of the 'Dublin Women's Police Force' were allowed to dwindle away.[67] Both Cumann na nGaedheal and Fianna Fáil governments failed to implement the demands of women's groups in this regard, one women's delegation being told in 1939 that 'the agitation for women police is an artificial business without any real roots in the country'.[68] Other reasons cited over the years were lack of funds and the lack of toilet facilities for women at Garda Barracks.[69] Official attitudes to the idea of women police were no doubt influenced by contemporary views regarding 'proper' roles for women during the 1920s and 1930s, attitudes that would be re-enforced by further legislation.

The legislation of the 1920s regarding women's role in society was but a foretaste of what would follow during the 1930s. Women's employment was the focus of significant legislation during this decade. One key development occurred in 1932 with the ban on married female primary school teachers. Among five reasons cited by government in support of this measure was the belief that women could not satisfactorily attend both to home and school duties, plus the fact that the removal of married women teachers would create more employment opportunities for other women. In addition, at a time of high unemployment, such a move would reduce social tensions in rural areas where double income couples were resented by families with at best a single income.[70]

In his study of this topic Eoin O'Leary has pointed to two significant factors. Firstly, although women comprised 60 per cent of its membership, the re-organisation of the INTO between 1917–19 by its General Secretary T.J. O'Connell, allied to its affiliation to the ITUC and Labour Party, saw women's influence in the organisation diminished. Earlier provision for the retention of two places on its Central Executive (CEC) for women was discontinued, and during the years 1932–1934 when the introduction of the marriage bar was under debate, there were no women on the CEC, nor were any women included in INTO delegations to the ITUC. In addition, O'Leary notes, 'O'Connell believed that an important motive behind the introduction of the marriage bar was government's wish to gain the rural vote'.[71] Despite its majority female membership, the ban was accepted reluctantly and under pressure by the INTO on the condition that existing teachers be exempted. Daly has pointed out that the INTO argument was based on the latter consideration rather than on the principle of a woman's right to equal treatment in the workforce.[72] Six years later, all women teachers were compelled to retire at age 60 rather than 65. As a result, female teachers who had not achieved 40 years' service before retirement did not qualify for a full pension. When de Valera became Minister for Education in 1939, O'Connell notes that during a series of interviews held by the INTO with him, 'this was one subject on which he was particularly adamant in his refusal even to give it any consideration'.[73]

A similar marriage bar was soon applied to the civil service. Pointing out that this measure was detrimental to single women also—ruining their promotional prospects—Mary Kettle, a consistent campaigner for the removal or modification of the ban, argued that 'women from their entry (to the service) until they reach the ages of 45 or 50 are looked on as if they were loitering with intent to commit a felony—the felony in this case being marriage'.[74] In a submission to the Commission of Inquiry into the Civil Service during the early 1930s, representatives of women civil servants argued that the marriage bar depreciated the value of all women because of some women. As it was mainly young women who retired to marry, they noted that the bar 'unfairly hits the experienced middle-aged women who will spend their lives in the service'.

One enterprising young woman found a way around the marriage bar. Vera Carey was appointed Leitrim County Librarian in 1936 at the age of twenty-five, married in 1940 and submitted her letter of resignation as required. Vera Carey McCarthy did not want to give up her job. When she was asked to stay on until a new Country Librarian was appointed, she agreed. Vera consulted her brother, a solicitor, who scrutinised the relevant government bill in detail, and discovered that while it required a woman in the public service to resign her post on marriage, nowhere in the bill did it forbid a married woman from applying for such a post. Vera subsequently applied for her old job, and as the most experienced and best qualified candidate, was re-appointed by Leitrim County Council in 1941. This decision had repercussions both at local level, with pressure being put on county councillors not to appoint her, and at national level where an amendment to the existing legislation was introduced to prevent a recurrence. Meanwhile, Vera continued to work as County Librarian until 1974.[75]

Ireland was not unique in passing such legislation. Throughout Europe governments cut the numbers of married women in employment, and increasingly those women who worked were channelled into the 'caring' occupations, school curricula emphasising domestic economy for girls. In Germany, the total number of married women employed in the postal service fell from 2,718 to 21 between 1922 and 1923.[76] Similarly, Italian fascists also limited female participation in the workforce. Women's salaries in Italy were cut 50 per cent in 1927, and in the 1930s the number of women working in government offices was reduced to 10 per cent. As in Ireland, women were limited to the lower sections of the civil service.[77] It was against this international background, allied to the effects of the Great Depression and the Irish economic war with Britain, that restrictions on women's employment were introduced in the 1930s.

The ostensible aim of the 1936 Conditions of Employment Act was to improve working conditions by imposing a maximum 48-hour working week, guarantee one week's paid holiday, and establish controls regarding overtime.[78] As such, it was in line with International Labour Office policy. But the bill, which had been drafted by the Minister for Industry and Commerce following detailed consultation with male trade union leaders, gave the minister power under Section 16 to prohibit and/or control the employment of women in certain industries:

> The Bill was recognised as a clear attempt to alleviate economic depression by removing women from the workplace and giving their jobs to men; it also gave unlimited power to the Minister.[79]

In particular, the Bill sought to restrict the number of working-class women in paid employment. O'Dowd has pointed out that implementation of such a bill would have been most unlikely north of the border given the number of Unionist linen barons employing large numbers of women in their factories. In the South, however, the expanding role of women in manufacturing under Fianna Fáil's protectionist policies engendered fear in labour circles that women would be used to undercut male employment and wage levels.[80]

The campaign by the IWWU against the implementation of Section 12 of the Act was carried out within the trade union movement, on the political front, and in the public arena through the media and public meetings. Within the trade union and labour movement, the women's case received little if any support. Male trade union leaders supported the proposed legislation, viewing with alarm rising male unemployment figures. In contrast the 1930s saw a marked increase in unskilled female employment, partly due to new light industries and partly to the mechanisation of some existing industries. By 1936 women accounted for 31 per cent of the manufacturing workforce compared with 26 per cent ten years earlier. Ironically, while this period saw an increase in female trade union membership, primarily within mixed unions, such unions 'rarely articulated the point of view of women workers, nor did they do anything to reduce inequalities in pay and career prospects for women workers'.[81] When confronted with strong opposition from within their own ranks of labour and trade unionism—and sometimes from women colleagues—women trade unionists remained 'a weak and financially vulnerable minority in a predominantly male movement'.[82] It was left to the Irish Women Workers' Union (IWWU) to carry the flag on behalf of women workers, and as noted earlier within this union too there were differences of opinion and concessions to prevailing views regarding married women and employment.

Louie Bennett and the IWWU executive were fearless in their confrontation with politicians on the proposed new Act, in particular the Minister, Seán Lemass. Section 12 of the Bill, published in May 1935, gave the Minister power to ban women workers from certain industries and to restrict the number of women workers within other industries. Bennett argued that:

> By this bill women's security of employment was placed unreservedly in the power of the Minister for Industry. They had no power to appeal against any arbitrary decision he might make, and it must be clearly understood that his motive was not concern for the welfare of women workers.[83]

In a letter to the *Irish Press* ahead of the Dáil debate on the Bill, Bennett responded to one critic who argued man's right to be the protector and breadwinner, asking what man would carry out this role for widows or elderly spinsters: 'If women were to claim as their birthright a life of "protection and idleness", would the State provide their dole, and would men pay further taxes to finance the collective needs of the female species?'[84] During a deputation by Bennett and her union colleagues to Lemass, he assured them that women's current employment would not be affected, his concern being directed at the new industries. The deputation did not believe this as word had already reached them of the planned re-allocation of traditionally female work to men in some of the Dublin laundries.[85]

While the IWWU stance received little support from trade unionists or politicians, it did receive strong support from women's groups at home and abroad. Among Irish groups who opposed the bill were the Irish Women's Citizens' Association (IWCA), the National Council of Women of Ireland (NCWI), the National University Women Graduates Association (NUWGA) and the Dublin University Women Graduates Association (DUWGA). In September 1935 the League of Nations Conference in Geneva planned to debate the issue of equality for women at work. In advance of this, the NCWI asked the IWWU to prepare a memorandum on the subject and to hold a conference to debate the status of women. A memorandum issued by Bennett on behalf of this conference, and forwarded to the Women's Consultative Committee at Geneva, noted Irishwomen's expectation that the establishment of a native government would have ensured female equality with men:

> In certain matters such as the citizenship laws, [women's] hopes have been justified, but more recent legislation shows a violent movement in the opposite direction, depriving women of fundamental liberties, and suggesting that the Government is permitting itself to be influenced by the incentive which is overthrowing democratic freedom and establishing bureaucratic dictatorships in certain European states.[86]

In addition to Irish women's 'disappointment and resentment' at the proposed legislative controls on women's employment, other areas of concern raised in the memorandum included the marriage bar in the public service, non-compulsory jury service for men and women, differential salary scales for male and female teachers, and the issue of nationality being recognised only through the father. Bennett sent a copy of this memorandum to President de Valera, who subsequently met a deputation of women to discuss the status of women in the Free State. The success of this meeting can be gauged from Bennett's report to the IWWU executive that the president 'could not see how men and women could be equal'.[87] When the League of Nations Conference passed a resolution to investigate the status of women in all member nations, the IWWU requested that Seán Lemass suspend Section 12 of the Conditions of Employment Bill pending examination by the International Labour Office in Geneva. This Lemass refused to do. The IWWU increased its publicity campaign, using posters, leaflets, newspaper articles and advertisements. Internationally, associated women's groups were kept informed of developments through the pages of the *International Women's News* (a continuation of a former suffrage paper). In this, details were published of Free State legislation affecting the status and equality of women. Many of the issues raised in this paper and other international women's journals reflected the growing restrictions on women during the 1930s, particularly under fascist regimes.

Following the establishment of the League of Nations inquiry in 1935, a protest meeting against the Conditions of Employment Act was held in Dublin's Mansion House. Many well-known women spoke against the proposed legislation, including Professor Mary Hayden, Hanna Sheehy Skeffington and Dorothy McArdle. Shades of suffrage activism emerged with the formation of a standing committee representing various women's organisations. Working in tandem with the IWWU this committee, of which Bennett was chair, initiated a further publicity campaign to oppose the bill and inform the public of its implications.[88]

In the Dáil, none of the three women TDs spoke for or against the proposed bill. On the other hand, as before, women Senators were most vocal in their opposition.[89] When it came to an attack on the rights of women, old political adversaries such as Jennie Wyse Power and Kathleen Clarke buried their differences.[90] Wyse Power recalled the hopes of those young girls who had lost their jobs following the 1916 Rising, but who had faith that 'when our own men are in power, we shall have equal rights'. Clarke, responding to the accusation that 'the feminists have run riot' over the Bill, stated that although she was sympathetic to the feminist movement, 'her opposition to Section 16 of the Bill was based on nationalist grounds, and specifically on the 1916 Proclamation which granted equal rights to all citizens'. Both women criticised Labour Party support for the Bill, Clarke wondering what Connolly's attitude would be, and pointing out that the proposed 'very dangerous' legislation represented 'the thin end of the wedge against women'.[91] An amendment to have the section deleted was moved by Clarke, and supported by both Wyse Power and Kathleen Browne. Ultimately, however, the amendment was defeated by 19 votes to 14.

Objection to working wives was not restricted to traditional Catholic circles. In February 1937, the *Irish Times*' leader page criticised marriages based on the 'fifty-fifty' principle of joint earners, declaring that 'one of the great tragedies of today (is) that marriage on the old-fashioned basis becomes increasingly difficult'. Noting that too often the 'fifty-fifty' principle prevailed without justification, the article stated:

Hundreds of married women, whose husbands already draw adequate salaries, hold jobs in Dublin today, thereby closing them against unmarried women, and often against men who are in dire need of work. Such cases, we think, demand investigation, not only on the score of justice, but also on the ground that a dangerous view of the marriage state is being inculcated. Some day, please Heaven! the nation will be so organised that work will be available for every man, so that he may marry and assume the burdens of a home, and for every women until she embarks upon her proper profession— which is marriage. In that more prosperous nation there will be no question of the woman who 'will not allow marriage to interfere with her career'.[92]

With the Conditions of Employment bill passed, the NCWI formed a Standing Committee to monitor all future legislation affecting women.[93] Louie Bennett was its chairwoman, Dorothy McArdle its vice-chair. This group, along with the NUWGA, the JCWSSW and the IWWU, would form an experienced and vocal coalition in opposition to any further restrictive legislation. And as they suspected, they did not have long to wait to exercise their skills. It was known that de Valera had been considering a new Constitution for some time. Mary Kettle, in an address to the NUWGA in December 1935 urged her audience to vigilance regarding the constitutional position of women, noting that while equality of citizenship had been conferred on women through the existing constitution and the proclamation of 1916, 'men had little by little begun to take away what they had conferred'.[94] In May 1936 de Valera abolished the Senate. In preparation for the introduction of his new constitution, de Valera established a commission to advise him as to how the reformed second house should be composed.[95] The abolition of the Senate had been expected, legislation to this effect having been introduced and held in abeyance since 1934. A series of senate rejections of government bills allied to its composition paved the way for this action. Lyons has noted that long before relations between Fianna Fáil and the Senate became acute, Seán Lemass had spoken in support of a Dáil elected Senate, commenting 'if there is to be a second house, let it be a second house under our thumb. Let it be a group of individuals who dare not let a squeak out of them except when we lift our fingers to give them breath to do it.'[96] It was therefore, not by coincidence, that the proposed new Constitution was introduced in the early summer of 1937 under single-chamber government.

Following the senate abolition, the JCWSSW sought a meeting with de Valera to discuss the constitutional and economic position of Irish women and their representation in a reformed Senate. After further letters, and two refusals, he finally met their representatives in January 1937.[97] The IWWU also attended this meeting, having forwarded a memorandum to the President with suggestions for the inclusion of women in the Second Chamber. General issues of concern regarding equality in law and employment were also raised by the delegation. Although de Valera promised to consider the proposals put forward by the women, his comments that 'any inadequacy in the representation of women in the legislature and in public bodies was attributable to the state of public opinion' and that 'it would be difficult to do anything to give women a larger place in public life while public opinion remains as it is' did not augur well.[98] Following this deputation Rosamund Jacob commented that de Valera 'badly needs to be taught a lesson, if only there were enough women with the guts to do it'.[99] An IWWU recommendation—supported by the JCWSSW—that to enable adequate representation of women in the new Senate a further panel should be included for nominations to represent Public Health and Social Services would appear to have been included in the panel 'Public Administration and the Social Services'. But as the new Senate became in fact a nominating body for TDs and county councillors for party loyalists or ex-politicians, the benefit to women was minimal. Maurice Manning has pointed out that while each Taoiseach had the power to nominate eleven members, between 1937 and 1977 only eleven women were so nominated.[100]

In May 1937 de Valera published his draft constitution. Not too much time was provided for debate on the matter as it was planned to hold a referendum on the constitution on the same day as the pending general election, 1 July. Political, not religious motives were the primary reasons for a new constitution; the need for a specifically Irish document with no reference to the British crown, and provision for a head of state to be elected by the people was considered paramount. Many other aspects of the 1922 and 1937 constitution retained much in common, particularly regarding executive responsibility, an independent judiciary, and a two-chamber parliament. But as Whyte points out, there was one other important difference between the two constitutions:

> The 1922 constitution had been a typical liberal-democratic document which would have suited a country of any religious complexion ... The corresponding articles of the 1937 constitution, however, were obviously marked by Catholic thought.[101]

Noting the gradual enforcement of Catholic moral standards through legislation over the previous decade, Whyte has described the constitution of 1937 as 'the coping stone of this development'. The social clauses of the constitution were particular examples of this ideal, and it was with these clauses that women's groups would find greatest difficulty. Articles 16, 40, 41 and 45 all contained clauses with specific references to women. Article 40, while stating that all citizens would be held equal before the law, noted that this would not prevent the State in its enactments having 'due regard to differences of capacity, physical and moral, and of social function'.[102] In Article 41(1), it was noted in particular that 'by her life within the home, woman gives to the State a support without which the common good cannot be achieved', going on in Article 41(2) to note the State's endeavour to ensure that 'mothers shall not be obliged by economic necessity to engage in labour to the neglect of their duties in the home'.[103] Article 45(2) declared that 'The State shall endeavour to ensure that the inadequate strength of women and the tender age of children shall not be abused, and that women and children shall not be forced by economic necessity to enter avocations unsuited to their sex, age or strength'.[104]

Immediately the text of the constitution was made public, women's groups sprang into action. The NUWGA, along with the JCWSSW and the IWWU, launched a campaign to have the offending clauses deleted. Within the NUWGA, three women professors—Mary Hayden, Mary Macken and Agnes O'Farrelly—along with Hanna Sheehy Skeffington were particularly vocal in their opposition. Having formed an emergency committee to co-ordinate its protest and to seek a meeting with de Valera, the NUWGA sought the deletion of the offending articles which, they argued, would 'leave the door open for reactionary legislation against women in every department', and the retention of Article 3 of the 1922 constitution which had guaranteed the equality of all citizens. Omission of the latter equality provision they described as 'sinister and retrogressive'.[105] Under Article 16 it was feared that voting rights could be removed from women on the grounds of incapacity or disability. Hanna's sister—Mary Kettle—was also very active in this campaign with the JCWSSW of which she was chairperson.

With such a short period before the referendum in which to influence politicians and voters, time was of the essence. A 'fighting fund', set up by the NUWGA, funded an active media campaign of advertisements on hoardings and in the press, along with a stream of letters and articles in the main newspapers articulating their objections to the clauses.[106] The

JCWSSW pointed out to women voters the manner in which their rights had been undermined, the offensive articles being described as 'an attack upon our fundamental rights as human beings and contrary to the principles of the founders of this state'.[107] The IWWU was also to the front in attacking the proposed articles, Louie Bennett's letter to de Valera in this regard receiving much publicity in *The Irish Times*. Pointing out that certain sections were dangerous 'not so much for what they actually state as because of their ambiguity and the implications that may be given to them', she stated that the IWWU objected to Articles 40, 41 and 45. The latter she argued was the most indefensible from a woman's point of view as 'it takes from women the right to choose their own avocation in life'.[108] Dorothy MacArdle wrote to de Valera in May 1937 outlining her complete agreement with Louie Bennett, commenting:

> The real crux is the question of employment. The language of certain clauses suggests that the State may interfere to a great extent in determining what opportunities shall be open or closed to women, and there is no clause whatever to counterbalance that suggestion or to safeguard women's rights in this respect.[109]

When, after intense lobbying de Valera received deputations from all the main women's groups, a number of modifications were conceded. Article 16 was amended to include the phrase 'without distinction of sex'; 'the inadequate strength of women' in Article 45 was replaced with 'the strength and health of workers, men and women', and a further reference to 'women' was replaced by 'citizens'. Further than this de Valera would not go. He remained convinced that the conceded amendment to Article 16 was not necessary, the phrase in question only having been removed to avoid insulting women by reminding them of how recently they had won the suffrage.[110] Lee has commented that by his particular attention to the place of woman 'within the home', de Valera made quite clear his opinion that this was the only proper place for her.[111] An example of this was his rejection of an amendment suggested by Louie Bennett substituting woman's work 'for the home' for the phrase 'life within the home'.[112] In his introduction of the Constitution in the Dáil de Valera emphasised his views. Stating that he did not care who said he was reactionary in his aim that the breadwinner 'who is normally and naturally the father of the family' should have sufficient income to do so and that women should not have to neglect their duties in the home by going out to work, he declared, 'I do not care what women's organisation there are ... I am going, as long as I live, to try and work for that.'[113]

This provision was to be honoured more in the breach than in the observance. Male wages were not raised to prevent mothers of poor families being forced to work outside the home, and the idea that Irish society placed special value on motherhood *per se* was 'an illusion fostered by the constitution' which diverted attention from the social and economic facts unpinning low marriage rates and high female emigration.[114]

At this point the IWWU ceased its involvement in the campaign, Bennett explaining in a letter to *Labour News* that while the IWWU still stood shoulder to shoulder with women's groups fighting for full equal rights for women in Ireland, there was a difference of opinion as to the best methods of carrying on that fight. Considering that the amendments attained had removed the really serious menace to the position of women, it was the belief of her committee that 'our task now is to direct public opinion in such a way as to prevent any possible attempts to draw from any Section of this Constitution an incitement to sex discrimination'[115] (see Chapter 8). The other groups involved were disappointed, recognising the weakening effect of such action. But they determined to carry on. After the Dáil passed the draft constitution on 14 June, the three remaining groups embarked on an intensive campaign urging voters to reject the constitution in the forthcoming referendum.

In addition to a series of charged public meetings, women voters were targeted in particular through the press, and through a postcard and poster campaign asking, 'do you realise that your rights are being filched from you under the new constitution?'[116] A handbill warned women that Article 40 left the door 'invitingly open to legislation against women' while also permitting class and sex distinction; article 41 was deemed to allow state interference in the home, while Article 45 indicated discrimination against working women in their choice of occupation.[117] Their protest campaign culminated in a public meeting in Dublin's Mansion House attended by 1,500 women. That de Valera was needled by this campaign is clear from attacks made by him on the women's stance during pre-election rallies when he told listeners, 'There is nothing in the Constitution which is an attack on women's rights, there is nothing in it to cause woman to fear that she will be denied any opportunity of earning her bread.'[118] Despite the efforts of the combined women's groups, the Constitution was passed by 685,105 votes to 526,945. Hanna Sheehy Skeffington commented that this result 'puts us back into the tyranny of the pots and pans'.[119] The reasons given why a majority of women did not vote against it are numerous, including party political loyalties, republican non-recognition of the Free State, and public acceptance of the Catholic social principles inherent in the constitution. Primarily, however, as Caitriona Beaumont has noted:

> For many women equality was an abstract concept which had little to do with the everyday necessities of life. For women who struggled to feed and clothe their families, a political debate raging in Dublin about women's equality was of little relevance.[120]

Despite their failure to achieve all the amendments they had fought for, it has been pointed out that those attained were not without significance. The modification of Article 45 to remove the phrase 'inadequate strength of women' was noteworthy in view of de Valera's insistence on the inclusion of that concept. Similarly, despite his protestations that the phrase 'without distinction of sex' was unnecessary, its subsequent inclusion in Article 16 'represented an important achievement for critics both inside and outside the Dáil'.[121] Lee has noted that despite winning the election, Fianna Fáil suffered a sharp setback in its popular vote— the first in five elections. Its share of the vote fell from 49.7 per cent to 45.3 per cent, and it lost its absolute Dáil majority, winning just half of the 138 seats.[122] In a radio broadcast in 1938 de Valera admitted that the women's campaign against the constitution had encouraged people to vote against it, and had lost Fianna Fáil votes.[123] Criticism of the women's stance outlived the campaign. In December 1937 *The Irish Press* denounced Mary Hayden and her fellow campaigners as enemies of the state, vilifying their uncompromising opposition to the restrictions on women implicit in the new constitution; their support of women's right to work saw them described as enemies of the Church.[124] Under the heading 'Women Graduates Again', its editorial of 17 December 1937 commented:

> It would seem that the body of women styling themselves the Emergency Committee of the National Women Graduates Association are still determined to carry on their campaign against *Bunreacht na hÉireann*, that they are not ashamed to rely on the most unblushing perversion and misrepresentation of its provisions with regard to the status and rights of women, in order to mislead the public with respect to its true purport ... this group

of University women are in actual revolt against the authority and teaching on the questions at issue of Pope Pius XI ... They are deliberately placing themselves in opposition to the advice, the solemn exhortation, the paternal admonition given by the venerated Head of the Catholic Church to all who would listen to his voice as to the position, the sphere, the duties of women ... We think ... it a case where the women of the country may well pray to be saved from the advocacy of the academic group who have constituted themselves their champions, who have set themselves in opposition to and in conflict with the principles laid down by the Pope for the guidance of the nations.

Were these then the steps that brought about what Mary Robinson has described as 'the non-participation of women in the new Irish state'?[125] For many who had been active within labour, nationalist, and feminist circles, the state that emerged from the mid-1920s became a travesty of what they had expected. The equality of all citizens and both sexes had been endorsed in the 1916 Proclamation and in the Constitution of 1922, forming women's expectations of their right to full participation in the life of the new state. Independence quickly saw the silencing of radicalism, particularly in regard to social legislation and the role of women. Political leaders between 1922 and 1937 displayed an attitude towards the role of women in the new state 'which was as remarkable for its consensus as it was for its conservatism'.[126] In particular, the opposition of Kevin O'Higgins and Éamon de Valera to a public role for women was instrumental in the passing of a series of restrictive legislative measures. The road map for the role and status of women in Ireland during the first fifty years of the state was established by criteria laid down by church and state during the 1920s and 1930s. By its actions during the 1920s regarding women's employment and their rights to jury service, the Cumann na nGaedheal government sent a very clear message to Irish feminists, 'the struggle for women's equality in the Free State was far from over.'[127] It is true that the campaign against the 1927 Juries Bill gave women's groups a focus, post-suffrage, that would be important in organising resistance to further restrictive legislation in the 1930s.[128]

From a long-term perspective, the effect of the 1927 Bill was the virtual exclusion of women from jury service for almost fifty years. Mary Robinson has noted that between 1963 and 1973 a total of nine women in the entire country applied to have their names inserted in the jury list. Only three of these actually served on a jury during that ten-year period.

Exploring the broader significance of this, Robinson has pointed out:

> Down the years the assessment of criminality has been an entirely male assessment. It is men alone who have decided on guilt in cases of rape, drunken driving causing death, murder, etc. The male jury has been addressed by male barristers, both for the State and for the particular defendant, and after verdict the sentence has been imposed by a male Judge.[129]

Rosaleen Mills, a feminist activist from the 1940s, recalled the outrage of her female colleagues that young girls charged with infanticide and prostitution were judged by twelve men.[130] The 1927 Bill remained in force until 1975 when two women challenged the constitutionality of the jury system as being discriminatory both on the grounds of sex and of property. The Supreme Court upheld their claim on both grounds and held that the relevant provisions of the Juries Act 1927 were incompatible with the Constitution.[131] In a vindication of women's claims made almost fifty years earlier, Mr Justice Walsh noted in his Judgment that 'the provision made in the Act of 1927, is undisguisedly discriminatory on the grounds of sex only'.[132] Similarly, Mr Justice Henchy observed, 'it is incompatible with the necessary diffusion of rights and duties in a modern democratic society that important public decisions, such as voting, or jury verdicts involving life or liberty, should be made by male citizens only.'[133]

Commenting that 'most descriptions of women's lives in independent Ireland provide a dreary litany of legislative and administrative restrictions on women's rights', Mary Daly has argued that the historiography of women in the early years of the Irish state, as articulated by Irish feminists during the past two decades, may have been unduly influenced by issues which loomed larger in women's lives in the 1980s than in the 1920s. Failure to assess the extent to which Irish women's lives were economically determined by factors predating the foundation of the state—factors which subsequently impinged on the political sphere—has meant, she argues, that many aspects of women's history have been misinterpreted, and in particular, little account has been taken of real, if modest gains by Irish women during the 1930s in the field of employment.[134] Notwithstanding Daly's arguments, the existence of such a 'litany' of restrictions—no matter how dreary—was a fact of life for most Irishwomen until the 1960s, affecting not only public perception of their role and status, but increasingly their employment opportunities. Regarding equality of citizenship, what economic determination justified the removal of jury rights from women? Why was the first government of the IFS so determined to keep women out of the public life of the nation?

Contemporary argument from women's groups during the 1920s and 1930s against restrictive legislation clearly articulate their concerns. Protesting against the implications of the Civil Service (Amendment) Bill of 1925, the IWCA stated that for women's organisations, the question is one of principle, pointing out that the Bill created 'a principle of sex disqualification which does not at present exist in our legislation' and that 'this attempt to legalise the exclusion of women however competent or suitable on grounds of sex alone is bitterly resented'.[135] The emphasis placed by the new government on social caution would be reflected in its policies towards women, and would be continued by successive governments. Emphasis on women's domestic function, seen not just as one aspect of women's experience, but as the sole normal function of women in the interests of the state, were articulated by politicians from both sides. Measures regulating contraception, employment and equal rights undertaken by the Cumann na nGaedheal government in the 1920s, were replicated and strengthened by the Fianna Fáil administration from 1932.[136] Despite major differences between the parties on constitutional and economic issues, they were at one in the area of social values:

> Mr Cosgrave refused to legalise divorce; Mr de Valera made it unconstitutional. Mr Cosgrave's government regulated films and books; Mr de Valera's regulated dance halls. Mr Cosgrave's government forbade propaganda for the use of contraceptives; Mr de Valera's banned their sale or import. In all this they had the support of the third party in Irish politics, the Labour Party.[137]

Writing in 1971, Whyte also commented that 'The Catholic populace gave no hint of protest. The Protestant minority acquiesced. The only real opposition came from a coterie of literary *men* (author's emphasis) whose impact on public opinion was slight.' What of the women's protests? Can this comment by Whyte be construed as proof of the effectiveness of successive governments' policies and the disappearance of Irish women from recorded public life? While the number of women involved in political and public life in the 1920s and 1930s may have been a small and unrepresentative minority, 'they do provide some clues about the vast majority of women who have remained invisible'.[138] While it has been argued that the 1936 Conditions of Employment Act could be regarded as a model of reforming labour legislation, it has also been pointed out that the act had been drafted by Seán Lemass following detailed consultation with *male* trade union leaders (author's emphasis).

These leaders roundly supported the power given by this Act to the Minister to regulate or prohibit women workers. Speaking in the Senate, Thomas Foran, President of the ITGWU, denounced the women who opposed the Act, asking, 'Do the feminists want here what occurs in certain industrial countries across the water where the men mind the babies and women go to the factories? Do they want that in this holy Ireland of ours?[139] Confronted with the power of both a trade union movement and a government that was predominantly male both in membership and leaders, women workers and their organisation were vulnerable and limited in their options. Restrictions on women's employment during the 1920s and 1930s were not confined to one class of worker; both educated middle-class and working-class women were the object of such legislation. By 1937, the Irish Free State was placed on a black-list at the International Labour Organisation at Geneva for its conduct in regard to women workers.[140]

An interesting fact emerges on examining the progress of the various bills directly affecting women through both the Dáil and the Seanad during the 1920s and 1930s. In Dáil debates, women deputies rarely spoke against such measures, and generally voted with the government of the day. Women Senators, of differing political allegiance, were most vocal and united in opposing such legislation. Despite the legacy of deeply-rooted civil war differences, 'the erosion of women's rights drew a united response from politically opposed women Senators'.[141] With the consolidation of a patriarchal view of women's domestic role as the sole normal function of womanhood in the interests of the state—a view shared and reinforced by women Dáil Deputies—the equality guaranteed to women under Article 3 of the Free State Constitution was steadily eroded. It was women Senators during this period, along with non-parliamentary women's organisations, who consistently opposed legislation which they believed aimed to restrict their role in the Irish Free State.

THE POLITICISATION
OF WOMEN MID-TWENTIETH
CENTURY

Women's effectiveness in social movement politics is a testament to their flexibility in attitude and approach to problem resolution, if reinforcing the outsider status of such activity. (FRANCES GARDINER, *Irish Women's Studies Reader*)

Given developments between 1924 and 1937 relating to women's public role and working life, what options were open to women to address their unequal citizenship? How might committed women attempt to ensure their voices were heard—and listened to—at a time of economic depression, increasing emigration and international conflict? Increasingly, those who had been active during the 1920s and 1930s came to believe that it was only through political action that change would be attained. What is interesting during the period 1937–1967 is the varying ways political action was interpreted.

At one of the largest public meetings held in opposition to the 1937 Constitution Hanna Sheehy Skeffington had proposed the formation of an independent political party for women.[1] In November that year, through the combined influence of the National University of Ireland Women Graduates' Association (NUWGA), the Joint Committee of Women's Societies and Social Workers (JCWSSW) and the National Council of Women of Ireland (NCWI), such a party was formed. Initially named the Women's Social and Political League, within six months it was renamed the Women's Social and Progressive League (WSPL). Lack of funding and a nationwide network of support necessary to underpin a new party were among the reasons posited for the change in title, as was the fact that public service employees were barred from joining a political party.[2] The new association included within its aims the organisation of women voters throughout the country to secure equal opportunities and equal pay for women, the promotion of women candidates as independent members of the Dáil, Seanad and public bodies, and 'constant vigilance and united action on all legislation affecting the interests of women'.[3] Non-party and non-sectarian, the party attracted women such as Hanna Sheehy Skeffington, her sister Mary Kettle, Mary Hayden, Mary Macken and Dorothy McArdle, all of whom had been active in earlier women's organisations, and all of whom had opposed the articles relating to women in the 1937 Constitution. Despite being a staunch republican and a long-time supporter of de Valera, McArdle had written to him in May 1937 stating that 'as the Constitution stands, I do not see how anyone holding advanced views on the rights of women can support it, and that is a tragic dilemma for those who have been loyal and ardent workers in the national cause'.[4]

At the inaugural meeting of the wSPL, McArdle announced that the new party was a 'humiliating necessity' made all the more vital by the failure of the anti-constitution campaign and the growing repression of women throughout Europe.[5] Mary Hayden pointed out that while up to this point women in public life in Ireland had generally been associated with one party, 'we want to have women in public life quite free from such party obligations and who will therefore be useful for promoting the best interest of women'.[6] In an *Open Letter to Women Voters of Ireland* prior to the general election of 1938, the wSPL pointed to the deterioration of women's position under the recent Constitution, listing the restrictions placed on women in recent years in the fields of employment and citizens' rights. Women voters were exhorted not to accept platitudes, 'DO NOT VOTE (sic) for any candidate, however plausible pre-election promises may be, unless you are satisfied that he or she will defend your interests and guarantee your equal right of citizenship.'[7] Despite their efforts, the only women returned to the Dáil that year were three widows of former deputies—the 'silent sisters', Brigid Redmond (FG), Mrs Reynolds (FG) and Mrs Rice (FF), 'obedient party women [who] have never shown any interest in questions affecting women'.[8]

In the General Election of 1943 four women stood as independent pro-woman candidates, endorsed by the wSPL—Hanna Sheehy Skeffington in South Dublin, Mary Corbett and Mary Anne Phillips in Tipperary, and Margaret Ashe in Galway West. All four women had significant public service experience. If elected, they hoped to form the nucleus of a Woman's Party.[9] Supported by the NUWGA, the Irish Housewives Association (IHA) and the Irish Women's Citizen's Association (IWCA), Hanna's manifesto argued:

> There can be no true democracy where there is not complete economic and political freedom for the entire nation, both men and women. How can there be effective administration where the only political machine is entirely controlled by one sex only? … Under the 1916 Proclamation Irish Women were given equal citizenship, equal rights and equal opportunities, and subsequent constitutions have filched these, or smothered them in mere 'empty formulae'.[10]

With slogans calling for 'Equal Pay for Equal Work', and 'Equal Opportunities for Women', the WSPL appealed to women voters for funding and practical assistance to help the election of 'Women not tied to the party machine who will act consciously and courageously in the public interest'.[11] Sheehy Skeffington's campaign relied primarily on volunteer workers and door-to-door canvassing. One such volunteer— Rosaleen Mills—noted that as they could not afford to hire a hall to hold a public meeting, they held a bicycle parade in the city centre displaying placards stating key points of Hanna's programme.[12]

While Sheehy Skeffington's campaign got positive support in *The Irish Times*, generally independent candidates, male or female, received little press coverage during the election campaign.[13] All four women were defeated. One of Sheehy Skeffington's supporters observed that among the reasons for her defeat was 'the fact that Irish women had made no inroads into Irish political life at either local or national level; they could not select candidates and were not part of a party machinery'.[14] In the aftermath of the election, reflecting on whether the Dáil was a fit place for women, Hanna concluded that the electorate obviously thought the answer was no:

> Our experiment, a bold enough challenge to masculine monopoly, failed … If women in Ireland are not yet sufficiently educated politically to vote for women the blame rests largely with the various political machines that disregard them save as mere voting conveniences. Certain blame, too, of course, attaches to the women themselves, those smug ones especially, who declare that they have 'no interest in politics'.[15]

The women candidates had succeeded, however, in keeping the issue of equality before both the politicians and the public. An interesting insight into perceptions of women at home and at work was revealed in the work of the Commission on Vocational Organisation (CVO) which was in session between the years of the 1938 and 1943 elections. The CVO was established by de Valera in 1939 to investigate vocational organisation in Ireland following the publication in 1931 by Pope Pius XI of his encyclical *Quadrogesimo Anno*, an encyclical which Lee has described as engendering the first serious, sustained discussion of social principles in the history of Irish Catholicism.[16] Of the twenty-five members appointed to the Commission, three were women, Louie Bennett of the Irish Women Workers' Union (IWWU), Lucy Franks of the Irish Countrywomen's Association (ICA) and Máire McGeehan. Six women's organisations were among the 174 groups giving oral evidence to the Commission, and included the IWWU, the ICA, the JCWSS, the NCWI and the Catholic Women's Federation of Secondary School Unions (CWFSSU).[17] Along with the ICA, the latter three groups represented 'home-makers', i.e. those women not gainfully employed but who worked full-time and unpaid in the home; as such, Clear has noted that 'the irony of this census designation was not lost on any of those giving evidence.'[18]

While the ICA evidence was heard under the Agricultural heading, the other three home-based groups formed a committee to give joint evidence to the Commission—the Joint Committee on Vocationalism (JCV), and were the object of particularly aggressive questioning by the Chairman, Michael Browne, Catholic Bishop of Galway. Browne consistently sought to reveal a hidden agenda on the committee's part. Questioning their commitment to women as home-makers, he asked if all such groups were not just feminist or suffragist in origin, whose real aim was the achievement of equality with men. Constant references were made to 'leisured ladies, philanthropists and slumming do-gooders'. The latter reference was in response to the women's proposal for the establishment of baby clinics to teach new mothers how to care for the babies, the issue of clean milk, and provision of nursery schools to care for older children where mothers had to work outside the home. Browne objected to the idea that working-class women needed training in how to look after infants. He professed that the main concern of the women's groups was with getting women out of the home to work, arguing that most women preferred to leave political matters to the men.[19]

The slur of 'slumming' was also made against the ICA, but in a more benign way. ICA delegates laughed off suggestions that they were all 'ladies of the manor', insisting on the democratic nature of their organisation, while admitting that not much headway had been made in poorer rural areas.[20] When the IWWU delegation gave evidence, Browne probed the implications of women at work, suggesting that the rise in factory employment for women contributed to male unemployment, and acted as a deterrent to marriage. Refuting such suggestions, Helena Molony pointed out that the IWWU was desperately concerned with male unemployment 'because we regard women as the greater part of the family and where the men are unemployed the women suffer'.[21] In its report to government in 1943, the CVO accepted that women in the home should be organised to enable them exert pressure on a range of issues including prices and food-supply, housing, education, health services and 'the social and moral environment of the community'. It did not, however, provide a permanent place for such home-makers on the proposed National Vocational Assembly, although provision for co-option was allowed.[22] Many of the issues raised by women's groups at the CVO would remain topical over the coming decade.

Despite its ambition to organise women voters country-wide, the WSPL remained essentially a middle-class, Dublin-based group. Even within Dublin, its experience during the 1943 general election reinforced the fact that ordinary Dublin women, many living in appalling slum conditions in extreme poverty, could not relate to its ideals of equality, viewing the latter as 'pie in the sky'.[23] Mills's memories of canvassing for Sheehy Skeffington highlighted the housing conditions of Dublin's poor. Calling to a house in Winetavern Street she recalled:

> There was just one door and one room, which had no window in it ... There was only a sort of bed in the room and a box and (the old woman who lived there) invited me to sit on the box and she sat on the bed. I began to talk to her, and felt ashamed to ask her anything or bother her with anything, she was living in really disgraceful conditions but yet she was dignified and polite and listened to me with care.[24]

The situation of Dublin's poor had been critical even before the war. Writing in *The Irish Press* in 1936, Dr Bob Collis, a Dublin paediatrician,[25] had pointed out that behind the veneer of Dublin's 'quaint old eighteenth century houses' existed the 'foulest slums of any town in Europe (into which) people are herded and live in conditions of horror'. Collis later wrote that 'the plight of the poor in the city was appalling', with ninety thousand living in one-roomed tenements without a proper water supply, ten thousand of whom 'existed in basement cellar rooms or old wine cellars'.[26] While the health of all slum dwellers was at risk from environmental factors due to overcrowding, lack of sanitation and hygiene, public health problems were not restricted to Dublin, with typhus, typhoid, infant enteritis, and tuberculosis present to a significant extent throughout the country.

In 1944, on taking up the post of Chief Medical Adviser to the Department of Local Government and Public Health, Dr James Deeny highlighted some of the challenges facing him:

We had the worst tuberculosis problem in Western Europe, the last louse-borne typhus in Western Europe, a chronic typhoid problem, a very high infant mortality rate with huge numbers of babies dying from enteritis, a high maternal mortality rate, workhouse hospitals, few medical specialists outside Dublin, decaying dispensaries, low standards, and the senior medical establishment more concerned with sport, gracious living and style than professional excellence ... And of course there was a war on.[27]

Between 1935 and 1941 enteritis in infants became endemic, causing 500–600 deaths per year. This figure rose to 1,000 per year from 1941, 600 of these in Dublin. Deeny's work revealed that the disease mainly affected the children of disadvantaged families, living in the poorer districts of Dublin. It was contagious, usually striking during the first month of life. In what he describes as 'a Dublin form of the disease', Deeny observed that the overwhelming factor influencing the onset of the disease was the low rate of breast-feeding and dependence on cow's milk.[28] As research in Britain had shown, 'the disease was related to poverty, over-crowding and the domestic infection of foods, particularly milk'.[29] Rickets was another serious Dublin health concern, caused by a shortage of calcium in the diet of the poor. Susceptibility to health problems was increased during World War II.[30] A number of individuals initiated projects to help those most at risk. Dr Robert Collis started the Marrowbone Lane Fund to help children discharged from hospital by providing nutritious food and improved housing conditions to prevent further illness. Judge Wylie and a group of supporters opened a number of non-profit-making restaurants providing simple nourishing meals at low cost. The Mount Street Club, initiated by Paddy Somerville Large, ran a co-operative for unemployed men, providing workshops for craftwork and plots of land to grow vegetable and fruit.[31] With social welfare provisions being quite inadequate to deal with the problems of the time and no services such as school meals, or meals on wheels, 'The old, children and the unemployed suffered particularly'.[32] In an address to the WSPL in the spring of 1940, Collis emphasised the need to reduce food prices to the poor. Citing research on the wives of unemployed men attending the Rotunda Hospital ante-natal clinic, based on minimum standards laid down by the League of Nations, he pointed out that only 6 per cent of such women were receiving enough protective food and only 8 per cent received enough food of any kind; 'on an average they were only getting half the minimum amount of food they required, and were, literally, in a state of semi-starvation,'[33]

With limited state social services available during the first thirty years of the state, the need for extensive voluntary work was great. Two early societies were the Women's National Health Association (WNHA) formed in 1907 (which focused on the prevention of tuberculosis and child mortality through improved standards of hygiene and clean milk), and the National Council of Women of Ireland (NCWI) formed in 1924 by Lucy Kingston (which in addition to other work promoted reforms regarding the health and well-being of women and children).[34] Another significant initiative was the founding of St Ultan's Children's Hospital in 1919 by Dr Kathleen Lynn and Madeleine ffrench-Mullen to care for sick infants from poor families. A unique development at St Ultan's was the establishment of a Montessori department at the hospital, which Dr Montessori visited a number of times.[35] There were in addition, however, what Kennedy has described as 'the two most important women's organisations—the Irish Countrywomen's Association (ICA) and the Irish Housewives' Association (IHA)—(both) based around the home'.[36] And indeed, these organisations *were* important, becoming the most significant representation of women's views on a broad range of issues from both a rural and urban perspective up to the 1960s.

'The housewives hold the purse-strings of the community, yet because they are unorganised they exercise little control over prices,' declared the Report of the CVO. Ireland's 'Emergency' (World War II) provided the impetus for such organisation. Although removed from direct involvement in World War II through its neutrality stance, the Irish Free State nonetheless suffered extreme shortage of imported goods such as tea, sugar, flour and fuel. No system of rationing had been introduced, and while 'Those who had money were buying sacks of sugar and flour, and chests of tea, (the) rest managed as best they could'.[37] As a result prices soared and goods became prohibitively expensive. During the years of the 'Emergency' the cost of living rose by two-thirds while wages rose by one-third, 'Unemployment, poverty, and above all, the social inequality of the Emergency regime, swung public opinion to the left.'[38] The women and children in Dublin, particularly the poor, took a tremendous beating:

> Wet turf with which to cook and heat, a short daily period of gas 'glimmer', shortages, deprivation and poverty. Wartime for the Lurgan people was relative prosperity; for the Dublin poor, it meant that their poverty and misery grew worse.[39]

Aware of the problems caused by the war, a young Dublin woman, Hilda Tweedy, contacted a group of friends to see what might be done to alleviate the situation. As a result, Tweedy, Andree Sheehy Skeffington and a group of like-minded women decided to send a petition to the government for Budget Day, 5 May 1941. Initially signed by 51 women—a figure which grew to 640—the petition was also presented to the opposition parties and the press the day before the budget. Among the list of items sought by the petitioners was national registration of all essential foodstuffs, with immediate and effective rationing to sell goods at standard prices within reach of all. The issue of equality of such rationing was paramount in their demands. In addition they called for a government fruit and vegetable market to supply retailers and control retail prices, controls on the production and distribution of food with fair prices for producer and consumer, and similar controls on the production, distribution and consumption of fuels, gas and electricity. Tweedy has recalled that the group also sought:

> . . . special measures to ensure that the poor and unemployed would be safeguarded against the rise in the cost of living, measures such as a proportional increase in unemployment allowance, a free milk scheme for nursing and expectant mothers and the raising of the age from five to eight years of children of the unemployed eligible for the free milk scheme. We urged the government to organise a comprehensive plan embracing all existing schemes for communal feeding centres, including cooking centres and mobile kitchens.[40]

The petition caught the imagination of the press, which gave it much coverage, dubbing it the 'Housewives Petition'. Louie Bennett and her sister Susan Manning (signatories to the petition) advised the group's leaders to build on the momentum generated by the petition to start a new women's organisation, Bennett offering the use of the IWWU hall for an inaugural meeting. In May 1942, with an initial membership of 12 the Irish Housewives Committee was formed, the title being amended in 1946 to the IHA. The IHA decided on four points from the Petition as the basis for their work—price control and rationing, transport, school meals, and salvage of waste.[41] Their methodology was to investigate thoroughly the matter in hand, then lobby TDs and senators, send letters to government and the press while contacting state and semi-state bodies, professional and trade associations for information and support.

Tweedy has noted that 'though small in number we quickly built up a reputation for reliability and tenacity of purpose', so much so that it is claimed that during de Valera's period as Taoiseach a file was kept by his Department on the activities of the IHA.[42] Key campaigns initiated by the IHA during its first year included issues later articulated by Deeny, and are summarised in the posters carried by members during a march through Dublin which stated 'The Children must be Fed', 'War on TB', 'Pure Milk', 'Clean Food', 'Fair Prices', and 'Give the Children Dinner and not Bread'.[43] In its campaign for a hot meal and one third of a pint of milk daily for school children, schools managers, doctors, TDs and members of Dublin Corporation were all lobbied. One Reverend gentleman on the school committee of Dublin Corporation argued that to feed children at school would break up the sanctity of the home. Tweedy has noted that such a charge was not made against those who could afford to send their children to boarding school.[44]

The new group was non-party and non-sectarian, and Tweedy has pointed to its feminist leanings, noting that pleas to governments were not enough; 'we needed committed women in political life, women in the places where the decisions were being made.'[45] Not surprisingly, therefore, the IHA endorsed the candidature of Hanna Sheehy Skeffington as an Independent candidate for the Dáil in 1943. While supportive of the new group, Hanna had been unhappy with its title. Writing in the first issue of *The Irish Housewife* in 1946, she explained her dislike of 'clumsy man-made words (that) remind us how little free we really are, so "housewife" is accepted more or less meekly by most women as we accept men's names in marriage and live in their inconveniently constructed houses'. Despite her reservations with the title of *Housewife*, Hanna now applauded the achievements of 'a band of energetic and determined women' in ending the black market and obtaining price controls. True to character she urged the group to further organisation and education in citizenship, pointing out with conviction—and humour—'The association needs more members, additional subscribers, investigators, workers, politically-minded women—much work remains to be done in '46. Go to it, housewives!'[46] The group's links with earlier feminist organisations was strengthened in 1947 when the Irish Women Citizens Association (formerly the iwslga) was incorporated into the iha; an important result of this was the formation of an international committee of the iha with members from both organisations dedicated to carry on the work of the iwca through its affiliation to the International Alliance of Women (iaw). Over the next fifty years, this international connection was to prove vital in expanding the knowledge and expectations of both the iha and Irish women's groups generally on issues of equality and rights.

Hanna Sheehy Skeffington's daughter-in-law, Andree, was one of the co-founders of the iha. A French woman with a strong social and feminist conscience, she married Hanna's only son Owen in 1935, and settled in Dublin. Both Andree and Owen joined the Labour Party, and became involved in its Pearse Street Council of Action which sought to monitor food and fuel prices in this deprived area. They soon discovered that despite the poverty and high price of goods, the question of housing and the cost of rent was the priority of the residents of the area, fear of eviction being more potent than the profiteering of local shopkeepers. The group adapted their work accordingly, acting as liaison between tenants, rent-collectors, landlords and Dublin Corporation Housing Department. Andree's skill and experience in dealing with such issues was a great advantage to the iha. While her mother-in-law had reservations about the title of the organisation, Andree felt that the newspaper's attempted put-down of the group as 'housewives' presented a challenge to women as homemakers 'to speak up for the women in the home'. Her mantra for the iha became 'educate, investigate, agitate', a *modus operandi* in which the group became particularly adept.[47]

During its first decade the iha continued to pressurise successive governments on issues ranging from the cost of living, public health and food hygiene to emigration and population problems. Particularly significant was its research and reportage into the Dublin milk supply. The iha investigated the composition and sourcing of Dublin milk, finding in 1942 that 35 per cent of this was untreated 'loose milk', liable to germ infection.[48] This finding coincided with Dr Deeny's concerns regarding infant enteritis. The iha continued its investigations during the war years, investigating creameries and co-operatives, asking schools and hospitals where they sourced their milk supply, and demanding of the Department a policy of tuberculin-tested and pasteurised milk. In March 1945 the Minister for Local Government and Public Health announced the appointment of a Tribunal of Inquiry into the supply of milk to Dublin, the terms of reference being to examine the supply of milk to distributors and consumers. In its evidence to the Tribunal, the IHA highlighted milk shortages during 1943, the difficulty of obtaining highest grade (tuberculin-tested) milk in some areas, the fact that only the better off could afford an adequate supply of milk, and the insufficient number of inspectors. It also sought provision of an adequate supply of cheap milk for all children under sixteen and for all nursing and expectant mothers. As a result of the Tribunal Tweedy noted that 'all milk sold (now) is pasteurised with the exception of highest grade milk and all milk is now produced under more hygienic conditions'.[49]

The cost of living had risen significantly during the war years. In August 1939 the Consumer Price Index was 173; by 1946 this had increased to 288. Goods which had cost twelve shillings in 1939 now cost twenty shillings.[50] In September 1946 the wages freeze was abolished and the Labour Court was established under the Industrial Relations Act. Pay increases would now be negotiated through the Court, the first of these 'Rounds' occurring later that year. Trade unionists were concerned that further pay increases would be offset by price increases. Articulating these concerns, Christy Ferguson of the Workers Union of Ireland (WUI) proposed that Dublin Trade Union Council (DTUC) 'invite labour bodies and women's organisations to a conference, for the purpose of initiating a campaign for the immediate control of prices'.[51] A conference was held on 17 January 1947, attended by the IHA, WSPL, the Labour Party and Clann na Poblachta. From this conference emerged the Lower Prices Council (LPC), with E.J. Tucker of the TUC as Chairman and Maureen O'Carroll as Hon Secretary. In addition to trade union and labour representation, the IHA, the WSPL and the JCWSSW were also represented on the committee. In recognition of the work done by the IHA in the area of price control Hilda Tweedy was elected as Hon. Secretary of the executive co-ordinating committee.[52] Offices were established with the help of the DTUC, and intensive investigation was conducted into the price of food, clothing and housing. With the establishment of an open and transparent mechanism to decide on price increases as one of its main objectives, the LPC organised extensive lobbying of TDs and media coverage. A contemporary newspaper report on the daily work of its Secretary, Maureen O'Carroll (later to be a Labour TD), noted that:

> Every morning 37 year old Mrs Maureen O'Carroll, Dublin housewife, goes shopping for 70,000 people. As secretary of the city's Lower Prices Council, she knows what the price of everything from food to fuel should be .... With seven children to look after—ages seven weeks to fourteen years—Mrs O'Carroll packs more action into one day than most people do in a week.[53]

The report noted that when overcharging is noted, the LPC buys the article concerned and sends the receipt to the Department of Industry and Commerce for action, reporting Mrs O'Carroll's comment that 'we give no second chances, even if it is only a farthing overcharge'. When questioned as to the methods used to maintain its 'incessant research into costs of production', Mrs O'Carroll responded mysteriously, 'We have our own methods.'

Tweedy has recounted that the LPC considered that an association of women's organisations could be an effective ally to combat the continuous rise in the cost of living and to work for a betterment of social conditions.[54] In October 1947 the LPC organised what became known as 'the Women's Parliament' in Dublin's Mansion House. Participating women debated issues relating to the cost of living and were allocated ministerial portfolios as re-enforcement of their right to commentate on the national housekeeping. Louie Bennett chaired the inaugural meeting, from which emerged the Women's National Council of Action (WNCA) as a subsidiary of the LPC. The WNCA produced six demands relating to the control of rents and food prices and the establishment of producer/consumer markets. The idea of a Women's Parliament attracted the attention of Myles na gCopaleen who wrote in his satirical column in *The Irish Times*:

> It says in the papers that more than 300,000 women in every county in Ireland will be represented at the Women's Parliament in Dublin—*to demand*—if you don't mind, 'Control of prices and an immediate reduction in the cost of essential goods and other commodities'. Hah? I well remember the day, and your poor father would bear me out in this, when into the newspapers the word 'women' never got! In those days respectability was the rage of course.[55]

The WNCA continued to concentrate on economic matters over 'respectability', and in 1949 a producer-consumer market was opened by Dublin Corporation at the Iveagh Market in Francis Street. This and the establishment in 1951 of a Prices Advisory Board (PAB) by the Minister for Industry and Commerce were two significant achievements of the WNCA. Through its work with the PAB and the LPC, the IHA was involved in consistent research and challenging of successive governments in relation to proposed price increases for more than twenty years. Tweedy has pointed out that:

> The IHA steadily built up a reputation for dedicated work on behalf of the consumer and particularly for women and children. This was recognised by the government and we may take some credit for the setting up of the Milk Tribunal, and of the Prices Advisory Board ... The willingness of government departments to receive deputations and discuss our memoranda, and on occasions to consult us (and) to include some of our suggestions in legislation, e.g. in public health and food hygiene regulations was proof of the value of our work.[56]

Some interventions by the IHA landed them in controversy. One such instance occurred in 1949 when a letter was received from the British Cultural Committee for Peace inviting the IHA to send a peace message to a World Congress for Peace due to be held in Paris. After full discussion it was decided to send a message. Aware that some participants at the Congress might be communist sympathisers, a very carefully drafted letter was composed emphasising the non-political ethos of the IHA, while calling on women to sink their political differences and work for peace. Although copies of this letter were sent also to the press, no paper published it at the time. Ten days later in a report referring to the 'Red' Dean of Canterbury's address to the Congress, a press headline noted that 'Irish Housewives Association sends message to Paris Peace Conference'.[57] Complaints from some members ensued, followed by individual and branch resignations and/or splits. While a letter of clarification from the IHA was published by some daily newspapers, the *Catholic Standard* failed to do so, preferring to run with the headline 'Message to Reds splits Housewives' Association'. Tweedy has described this episode as very damaging to the organisation, providing an example of what the fear of communism at this time could do.

These charges of communist leanings proved very upsetting and disrupting for the organisation, and stuck with the IHA for some time. In 1950 it was included among a list of 'communist-dominated' organisations published in *The Cavalcade*. In 1952, the *Roscommon Herald* suggested in an article on 'Dangerous Trends in Ireland' that the IHA had been involved with rioting in O'Connell Street, and 'had always been used as a medium of expression' by Marxists, communists or fellow-travellers. Legal action was taken in both cases, with apologies being published in the relevant papers, although in the case of the *Roscommon Herald* this took place only after a writ for libel was issued. As a non-national, Andree Sheehy Skeffington felt particularly vulnerable, recalling that during the early 1950s 'I felt what I had never felt before, that I was an alien'.[58] On hearing that a local priest had advised women parishioners either not to join the IHA (which he described as anti-Catholic), or to join and control it, Andree decided to confront him. When, by arrangement, she called to the priest's house, before any conversation took place he asked her if she was a Catholic. She replied that she had been so baptised, but was not a practicing Catholic, at which point he ended the interview.[59]

Another contentious issue during this period was the 'Mother and Child' proposal. In his assessment of key problems facing him when he started work in the Department of Local Government and Public Health in 1944, Dr James Deeny had included the high rate of maternal mortality in the state. There was a significant difference in the rate of such deaths within and outside Dublin. By 1940, 50 per cent of births in Dublin city and county took place in the city's three maternity hospitals, resulting in Dublin's maternal mortality rate being one-fifth of the national average.[60] In addition one-third of all beds in the three Dublin maternity hospitals were occupied by pregnant women suffering from toxaemia, malnutrition, anaemia and other factors which made hospitalisation necessary for a few weeks before delivery to build up their health.[61] The extent of the problem, allied to the huge problem of infant mortality, moved Deeny to recommend a scheme for the care of women and children as a priority. From his experience in Belfast when the free medical care scheme was introduced for insured workers, Deeny had noted that those most in need of such care, i.e. wives and children, were not covered by the scheme, it being confined to insured workers, employed or unemployed. His views in this area were reflected in the draft White Paper for reform of the health services drawn up by him at the request of the Minister, Seán MacEntee. Passed in 1947 as the Health Act, this wide-ranging plan contained much of the provisions included in what became known as 'The Mother and Child Bill'. In fact, it was Deeny who gave it this name while working on the White Paper in 1946, considering that 'no one could oppose a scheme with a name like that'.[62] Little did he anticipate the controversy that would ensue. With Fianna Fáil out of office in 1948, the matter came to a head during the term of the new Inter-party government 1948–1951. Most associated with Dr Noël Browne, Minister for Health in that government, the 'Mother and Child' bill drew the wrath of both the hierarchy and medical consultants. The IHA supported the scheme, in March 1951 unanimously passing a resolution in its favour, sending a letter to the press to that effect.

The association's awareness of the problems facing women and children in the area of health through their own research would have been heightened by the level of debate on the issues, and perhaps influenced by an excellent pamphlet produced by the Department of Health. This pamphlet is particularly noteworthy for being produced at a time when official publications were, to say the least, unexciting. Citing the 1916 Proclamation promise of 'cherishing all the children of the nation equally', through its extensive use of photographs and illustration, and clearly worded text, the seventeen-page document explained the content of the bill in an attractive and professional manner. In his introduction, Dr Browne noted that when the new service was fully operational, all mothers who chose to avail of it for themselves and their children could do so 'as a right of their nationhood, and without any mark of the Poor Law, or any means test'.[63]

When the matter came to a head, and Browne's resignation was imminent, the Committee of the IHA notified its support of the proposed bill to the Taoiseach, stating their belief that 'the principle of equal opportunities, enshrined in our Constitution, should be applied in the sphere of health to those least able to fend for themselves: the mothers and children of Ireland'.[64] Following Browne's resignation, the IHA report for 1950–51 declared that despite its non-party and non-sectarian ethos, the organisation could not but deplore the manner in which an issue vital to the health of the nation was handled, stating, 'We re-affirm our belief in the equal rights of all Irish women to happy motherhood, and deplore the resignation of a Minister for Health who had done so much in his term of office for the health of the community.'[65] Many women activists of the time supported Browne, and were sometimes the object of amusing, rude and/or abusive behaviour by those who opposed him. At one large public meeting, Tweedy has recalled being 'on the back of a lorry' with two other IHA members and

Browne in support of the scheme: 'Every time the would-be speakers raised the megaphone, their words were drowned out by the crowd singing "Faith of our Fathers".[66] In the lead-up to the General Election of 1951 (which followed shortly after Browne's resignation) Rosaleen Mills and some friends—all canvassers for Browne—attended a public meeting in Dolphin's Barn addressed by Seán MacBride. As they approached the meeting, their way was barred by what Mills described as 'five or six thugs', who refused to let them through, threatening to puncture their tyres and to throw Mills into the canal. The women were made of stern stuff, however, and persevered.[67]

While it can be argued that during its first decade the IHA was home-centred, 'defin(ing) women's concerns in the wider society as those which extended their domestic nurturing concerns',[68] it has also been noted that housewives' interests were defined very broadly by the group, and were in no way limited or determined by the organisation's largely middle-class urban membership.[69] Tweedy herself has confirmed that 'until 1948 we had been very busy with domestic issues'.[70] Following its first attendance at an IAW congress in 1949, Tweedy notes that the delegation were 'greatly cheered to find women in other countries were facing the same problems, only the emphasis differed'. With renewed enthusiasm the IHA set up networks to liaise with the commissions of the IAW and to monitor laws and conditions affecting women in Ireland.

Their first effort was to press for equal pay, making representations to both government and trade unions. Tweedy recounts that the only support they got was from Louie Bennett and the IWWU; other unions just did not want to hear about equal pay. And, as the IHA discovered, not all women favoured the idea either, fearing a threat to their husband's jobs. 'It was the same with other reforms we hoped to initiate. Women were nervous about innovations; we had to gain their support first.'[71] The IHA was represented at each IAW Congress from 1949 to 1992, that of 1961 being held in Dublin. While maintaining its high profile on prices and consumer affairs during the 1950s and 1960s, other issues advocated by the IHA included the raising of the marriage age, the need for women police, and equality of jury service for men and women.

On a number of occasions members of the IHA committee stood in local and national elections. Jean Coote ran as an independent for Dublin Corporation while serving as IHA Chairwoman. In 1957 the IHA nominated three of its most experienced members for the general election of that year, Kathleen Swanton, Beatrice Dixon and Mairéad McGuinness. In what was described as 'a great learning experience for the IHA', the organisation put its full weight behind the candidates, raising funds, canvassing and distributing election literature, even hiring a lorry and megaphone. Tweedy has recalled that the lorry was stopped 'wherever we saw a few people together (and we) addressed them through the megaphone, asking for support for our candidates'.[72] None of the women was elected, although Beatrice Dixon was only eliminated on the 7th count (at the same time as outgoing Minister Seán MacBride), and Kathleen Swanton was elected to Dublin Corporation at the next local election. With the backing of the organisation, the IHA Hon. Secretary, Carmel Gleeson, won a seat as an independent candidate for Dublin County Council in the local elections of 1966.[73] Tweedy has commented that through its participation in the electoral process, the IHA drew attention to the need for representation of women by women, highlighting the gross imbalance of the sexes in government. Although 1966 was the last occasion the IHA put forward candidates from its own ranks, it continued to encourage women to stand for Dáil, Senate and Local Government seats, and at each election wrote to the press seeking support for women candidates.

Towards the end of the 1960s international developments instigated significant changes in women's demands. At the IAW congress in London in 1967, IHA delegates learned that the UN Commission on the Status of Women had issued a directive to women's international non-governmental organisations asking affiliates to examine the status of women in their own countries and, where necessary, urge their governments to set up a national commission on the status of women.[74] This news set in train a chain of events that would dramatically change the status of women in Ireland.

Constituting 'a significant minority', Hilda Tweedy and Andree Sheehy Skeffington became prominent among a new generation of urban women who would challenge existing norms, and would in time develop for women in Ireland the real meaning of citizenship.[75] Rural women too organised to improve conditions for farming women. The Irish Countrywomen's Association (ICA) had been formed originally as the Society of United Irishwomen (UI) in 1910, an affiliate of the co-operative movement through its connection with the Irish Agricultural Organisation Society (IAOS). Its founder was Mrs Harold Lett, a farmer and Vice-President of the County Wexford Farmers' Association.[76] Bourke has noted that the founders were initially drawn from the aspiring middle-class.[77] Following a presentation to the AGM of the IAOS, at which the UI stressed the need for women's co-operation for the IAOS to achieve its full potential, it was agreed that formation of branches of the UI would be encouraged close to co-operative societies.[78] While much assistance was received from the IAOS, including the provision of an office at its Dublin headquarters, Plunkett House, the UI remained an independent association. A short history of the organisation produced in 1950 indicates that early concerns of the organisation included the training of village nurses (later handed over to the Queen's Institute), the provision of clean milk, and the establishment of cottage industries.[79] Organisationally based on a system of guilds set up in areas with a population of less than 3,000, membership fluctuated during the period of unrest commencing in 1914 with World War I, continuing into the 1920s in the aftermath of civil war. By 1927 the number of guilds had dropped from its earlier number of 49 to just over a dozen.

Following debate over many years on the political inference of its name, in 1934 the new title of ICA was adopted. An article in the *Farmers' Gazette* in 1935 noted that the new organisation would be 'more adaptive to the times, more developed and possible (*sic*) freer in its mode of activity'.[80] Commenting that the ICA represented a continuation rather than a new beginning, it pointed out that under the new Constitution 'general decentralisation makes the Guilds more independent and gives the countryside a prior importance to the Dublin group'. By 1937 the number of Guilds had increased to 70, rising to 218 by 1948.[81] While continuously seeking to empower countrywomen within their own community, the focus of the ICA remained narrow, concentrating on particular rural issues without addressing wider issues of citizenship for Irishwomen. In this it differed from other women's organisations concerned with equality and opportunity for women. Ferriter has noted that the ICA arguments in the 1940s for training farmers' daughters 'based on the dignity of labour on the land and in the home' were in line with nationalist views on education: 'the ICA (tended) to frame its ideals and goals in a national context; never were these women's issues alone. Rather they were national issues which were of concern to women.'[82]

Speaking in 1939 (two years after passing of the new Constitution), a future ICA President, Alice Ryan, stated that the organisation should 'challenge the man's saying "a woman's place is in the home" to "a woman's place is where she can best help her home"'.[83] The ethos of the ICA has been described as 'not (wishing) to challenge traditional axioms, but to reshape them'.[84] Women were encouraged not only to be assertive in the running of the family unit, but also to seek representation on local decision-making councils and authorities. By 1950 it was noted that one of the most valuable functions of the ICA was its training of women for leadership and participation in public life, and to this end it sought to instil confidence in women through training in public speaking. Themes documented during its early years remained on the agenda of the ICA over the next fifty years—'improvement in the conditions of (women's) rural environment, in their education and business knowledge and methods, the definition of their relationship with other organisations, official and voluntary'.[85] Emphasis on training and education in housewifery, arts and crafts remained a constant, with community development, leadership courses and marketing skills being added over the years. The opening of The Country Shop by Muriel Gahan in Dublin during the early 1930s as a most successful outlet for the sale of country crafts produced by members was added to in 1947 by the initiation of Country Markets. The symbolism of women 'doing business by themselves, for themselves' was potent; women 'were often astonished and flattered by the size of their monthly cheques which they could show with pride to their menfolk as quite worthy to confront the creamery cheque'.[86] Financial independence was seen as a crucial step in empowerment and self-confidence. Olivia Hughes, former ICA president and an organiser of the country markets, looking back on forty years involvement in rural affairs, commented in 1959 that 'The countrywoman's chief need is for money which she can call her own'.[87] From an urban perspective, Rosaleen Mills had also pointed to the dilemma facing working women forced to surrender financial independence if they wished to marry and concentrate on homemaking skills: 'the awful snag is that if a woman wants herself to do this she has no money; she is not paid.'[88]

As outlined above, the ICA was one of a number of women's organisations which appeared before the CVO. In its evidence to the Commission, the ICA argued the need for countrywomen to be represented vocationally in a separate category from farmers and other women working in the home because of their unique position in being both producers and consumers and the impossibility of distinguishing their remunerative work from their home and life maintenance work.[89] Pointing out that the ICA played an important part in training women for public life and giving them confidence in public speaking and organisation, its delegation led by Muriel Gahan responded firmly—but negatively—to a suggestion by some Commission members that they merge with other rural organisations such as Muintir na Tíre, stating that in mixed organisations 'men did most of the talking and women were left out'.[90] Shades of IWWU arguments of the need for a separate women's union! Mamo McDonald (President of the ICA in the 1980s), has recounted that in the early 1940s, when a South Tipperary farmer was unable to attend the AGM of his Co-op and sent his wife to represent him, all the men present turned her out. Interestingly, the woman concerned—Olivia Hughes—a long-time ICA member and future President, went on to start the Country Markets. McDonald highlighted this incident in reference to a comment by Horace Plunkett (founder of the Co-operative movement in the 1880s) that in organising the whole of rural life '(we) have attempted to enlist only half the rural population —the male half'.[91]

In her perceptive essay, *The State, Irish Women and Running Water*, Daly has examined the contrasting rate of progress in the supply of electricity and piped water to rural areas, revealing a gender bias favouring the former over the latter.[92] The differing priorities towards provision of electricity and piped water reveals much about the status of women in rural Ireland at this time. Electricity was seen primarily as a means of improving leisure and social facilities, initially through radio and later television rather than an aid to reducing housework. The fact that men used leisure products, while household appliances were primarily of benefit to women, is not without significance. And water, as the 'greatest labour saving device',[93] remained very low on the agenda of many men.

A comparison between rural and urban areas in the provision of these services reveals significant differences. In 1946 the majority of urban houses had access to electricity but few rural homes had this service. That same year, 92 per cent of urban homes had piped water and 35 per cent had a fixed bath; by comparison over 91 per cent of rural homes had to rely on a pump, well or stream, and less than 4 per cent had a fixed bath.[94] In 1947 the ESB began its rural electrification campaign, and by 1956 over half of all rural households had been connected. During the 1950s, however, the gap between town and country regarding water and sanitary services widened. By 1961, 97 per cent of urban homes had running water, while in contrast only 12 per cent of rural homes in 1960 had a water supply, very often less than adequate, being drawn from a roof tank or a nearby well.[95]

The post-war Government commitment to an intensive rural electrification scheme, and to spending on roads, houses and other infrastructure to improve life in rural areas, was not matched in regard to piped water. Seán MacEntee, Minister for Local Government and

Public Health, appears to have been the first government minister committed to this issue, establishing in 1947 a committee to report on the implementation of piped water to areas where no supply existed. While the Minister linked the issue with the need to improve conditions of life for those in rural areas, particularly those who worked on the land, James Deeny, chief medical adviser in MacEntee's department, specifically associated the issue with the quality of women's lives:

> Men, all over the world, are singularly lacking in thought for the welfare of their womenfolk. While any drudgery or inconvenience in man's work will soon be lightened by intervention or improvisation, for women little or no effort is made to ease the burden of their monotonous household tasks. All over the country hundreds of thousands of women depend for every drop of water on half filled cans—drawn laboriously from surface wells sometimes hundreds of yards away ... the mother or housewife deserves most from the community; the provision of piped water and better still a domestic hot water system should be our first consideration in household planning.[96]

The views of MacEntee and Deeny were not widely shared. The committee established by MacEntee was disbanded in 1948 following a change in government, and successive Ministers concentrated on improved housing standards without reference to water connection.[97] Experience of the ESB campaign for rural electrification from the late 1940s had seen the ICA acquire much skill in lobbying and pressuring relevant groups and politicians. This experience was now brought to bear in a renewed campaign for piped water with the Department of Local Government enlisting the aid of the society. At a conference on the subject held in the ICA's residential college, An Grianán, in 1960, civil servants, clerics and politicians all spoke in favour of its implementation. Among the speakers, Dick Roche of the Department of Local Government described piped water as 'the first and greatest of domestic labour saving devices'.[98] Minister Neil Blaney laid the blame for inaction on its implementation on men, expressing surprise that women had tolerated it for so long.

During 1961 the ICA co-operated with the Department in organising an exhibition which toured Ireland explaining the benefits of running water. The general election of that year gave a further boost to the campaign, Taoiseach Seán Lemass declaring it to be 'perhaps the most significant measure ever taken to improve the conditions of people in rural areas'.[99] The ICA efforts received most severe criticism from the National Farmers' Association (NFA) who argued that implementation of the scheme would result in higher rates on agricultural land. In addition to a clash between male and female rural organisations—the NFA versus the ICA—there were undercurrents of class difference and inter-departmental power politics.[100] Whereas this campaign aimed to bring water to all households, rich and poor, previous grant schemes had been availed of mainly by more prosperous farmers because much of the cost remained to be borne by the consumer. Opposition from the NFA and supportive politicians was effective, and resulted in a departmental shift away from the originally planned regional water schemes to smaller group schemes. This transferred much of the initiative for promoting rural water schemes away from central government to the local community, 'where women were forced to assume an even more active role—canvassing neighbours, collecting down payments, and raising consciousness of the value of such amenities'.[101] Through its high profile involvement in this campaign, the ICA gained further extensive experience in public participation. Becoming expert in what has been described as 'quiet revolutions', the organisation proved that 'they now had the status and the authority to lead'.[102]

ICA membership in 1938 was in excess of 2,000; by 1965 this figure had risen to over 20,000.[103] The organisation built strong international links through its affiliation with the Associated Country Women of the World (ACWW) in 1933. Like early feminist groups, the ICA 'had looked outwards, long before it became nationally fashionable to do so', although its emphasis was firmly on 'providing a mirror which illustrated that the problems and preoccupations of rural Ireland were by no means unique'.[104] A similar path would be taken by the IHA following its alliance with the IAW in 1949.

CONCLUSION

Ireland in the 1940s has been described as 'a state where gendered political forces had limited women's access to political and economic power'.[105] The broadly accepted view that the 'proper' place for married women was in the home, a view promulgated by politicians, trade unionists and the churches, had been reinforced by legislative restrictions placed on the employment of married women during the 1930s. True, women had the vote, but there was little female representation in political life, and the first twenty years of the Free State had seen little advancement of women in public life generally.[106] In recounting the formation of the IHA, Tweedy noted that its founders in 1941 were all home-based young married women, as 'it was quite unusual for married women to work outside the home and quite difficult for them to find jobs'. She herself was turned down for a job teaching twelve-year-old girls precisely because she was married and 'it would not be nice for the girls if you became pregnant'.[107] Given the climate of the time, what were the options for this younger generation of women if they wished to improve the position of women? Was it perhaps a shrewd move to use the 'home-maker' card, concentrating on the areas of health, hygiene and consumer issues publicly accepted as part of women's traditional role?[108] Or in fact, was it the only option available?

It has been argued that the feminism of mid-twentieth-century Ireland was almost identical to the maternalist feminism of early twentieth-century Europe, women's interests being defined as those which reflected women's domestic concerns in the wider society.[109] Nonetheless, in promoting the values of domesticity—while simultaneously legitimating women's public relationship to politics, the State, community, workplace and marketplace—the dual nature of such maternalism frequently resulted in hostility from male-dominated centres of power. The reaction of Bishop Browne to women's groups giving evidence to the CVO was one example of such hostility. While the presence of hostility can be interpreted as the awareness of a threat to the status quo, too often the views of women were not even considered when measures were drafted which could affect their lives. One such instance occurred in 1943 when de Valera appointed an interdepartmental committee to consider government subsidies for the building of a second house on farms to facilitate earlier marriage. No woman was appointed to the committee, nor was any woman or woman's organisation asked for an opinion on the proposal.[110] Similarly, on the matter of children's allowances (introduced in 1944) no women's groups were consulted.

The payment of children's allowances had first been proposed in 1938 by James Dillon and over the next five years would be the subject of an interdepartmental committee, engendering much divisiveness and political in-fighting. Its subsequent progress in the Dáil was the subject of much conflicting debate. It is worth noting that while it was a newly elected Liam Cosgrave who first suggested that payment of such an allowance should be paid directly to mothers, a view supported by a number of other deputies, there is no record of a campaign or opinion on the matter by any women's group.[111] This omission has been described as indicative of the middle-class nature of existing women's groups and their lack of empathy with the concerns of the majority of women.[112] While the IHA had only been formed in the year before the Bill passed through the Dáil, the absence of feminist debate on the issue indicates a particularly significant missed opportunity.

The 1950s—generally regarded as a bleak era of economic and social depression—can in retrospect be viewed as a significant turning point for Irish women. While the major developments in the field of employment and equality were not debated realistically in the public arena until the late 1960s, the seeds for subsequent change were nurtured by the groundwork of organisations ten–fifteen years earlier. It was through organisations such as the IHA, the ICA, and other groups focused on the support of women in the home, the JCWSSW and professional bodies such as the INTO that 'women honed the political skills of organisation and lobbying which would help them move forward in public life'.[113]

While never claiming to be a feminist organisation, the ICA with its ever-growing membership extending to all corners of Ireland, played a most influential role in the empowerment of rural women. The 1950s has been described as the most important decade in its history, being 'productive, lively and forward-looking'.[114] During these years—with more than 350 Guilds—the ICA expanded its educational facilities, obtained a grant-in-aid from the government, successfully lobbied funds from abroad which enabled them to open their own residential college, An Grianán in County Louth, employed full-time organisers to tour the country to increase membership and encourage women's participation in rural trade, education and social activities; 'It became comfortable in its confidence to achieve practical results. It learned how to project itself and in the process became a highly professional organisation.'[115] And, politicians began to recognise this. Opening an ICA Country Fair in 1950, the Minister for Agriculture, James Dillon, advised members to challenge their daughters not to marry until they had hot and cold water connected to their homes. Ferriter has pointed to significant semantic changes in the demands of the ICA executive by the 1950s 'as it prepared to move beyond confined spheres and to define its goals accordingly'.[116]

Through the influence of such organisations, the 1950s can be seen as a decade of incipient change in the confidence and empowerment of women in Ireland. By working within these groups, women became accustomed to questioning political and social issues. While not articulated in full until the late 1960s, the preparatory work of the IHA, the ICA and groups such as the WSPL and JCWSSW paved the way for an explosion of demands that emerged from 1968. From this point on, such demands could not be dismissed as representing only elite middle-class groups or rural women in isolation from national and international developments.

The overview of issues relating to women in independent Ireland outlined above has omitted a significant segment of Irish women, i.e. those who emigrated. As detailed in earlier chapters, significant numbers of women had emigrated from Ireland from the mid-nineteenth century. During the 1930s emigration steadily increased, and as a result of the Great Depression became concentrated on the UK. Female emigration to the UK fell during the war-years, but increased substantially post-war. Of every 100 girls in Connaught between the ages of 15 and 19 years in 1946, forty-two had left by 1951.[117] A number of sources indicate interesting reasons for this increase. While unemployment at home remained the principal criteria, a number of other factors contributed, with better pay, conditions and higher status abroad being significant reasons. The fact that many emigrant girls took up domestic jobs in Britain which they would not take up at home was explained by a lack of stigma attached to such work in Britain, the point being made that 'in England … they respect you for your work'.[118] It was noted that 'the rising emigration of young women meant that they were placing their personal interest above those of family and society'.[119] The majority of female emigration continued to be from rural areas. Of 122,954 women who applied for travel permits to work in Britain between 1943 and 1951, 68 per cent came from rural Ireland.[120] Noting the gendered dimension of this problem, it has been suggested that the widening gap in material standards between urban and rural life may also have played a part in this female exodus.[121] Ferriter has commented that many women rejected the built-in assumption of a gendered state by 'voting for change with their feet and emigrating'.[122]

Following World War II, the numbers of emigrant women entering domestic service declined as other areas of work opened up, including shop, restaurant, pub, and factory employment. Increasingly, girls were better educated, one study noting that the education of farmers' daughters 'places them at variance with their environment'.[123] Land Commission reports confirmed that second-level education was a significant catalyst in the decision of many farmers' daughters to emigrate. One area that attracted many such girls was nursing. In 1943 the Irish Nurses Organisation (INO) had noted that 'for the first time since nursing became a professional career Ireland (is) faced with a shortage of nurses due to emigration'.[124] Nursing journals noted increased demands for Irish nurses in post-war Britain. In addition to the emigration of qualified nurses, a significant number of girls who could not afford the fees charged by Irish training hospitals, left to take up training in England. Nursing as a career was not popular with English girls, who disliked the discipline and hard work involved.[125] The resulting shortage of nurses created a demand for Irish trainees. Women in other professions, including doctors and teachers, also emigrated in increasing numbers, with Irish graduates finding employment without difficulty.

Another group of emigrants that have been generally overlooked are the members of religious orders that made up Ireland's large missionary population. The foundation of orders such as the Columban Missionary Sisters and the Holy Rosary Sisters of Killeshandra in the 1920s at a time of intense idealism in post-civil war Ireland, was followed a decade later by 'possibly the most innovative of the Irish Missionary orders', the Medical Missionaries of Mary founded in 1936 by Marie Martin.[126] These developments occurred at a time when devotional Catholicism was reaching a peak, in particular the cult of Mary. The 1950 promulgation of the dogma of Mary's assumption into heaven, followed in 1954 by 'the Marian year' decreed by Pius XII, resulted in that decade being the high point of female religious vocations in twentieth-century Ireland.

Associated with the development of these new orders—and particularly relevant in the missionary context in which they operated—was the quest for professional qualification in surgery and obstetrics, Rome's 'forbidden skills'.[127] This involved a double battle on the part of the Sisters, firstly with the medical schools, and then with Rome. Finally, in February 1936, permission was granted in Canon 489 'Maternity training for missionary sisters'. Concern on the part of the papacy in 1950 that Sisters required additional training across a wide range of disciplines, particularly in theology, scriptural studies and school curricula, initiated an influx of female religious into higher degrees and lectureships at third level. The Pontifical Institute of Regina Mundi established in Rome in 1954 offered three-year religious courses for both lay and religious women. Many of those returned to positions of responsibility within novitiates and 'brought back a new concept of the mission of religious orders'.[128]

In the wake of the Report of the Commission on Emigration (published in 1954), public attention was focused on government policies towards rural Ireland, and in particular on the relationship between emigration, late marriages and the quality of rural life.[129] There appears to have been little public debate on the loss to the country of so many educated young people. One TD had addressed this issue in 1948, referred to the failure 'to retain any percentage of the cream of young Ireland to build up the nation. From our universities and secondary schools, thousands of brilliant graduates and students have had to seek employment in Britain.'[130] A survey of intending emigrants in County Cavan during the 1960s showed that the majority of girls with secondary education would emigrate even if a job was available.[131] It has sometimes been suggested that without the safety valve of male unemployment during the 1940s and 1950s, serious social and political unrest may have emerged in the state. There is no doubt that Ireland lost some of its brightest young people during these years. What effect the loss of so many young women may have had on the women's movement mid-century can only be surmised.

From the mid-1960s, there emerged a discernible change in attitude regarding women's rights and status, both on the part of women themselves, and successive governments. While much change effected from the 1970s was the result of international developments—in particular Ireland's membership of the EEC from 1973—before such influences took effect a number of important domestic developments occurred in the field of family legislation. The 1964 Guardianship of Infants Act gave parents joint guardianship of their children, and in cases of dispute, allowed courts to make decisions on custody and access. The Succession Act of 1965 reformed the law regarding the estates of those who died without making a will, or who had failed to make provision for the surviving spouse. Prior to the passing of this latter act it was possible for one spouse to exclude the other from any share in his or her estate. While applicable across the general population, failure to make provision for widows was particularly relevant in farming communities, where the 'heir at law'—generally the oldest son—could inherit property in preference to the widow and other children.

Another problem in rural areas was the common practice of a man leaving money to the church for masses to be said after his death, often ignoring the needs of his wife and family. Kennedy has related the recollections of the then Minister for Justice, Charles Haughey, on the hostility shown to the bill in many quarters. Haughey recounted being approached by church authorities on the issue of money left for masses, the clergy pointing to the physical impossibility of saying the requested number of masses. This spurred him to examine the issue of inheritance, following which 'he became incensed by what he saw, by what the position was, that a man could ignore his wife in his will'.[132] Haughey's father had died at the age of forty-five, leaving a widow and seven children, and he acknowledged this personal perspective of widowhood probably influenced his thinking on the issue. Under the provisions of the Succession Act a surviving spouse became entitled to a proportion of the estate whether a will was made or not, the proportion depending on whether there were children to the marriage.

A notable development from the 1960s was the politicisation of widows in Ireland, described by June Levine as 'being ahead of their time in (their) recognition of the relationship between the personal and the political realms of life'.[133] The National Association of Irish Widows (NAIW), formed in 1967 by Eileen Proctor, played an important role in winning acknowledgement of the problems facing one-parent families. Initially formed as a support group for widows (of whom there were 129,793 in 1967), the organisation grew to seventeen branches nationwide.[134] Becoming more militant in the 1970s with street protests and mass meetings, the NAIW achieved increased social welfare allowances for widows with dependent children, and support for dependent children up to 18 years, or 21 years if at third-level education.[135] A further group of widows to become active during the 1960s were the widows of public servants, who were excluded from the provisions of the 1935 Widow's and Orphan's Act. Kennedy has argued that Haughey's attention to the needs of widows was further demonstrated in provisions he made in the late 1960s regarding this group. Yet, as Bríd Ní hÉigeartaigh has recounted, the Widows and Orphans pension scheme introduced in 1968 for public servants 'left out all the widows'.[136] The scheme provided for *wives* of civil servants, and excluded widows of civil servants who died before 23 July 1968.

Winifred Delaney and Rita Fay formed the Association of Widows of Civil Servants (AWCS) to campaign for the admission of pre-1968 widows to the pension scheme, a campaign that lasted until 1986 when they were granted full pension rights.[137] During these years the group lobbied successive Ministers for Finance, conducting a most earnest and vocal campaign, leading one Minister, George Colley, to describe them as 'a group of well-heeled articulate women only concerned with their own welfare'.[138] Ní hÉigeartaigh has pointed out that while the leaders of the group were articulate, they represented many widows who had nothing to live on, and who were neither well-heeled nor articulate. During the

1970s, the AWCS made use of the fact that some post-1968 widows—whose husbands had deliberately refused to join the new scheme—were being admitted on the basis of their husband's medical condition or state of mind. Their letter to John Kelly TD stated that:

> It could be argued that, if a husband's medical condition justified the admission of his widow to full benefit of the Pension Scheme which he had not joined, then, as the husbands of the pre-1968 widows suffered from the most incurable condition of all—death—the claim of these widows to the right to participation in the scheme is irrefutable.[139]

Starting with Haughey in 1969, a series of amendments were made allowing widows entry to the scheme on a phased basis, culminating in 1986. By this time, many of the qualifying widows were quite elderly, or had since died.

Towards the end of the 1960s international developments instigated significant changes in women's demands. Two key influences in this regard were the United Nations and the European Union. A brief look at the evolution of the EU demonstrates Irish enthusiasm for membership.

The first European Treaty was signed in Paris in 1951 between six member states, France, Germany, Italy, Belgium, the Netherlands and Luxembourg. Six years later, the Treaty of Rome officially created the European Economic Community (EEC) and was signed by the same six countries. In 1948 Ireland had signed the Convention creating the Organisation for European Economic Cooperation (OECC); that same year Ireland was a founding member of the Council of Europe, and a branch of the International Committee of the Movement for European Unity had been formed in Dublin.[140] There was widespread interest in Ireland in the 1950s towards membership of the EEC, particularly articulated by the Taoiseach, Seán Lemass. Ireland's first formal application for membership in July 1961 was unsuccessful. While economic and neutrality considerations were cited as reasons for non-admission at this stage, the hostility of General de Gaulle to British membership was a factor that undoubtedly impeded Irish entry during the 1960s.

Post-World War II, the issue of equality between the sexes was addressed by both the United Nations and the emerging EEC. It was Article 119 of the Treaty of Rome that introduced the first provision on gender equality in the early European Community, with its introduction of the principle of equal pay for women and men for equal work.

Subsequently, this principle would be used extensively to ensure equality between men and women in employment, being reinforced in subsequent Treaties. Through its contact with European women's groups during the 1950s and 1960s, both in the IAW and in consumer groups, the IHA was kept informed of developments regarding equality issues in the EEC. From 1949 the IHA had been represented at triennial congresses of the IAW, the 1961 congress of the IAW being held in Dublin.[141] In addition, IHA delegates attended conferences held by European women examining issues relating to women in the new Europe, and—wearing its consumer hat—the IHA received government funding to send delegates to conferences held by the OEEC.

In 1967, members of the IHA and the Business and Professional Women's Clubs (BPW) attending separate international congresses in Europe, learnt of a development that would, in time, radically affect Irishwomen. The UN Commission on the Status of Women had issued a directive to women's international non-governmental organisations, asking them to examine the status of women in their own countries, and where necessary, to urge their governments to set up a national commission on the status of women.[142] The IHA and the BPW decided to work together on the setting up of such a commission. Following a meeting in Dublin on 30 January 1968 attended by representatives of a dozen women's groups, it was decided to establish an ad hoc committee to work for a limited period, researching the need for a national commission. The resulting committee elected Hilda Tweedy (IHA) as chair, Dr Blanche Weekes (BPW) as honorary secretary, and Dr Hazel Boland, Women's International Zionist Organisation (WIZO) as honorary treasurer. In addition to these three groups, other organisations with permanent representatives on the ad hoc committee were: the NAIW, Association of Women Citizens, Irish Council of Women, ICA, Soroptimists Clubs of Ireland, Dublin University Women Graduates Association (DUWGA), UCD Women Graduates, with Rosaleen Mills an Independent.

It was decided not to publicise the work of the committee but to concentrate on garnering relevant information from its constituent members. Topics investigated included discrimination against married women in obtaining employment, exploitation of women in part-time work, payment of income tax, provision of pensions, retirement age for women workers, and the monitoring of advertisements offering lower pay to women with the same qualifications as men. It was agreed that 'women had to be educated to expect equal pay'.[143] The availability of educational facilities for girls wishing to study science and higher mathematics in preparation for non-traditional jobs, and of training and re-training in employment 'were hotly debated subjects'.[144]

On hearing that ICTU planned to discuss a resolution to government seeking the establishment of a Commission on the Status of Women, the ad hoc committee decided in May 1968 to go public and issue a press statement announcing its existence. While they much appreciated the support of ICTU, it was felt by all that such a demand should come from women's organisations. ICTU in turn unanimously passed its resolution on the matter. A memorandum was sent to the Taoiseach, Jack Lynch, by the ad hoc committee on 8 October 1968 requesting him to set up a National Commission on the Status of Women and to meet a deputation in this regard.[145] The committee was left waiting over a year for a response. During this time, the committee continued its investigations and monitoring of advertisements, lobbying candidates in the 1969 general election on the matter, and gathering information about similar commissions in Denmark and Canada. It was decided that the Commission should comprise equal numbers of women and men, with an independent chair. Dr Thekla Beere was their choice for the latter.

Twelve months after their original letter, the ad hoc committee again wrote to Jack Lynch requesting him to receive a deputation, and arranged a press conference for 12 November. On 7 November 1969, a reply was received from Lynch stating he was recommending the setting up of a National Commission, a fact confirmed by Lynch the following day at the annual dinner of the Soroptimists Club in Cork. While pleased and relieved at Lynch's announcement, the ad hoc committee were still keen for him to receive a deputation, a situation that was exacerbated when they learned of a suggestion that certain public service pay-claims be referred to the new Commission. Writing to the Taoiseach in December 1969, the ad hoc committee pointed out that the terms of reference and mandate of the Commission were not yet known and that they 'deplore(d) the suggestion that the setting up of a Commission should be used to delay action on any of the points mentioned in our Memorandum'.[146]

In this context, some correspondence in the National Archives shed light on government thinking at this time. In November 1968 a letter from the office of the Minister for Labour to the Department of the Taoiseach on the issue of equal pay differentiates between the private and public sectors. In regard to the former, the Minister felt it was the responsibility of the trade unions to attain this objective through negotiating pay agreements with employers. In the public sector, the

Minister had suggested to the Minister for Finance that the principle of equal pay 'be generally considered'. The letter stated that the Minister felt that 'public opinion would not favour the general removal of barriers on the employment of married women in public employment in view of the substantial extent of male unemployment'.[147] The Minister did accept, however, that married women were being employed to a greater extent in the public sector, and that the general policy on this issue would have to be reviewed. A letter from the Department of Finance to the Taoiseach's Private Secretary in August 1969 accepted that pressure for equal pay was likely to increase, but noted the Finance Minister's concern regarding the cost of its introduction, particularly in the context of industrial competitiveness. The Minister concluded that the establishment of a Commission as suggested by the ad hoc committee 'would provide the government with an answer to groups seeking to force them to move too precipitately towards equal pay'.[148] The ad hoc committee were invited to meet with the Minister for Finance, Charles Haughey, who confirmed that the setting up of the Commission was imminent. Subsequently its terms of reference were published:

> To examine and report on the status of women in Irish society, to make recommendations on the steps necessary to ensure the participation of women on equal terms and conditions with men in the political, social, cultural and economic life of the country, and to indicate the implications generally—including the estimated cost—of such recommendations.[149]

In April 1970 the members of the Commission were announced with Dr Thekla Beere as its chair. Beere, the first woman to be appointed secretary to a government department, had a distinguished academic career, graduating from Trinity College Dublin in 1922 in both law and legal and political science.[150] Despite her dual degree, she was unable to obtain employment except as a grade 3 temporary clerk in the Central Statistics Office. Awarded a two-year Rockefeller Scholarship, Beere studied at Harvard and Berkeley. On her return to Ireland she returned to the civil service as a technical assistant, on a low pay rate similar to junior executive officer. With little promotional opportunities, Beere assessed her options and decided to move down a level to staff officer, from which point she could move upwards. Eventually promoted to higher executive, Beere expected to be left at that point for some time, but staff shortages during the war years opened up vacancies, and she applied for and obtained Assistant Principal Officer. Subsequent promotion saw her become Principal Officer and then Assistant Secretary in the Department of Industry and Commerce. During Seán Lemass's period as Minister in the new Department of Transport, Marine, Tourism and Power, Beere was promoted to Secretary of the Department in 1959. Throughout her civil service career—despite her qualifications and promotions—at no stage did she receive equal pay with her male colleagues.[151] Beere viewed her appointment as chair of the Commission in 1970 with mixed feelings—on the one hand she had just completed three years work on the Devlin Commission on the Public Service, and was looking forward to enjoying her retirement. However, she accepted the role 'because I felt it was my duty as a woman, and I felt I should do my best to help women'.[152] Beere later referred to the awareness gained by herself and other Commissioners during their work of the legal and economic difficulties faced by many women, and the often established views of some male trade unionists towards women's work.[153]

Having attained its objective, the ad hoc committee met in May 1970 to wind up its affairs, expressing satisfaction with the terms and composition of the Commission, and with the appointment of two of its members to the Commission. In 1971, the Commission published an interim report on Equal Pay, its full report being published in 1972. From a total of 49 wide-ranging recommendations, 17 related to equal pay and women's working conditions, others highlighting issues to be taken up by women's groups, trade unions, etc. It recommended the abolition of sex discrimination in employment, the provision of twelve weeks' maternity leave, training facilities for women, and the removal of discrimination and/or inequities regarding women in education, social welfare, taxation, political and cultural life.[154] Two key recommendations by the Commission were the introduction of an allowance for unmarried mothers rearing children on their own, and a payment to be made to mothers in the home. The former measure was introduced in 1973, but the latter has never been implemented. In line with another recommendation of the Commission that children's allowances be paid directly to mothers, this measure was passed by government within the provisions of the Social Welfare Act 1974. The Dáil deputy who had first proposed such a measure some thirty years earlier—Liam Cosgrave—was Taoiseach when the measure finally passed.

To ensure implementation of the Commission's recommendations, and to act as a co-ordinating body for women's organisations, a permanent Council for the Status of Women (csw) was established in 1972, with Hilda Tweedy as its first chairperson. Seventeen women's groups initially joined the csw, soon rising to thirty plus.[155] With no government aid before 1975, the work of the csw was carried out by volunteers, its meetings held in rooms provided free of charge by the DUWGA and the ICA. It has been noted that while none of the groups were radical in a feminist sense 'even the notion of such a body would have been radical before the activities of the early seventies'.[156] Despite Ireland's membership of the EEC from 1973, the Irish government tried to postpone implementation of equal pay in the public service, due to become law in January 1976. Following a legal challenge against the government by the Chairwoman of the Women's Political Association (WPA), the European Commission rejected the Irish government's application for derogation from its directive on equal pay which was made binding, retrospectively from February 1976.

The cumulative effect of the Report of the Commission on the Status of Women, the formation of the csw, the emergence of radical women's liberation groups, and pressure from Europe, produced during the 1970s a series of legislative measures that transformed many key areas of women's lives, particularly those relating to equal pay and opportunity, the elimination of the marriage bar, provision of paid maternity leave, and a series of social welfare benefits regarding widows, deserted wives and single mothers. In a progress report in April 1975 on the implementation of the recommendations of the Commission on the Status of Women, Thekla Beere pointed out that '50 per cent of our recommendations have been implemented or are in the process of implementation, 30 per cent have been accepted in principle, and work is proceeding towards their implementation. On 20 per cent I can find no action.'[157] In 1974 the Minister for Finance Michael O'Leary set up the Women's Representative Committee (WRC) to monitor progress towards the implementation of the Commission's recommendations. Chaired by Eileen Desmond TD, the WRC consisted of nominees of the ICTU and FUE, the csw, the Economic and Social Research Institute (ESRI) and a legal representative of the Minister. Following its disbandment in 1976 after the production of a progress report, the Employment Equality Agency (EEA) was established in 1977, with Sylvia Meehan as its first chairperson.[158] Interestingly, in light of the Beere progress report in 1975, that of the WRC in 1976 showed there to have been 75 per cent implementation of the commission's recommendations, with partial implementation of a further 17 per cent.[159]

During the early years of the twentieth century radical suffrage groups using militant tactics had emerged, inspired by a combination of impatience with government inaction, and with the conservative gradualist approach of earlier suffragists. Generally these were women of a younger generation, impatient for change, and more conscious of feminist demands worldwide. Through their militancy, much press coverage and notoriety was attained. Relations with the older groups, while strained at times, generally remained cordial, particularly in Ireland where both camps co-operated on the core issues of the day. An analogy between this and the emergence of a women's liberation—as opposed to a women's rights—movement in Ireland from 1970 can be seen to exist to a degree. The Irish Women's Liberation Movement (IWLM), and later Irish Women United (IWU) have been described by Tweedy as 'justifiably angry young women, who expected immediate responses to their demands, looked upon the *ad hoc* committee, and the CSW as "establishment", and anything we did, or had done, was suspect to them'.[160] Tweedy notes that the CSW group resented this, fearing the methods of the younger group would result in a backlash and further delay in the reforms it sought. She points out that although there were confrontations, the CSW found that some issues raised by the new groups 'were pinpointing areas of discrimination which needed investigation and which the Council should address'.[161]

While many of the issues raised by both IWLM and IWU were similar to the concerns of the CSW, their means of articulating concern was radical confrontation allied to expressive and spontaneous action. Methods used by the women's liberation groups included consciousness raising, public demonstrations, and very effective use of media, written, radio and television—not surprising since many members were journalists and broadcasters. From early 1971, a number of key examples of successful publicity strategy by the IWLM included the publication of its manifesto *Chains or Change? The Civil Wrongs of Irish Women,* their presentation of an entire edition of *The Late Late Show* on Irish TV during which 'IWLM women on the panel raised hitherto unspoken issues and taboo topics for women ... on a range of social and sexual matters',[162] and a highly publicised 'Contraceptive Train' to Belfast. Conflict over the definition of feminism and structural inadequacies led to the disintegration of IWLM later that year.

A number of single-issue organisations emerged from 1972, each becoming effective pressure groups.[163] A key area of disagreement between the CSW and IWLM was the issue of contraception. While central to the demands of women's liberation groups, Tweedy has recounted, in 1974 the csw could not obtain consensus amongst its affiliates on the issue of family planning, despite the fact that the 1972 Commission had included such provision in its recommendations.[164]

During the 1970s it can be seen that many of the objectives of women's organisations over the previous hundred years began to be attained. During that hundred-year span, a series of women's groups had emerged, often with a particular demand relevant to the situation of women at the time, but all imbued with the underlying aim of improving the economic, political and social role of women in Ireland. Generally small in number and middle-class in nature, over the decades such groups continued to articulate concern on particular issues relevant to women. They were not joined in any great numbers by the mass of Irish women, a fact possibly explained by a number of factors, including economic circumstances, the overwhelming rural nature of Irish society for most of this period, acceptance of traditional attitudes towards women's role, religious influence, all reinforced by government policy. Other considerations for the lack of women's participation are political antipathy, poverty, high rates of female emigration, and apathy among those many women described by Hanna Sheehy Skeffington as having 'no interest in politics'.[165] Yet there survived throughout this period a core group of activists who, although sometimes disagreeing on priorities or methodology, continued an often-lonely campaign to achieve change for the betterment of women in Irish society.

A number of clear stages emerge from this study. Firstly, those women activists of the late nineteenth century who sought equality in education, property rights and suffrage. During the early years of the twentieth century, the suffrage campaign dominated, in both its militant and non-militant phases, both influenced in turn by political and nationalist developments. From the early years of the newly independent state, women's groups articulated opposition to restrictive legislation on the employment and public rights of women, culminating in opposition to clauses regarding women in the Constitution of 1937. Between the 1940s and 1960s three main groups emerge to speak on behalf of women, the jcwssw, the iha and the ica. Working to different agendas relative to the groups they represented, as with earlier groups, these organisations worked together on issues of common concern. It is no surprise therefore that members of all three groups were involved in the establishment of the ad hoc committee in 1968, and the subsequent csw.

Linda Connolly has referred to the 'thread of historical continuity' that existed between the earlier and later women's movement.[166] That such a thread existed is without doubt, fragile though it appeared at times. The overlap of women from earlier groups into the formation of mid-century organisations—and into the new developments from 1968—ensured its continuance. Ultimately, such long-term activism resulted in the Commission on the Status of Women and the formation of the csw. Using its significant experience and inherited traditions of political lobbying and international connections, the csw continued the work of pioneering women's groups in an environment becoming increasingly more open to change. That is not to say that all was achieved; far from it. Many issues regarding equality and discrimination continued to be problematic, often needing legal or European intervention for attainment. From the 1970s, agencies such as the EEA and the csw continued activism in these areas. While articulating differing priorities, the 1970s saw a coalition of forces in the cause of women reflecting both the pioneering work of earlier generations, and the need for continued work on the journey towards equality, emancipation and empowerment.

EPILOGUE: A WOMAN'S WORLD?

Like most historic peoples
We are defined
By what we forget,

By what we never will be:
Star-gazers,
Fire-eaters.
It's our alibi

For all time
That as far as history goes
We were never
On the scene of the crime.

EAVAN BOLAND, '*It's a Woman's World*'[1]

Between 1870 and 1970 Ireland as a nation had undergone many changes, from colonial state through armed uprising, civil war, partition and independent republic. The significant societal changes that occurred during this period were sometimes, although not always, the result of political upheaval. Through all such transitions, the people of the country were forced to cope, to adapt, and to survive. This they did in a variety of ways, sometimes benefiting from change, other times becoming its victims.

The focus of this study has been to trace the role, status and voice of Irish women during these years. Two distinct profiles emerge from the 1870s onwards, one questioning, the other accepting. The questioning profile begins somewhat tentatively, seeking social justice for those in need. Gradually that questioning becomes more focused on women themselves, and over the decades more persistent. Always a minority, the questioners are to be found throughout the entire period and beyond.

The accepting profile is, without doubt, the majority. Spread across all classes of society, its members reflect the majority population as a whole, accepting of authority, of one's place in society, of tradition. Among this majority, Irish women from both rural and urban backgrounds lived out their lives within the social and economic confines of the class into which they had been born. For many at the lower end of the class hierarchy, life was very often a struggle to survive against harsh conditions in both town and country. Life was easier for those of a more comfortable class, but here too, social convention and economic priorities dictated their life choices. From within both socio-economic groups, those who could not, or who would not be accommodated within such strictures, were forced to leave. At times, a decision to leave was not merely an alternative, but a firm rejection of the available life-style options. In exercising this decision, many moved closer to the ranks of the questioner.

The voice of the questioner can be found throughout the entirety of this period in active campaigns to advance the opportunities available to women, varying in emphasis according to political circumstances and conditions. While the individuals involved at any one time may have had quite different political and/or social allegiance, these campaigns built one on the other, each attainment giving strength to further demands. During the first fifty years of this study, the quest for equality of education at all levels allied to the achievement of the married women's property acts became interspersed with demands for increased employment opportunities for women and the political franchise. The latter movement was without doubt the child of the educational and married women's property campaigns. Its two distinct stages—late nineteenth century constitutional and early twentieth century radical—reflected both differing times and attitudinal changes between generations. The noisy, forceful suffragettes of pre-World War I years were the product of achievements won by a previous generation, a pattern to be repeated some fifty years later.

In many ways it can be argued that the most groundbreaking gains for women were attained during the first half of this study. During the years 1870–1922, significant improvements were obtained for women in education, property rights, local and parliamentary suffrage, and expansion of working opportunities. In contrast, the following thirty years saw a contraction of women's rights and work opportunities, emphasis being placed on women in the home. Education was one of the key determinants effecting significant change in the lives of women in

Ireland. Nineteenth-century developments at second and third level can be seen to have benefited middle-class women primarily, but the importance of primary education should not be overlooked. It was at primary level that the majority of females attended, becoming more literate than earlier generations, and attending in higher numbers than their brothers. This latter fact, allied to the socio-economic circumstances of the time, can be seen as a deliberate employment strategy by parents. Post-independence, increasing participation by girls in second-level education is reflected in the number of girls sitting the Intermediate examination equalling that of boys by the early 1950s.

Following the introduction of free second-level education in the 1960s, the number of girls attending second-level outnumbered boys by 1971. Examination results for 1967–1972 show a higher percentage of girls passing both Intermediate and Leaving certificate examinations, with male and female results for Honours Leaving Certificate in the same period becoming almost identical. This pattern was not reflected at third level, however. The 1965 *Investment in Education* report had noted that of those achieving honours Leaving Certificate in 1963, 43 per cent of boys went to university but only 19 per cent of girls did so. The report of the Commission on the Status of Women in 1972 pointed out that between 1964 and 1969 women comprised one-third of all full-time students in the NUI and University of Dublin. The Commission's hope that changing societal attitudes and removal of the marriage bar would redress the imbalance began to be realised from the 1970s.

The expansion of female religious orders during the first half of the nineteenth century opened up new career opportunities for Irishwomen at home and abroad. The initiators of this new religious life for women were radical, independent women who saw a need for their work in society, and determined to do it. Forced to establish formal religious orders by local bishops, they reluctantly agreed to do so in the interests of their work. Their successors were less vocal, more compliant, working within a framework of a highly organised church and Episcopal control. The continuance of such acquiescence by further generations of nuns, promulgated through their key role within education and health, would have implications for women's self-image both within and outside the convent for many decades. Nonetheless, the presence of such a body of female religious into the mid-twentieth century presented to the laity the relatively novel image of a powerful group of women, active in many key aspects of state services, and church ministry. Through their prominent role in female education, and in their capacity as owners and matrons of hospitals, industrial schools and orphanages throughout the country, 'these women were major players in church-state relations below the official level of the Catholic hierarchy'.[2]

Nineteenth-century activists had voiced their concerns on a number of issues regarding women's rights within marriage and the family. The first significant development for women during this period was the successful campaign for the legal right of married women to own property in their own name. It is noteworthy that the Act of 1882 which conferred this right (with some alterations between 1884 and 1907) essentially remained unchanged until the Married Women's Status Act of 1957. This latter Act allowed a married woman to make her own contracts without her husband's consent, to sue and be sued on them, and allowed one spouse to sue another in court. In the Senate debate on the Bill, Owen Sheehy Skeffington, while generally welcoming the bill, disagreed with the suggestion of a colleague that women now possessed equal rights, pointing to the restrictions on married women workers. Another Senator, Dr O'Connell, worried about the effect of the Bill on the already low marriage rate, argued that 'one of those wary gentlemen who would like to be sure that he would be the member of the matrimonial team who would always wear the trousers, if it were to be different, (might) think twice before entering into this bond'.[3]

Other particularly relevant developments in family law during the 1960s were the Guardianship of Infants Act 1964 which gave parents the right to joint guardianship of their children, and the Succession Act of 1965 which gave a woman the same rights to her husband's estate as he had to hers, and specified the shares of spouses and children on intestacy. The Family Home Protection Act of 1976 ensured that the family home could not be sold or mortgaged without the consent of both spouses. Welcome as this Act was, it stopped short of securing a joint legal right to ownership of the family home.

Campaigners on women's issues during the late nineteenth century were tenacious in pursuit of their aims, pressing for reform of the many legal and social measures discriminating against women. Their *modus operandi* was to gain acceptance of their objectives by means of appeals to politicians, public lectures and letters to the press, all conducted in a strictly constitutional manner in keeping with the social mores of the day. Results in the field of education, property rights and moral reform were attained quicker than political rights. A significant break-through in regard to the latter was achieved in the Poor Law and Local Government provisions for qualifying women at the end of the century.

While many of the above attainments initially benefited only women of some means, the breaking of the sex barrier was crucial for future developments. The legacy of such attainments, allied to the example of early activists, laid the foundations for the new generation of women who became active in the early 1900s. Adopting a more radical outspoken approach, this second phase of the women's movement interacted with the many political and social questions surfacing in Ireland up to the foundation of the new state. As political conditions nationally and internationally became more acute, women took differing approaches on issues such as war, pacifism and nationalist objectives. A core group struggled to maintain feminist ideals, sometimes within, sometimes outside formal political organisation. Generally, it is women from this group who are found to the fore of campaigns regarding women's issues during the 1920s and 1930s in the new southern state. Unionist women opposed to Home Rule organised in 1911 into the successful UWUC. While non-feminist, this outlived other contemporary women's groups 'continuing to introduce women to unionism and to political activity'.[4] From 1922, however, this study focuses primarily on the Irish Free State/Republic of Ireland.

The political and constitutional status of women within the new Irish state in 1922 appeared to meet all feminist demands of the previous decade. Equal suffrage and opportunities for public office were guaranteed within the constitution, principles drawn from the proclamation of 1916, and strengthened by the active role of women in nationalist life from 1916. Given the high profile of women such as Constance Markievicz, Jennie Wyse Power, Mary MacSwiney, Dr Kathleen Lynn, Hanna Sheehy Skeffington, Kathleen Clarke to name but a few, it was not unreasonable to expect that women would continue to play a prominent and meaningful role in the development of the new state. Yet, time would show that this period was in fact the peak of women's political involvement until the early 1980s. A number of factors contributed to this development—the strong anti-Treaty stance of many nationalist women, the lack of a cohesive women's movement post-suffrage, and the development of an authoritarian society with traditional views regarding women. Bitter post-civil war political differences accentuated the problem. MacSwiney, Markievicz, Lynn and Caitlín Brugha—all elected in the 1923 General Election—abstained because of their anti-Treaty stance. By the election of 1927, the only woman in the Dáil was Margaret Collins O'Driscoll, sister of Michael Collins.

Over the coming decade, a recurring pattern emerged in regard to women elected to the Dáil—they were all widows or sisters of dead patriots. Generally voting with the government of the day, and conservative in regard to women's issues, they became known as 'the silent sisters'. From the total number of 650 TDs elected to the Dáil in the period 1922–1977, only 24 were women (less than 4 per cent over 55 years). Only five of these women did not fall into the 'dead-relative' category. Even more striking is the fact that in the first 57 years of independence, 15 of the 26 counties never once elected a woman TD. Maurice Manning has noted that women TDs always placed party before sex, never defying the party whip or taking a major initiative on women's issues. Their hard work on behalf of constituents was combined with 'a sense of knowing their place in a male-dominated political world—and keeping to it. And since the electors kept sending back the same women to the Dáil, this presumably is what they wanted'.[5]

It would appear that the women elected to the Dáil were not the only 'silent sisters'. Despite the valiant efforts of women's groups from the 1920s, the non-politicisation of most Irish women on issues directly affecting their role and status in the state, and in effect their non-use of the suffrage in anything other than party political concerns, was a serious impediment in preventing or changing restrictive measures introduced during the first thirty years of the state. In part a legacy of the sublimation of women's issues to national questions from 1914, and the non-feminist agenda of many women who became active in the nationalist movement post-1916, the diminishing public visibility of women from the 1920s was strengthened by the deepening Catholic ethos and conservative values of the Irish Free State. Notable exceptions to this pattern were a number of women members of the 1922–1936 Senate, in particular Jennie Wyse Power, Kathleen Clarke, Eileen Costello and Kathleen Brown, who—across party lines—consistently opposed legislation which sought to restrict the role of women. Clancy has pointed to the discrepancy between the united response from politically opposed women Senators to the erosion of women's rights, and a similar united response across party political differences in the Dáil supporting such legislation.[6]

A notable factor throughout this study has been the significant amount of female emigration. The scale of Irish emigration generally was unique, and was particularly so in regard to Irish women. J.J. Lee, in his seminal study *Ireland 1912–1985*, has pointed to the evasion of responsibility for emigration throughout this period by a series of politicians and the more privileged business, professional and large farming classes. Emigration was portrayed as a random choice by those foolish enough—or daring enough—to seek to better themselves by leaving Ireland. De Valera's idealised Ireland of a people satisfied with frugal comfort was in fact an Ireland wherein life was distinctly more frugal for some than for others, with choice being particularly lacking.[7] Views articulated by Alexis Fitzgerald (later Senator) in a reservation to the report on the Commission on Emigration have been seen to reflect those widely held among the possessing classes, with 'no hint that emigration was intimately related to the wealth, power and privilege structure of the society, to the accident of birth according to class and geographical location'.[8]

Concern with female emigration had been voiced from the early 1900s, continuing with the ever-increasing figures over the decades which resulted in Ireland boasting the highest rate of female emigration of any European country between 1945 and 1960. Early twentieth-century commentators argued that Irish girls, beguiled by expectations of high wages abroad, were turning their back on the simple life and putting themselves and their souls at risk. By the 1930s, outside influences—in particular the cinema—were blamed for adding to the outpouring of female emigrants. Commenting that it was more likely that girls were fleeing from 'the fate staring at them in the wizened faces of their own mothers and unmarried aunts', Lee points out that the cinema cannot be blamed for earlier generations of female emigrants, citing Æ's 1912 remarks that 'Many a young Irish girl must have looked on the wrinkled face and bent back and rheumatic limbs of her mother, and grown maddened in a sudden passion that her own fresh young life might end just like this'.[9] Huge increases in the number of female emigrants in the post-World War ii era saw concern for their sexual morality being increasingly voiced, with a prohibition on such emigration being mooted by one politician. The seriousness of the emigration crisis facing the country by mid-century is emphasised by Lee's figure that 'four out of every five children born in Ireland between 1931 and 1941 emigrated in the 1950s'.[10]

Those women who stayed in Ireland post-independence faced limited options. While employment opportunities for women expanded from the early 1900s, women were paid less than men, usually at the lower grades. This applied across the spectrum of areas in which most women were employed—clerical/white collar work, teaching and nursing, and in manufacturing and service areas. If a woman did not marry and continued in employment, promotional opportunities were limited, with priority being given to men. The Brennan Commission reporting in the 1930s on the organisation and efficient working of the Civil Service noted that 'if a woman recruited to the post married after eight or ten years, the main purpose for which she had been employed entirely fails, and she has, moreover, during that time been blocking the way of a man who could give good value for the service in question'.[11] Differential pay rates between the sexes was justified by the Commission as accepted by Irish society and outside the remit of the Civil Service to alter, pointing out that 'if the Government were to grant equal pay the result would be a disproportionate influx (of women) into State employment'. Reflecting traditional views across the classes on the 'proper' role of women, the majority of women did not work outside the home after marriage, a situation that was enforced in law for those in the public service from the 1930s. Despite a significant increase in the number of women working in manufacturing industries from the 1930s, the ideal for most families, reinforced by the trade union movement, was that married women should not be employed.

Strong participation by women in events leading to the establishment of the Irish Free State in 1922 led many to assume that the new government would welcome a continuance of such participation. Constitutional provisions regarding equality underpinned this expectation. Within two years, however, the first hint of restriction was introduced, a precedent for further legislative constraints over the next decade. In protest against these measures, a further phase of women's activism emerged. During the first thirty years of the new state such activists included veterans of the suffrage, labour and nationalist movements as well as a younger generation of women. The experienced and the novice both sought ways to progress women's role despite the odds being increasingly stacked against them. The work of organisations such as the Women's Citizens Association, the Joint Committee of Women's Societies and Social Workers (JCWSSW), the Women Graduates Associations and the Irish Women Workers' Union during the 1920s and 1930s emphasised the need for a political voice for women on decisions affecting equality and opportunity.

The formation of the Women's Social and Progressive League following the passing of the 1937 constitution was an attempt to formally politicise women activists to achieve the election of more female politicians. Its failure to do so must be measured by the forces against which women's groups were pitted, the conservative nature of Irish society with its emphasis on a non-public role for women, the non-involvement of the majority of women in political debate, and above all the male-dominated party political system which did little to encourage women—unless they happened to be the bearer of a politically useful name.

Increasingly confined to the home from the 1930s, what options were open to women anxious to participate in and contribute to public life in Ireland? Was it through the use of the very acceptable home base that such participation could be achieved? It is perhaps no accident that the long established Irish Countrywomen's Association (ICA), and the newly established Irish Housewives Association (IHA)—both groups representing women within the home—became increasingly more articulate and listened to by official sources from the 1940s onwards. Concentrating on the improvement of conditions and provision of educational opportunities for rural women, the ICA was particularly active in the establishment of country markets, and in rural electrification and water schemes during the 1940s and 1950s. The IHA, initially concerned with the fair distribution of household goods during the war years, very quickly articulated its concerns on the health and well-being of women and children, particularly those living in poverty and slum conditions. It too attempted to gain direct political representation by participating in local and national elections. Its increasing involvement in consumer issues would in time lead to the establishment of the Consumers Association of Ireland in 1966.

While both the ICA and the IHA were represented on international women's groups, it was the IHA in particular which focused on issues of women's equality, monitoring developments in both the national and international arena. Ultimately the influence of the IHA and a number of other women's groups active during the 1950s and 1960s—allied to international developments regarding the role and status of women in society—resulted in the formation of the first Commission on the Status of Women in April 1970.

The post-World War II decade in Ireland marked a particularly low point in the status of Irishwomen. However, despite the dismal economic condition of 1950s Ireland, from a female perspective the mid-decade years can be viewed as a crossroads. Behind lay restrictions—and attainments—to date. Ahead beckoned further equality, demonstrated by domestic legislation regarding married women, property and succession rights, the abolition of the ban on primary school teachers in 1958, and above all, the influence of Ireland's pending membership of the European Economic Community with significant knock-on effects for women's rights. While the latter was not apparent in 1958, the groundwork was being prepared by groups such as the IHA, the JCWSSW, and eventually the ad hoc committee. As in earlier years, when changing styles of women's activism had emerged in reaction to social and political circumstances, the 1970s would see an explosion of radical women's groups seeking a broader agenda of reform than they recognised in the ad hoc aspirations. Reflecting international trends, the Irishwomen's Liberation Movement was formed in Dublin in the early 1970s, followed by a series of women's groups focusing on a particular agenda. Looking back over the history of women's organisation, with highs and lows of achievement at differing times, there is no doubt that developments during the 1970s embodied the pinnacle of a century of determined activity to improve the role and status of women in Irish society. The hackneyed political phrase 'a lot done, a lot more to do' still applied, however. The 1972 report of the Commission on the Status of Women, while detailing many instances of actual discrimination against women, noted that their removal would still leave untouched a larger and more subtle area of discrimination, in particular:

> . . . the stereotyped role that is assigned to women, the inculcation of attitudes in both boys and girls in their formative years that there are definite and separate roles for the sexes and that a woman's life pattern must be predominantly home-centred while the man's life pattern will be predominantly centred on employment. It is from this type of cultural mould that formal discrimination arises, and it is only by the removal of such traditional attitudes that women can hope to achieve complete self-fulfilment and equal participation in all aspects of the community.[12]

In 1932, the *International Women's News* reported the presentation in Dublin of a municipal robe to independent councillor Mary Kettle by a group of over 100 feminists as 'a gesture to honour a woman who has upheld the dignity of her sex in public affairs and who has ever been a consistent feminist'.[13] In her response, Kettle noted that her aim on entering public life had been 'to give children a square meal and women a square deal', commenting that 'the latter has been much harder than the former'.[14] When Mary Robinson was elected President of Ireland in 1990, she noted that in her election, the women of Ireland—who had traditionally rocked the cradle—had 'rocked the system'.[15] While their number may have been small, this study has shown that from 1870 there have been always some women attempting to 'rock the system'.

REFERENCES

Introduction (pages XVII–XX)
1. Mary Robinson, 'Women & the New Irish State' in Margaret MacCurtain and Donncha Ó Corráin (eds), *Women in Irish Society: The Historical Dimension* (Dublin 1978).
2. Maria Luddy and Cliona Murphy (eds), *Women Surviving: Studies in Irish Women's History in the 19th and 20th centuries* (Dublin 1990).
3. Deirdre Beddoe, *Discovering Women's History* (London 1983).
4. MacCurtain and Ó Corráin, *Women in Irish Society*.
5. Mary E. Daly, 'Women in the Irish Workforce from Pre-Industrial to Modern Times', in *Saothar 7* (1981).
6. V. H. Galbraith, *Why We Study History* (London 1944).

Chapter 1 (pages 1–20)
1. Richard J. Evans, *The Feminists: Women's Emancipation Movements in Europe, America and Australasia 1840–1920* (London 1977), p. 34.
2. Mary Wollstonecraft, *A Vindication of the Rights of Woman*, Prefatory Note by Elizabeth Robins Pennell (ed.) to 1891 edition (London), p. vii.
3. Deirdre Raftery, *Women and Learning in English Writing 1600–1900* (Dublin 1997), p. 71.
4. Wollstonecraft, *Vindication*, p. 53.
5. Ibid, p. 210.
6. Raftery, *Women and Learning*, pp 73–4.
7. J. Mill, article on 'Government', in Encyclopaedia Britannica, Supplement to 4th, 5th and 6th editions, VOL. 4 (1820), p. 500.
8. Dolores Dooley, 'Anna Doyle Wheeler', in Mary Cullen and Maria Luddy (eds), *Women, Power and Consciousness in 19th-Century Ireland* (Dublin 1995), p. 26. (Wheeler was active in Co-operative and Utilitarian groups in France and London and was a close ally of Robert Owen and Jeremy Bentham; through this circle she met Thompson, an economist and theorist in the Co-operative Movement.)
9. W. Thompson (London 1825). While Thompson is cited as the sole author, an 'Introductory letter' clarifies Wheeler's contribution; Dooley, 'Anna Doyle Wheeler', p. 26.
10. Evans, *The Feminists*, p. 64.
11. Evans, *The Feminists*, p. 63.
12. Andrew Rosen, *Rise Up Women! The Militant Campaign of the Women's Social and Political Union 1903–1914* (London and Boston 1974), pp 8–9.
13. Evans, *The Feminists*, p. 64.

14. Maria Luddy, 'Women and Politics in Ireland, 1860–1918', in Angela Bourke et al (eds), *The Field Day Anthology of Irish Writing* VOL. V, *Irish Women's Writing and Traditions* (Cork 2002), p. 71.

15. Evans, *The Feminists*, p. 34.

16. H. Blackburn, *A Record of the Women's Suffrage Movement in the British Isles* (London 1902).

17. 'The Women of Ireland', in *Dublin University Magazine*, May 1939, pp 591–2.

18. 'Womanhood and its Mission', in *Dublin University Magazine, Part 1* (1859), p. 628.

19. *Report of Statistical and Social Inquiry Society of Ireland* (Dublin 1863), v. 3, p. 138.

20. Rosen, *Rise Up Women!*, p. 5.

21. George Dangerfield, *The Strange Death of Liberal England* (London 1966), p. 138.

22. Evans, *The Feminists*, p. 24.

23. Joseph Lee, *The Modernisation of Irish Society 1848–1918* (Dublin 1973 and 1989), p. 1.

24. Maria Luddy, *Field Day*, p. 71.

25. Evans has noted that Mill's essay, *The Subjection of Women* (London 1869) became 'the feminist bible', cited in Evans, *The Feminists*, p. 18.

26. Blackburn, *A Record of the Women's Suffrage Movement*, pp 53–6; also *Reports of the Irish Women's Suffrage and Local Government Association 1896–1918* (IWSLGA), preface to 1918 report.

27. Blackburn, *A Record of the Women's Suffrage Movement*, p. 140.

28. J.S. Mill to Thomas Haslam 17 August 1867, Historical Library, Quaker House, Rathfarnham, Dublin 16.

29. Carmel Quinlan, *Genteel Revolutionaries, Anna and Thomas Haslam and the Irish Women's Movement* (Cork 2002), p. 113.

30. *Report of Statistical and Social Inquiry Society of Ireland* (Dublin 1868), v. 4, p. 457.

31. Volume of Women's Suffrage pamphlets, The Women's Library (formerly the Fawcett Library), London, ref. 396.11.

32. *Women's Suffrage Journal*, 1870, 1871, 1873, 1874.

33. Cited in Quinlan, *Genteel Revolutionaries*, p. 113.

34. *Women's Suffrage Journal*, October 1871, p. 109.

35. Quinlan, *Genteel Revolutionaries*, pp 114–17.

36. Maria Luddy, 'Isabella M.S. Tod', in Cullen and Luddy (eds), *Women, Power and Consciousness*, pp 215–16.

37. Ibid, pp 216–17.

38. IWSLG, 1918 Report, preface p. 3.

39. Quinlan, *Genteel Revolutionaries*, Introduction pp ix–x.

40. *The Women's Advocate*, NO. 1 (Dublin, April 1874), pp 1–2.

41. *Irish Citizen*, 21 March 1914.

42. Quinlan, *Genteel Revolutionaries*, p. 122.

43. Mary Cullen, 'Anna Maria Haslam', in Cullen and Luddy (eds), *Women, Power*

and Consciousness, p. 174.

44. Quinlan, *Genteel Revolutionaries*, p. 122. Among early male supporters were Charles Eason, Abraham Shackleton, Henry Allen, and MPS T.W. Russell, Maurice Brookes, Colonel Taylor, William Johnston and Sergeant-At-Arms, David Sherlock.

45. Cullen, 'Anna Maria Haslam', p. 174; Quinlan, *Genteel Revolutionaries*, p. 125.

46. Cullen, 'Anna Maria Haslam', p. 175.

47. Evans, *The Feminists*, p. 144.

48. The Primrose League (Conservative) was established in 1885, the Women's Liberal Association in 1886 and the Women's Liberal Unionist Association in 1885.

49. Ian d'Alton, 'Southern Irish Unionism', in *Transactions of the Royal Historical Society*, 5th series, 23, 1973, p. 85; also R. Fulford, *Votes for Women* (London 1957), p. 94.

50. Rosen, *Rise Up Women!*, p. 12.

51. IWSLG, *Annual Report 1918* (preface).

52. Rosen, *Rise Up Women!*, p. 10.

53. House of Commons Debates (H.C.Deb.), 4s, 37, 18 February 1896, p. 631.

54. H.C.Deb., 4s, 37, 2 March 1896, p. 1450.

55. DWSA, *1897 Report*, p. 5.

56. H.C.Deb., 4s, 45, 3 February 1898, pp 1202–20.

57. DWSA, *1898 Report*, p. 6.

58. IWSLGA, *Annual Report* 1903, p. 7.

59. Rosemary Cullen Owens, *Smashing Times: A History of the Irish Women's Suffrage Movement 1889–1922* (Dublin 1984 and 1995), p. 34.

60. Evans, *The Feminists*, p. 1.

61. Barbara Bodichon, quoted in Deirdre Rafterty, 'Frances Power Cobbe', in Cullen and Luddy (eds), *Women, Power and Consciousness*, p. 91.

62. Ibid, p. 106.

63. Evans, *The Feminists*, p. 63.

64. Quoted in Rafferty, 'Frances Power Cobbe', p. 107.

65. Luddy, 'Women and Politics in 19th-Century Ireland', in Maryann Gialanella Valiulis and Mary O'Dowd (eds), *Women and Irish History: Essays in honour of Margaret MacCurtain* (Dublin 1997), p. 102.

66. *Irish Citizen*, 21 March 1914.

67. Luddy 'Isabella M.S. Tod', p. 213. Two further CDAS were introduced in 1866 and 1869.

68. Maria Luddy, 'Irish Women and the Contagious Diseases Acts 1864–1886', in *History Ireland*, 1, 1 (Spring 1993), p. 32.

69. Quinlan, *Genteel Revolutionaries*, p. 82.

70. Ibid.

71. Luddy 'Isabella M.S. Tod', p. 213. The initial exclusion of women from the NARCDA resulted in the formation of the LNA. Luddy notes that while women were later admitted to NARCDA, the society was run by men, with little female impact on policy.

72. Quoted in Cullen, 'Anna Maria Haslam', p. 171.
73. Luddy, 'Irish Women and the Contagious Acts', p. 33.
74. Ibid.
75. Quinlan, *Genteel Revolutionaries*, p. 77.
76. Ibid, p. 100.
77. Ibid, p. 99.
78. Ibid, p. 83.
79. Luddy, 'Women and Politics', p. 72,
80. Quinlan, *Genteel Revolutionaries*, p. 104.
81. Cullen, 'Anna Maria Haslam', pp 172–3.
82. Quoted in Luddy, 'Isabella M.S. Tod', p. 215.

Chapter 2 (pages 21–56)
1. Quoted in Deirdre Raftery, *Women and Learning in English Writing 1600–1900* (Dublin 1997), p. 103.
2. Quoted in Raftery, *Women and Learning*, p. 61.
3. David Fitzpatrick, 'A Share of the Honeycomb': Education, Emigration and Irishwomen', in Mary Daly and David Dickson (eds), *The Origins of Popular Literacy in Ireland: Language Change and Educational Development 1700–1920* (Dublin 1990), p. 167.
4. Anne V. O'Connor, 'Education in Nineteenth-Century Ireland', in Angela Bourke et al (eds), *The Field Day Anthology of Irish Writing*, VOL. V, *Irish Women's Writing and Traditions* (Cork 2002), p. 648.
5. Maria Luddy, *Women in Ireland 1800–1918: A Documentary History* (Cork 1995), p. 90.
6. John Logan, 'The Dimensions of Gender in Nineteenth-Century Schooling', in Margaret Kelleher and James H. Murphy (eds), *Gender Perspectives in Nineteenth-Century Ireland* (Dublin 1977), p. 45.
7. Ibid.
8. Ibid, p. 46. Logan notes that in 1848 the Commissioners published *The Agricultural Class Book*, a theoretical introduction to farming for boys, which included sections on kitchen management for girls.
9. Fitzpatrick, 'A Share of the Honeycomb', p. 172, cited in Logan, 'The Dimensions of Gender', p. 40.
10. Rita M. Rhodes, *Women and the Family in Post-Famine Ireland* (New York and London 1992), p. 205.
11. Ibid, p. 195.
12. Ibid, p. 203.
13. Ibid, p. 201.
14. Logan, 'A Share of the Honeycomb', cited in Logan, 'The Dimensions of Gender', p. 40.
15. Kerby A. Miller with David N. Doyle and Patricia Kelleher, '"For love and liberty": Irish women, migration and domesticity in Ireland and America, 1815–1920', in Patrick O'Sullivan (ed.), *Irish Women and Irish Migration* (London 1995), p. 46.

16. Rhodes, *Women and the Family*, p. 210.
17. Myrtle Hill and Vivienne Pollock, *Image and Experience* (Belfast 1993), p. 108.
18. Tony Fahey, 'Nuns in the Catholic Church in Ireland in the Nineteenth Century', in Mary Cullen (ed.), *Girls Don't Do Honours: Irish Women in Education in the 19th and 20th Centuries* (Dublin 1987), p. 17.
19. Ibid, p. 20.
20. Ibid, p. 19.
21. Anne V. O'Connor, 'Education in Nineteenth-Century Ireland', p. 648.
22. Fahey, 'Nuns in the Catholic Church', p. 18.
23. Ibid, p. 25.
24. Logan, 'The Dimensions of Gender', p. 48.
25. Ibid, p. 49.
26. J.J. Lee, 'Women and the Church since the Famine', in Margaret MacCurtain and Donncha Ó Corráin (eds), *Women in Irish Society: The Historical Dimension* (Dublin 1978), pp 41–2.
27. Luddy, *Women in Ireland*, p. 108.
28. Anne V. O'Connor, 'The Revolution in Girls' Secondary Education in Ireland, 1860–1910', in M. Cullen (ed.), *Girls Don't Do Honours*, p. 36.
29. Ibid, p. 38.
30. Ibid, p. 41.
31. Ibid, p. 43.
32. Ibid.
33. Ibid, p. 44.
34. Maria Luddy, 'Isabella M.S. Tod', in Mary Cullen and Maria Luddy (eds), *Women, Power and Consciousness in 19th-Century Ireland* (Dublin 1995), p. 210.
35. O'Connor, 'The Revolution in Girls' Secondary Education', p. 44.
36. Quoted in Eibhlín Breathnach, 'Charting New Waters: women's experience in higher education, 1879–1908', in M. Cullen (ed.), *Girls Don't Do Honours*, p. 58.
37. O'Connor, 'Education in Nineteenth-Century Ireland', p. 652.
38. O'Connor, 'The Revolution in Girls' Secondary Education in Ireland', p. 44.
39. Hill and Pollock, *Image and Experience*, p. 109.
40. O'Connor, 'Education in Nineteenth-Century Ireland', p. 653; Breathnach, 'Charting New Waters', p. 46.
41. Quoted in O'Connor, 'The Revolution in Girls' Secondary Education', p. 46.
42. Breathnach, 'Charting New Waters', p. 68.
43. O'Connor, 'The Revolution in Girls' Secondary Education', pp 47–8.
44. *The Weekly Freeman*, cited in O'Connor, 'The Revolution in Girls' Secondary Education', p. 50.
45. P. Heffernan, *The Heffernans and their Times: A Study in Irish History* (London 1941), cited in Senia Paseta, *Before the Revolution: Nationalism, Social Change and Ireland's Catholic Elite, 1879–1922* (Cork 1999), p. 5.
46. Paseta, *Before the Revolution*, p. 6.
47. F. Hacket, *Ireland: A Study in Nationalism* (New York 1918), cited in Paseta, *Before the Revolution*, p. 6.
48. Paseta, *Before the Revolution*, p. 6.

49. Breathnach, 'Charting New Waters', p. 62.
50. Ibid, p. 59.
51. Ibid, pp 66–7.
52. Norman Atkinson, *Irish Education: A history of educational institutions* (Dublin 1969), p. 117.
53. Breathnach, 'Charting New Waters', p. 68; Anne V. O'Connor, 'Education in Nineteenth-Century Ireland', pp 653–4.
54. Breathnach, 'Charting New Waters', p. 60.
55. Ibid, p. 69.
56. Ibid, p. 71.
57. Eibhlin Breathnach, 'Women and Higher Education in Ireland 1879–1914', in *The Crane Bag*, VOL. 4 NO. 1 (1980), pp 51–2.
58. Paseta, *Before the Revolution*, p. 10.
59. Ibid, p. 16.
60. Ibid, p. 18.
61. Breathnach, 'Charting New Waters', pp 77–8.
62. Paseta, *Before the Revolution*, p. 140.
63. E.T. O'Dwyer, *Technical Instruction* (Dublin 1900), cited in Paseta, *Before the Revolution*, p. 139.
64. D.M. O'Kane, *Woman's Place in the World*, cited in Paseta, *Before the Revolution*, pp 139–40.
65. Breathnach, 'Charting New Waters', p. 77.
66. Ibid, p. 78.
67. Rev. Seán Ó Catháin, S.J., 'Education in the New Ireland', in Francis MacManus (ed.), *The Years of the Great Test 1926–39*, pp 104–105. By 1939 there were six such colleges.
68. Donald H. Akenson, *A Mirror to Kathleen's face* (Toronto 1973), p. 33.
69. J.J. Lee, *Ireland 1912–1985* (Cambridge 1989), p. 130.
70. Akenson, *A Mirror to Kathleen's face*, p. 65.
71. Atkinson, *Irish Education*, p. 102.
72. Akenson, *A Mirror to Kathleen's face*, p. 66.
73. Ibid, p. 68; Akenson notes that the average daily attendance expressed as a percentage of average numbers on school roles increased from 73.3 per cent in 1921 to 83.3 per cent in 1950–51 (all figures for the twenty-six counties).
74. Finola Kennedy, *Cottage to Crèche: Family Change in Ireland* (Dublin 2001), p. 125.
75. Atkinson, *Irish Education*, p. 166.
76. F.S.L. Lyons, *Ireland Since the Famine* (Great Britain 1973), p. 650.
77. Ó Catháin, 'Education in the New Ireland', p. 112.
78. Lyons, *Ireland Since the Famine*, pp 650–51.
79. Quoted in Kennedy, *Cottage to Crèche*, p. 66.
80. Kennedy, *Cottage to Crèche*, p. 170.
81. Atkinson, *Irish Education*, p. 161.
82. Ó Catháin, 'Education in the New Ireland', pp 108–10.
83. Akenson, *A Mirror to Kathleen's face*, p. 35.

84. Lee, *Ireland 1912–1985*, p. 134.
85. Akenson, *A Mirror to Kathleen's face*, p. 67.
86. Lee, *Ireland 1912–1985*, p. 132.
87. Ó Catháin, 'Education in the New Ireland', p. 105.
88. Terence Brown, *Ireland, A Social and Cultural History 1922–79* (London 1981), p. 248.
89. Lyons, *Ireland Since the Famine*, p. 646.
90. Brown, *Ireland, A Social and Cultural History*, p. 248.
91. Akenson, *A Mirror to Kathleen's face*, p. 34.
92. Kennedy, *Cottage to Crèche*, p. 130.
93. Alexander J. Humphreys, *New Dubliners: Urbanization and the Irish Family* (London 1966), p. 150.
94. Ibid, p. 127.
95. Tony Farmar, *Ordinary Lives: Three Generations of Irish Middle Class Experience 1907, 1932, 1963* (Dublin 1991), p. 168.
96. Ibid, pp 166–7, p. 170.
97. Conrad M. Arensberg and Solon T. Kimball, *Family and Community in Ireland* (3rd edition, Clasp Press, Co. Clare 2001), p. 376.
98. Ibid, p. 378.
99. Ibid.
100. Ibid, pp 379–80.
101. Humphreys, *New Dubliners*, p. 132.
102. Ibid, p. 126.
103. Ibid.
104. Ibid, pp 218–19.
105. Farmar, *Ordinary Lives*, pp 178–9.
106. Humphreys, *New Dubliners*, pp 204–5.
107. Atkinson, *Irish Education*, p. 178.
108. Ibid, pp 178–9.
109. Lee, *Ireland 1912–1985*, p. 136.
110. Atkinson, *Irish Education*, pp 184–5; D.H. Akenson, *Education and Enmity: The Control of Schooling in Northern Ireland 1920–1950* (Newton Abbot 1973), p. 180.
111. Akenson, *Education and Enmity*, p. 162.
112. Ibid, p. 163.
113. Lee, *Ireland 1912–1985*, p. 414.
114. John Hume speaking on The Late Late Show, RTÉ Television, 6 February 2004.
115. Akenson, *A Mirror*, p. 143.
116. Brown, *Ireland, A Social and Cultural History*, p. 250.
117. Lyons, *Ireland Since the Famine*, p. 651.
118. Akenson, *A Mirror to Kathleen's face*, p. 146.
119. Brown, *Ireland, A Social and Cultural History*, p. 254; the source cited by Brown is Seán O'Connor, 'Post-Primary Education Now and in the Future', in *Studies*, VOL. LVII (1968), pp 233–51.
120. Kennedy, *Cottage to Crèche*, p. 54.
121. Ibid, p. 124.

122. Ibid, p. 131.

123. *Report of the Commission on the Status of Women* (Stationery Office, Dublin 1972), p. 202, paragraph 518.

124. Ibid, p. 203, para. 520.

125. Ibid, p. 208, para. 531.

126. Ibid, p. 209, para. 533.

127. Ibid, p. 210, para. 536

128. Ibid, pp 102–3, para. 240.

129. Ibid, p. 212, para. 541.

130. Ibid, pp 214–15, para. 543 and 544.

131. Ibid, pp 216–17, para. 547.

Chapter 3 (pages 57–78)

1. Mary E. Daly, *The Famine in Ireland* (Dublin 1986), p. 117.

2. J.J. Lee, 'Women and the Church since the Famine', in Margaret MacCurtain and Donncha Ó Corráin (eds), *Women in Irish Society: The Historical Dimension* (Dublin 1978), p. 39.

3. Lee, 'Women and the Church', p. 40.

4. Caitríona Clear, 'The Limits of Female Autonomy: Nuns in Nineteenth-Century Ireland', in Maria Luddy and Cliona Murphy (eds), *Women Surviving: Studies in Irish Women's History in the 19th and 20th Centuries* (Dublin 1990), p. 27.

5. Caitríona Clear, 'The Re-emergence of Nuns and Convents, 1800–1962', in Angela Bourke et al (eds), *The Field Day Anthology of Irish Writing*, VOL. IV, *Irish Women's Writings and Traditions* (Cork 2002), p. 517.

6. Richard J. Evans, *The Feminists* (London 1977), pp 29–30.

7. Mary Peckham Magray, *The Transforming Power of the Nuns: Women, Religion, and Cultural Change in Ireland, 1750–1900* (New York and Oxford 1998), pp 5 and 128.

8. Tony Fahey, 'Nuns in the Catholic Church in Ireland in the Nineteenth Century', in Mary Cullen (ed.), *Girls Don't Do Honours: Irish Women in Education in the 19th and 20th Centuries* (Dublin 1987), p. 7.

9. Ibid, p. 8.

10. Ibid, p. 9. Magray in *The Transforming Power of the Nuns* has pointed out that while this organisation received Papal approval in 1688, its sisters were considered lay rather than religious women. This remained the Church view until 1749 when Pope Benedict XIV's *Quantus Iusto* conceded the right of religious women to form a new style of religious community (Magray, p. 8).

11. Clear, 'The Re-emergence of Nuns', p. 517.

12. Clear, 'The Limits of Female Autonomy', p. 27.

13. Ibid, p. 28. See also Fahey, 'Nuns in the Catholic Church', p. 10.

14. Fahey, 'Nuns in the Catholic Church', p. 11.

15. Clear, 'The Limits of Female Autonomy', p. 36.

16. Ibid, p. 30.

17. Ibid, p. 31.

18. Fahey, 'Nuns in the Catholic Church', p. 10.
19. Clear, 'The Re-emergence of Nuns', p. 523.
20. Clear, 'The Limits of Female Autonomy', pp 28–9; Fahey, 'Nuns in the Catholic Church', p. 10.
21. Clear, 'The Limits of Female Autonomy', pp 33–4; Clear notes that Loreto convents in Navan, Fermoy, Letterkenny, Omagh and Killarney were all forced by local Bishops to cut ties with Rathfarnham.
22. Clear, 'The Limits of Female Autonomy', p. 32.
23. Ibid, pp 34–6.
24. Ibid, p. 35.
25. Ibid, pp 31–2.
26. Magray, *The Transforming Power of the Nuns*, p. 122.
27. Clear, 'The Limits of Female Autonomy', pp 36–7.
28. Magray, *The Transforming Power of the Nuns*, p. 126.
29. Clear, 'The Limits of Female Autonomy', p. 45.
30. Magray, *The Transforming Power of the Nuns*, p. 129.
31. Ibid, pp 92–3.
32. Ibid, p. 89.
33. Ibid.
34. Ibid, pp 128–9.
35. Ibid, p. 11.
36. Ibid, p. 121.
37. Clear, 'The Limits of Female Autonomy', pp 42–3.
38. Ibid, pp 43–4.
39. Fahey, 'Nuns in the Catholic Church', p. 26.
40. Maria Luddy, *Women in Ireland 1800–1918: A Documentary History* (Cork 1995), p. 80.
41. Luddy, *Women in Ireland*, p. 82.
42. Caitríona Clear, 'Walls Within Walls: Nuns in Nineteenth-Century Ireland', in Chris Curtin, Pauline Jackson, Barbara O'Connor (eds), *Gender in Irish Society* (Galway 1987), pp 148–9.
43. Jacinta Prunty, 'Margaret Louisa Aylward', in Mary Cullen and Maria Luddy (eds), *Women, Power and Consciousness in 19th-Century Ireland* (Dublin 1995), pp 78–9.
44. Ibid, p. 79.
45. Ibid, p. 60; the full title of this charity was *The Ladies Association of Charity of St Vincent de Paul for the Spiritual and Temporal Relief of the Sick Poor*.
46. Ibid, pp 62–3. Prunty notes that within five years Aylward's branch numbered 148 lady visitors, with its effects extending beyond its parish boundaries as it assisted the establishment of several other city and suburban branches.
47. Ibid, p. 71.
48. Ibid, pp 72–3; St Brigid's Orphanage had sent the child to a nurse in Saggart, Co. Dublin, after her father's death in 1858. Unknown to Aylward, the child had been abducted to France. Following legal proceedings issued by the mother, Aylward was ordered to produce the child in court.

49. Ibid, p. 75.
50. Ibid, pp 77–8.
51. Magray, *The Transforming Power of the Nuns*, p. 130.
52. Prunty, 'Margaret Louisa Aylward', p. 81.
53. Ibid.
54. Ibid.
55. Fahey, 'Nuns in the Catholic Church', p. 15.
56. Ibid, p. 29.
57. Maria Luddy, 'Philanthropy in Nineteenth-Century Ireland', in Angela Bourke et al (eds), *The Field Day Anthology of Irish Writing*, VOL. V, p. 692.
58. Magray, *The Transforming Power of the Nuns*, p. 130.
59. Mary Cullen, 'Anna Maria Haslam', in Cullen and Luddy (eds), *Women, Power and Consciousness*, p. 64.
60. Maria Luddy, 'Women and Charitable Organisations in Nineteenth-Century Ireland', in *Women's Studies Int. Forum*, VOL. 11 NO. 4 (1988), p. 301.
61. Margaret MacCurtain, 'The Real Molly Macree', in A.M. Dalsimer (ed.), *Visualising Ireland: National Identity and the Pictorial Tradition* (Boston and London 1993), p. 14.
62. *English Woman's Journal*, VOL. 3 (1859), p. 357.
63. *English Woman's Journal*, VOL. 9–10 (1862–3), pp 30–33.
64. Rosemary Raughter, 'A Natural Tenderness: The Ideal and the Reality of Eighteenth-Century Female Philanthropy', in Maryann Gialanella Valiulis and Mary O'Dowd (eds), *Women and Irish History* (Dublin 1997), p. 73.
65. Anne O'Connell, 'Charlotte Grace O'Brien', in Cullen and Luddy (eds), *Women, Power and Consciousness*, pp 231–62.
66. Luddy, 'Philanthropy in Nineteenth-Century Ireland', p. 691.
67. Prunty, 'Margaret Louisa Aylward', p. 65.
68. Luddy, 'Women and Charitable Organisations', p. 303. Only seventeen years old when she began her work of saving children from the Dublin streets, Ellen Smyly had to be accompanied by an elderly lady as it was not considered seemly for a young girl to go about the streets on her own.
69. Prunty, 'Margaret Louisa Aylward', p. 62.
70. Ibid, pp 65–6.
71. Ibid, pp 66–7.
72. Ibid, p. 67.
73. Luddy, 'Philanthropy in Nineteenth-Century Ireland', p. 693.
74. Raughter, 'A Natural Tenderness', p. 86.
75. Maria Luddy, *Women and Philanthropy in Nineteenth-Century Ireland* (Cambridge 1995), pp 4–5.
76. Evans, *The Feminists*, p. 33.
77. Ibid, p. 30.
78. Luddy, 'Philanthropy in Nineteenth-Century Ireland', p. 691.
79. Ibid, p. 692.
80. Ibid, pp 692–3.
81. Evans, *The Feminists*, pp 148–50.

82. Luddy, 'Philanthropy in Nineteenth-Century Ireland', p. 693.
83. Raughter, 'A Natural Tenderness', p. 88.
84. Luddy, 'Philanthropy in Nineteenth-Century Ireland', p. 693.

Chapter 4 (pages 81–107)
1. This chapter is based on material in Rosemary Cullen Owens, *Smashing Times: A History of the Irish Women's Suffrage Movement 1889–1922* (Dublin 1984 and 1995).
2. Mary Colum, *Life and the Dream* (New York 1947), pp 153 and 174.
3. H. Sheehy Skeffington, 'Reminiscences of an Irish Suffragette', in A.D. Sheehy Skeffington and Rosemary Owens (eds and publs), *Votes for Women: Irish Women's Struggle for the Vote* (Dublin 1975), p. 12.
4. Christabel Pankhurst, *Unshackled* (London 1959), p. 41.
5. Andrew Rosen, *Rise Up Women! The Militant Campaign of the Women's Social and Political Union 1903–1914* (London and Boston 1974), p. 27.
6. E. Pankhurst, *My Own Story* (London 1914), p. 18.
7. J.H. and M.E. Cousins, *We Two Together* (Madras, India 1950), p. 169.
8. Hanna Sheehy Skeffington, 'Reminiscences' p. 12; Cousins and Cousins, *We Two Together*, p. 164; also *Report of Irish Women's Suffrage and Local Government Association* (Dublin 1908).
9. Cousins and Cousins, *We Two Together*, p. 185.
10. Cullen Owens, *Smashing Times*, pp 42–3.
11. *Irish Women's Suffrage Federation Annual Report* (1911–1912).
12. *Irish Citizen*, 7 May 1913; among societies affiliated in 1913 were the Dublin-based IWRL, Belfast Women's Suffrage Society, six branches of the Munster Women's Franchise League, Connaught Women's Franchise League, Warrenpoint and Rostrevor Suffrage Society, along with societies in Newry, Lisburn, Nenagh, Birr, Armagh, Portrush, Bushmills, Ballymoney and Derry.
13. H. Chenevix, 'Louie Bennett', in *Irish Housewife* (1959), p. 36.
14. For a comprehensive account of the life and work of Louie Bennett see Rosemary Cullen Owens, *Louie Bennett* (Cork 2001).
15. Cullen Owens, *Louie Bennett*, pp 14–15.
16. Cousins and Cousins, *We Two Together*, p. 185.
17. *Irish Citizen*, 2 November 1912, p. 191, and 17 May 1913, p. 417.
18. A. Birrell to J. Dillon, 15 January 1912 Trinity College Dublin, Dillon papers, MS 6799, item 182 a.
19. H. Sheehy Skeffington, 'Reminiscences', p. 18.
20. Letter reprinted in *Irish Citizen*, 3 August 1912.
21. *Freeman's Journal*, 1 April 1912.
22. Markievicz, Lynn, Wyse Power, Chenevix, Dudley Edwards and Cruise O'Brien (a sister of Hanna Sheehy Skeffington) were all known suffrage supporters. Lynn, also a committed nationalist, later established St Ultan's Hospital for Sick Children; Jennie Wyse Power, in her youth a member of the Ladies Land League, was vice-president of Sinn Féin at this time. Delia Larkin was the first secretary of the Irish Women Workers Union, formed in 1911.

23. *Irish Citizen*, 8 and 15 June 1912; this composite reference covers the three quotes cited.

24. *Irish Citizen*, 22 June 1912.

25. One group of four served two months in prison, the remaining four served five of their six-month sentence.

26. *Irish Citizen*, 22 June 1912.

27. *Evening Telegraph*, 8 July 1912.

28. *Evening Telegraph*, 9 July 1912.

29. *Evening Telegraph*, 8 July 1912.

30. Great disparity emerged as to the type of hatchet involved. Irish and English suffragettes claimed it was only a toy hatchet of the type used for breaking toffee, *Irish Citizen* 10 August 1912; Marie Johnson, at the time a member of the IWSS in Belfast, claimed that it was a small axe, thrown not by Mary Leigh, but by Helena Molony, 'a very extreme Republican, simply anti-British', letter from M. Johnson to A. Sheehy Skeffington 24 January 1972 (N.L. Woman Suffrage Collection, MS 21, 194–7). However, the accused woman, Mary Leigh, stated that she ran up to the carriage and dropped into it a small hatchet with a note attached stating, 'This is a symbol of the extinction of the Liberal Party for evermore', transcript of interview with Mary Leigh, 1965 (David Mitchell Collection of Suffrage Research, Museum of London, ref. 73.83/49).

31. *Evening Herald*, 19 July 1912; also *Evening Telegraph*, 19 July 1912.

32. *Evening Telegraph*, 20 July 1912.

33. NAI, CSO, Police and Crime Reports 1886–1914, carton 4.

34. *Irish Citizen*, 3 August 1912.

35. *Irish Independent*, 20 July 1912.

36. Ibid.

37. K. Tynan, *The Years of the Shadow* (London 1919), p. 109.

38. *Irish Citizen*, 27 July 1912.

39. *Irish Independent*, 19 July 1912.

40. *The Leader*, 3 August 1912.

41. *Sinn Féin*, 27 July 1912; *Irish Citizen* 3 August 1912.

42. Cited in Rosen, *Rise Up Women!*, p. 143.

43. *Sinn Féin*, 17 August 1912.

44. *Sinn Féin*, 24 August 1912.

45. Hanna Sheehy Skeffington, 'Reminiscences', p. 23.

46. Lizzie Baker was released on 18 August 1912 on health grounds.

47. A. Birrell to J. Dillon, 15 August 1912 (Dillon Papers TCD) MS 6799, no. 186.

48. George Dangerfield, *The Strange Death of Liberal England* (London 1966), p. 185; Rosen, *Rise Up Women!*, p. 193. The suffrage press noted that T.M. Healy was the only member of the Irish Parliamentary Party to oppose this bill, *Irish Citizen*, 26 April 1912.

49. The Act was first applied in Ireland in June 1913 when 3 members of the IWFL went on hunger-strike in Tullamore prison and were released under the terms of the Act five days later.

50. *Irish Citizen*, 5 July 1913.

51. Ibid.
52. Ibid.
53. Forcible feeding was re-introduced in England later in 1913 due to difficulties in re-arresting prisoners, and to their involvement in illegal activities while free on licence.
54. *Evening Telegraph,* 3 May 1913. The Bill proposed the parliamentary franchise for women householders and wives of householders of twenty-five years and over.
55. NAI, CSORP 13437, 1914, Attorney General to Asst. Under Secretary.
56. NAI, CSORP 13437, 20 July 1914, Under Secretary to Crown Solicitor.
57. Lloyd George papers (Typescript of speech 24 October 1913), House of Lords Record Office, c/36/1/18.
58. Hanna Sheehy Skeffington, 'Reminiscences', pp 13–14.
59. Cousins and Cousins, *We Two Together,* pp 189–90.
60. Hanna Sheehy Skeffington, 'Reminiscences', pp 24 and 26.
61. *The Leader,* 19 March 1910. It was Moran who first referred to Irish suffragists as 'Suffs' and 'Suffers'.
62. *Catholic Bulletin,* VOL 11, 1912. This common stereotype of suffrage campaigners was noted by Hanna Sheehy Skeffington when she referred to 'the myth of the hard-faced, man-hating spinster' being dispelled by the pleasing impression and courage of suffrage activists and visiting speakers, 'Reminiscences', p. 14.
63. *Irish Citizen,* 27 July 1912.
64. Rev. D. Barry S.T.L., 'Female Suffrage from a Catholic Standpoint' in *Irish Ecclesiastical Record,* 4s 26 (September 1909).
65. Cousins and Cousins, *We Two Together,* p. 150.
66. *Irish Citizen,* 1913.
67. *Church of Ireland Gazette,* 29 May 1914.
68. *National Student,* January 1914.
69. Hanna Sheehy Skeffington, 'Reminiscences', p. 17.
70. *Votes for Women,* reprinted in *Irish Citizen,* 1 March 1913.
71. Sheehy Skeffington papers, NLI MS 22664.
72. *Irish Citizen,* 20 September 1913.
73. NAI, CSORP 13437, 5 August 1914, Crown Solicitor to Under Secretary.
74. Hanna Sheehy Skeffington, 'Reminiscences', p. 18.
75. For a detailed study of the relationship between suffrage and labour activists see Rosemary Owens, 'Votes for Women, Votes for Ladies: Organised Labour and the Suffrage Movement, 1876–1922', in *Saothar* 9, Journal of the Irish Labour History Society (1983).
76. *Irish Citizen,* 27 September 1913.
77. *Irish Citizen,* 4 January 1913.
78. *Worker's Republic,* 18 December 1915.
79. *Bean na hÉireann,* March 1910.
80. *ITUC Report 1912,* p. 52.
81. Hanna Sheehy Skeffington, 'Reminiscences', p. 17.
82. *Irish Citizen,* 7 February 1914. At this Belfast meeting Louie Bennett stated in

response that this had not been her experience of Dublin working people.

83. *ITUC Report 1914*, pp 77–9.
84. *Irish Citizen*, 28 December 1912.
85. *Irish Citizen*, 13 November 1913.
86. It was Sylvia Pankhurst's appearance on this platform that precipitated her expulsion from the WSPU.
87. *Irish Worker*, 4 April 1914.
88. R.M. Fox, *Louie Bennett, Her Life and Times* (Dublin 1958), p. 45.
89. J. Connolly, *The Re-Conquest of Ireland* (Dublin 1917), p. 291.
90. Helena Molony, 'James Connolly and Women', in *Dublin Labour Year Book 1930*, p. 32.

Chapter 5 (pages 108–126)
1. *Irish Citizen*, 1 March 1913.
2. J.H. and M.E. Cousins, *We Two Together* (Madras, India 1950), p. 164.
3. *Bean na hÉireann*, November 1909, pp 5–6.
4. See Elizabeth Cady Stanton, 'Selections from the History of Woman Suffrage', in Alice S. Rossi (ed.), *The Feminist Papers* (2nd ed., New York 1974), pp 413–58.
5. *Irish Citizen*, 23 May 1914.
6. *Irish Independent*, 2 June 1914.
7. *Freeman's Journal*, 30 May 1914.
8. *Irish Independent*, 28 May 1914.
9. *Irish Citizen*, 28 March 1914 and 9 May 1914.
10. *Irish Citizen*, 2 May 1914.
11. Press cutting of letter from Agnes O'Farrelly in scrapbook in Sheehy Skeffington papers, NLI, MS 21616–21656. Neither name of paper nor exact date is given, but 1911 is written in pencil in margin.
12. *Irish Citizen*, 30 May 1914.
13. *Bean na hÉireann*, April 1909.
14. Ibid.
15. Constance de Markievicz writing in *Bean na hÉireann*, July 1909, under her pen-name of Maca.
16. Sheehy Skeffington Papers, NLI, MS 34133 (iii).
17. Copy of letter from P.H. Pearse to C. Doyle, 30 November 1913, NLI, MS 10486.
18. *Irish Volunteer*, 4 April 1914.
19. Jacqueline van Voris, *Constance de Markievicz in the Cause of Ireland* (University of Massachusetts Press 1967), p. 132.
20. *Irish Citizen*, 11 April 1914. At a meeting of Galway City branch of Cumann na mBan in August 1914, it was regretted that only a hundred men had joined the Volunteers; women present were asked to use their influence to get their brothers and sweethearts to join.
21. Diane Urquhart, '"The Female of the Species is more Deadlier than the Male"?, The Ulster Women's Unionist Council, 1911–40', in Janice Holmes and Diane Urquhart (eds), *Coming into the Light: The Work, Politics and Religion of Women*

in Ulster 1840–1940 (Belfast 1994), p. 94.

22. *Freeman's Journal*, 6 May 1914.
23. *Irish Independent*, 8 May 1914.
24. Ibid.
25. Quoted in Urquhart, 'The Female of the Species', p. 102.
26. Quoted in Margaret Ward, *In Their Own Voice: Women and Irish Nationalism*, (Dublin 1995), pp 42–3.
27. *Irish Citizen*, 4 July 1914.
28. *Irish Citizen*, 11 July 1914.
29. *Irish Citizen*, 25 July 1914.
30. *Irish Citizen*, 8 August 1914.
31. Minutes of the Conference of Women Delegates to the all-Ireland conference, 12 May 1917, later known as Cumann na dTeachtaire, Sheehy Skeffington Papers, NLI, MS 21,194.
32. Ibid, copy of letter sent to Sinn Féin executive, 1 August 1917. The women proposed by the delegates were Kathleen Clarke, Áine Ceannt, Kathleen Lynn, Jennie Wyse Power, Helena Molony and Mrs Ginnell.
33. Ibid, 17 September 1917.
34. Ibid, 2 October 1917.
35. Ibid, 16 October 1917.
36. *Irish Citizen*, November 1917.
37. Cumann na dTeachtaire minutes, 2 April 1918, General Meeting.
38. Ibid.
39. Ibid, 30 January 1919.
40. For details see Rosemary Cullen Owens, *Smashing Times: A History of the Irish Women's Suffrage Movement 1889–1922* (Dublin 1984 and 1995), p. 118.
41. Ibid, pp 120–22.
42. Ibid, pp 122–4.
43. *Irish Citizen*, August 1918.
44. IWFL Report for 1918 in the *Irish Citizen*, April 1919.
45. *Irish Citizen*, December 1918.
46. See Rosemary Cullen Owens, *Louie Bennett* (Cork 2001), pp 76–7; manoeuvrings between Labour and Sinn Féin as to whether Labour should contest this election may have played a role in her decision. Ultimately, Labour withdrew from the election.
47. *Sinn Féin, An Appeal to the Women of Ireland* (Dublin 1918).
48. *Sinn Féin 10th Convention Report*, October 1917.
49. *Irish Citizen*, December 1918.
50. Sheehy Skeffington papers, NLI, MS 24, 107.
51. *Irish Citizen*, April 1919.
52. *Irish Citizen*, February 1920.
53. *Irish Citizen*, November 1917.
54. Brian Farrell, 'Markievicz and the Women of the Revolution', in F.X. Martin (ed.), *Leaders and Men of the Easter Rising: Dublin 1916* (London 1967), p. 235.
55. Ibid.

56. Damien Doyle, 'Rosamund Jacob (1888–1960)', in Mary Cullen and Maria Luddy (eds.), *Female Activists: Irish Women and Change 1900–1960* (Dublin 2001), p. 176.
57. *Irish Citizen*, May 1919.
58. Margaret Ward, *Hanna Sheehy Skeffington: A Life* (Cork 1997), p. 221.
59. Ibid, pp 249–50.
60. Memoirs of Marie Johnson in Sheehy Skeffington papers, NLI, MS 21,194 (1).
61. Quoted in Ward, *Hanna Sheehy Skeffington*, p. 251.
62. Ward, *Hanna Sheehy Skeffington*, p. 249.
63. Margaret O'Callaghan, 'Women and Politics in Independent Ireland, 1921–68', in Angela Bourke et al (eds), *The Field Day Anthology of Irish Writing*, VOL. V (Cork 2002), p. 122.
64. P.S. O'Hegarty, *The Victory of Sinn Féin* (Dublin 1924), pp 56–8 and 102–5.
65. Ibid.

Chapter 6 (pages 127–154)

1. Richard Evans, *Comrades and Sisters: Feminism, Socialism and Pacifism in Europe 1870–1945* (Sussex 1987), Chapter 5. See also Jill Liddington, *The Long Road to Greenham: Feminism and Anti-Militarism in Britain since 1920* (London 1989), pp 37, 56, 58–9, 63.
2. Richard J. Evans, *The Feminists: Women's Emancipation Movements in Europe, America and Australasia 1840–1920* (London 1977), pp 251–2.
3. For a detailed study of Pacifism in Ireland see Rosemary Cullen Owens, *Louie Bennett* (Cork 2001).
4. Margaret Mulvihill, *Charlotte Despard: a Biography* (London 1989), p. 103.
5. Liddington, *The Long Road*; see also Adele Schreiber and Margaret Mathieson, *Journey Towards Freedom* (Denmark 1995). Addams was awarded the Nobel Peace Prize in 1931.
6. *Irish Citizen*, 21 November 1914.
7. Louie Bennett to Hanna Sheehy Skeffington, 1 October 1914, SSP,NLI MS 22,667 (2).
8. *Irish Citizen*, 11 December 1915.
9. Ibid.
10. Louie Bennett, 'Women of Europe, When will your call ring out?', in *Jus Suffragii*, 1 March 1915.
11. Gertrude Bussey and Margaret Timms, *Pioneers for Peace: Women's International League for Peace and Freedom 1915–65* (London 1965), p. 18; also Liddington, *The Long Road*, pp 94–6.
12. Diaries of Lucy O. Kingston, March 1915 (hereafter Kingston Diaries), Private collection.
13. Anne Wiltshire, *Most Dangerous Women: Feminist Peace Campaigners of the Great War* (London and Boston 1985), pp 88–90; also Mulvihill, *Charlotte Despard*, p. 115.
14. *Irish Citizen*, 24 April 1915. The delegates were Hanna Sheehy Skeffington, Margaret McCoubrey and Mrs Metge (IWFL), Louie Bennett, Miss Moser and

Mrs Isabella Richardson from the recently formed Irish Committee, and Helen McNaghten from the Northern Committee of the IWSF.

15. Evans, *Comrades and Sisters*, pp 127–9. For an Australian perspective see Darryn Kruse and Charles Sowerwine, 'Feminism and Pacifism: "Woman's Sphere" in Peace and War', in *Australian Women, New Feminist Perspectives* (Melbourne 1986).

16. *Irish Citizen*, 12 September 1914.

17. *Irish Citizen*, 27 February 1915; for an examination of the conflicting positions of nationalist, unionist and pacifist feminists in Ireland see Dana Hearne, 'The Irish Citizen 1914–1916: Nationalism, Feminism and Militarism', in *Canadian Journal of Irish Studies* 18, NO. 1 (1992), pp 1–14.

18. *Irish Citizen*, 22 May 1915.

19. Ibid.

20. Bennett to Hanna Sheehy Skeffington, 12 May 1915, SSP, NLI MS 22,674.

21. *Irish Citizen*, 10 April 1915.

22. *Irish Citizen*, 22 May 1915; published later in 1915 in pamphlet form.

23. R.M. Fox, *Louie Bennett: Her Life and Times* (Dublin 1958), p. 48.

24. *Irish Citizen*, 20 February 1915.

25. Bennett to Hon. Sec., ICWPP, 19 October and 26 November 1915, 5 and 18 January 1916, 14 February 1916 (WILPF Colorado); also Bennett to Hanna Sheehy Skeffington, 19 June 1915, SSP, NLI MS 22,648 (11).

26. Bennett to Chrystal MacMillan, 5 January 1916 (WILPF Colorado).

27. Bennett to Chrystal MacMillan, 29 January 1916 (WILPF Colorado).

28. First yearly report of the Women's International League (WIL) October 1915-October 1916 (WILPF Papers, British Library of Political and Economic Science (hereafter WILPF Papers BLPES).

29. *Irish Citizen*, October 1916.

30. Rosa Manus to Louie Bennett, 18 December 1916 (WILPF Colorado).

31. Minutes of Executive Committee, Irishwomen's Suffrage Federation, 30 June 1917, SSP, NLI MS 21,196.

32. Bennett to Chrystal MacMillan, 15 January 1916 (WILPF Colorado).

33. Fox, *Louie Bennett*, p. 57.

34. Bennett to Hanna Sheehy Skeffington (in folder marked May–September 1916), SSP, NLI MS 22,279(6).

35. Letter from IIL to Messrs Lloyd George, Redmond and Dillon, 13 June 1916, sent to Rosa Manus, 12 July 1916 (WILPF Colorado).

36. IIL to ICWPP, January 1917 (WILPF Colorado).

37. Bennett to Rosa Manus, ICWPP, 8 May 1917.

38. This read: CONRAD EADAR-NÁISÚNTA BAN NA H-ÉIREANN.

39. 'London Letter', in *Irish Citizen*, November 1918.

40. Mulvihill, *Charlotte Despard*, p. 132.

41. *Irish Citizen*, November 1918; also WIL—Special Executive Meeting, 22 October 1918 (WILPF Papers BLPES).

42. Fox, *Louie Bennett*, p. 74.

43. Bennett to Dr Aletta Jacobs, 7 November 1918 (WILPF Colorado).

44. Hanna Sheehy Skeffington had also been chosen as a delegate but was refused a passport, *Irish Citizen*, June/July 1919.

45. This remains the name and headquarters of the organisation. Proximity to the League of Nations offices was among the reasons for this location.

46. WILPF Colorado, May 1919.

47. Bennett, Hon. Sec. IIL, 'To the Smaller Nations', June 1919 (WILPF Colorado).

48. Bennett to Emily Greene Balch, 2 October 1920 (WILPF Colorado).

49. Ibid.

50. Bennett to Balch, 2 November 1919 (WILPF Colorado).

51. Bennett to Balch, 1 January 1920, (WILPF Colorado).

52. Helena Swanwick, *I Have Been Young* (London 1935), p. 336; also Minutes of Executive Committee and Report of WIL, October 1920–January 1922 (WILPF Papers BLPES).

53. Jane Addams Memorial Collection, University of Illinois, Chicago (I am indebted to Eibhlín Breathnach for this reference).

54. American Commission 1921, pp 979, 998.

55. Ibid, p. 979.

56. Ibid, pp 1002–3.

57. Ibid, p. 1046.

58. Ibid, p. 1051–2.

59. Charlotte H. Fallon, *Soul of Fire: A Biography of Mary MacSwiney* (Cork and Dublin 1986), p. 68.

60. *Irish Women and the Irish Republican Army*, Broadsheet, NLI, ILB 300 P12 (Item 94).

61. Bennett to Balch, 21 March 1921 (WILPF Colorado).

62. R. Fanning, M. Kennedy, D. Keogh, E. O'Halpin (eds.), *Documents on Irish Foreign Policy*, VOL. 1, 1912–22 (Dublin 1998), Document no. 11, p. 17.

63. Fanning et al, *Documents on Irish Foreign Policy*, Document no. 103, p. 179.

64. Rosamund Jacob Diaries (hereafter Jacob Diaries), NLI, MS 32,583, nos. 1–170, 1897–1960; this ref. 21 January 1922, diary no. 40.

65. Balch to Bennett, 25 January 1922 (WILPF Colorado).

66. Bennett to Balch, 30 January 1922 (WILPF Colorado); Bennett's reservations regarding the attitude of women in the Republican movement would be repeated later in 1922 with regard to the Irish Labour Party and over the coming years within WILPF in Ireland.

67. Bennett to Sir James Craig, 10 June 1922 (WILPF Colorado).

68. SSP, NLI MS, 21,194, (no. 45); also Fox, *Louie Bennett*, pp 76–9; A. Gaughan, *Thomas Johnson* (Dublin 1980), pp 207–8.

69. Report by Marie Johnson to fourth Congress of WILPF, Washington, 1924, (WILPF Colorado).

70. Fox, *Louie Bennett*, p. 80.

71. Bennett to Balch, 12 October 1922 (WILPF Colorado).

72. Kingston Diaries, 1 December 1920.

73. Jacob Diaries, 12 July 1922, NLI, MS 332,582, NO. 41.

74. Bennett to Balch, 12 October 1922 (WILPF Colorado).

75. Kingston Diaries, 2 November 1922.

76. Ibid, 3 January 1923.

77. Annual Report of Irish Section, Women's International League 1922–3 (WILPF Colorado).

78. Ibid.

79. *Report of the Fourth Congress of the Women's International League for Peace and Freedom*, Washington, May 1924 (WILPF Colorado).

80. Bussey and Timms, *Pioneers for Peace*, p. 53.

81. Lucy Kingston to Madeleine Doty (WILPF International Secretary 1925–7), 26 February 1926; Rosamund Jacob to Madeleine Doty, 23 March 1926 (WILPF Colorado); other committee members were Sybil Le Brocquy, Mrs M'Clintock Dix, Marie Johnson, Miss Molyneux, Miss Mills, Mrs J. Richardson, Miss M. Stephens, Miss G. Webb.

82. Kingston to Doty, 1 January 1926 (WILPF Colorado).

83. Bennett to Doty, 16 February 1926 (WILPF Colorado).

84. Fox, *Louie Bennett*, pp 88–9.

85. Jacob Diaries, 19 April 1926, NLI, MS 332, 582, NO. 53.

86. Report of the Fifth Congress of WILPF, Dublin, 8–15 July 1926 (WILPF Colorado).

87. Ibid, p. 63.

88. Jacob Diaries, 12 July 1926, NLI, MS 332,582, NO. 53.

89. Fox, *Louie Bennett*, p. 89.

90. Swanwick, *I Have Been Young*, pp 450–52.

91. *International Woman Suffrage News*, August–September 1926.

92. Mary Sheepshanks (WILPF International Secretary 1927–30) to Louie Bennett, 20 November 1928 (WILPF Colorado).

93. Sinn Féin to WILPF, 25 October 1929 (WILPF Colorado).

94. Kingston Diaries, 1 November 1929.

95. Bennett to Sheepshanks, 30 November 1929 (WILPF Colorado).

96. Una M'Clintock Dix to Sheepshanks, 1 February 1930 (WILPF Colorado).

97. Kingston Diaries, 13 December 1929.

98. M'Clintock Dix to Sheepshanks, 1 February 1930 (WILPF Colorado).

99. Rosamund Jacob to Camille Drevet (WILPF International Secretary 1930–34), 9 April 1931 (WILPF Colorado).

100. An Irish branch of WILPF was reconstituted in 1991 in the wake of the Gulf War.

101. Evans, *Comrades and Sisters*, pp 130, 150–51.

Chapter 7 (pages 157–189)

1. Finola Kennedy, *Cottage to Crèche: Family Change in Ireland* (Dublin 2001), p. 57.

2. Ibid, p. 21; Kennedy compares this figure with two in three men who were married at this age in 1980.

3. Ibid, p. 22; the figure for 1998 (over one hundred and thirty years later) was 16,800.

4. Quoted in Kennedy, *Cottage to Crèche*, p. 23.

5. Quoted in Kennedy, *Cottage to Crèche*, p. 22.

6. James Deeny, *To Cure and to Care: Memoirs of a Chief Medical Officer* (Dublin 1989), p. 115.

7. Ibid, p. 84.

8. Kennedy, *Cottage to Crèche*, p. 33.

9. Ibid, pp 32–3.

10. Ibid, p. 35.

11. C.S. Andrews, *Dublin Made Me: An Autobiography* (Dublin 1979), p. 18. Andrews also notes there was an equally well-founded fear of 'consumption', which in addition to being deadly, was regarded as a rather shameful disease (p. 19).

12. Deeny, *To Cure and to Care*, pp 92 and 115.

13. Ibid, pp 115–16.

14. Mary E. Daly, *Dublin—The Deposed Capital: A Social and Economic History 1860–1914* (Cork 1985), p. 266.

15. Deeny, *To Cure and to Care*, p. 116.

16. Kennedy, *Cottage to Crèche*, p. 36.

17. Kevin C. Kearns, *Dublin Tenement Life: An Oral History* (Dublin 1994), p. 14.

18. Kennedy, *Cottage to Crèche*, p. 36.

19. Ibid, p. 37.

20. Deeny, *To Cure and to Care*, p. 85.

21. David Fitzpatrick, 'Marriage in Post-Famine Ireland', in Art Cosgrove (ed.), *Marriage in Ireland* (Dublin 1985), p. 116.

22. Mary E. Daly, *The Famine in Ireland* (Dublin 1986), p. 117.

23. Rita M. Rhodes, *Women and the Family in Post-Famine Ireland* (New York and London 1992), p. 4.

24. Ibid.

25. Daly, *The Famine in Ireland*, p. 117.

26. Joseph Lee, *The Modernisation of Irish Society 1848–1918* (Dublin 1973 and 1989), p. 1.

27. Daly, *The Famine in Ireland*, p. 117.

28. Lee, *The Modernisation of Irish Society*, p. 1. Rhodes has noted that later marriage, permanent celibacy and emigration had existed pre-famine in the land-conscious and market-oriented eastern region of the country, Rhodes, *Women and Family*, p. 6.

29. Lee, *The Modernisation of Irish Society*, pp 2–3.

30. Rhodes, *Women and the Family*, p. 85.

31. Quoted in Rhodes, *Women and the Family*, p. 21.

32. Hasier R. Diner, *Erin's Daughters in America* (Baltimore and London 1983), p. 7.

33. Ibid.

34. Art Cosgrove, *Marriage in Ireland*, p. 3.

35. Caoimhín Ó Danachair, 'Marriage in Irish Folk Tradition', in *Marriage in Ireland*, p. 103.

36. Kennedy, *Cottage to Crèche*, p. 22.

37. David Fitzpatrick, 'The Modernisation of the Irish Female', in Patrick

O'Flanagan, Paul Ferguson, Kevin Whelan (eds), *Rural Ireland 1600–1900: Modernisation and Change* (Cork 1987), p. 170.

38. Conrad M. Arensberg and Solon T. Kimball, *Family and Community in Ireland* (3rd edition, Clasp Press, Co. Clare 2001), p. 131.
39. Ibid, pp 130–31.
40. Fitzpatrick, 'The Modernisation of the Irish Female', p. 170.
41. Quoted in Rhodes, *Women and the Family*, p. 95.
42. Arensberg and Kimball, *Family and Community*, p. 132.
43. Ibid.
44. Ibid.
45. Fitzpatrick, 'The Modernisation of the Irish Female', p. 170.
46. Arensberg and Kimball, *Family and Community*, pp 134–5.
47. Quoted in Rhodes, *Women and the Family*, pp 95–6.
48. Quoted in Rhodes, *Women and the Family*, p. 96.
49. Arensberg and Kimball, *Family and Community*, pp 109–10.
50. Fitzpatrick, 'The Modernisation of the Irish Female', p. 170.
51. Quoted in Kennedy, *Cottage to Crèche*, p. 126.
52. J.J. Lee, 'Women and the Church since the Famine', in Margaret MacCurtain and Donncha Ó Corráin (eds), *Women in Irish Society: The Historical Dimension* (Dublin 1978), p. 39.
53. The linen industry in the Belfast region provided the only exception to this.
54. Rhodes, *Women and the Family*, pp 85–6.
55. Arensberg and Kimball, *Family and Community*, p. 77.
56. Lee, 'Women and the Church since the Famine', p. 39.
57. Rhodes, *Women and the Family*, p. 102.
58. Lee, 'Women and the Church since the Famine', p. 38.
59. Elizabeth Malcolm, '"The House of Strident Shadows": the Asylum, Family and Emigration in Post-Famine Rural Ireland', in *Medicine, Disease and the State in Ireland 1650–1940* (Cork 1999), p. 184. Citing Joanna Bourke, *Husbandry to Housewifery: Women, Economic Change and Housework in Ireland, 1890–1914* (Oxford 1993), Malcolm notes that at the turn of the twentieth century, the average marriage age for men was thirty years and for women twenty-six years; by 1911, however, 27 per cent of men and 25 per cent of women in the age range forty-five to fifty-four years had never married.
60. Fitzpatrick, 'The Modernisation of the Irish Female', p. 169.
61. Arensberg and Kimball, *Family and Community*, p. 135.
62. Lee, *The Modernisation of Irish Society*, p. 4; Malcolm, 'The House of Strident Shadows', p. 184.
63. Malcolm, 'The Asylum, Family and Emigration', p. 184.
64. Lee, 'Women and the Church since the Famine', p. 38.
65. Malcolm, 'The Asylum, Family and Emigration', p. 185.
66. Quoted in Enda Delaney, *Demography, State and Society: Irish Migration to Britain 1921–1971* (Liverpool 2000), p. 54.
67. Rhodes, *Women and the Family*, p. 115.
68. Fitzpatrick, 'The Modernisation of the Irish Female', p. 173.

69. Rhodes, *Women and the Family*, p. 116.
70. Fitzpatrick, 'The Modernisation of the Irish Female', p. 176.
71. Malcolm, 'The Asylum, Family and Emigration', p. 185; Lee, *The Modernisation of Irish Society*, p. 5.
72. Rhodes, *Women and the Family*, p. 194.
73. Mary E. Daly, *Women and Work in Ireland* (Dundalk 1997), pp 19 and 22.
74. Delaney, *Demography, State and Society*, p. 21.
75. Daly, *The Famine in Ireland*, p. 115.
76. Arensberg and Kimball, *Family and Community*, p. 95.
77. Ibid, p. 102.
78. Pauric Travers, '"There was nothing for me there": Irish female emigration, 1922–71', in Patrick O'Sullivan (ed.), *Irish Women and Irish Migration* (London 1995), p. 147.
79. Malcolm, 'The Asylum, Family and Emigration', p. 180.
80. Ibid, p. 185.
81. Fitzpatrick, 'Marriage in Post-Famine Ireland', p. 116.
82. Kerby A. Miller with David N. Doyle and Patricia Kelleher, '"For love and liberty": Irish women, migration and domesticity in Ireland and America, 1815–1920', in *Irish Women and Irish Migration*, p. 51.
83. David Fitzpatrick, '"A Share of the Honeycomb": Education, Emigration and Irishwomen', in Mary Daly and David Dickson (eds.), *The Origins of Popular Literacy in Ireland* (Dublin 1990), p. 167.
84. Diner, *Erin's Daughters in America*, pp 28–9.
85. Fitzpatrick, 'A Share of the Honeycomb', pp 167–8, 173.
86. Rhodes, *Women and the Family*, p. 248; Ide O'Carroll, *Models for Movers: Irish Women's Emigration to America* (Dublin 1990), p. 18.
87. Rhodes, *Women and the Family*, pp 270–71.
88. Fitzpatrick, 'A Share of the Honeycomb', p. 168.
89. Ibid, pp 170–72.
90. Ibid, pp 177–8.
91. Ibid, p. 181.
92. Malcolm, 'The Asylum, Family and Emigration', p. 185.
93. Ibid, p. 186.
94. Diner, *Erin's Daughters in America*, p. 19.
95. Dympna McLoughlin, 'Women and sexuality in nineteenth-century Ireland', in *The Irish Journal of Psychology*, 15, 2 and 3 (1994), p. 274.
96. Dympna McLoughlin, 'Workhouses and Irish Female Paupers 1840–1870', in Maria Luddy and Cliona Murphy (eds), *Women Surviving: Studies in Irish Women's History in the 19th and 20th Centuries* (Dublin 1989), pp 134–5; also Dympna McLoughlin, 'Superfluous and unwanted deadweight: the emigration of nineteenth-century Irish pauper women', in Patrick O'Sullivan (ed.), *The Irish Worldwide, History, Heritage, Identity*, VOL. 4, *Irish Women and Irish Migration* (London 1995), pp 76–7. In the latter, McLoughlin notes that it could take up to five years before a mother/parent had saved enough money to send for children left in the Workhouse.

97. McLoughlin, 'Women and sexuality in nineteenth-century Ireland', p. 272.

98. Ibid, p. 273.

99. Arensberg and Kimball, *Family and Community*, pp 208–9.

100. Ibid, p. 205.

101. Ibid, p. 208.

102. Quoted in Maria Luddy, 'Moral Rescue and Unmarried Mothers in Ireland in the 1920s', in *Women's Studies*, VOL. 30 NO. 6 (2001), p. 798.

103. Luddy, 'Moral Rescue', p. 799.

104. Ibid, p. 806. Luddy notes that in one such home 50 per cent of babies died in 1930.

105. Ibid, p. 799.

106. Ibid, p. 801

107. Paul Michael Garrett, 'The abnormal flight: the migration and repatriation of Irish unmarried mothers', in *Social History*, VOL. 25 NO. 3 (October 2000), p. 333; Luddy, 'Moral Rescue', pp 805–6.

108. Garrett, 'The abnormal flight', p. 336.

109. Ibid, p. 331.

110. Ibid, p. 334; Garrett has pointed to a racist sub-text in such arrangements whereby white American Catholics could acquire white babies.

111. Ibid, pp 340–41.

112. Luddy, 'Moral Rescue', p. 813.

113. A. O'Connor, 'Women in Irish Folklore; the Testimony Regarding Illegitimacy, Abortion and Infanticide', in Margaret MacCurtain and Mary O'Dowd (eds), *Women in Early Modern Ireland* (Dublin 1991), pp 310–11.

114. Ibid, p. 308.

115. Dympna McLoughlin, 'Workhouses and Irish Female Paupers', pp 137 and 141.

116. Kennedy, *Cottage to Crèche*, p. 38.

117. Mary Clancy, 'Aspects of Women's Contribution to the Oireachtas Debate in the Irish Free State, 1922–37', in Maria Luddy and Cliona Murphy (eds.), *Women Surviving*, pp 214–15.

118. Cited in Kennedy, *Cottage to Crèche*, p. 38.

119. Kennedy, *Cottage to Crèche*, pp 37–8.

120. Ibid, p. 38.

121. F.P. Powell, *The Politics of Irish Social Policy* (Dyfed 1992), quoted in Garrett, 'The Abnormal Flight', p. 342.

122. Garrett, 'The Abnormal Flight', p. 342.

123. Elizabeth Steiner Scott, '"To Bounce a Boot Off Her Now and Then …": Domestic Violence in Post-Famine Ireland' in Maryann Gialanella Valiulis and Mary O'Dowd (eds), *Women and Irish History* (Dublin 1997), p. 131.

124. Ibid, p. 137.

125. Ibid, p. 125.

126. Joanna Bourke, *Husbandry to Housewifery: Women, Economic Change and Housework in Ireland, 1890–1914* (Oxford 1993), quoted in Steiner Scott, 'To Bounce a Boot Off Her', p. 135.

127. Steiner Scott, 'To Bounce A Boot Off Her', p. 126.

128. Kevin C. Kearns, *Dublin Tenement Life*, p. 51.

129. Ibid.

130. Lee, 'Women and the Church since the Famine', p. 41.

131. Brendan M. Walsh, 'Marriage in Ireland in the Twentieth Century', in Cosgrove (ed.), *Marriage in Ireland*, p. 137.

132. Rhodes, *Women and the Family*, p. 254.

133. Mona Hearn, 'Life for Domestic Servants in Dublin, 1880–1920', in Luddy and Murphy (eds), *Women Surviving*, p. 149.

134. Ibid, p. 150.

135. Daly, *Dublin—The Deposed Capital*, p. 142. Daly comments that these figures no doubt reflect the substantial movement of military and civil service personnel.

136. Hearn, 'Life for Domestic Servants', pp 154–5.

137. G. Sweeney, *In Public Service* (Dublin 1990), quoted in Kennedy, *Cottage to Crèche*, p. 57.

138. Andrews, *Dublin Made Me*, pp 4–7.

139. M. Hearn, *Below Stairs: Domestic Service Remembered* (Dublin 1993), quoted in Kennedy, *Cottage to Crèche*, p. 56.

140. Farmar, *Ordinary Lives* (Dublin 1991), p. 25.

141. Ibid, p. 19.

142. Daly, *Dublin—The Deposed Capital*, p. 278.

143. Bourke, *Husbandry to Housewifery*, p. 207.

144. Anne O'Dowd, 'Women in Rural Ireland in the Nineteenth and early Twentieth Centuries—How the Daughters, Wives and Sisters of Small Farmers and Landless Labourers Fared', in *Rural History*, 5, 2, (1994), pp 179–80.

145. Ibid. p. 180.

146. David Smith, '"I Thought I Was Landed!": The Congested Districts Board and The Women of Western Ireland', in *Éire-Ireland*, XXXI, 3 and 4 (1996), p. 219.

147. Bourke, *Husbandry to Housewifery*, pp 208–9.

148. Arensberg and Kimball, *Family and Community*, p. 127.

149. Ibid, p. 321.

150. Ibid.

151. Bourke, *Husbandry to Housewifery*, p. 209.

152. Ibid, pp 210–11.

153. Ibid, p. 211.

154. Arensberg and Kimball, *Family and Community*, pp 35–9.

155. Mary E. Daly, '"Turn on the Tap": The State, Irish Women and Running Water', in Valiulis and O'Dowd (eds), *Women and Irish History*, p. 209.

156. Bourke, *Husbandry to Housewifery*, pp 213–14.

157. Daly, 'Turn on the Tap', pp 210 and 218.

158. Ibid, p. 208.

159. Ibid, p. 213.

160. Ibid, pp 210–11,

161. Ibid, pp 215–17.

162. Deeny, *To Cure and to Care*, pp 97–8.

163. Daly, *Dublin—The Deposed Capital*, p. 118.

164. Ibid, pp 120–21.

165. Kearns, *Dublin Tenement Life*, pp 6–7.

166. Daly, *Dublin—The Deposed Capital*, p. 283.

167. Kearns, *Dublin Tenement Life*, p. 7.

168. Daly, *Dublin—The Deposed Capital*, pp 279–81.

169. Ibid, p. 308.

170. Kearns, *Dublin Tenement Life*, p. 8.

171. The classification of housing and of accommodation was based on the number and quality of rooms and windows. For further detail see Daly, *Dublin—The Deposed Capital*, p. 278

172. Daly, *Dublin—The Deposed Capital*, p. 286.

173. Kearns, *Dublin Tenement Life*, p. 9.

174. Daly, *Dublin—The Deposed Capital*, pp 289 and 301; Kearns, *Dublin Tenement Life*, p. 9.

175. Kearns, *Dublin Tenement Life*, pp 12–13.

176. Ibid, p. 13.

177. Daly, *Dublin—The Deposed Capital*, p. 270.

178. Ibid, p. 272.

179. Ibid, pp 285–6.

180. Ibid, pp 288–9.

181. Ibid, p. 289.

182. Ibid, p. 263.

183. Ibid, pp 263–4.

184. Ibid, p. 268.

185. Ibid, pp 268–9.

186. Ibid, p. 306. The Census also indicated that the majority of tenement families were Dublin-born, the majority unskilled labourers, with a significant proportion of illiteracy.

187. Kearns, *Dublin Tenement Life*, pp 32–3.

188. Ibid, p. 33.

189. Quoted in Kennedy, *Cottage to Crèche*, p. 58.

190. Ibid.

Chapter 8 (pages 190–214)

1. Theresa Moriarty, *Work in Progress: Episodes from the history of Irish women's trade unionism* (Belfast and Dublin 1994).

2. Miriam Daly, 'Women in Ulster', in Eiléan Ní Chuilleanáin (ed.), *Irish Women: Image and Achievement* (Dublin 1985), p. 56.

3. Mary E. Daly, *Women and Work in Ireland* (Dundalk 1997), pp 28–9.

4. Mary E. Daly, *Dublin—The Deposed Capital: A Social and Economic History 1860–1914* (Cork 1985), p. 42.

5. Christine Hynes, 'A Polite Struggle: The Dublin Seamstresses' Campaign, 1869–1972', in *Saothar* 18 (1993), p. 35; Daly, *Dublin—The Deposed Capital*, p. 42.

6. *Englishwoman's Journal,* October 1862, pp 107–11.
7. Ibid.
8. Ibid.
9. The following account is based on Hynes, 'A Polite Struggle', pp 35–9.
10. Hynes, 'A Polite Struggle', p. 38.
11. Ibid, 39.
12. Moriarty, *Work in Progress,* pp 1–2.
13. Ibid, p. 2.
14. Ibid, p. 3.
15. Ibid, p. 5.
16. Theresa Moriarty, 'Mary Galway (1864–1928)', in Mary Cullen and Maria Luddy (eds.), *Female Activists: Irish Women and Change 1900–1960* (Dublin 2001), p. 12.
17. Ibid, p. 11.
18. Moriarty, *Work in Progress,* pp 7–9.
19. Daly, 'Women in Ulster', p. 57.
20. Moriarty, *Work in Progress,* p. 10; her only absence during that period was during the Belfast linen strike of 1906.
21. Moriarty, 'Mary Galway', p. 23.
22. Quoted in Moriarty, 'Mary Galway', p. 20.
23. Moriarty, 'Mary Galway', p. 26.
24. Quoted in Moriarty, 'Mary Galway', p. 26.
25. Quoted in Daly, 'Women in Ulster', p. 55.
26. Dermot Keogh, 'Michael O'Lehane and the Organisation of Linen Drapers' Assistants', in *Saothar* 3 (1977).
27. Mary E. Daly, 'Women and Trade Unions', in Donal Nevin (ed.), *Trade Union Century* (Cork 1994), p. 107.
28. Keogh, 'Michael O'Lehane', p. 37.
29. Brid Smith, 'Cissy Cahalan, A Tribute', in *Labour History News,* NO. 8 (Autumn 1992), p. 14.
30. Mats Grieff, '"Marching Through the Streets Singing and Shouting": Industrial Struggle and Trade Unions Among Female Linen Workers in Belfast and Lurgan, 1872–1910', in *Saothar* 22 (1997), p. 29.
31. Rosemary Owens, '"Votes for Ladies, Votes for Women": Organised Labour and the Suffrage Movement, 1876-1922', in *Saothar* 9 (1983), pp 35–6.
32. For a detailed study of Bennett see Rosemary Cullen Owens, *Louie Bennett* (Cork 2001).
33. R.M. Fox, *Louie Bennett: Her Life and Times* (Dublin 1958), p. 42.
34. Cullen Owens, *Louie Bennett,* p. 66.
35. Owens, 'Votes for Ladies, Votes for Women', p. 38.
36. Profile of Bennett by Ann Daly in *Irish Press,* 2 May 1955.
37. Louie Bennett, 'With Irish Women Workers', in *Irish Economist,* VOLS 7–8 (August 1922), pp 294–301.
38. Bennett to Cecil Watson, Court Laundry, Dublin, 21 September 1917 (private collection of Robert Tweedy, former Manager of the Court Laundry).
39. Mary Jones, *These Obstreperous Lassies: A History of the Irish Women Workers'*

Union (Dublin 1988), p. 25.

40. Bennett, 'With Irish Women Workers', p. 298.
41. *Irish Times*, 28 February 1919.
42. *Irish Citizen*, July 1917.
43. *Irish Citizen*, November 1919.
44. *Irish Citizen*, December 1919.
45. Louie Bennett, 'Women and the Labour Movement', in *Dublin Labour Year Book* (Dublin, 1930), p. 40.
46. C. Cahalan, 'Women and the Irish Labour Movement', in ibid, p. 48.
47. Helena Molony, 'James Connolly and Women', in ibid, p. 32.
48. Ellen Hazelkorn, 'The Social and Political Views of Louie Bennett, 1870–1956', in *Saothar* 13 (1988), p. 36.
49. Ibid.
50. *Irish Citizen*, October 1919.
51. Marion S. Duggan to Hanna Sheehy Skeffington, 10 September 1920, SSP NLI MS 22,693 (5).
52. *ITUC Report 1918*.
53. *Irish Citizen*, February 1920.
54. Jones, *These Obstreperous Lassies*, p. 59.
55. J.J. Lee, *Ireland 1912–1985: Politics and Society* (Cambridge 1989), pp 124–7.
56. Jones, *These Obstreperous Lassies*, p. 87.
57. IWWU Executive Minutes 16 January 1930, quoted in Jones, *These Obstreperous Lassies*, p. 96.
58. Bennett, 'Women and the Labour Movement', p. 39.
59. Daly, 'Women and Trade Unions', p. 110.
60. Astrid McLaughlin, '"Received with politeness, treated with contempt": The story of women's protests in Ireland against the regressive implications of sections of the Conditions of Employment Act (1936) and Bunreacht na hÉireann, The Irish Constitution of 1937', unpublished MA thesis, University College Dublin (1996).
61. *Irish Press*, 14 May 1935.
62. Jones, *These Obstreperous Lassies*, p. 126.
63. ITUC, 41st Annual Report 1935; *Irish Times*, 3 August 1935.
64. ITUC, Report 1935.
65. Ibid.
66. Ibid.
67. *Irish Times*, 21 November 1935; also *The Republican Congress*, 30 November 1935.
68. Margaret Ward, *Unmanageable Revolutionaries: Women and Irish Nationalism* (London and Dingle 1983), pp 236–7.
69. Mary Daly cited in Liam O'Dowd, 'Church, State and Women', in Chris Curtin, Pauline Jackson, Barbara O'Connor (eds), *Gender in Irish Society* (Galway 1987), p. 27.
70. IWWU, Annual Report 1937–8, p. 5; see also Ward, *Unmanageable Revolutionaries*, p. 241.
71. *Labour News*, 26 June 1937.

72. Louie Bennett, Presidential Address to Irish Trade Union Congress 1932.

73. Mary E. Daly, 'Women, Work and Trade Unionism', in Margaret MacCurtain and Donncha Ó Corráin (eds.), *Women in Irish Society: The Historical Dimension* (Dublin 1978), pp 76–7.

74. Seamus Cody, John O'Dowd, Peter Rigney (eds.), *The Parliament of Labour: 100 Years of the Dublin Council of Trade Unions* (Dublin 1986), pp 171–7.

75. *The Torch*, 26 July 1941.

76. Rosemary Cullen Owens, interview with Lady Eleanor Wicklow (Eleanor Butler), May 1987.

77. *Irish Times*, 17 September 1945.

78. *Irish Times*, 5 and 13 September 1945.

79. Mai Clifford, 'They gave us one week but we wanted two', in *Labour History News* (Autumn 1986), p. 12.

80. Jones, *These Obstreperous Lassies*, pp 231–2.

81. Daly, 'Women and Trade Unions', p. 109.

82. Fox, *Louie Bennett*, pp 67–8.

83. Quoted in Miriam Daly, 'Women in Ulster', p. 58.

84. Daly, 'Women, Work and Trade Unionism', pp 73–4.

85. Ibid, p. 74.

86. Daly, 'Women and Trade Unions', p. 109.

87. Marianne Heron, *Sheila Conroy: Fighting Spirit* (Dublin 1993), p. 31.

88. Ibid, p. 30.

89. Daly, 'Women and Trade Unions', pp 113–14.

Chapter 9 (pages 215–247)

1. Mary E. Daly, *Women and Work in Ireland* (Dundalk 1997), p. 1.

2. Mary E. Daly, '"Oh, Kathleen Ni Houlihan, Your Way's a Thorny Way!": The Condition of Women in Twentieth-Century Ireland', in Anthony Bradley and Maryann Gialanella Valiulis (eds), *Gender and Sexuality in Modern Ireland* (Amherst, Mass 1997), p. 105; also Daly, *Women and Work*, pp 1–2.

3. Mary E. Daly, 'Women in the Irish Workforce from Pre-Industrial to Modern Times', in *Saothar* 7 (1981), p. 75.

4. Daly, *Women and Work*, pp 2 and 22; Daly notes that farmers' wives ranged from 40 per cent of women in agriculture in the counties of Leinster to 75 per cent in Leitrim and Mayo (Daly, 'Women in the Irish Workforce', p. 75 and fn 8, p. 81).

5. Quoted in Maria Luddy, 'Women and work in nineteenth- and early twentieth-century Ireland: an overview', in Bernadette Whelan (ed.), *Women and Paid Work in Ireland 1500–1930* (Dublin 2000), p. 45.

6. Joanna Bourke, *Husbandry to Housewifery: Women, Economic Change, and Housework in Ireland, 1890–1914* (Oxford 1993), p. 26.

7. Daly, 'Oh, Kathleen Ni Houlihan', p. 106.

8. Daly, *Women and Work*, p. 2.

9. Ruth Dudley Edwards, *An Atlas of Irish History* (London 1973), p. 214.

10. Daly, *Women and Work*, pp 3 and 56.

11. Mary Cullen, 'Breadwinners and Providers: Women in the Household Economy of Labouring Families 1835–6', in Maria Luddy and Cliona Murphy (eds), *Women Surviving* (Dublin 1989), p. 85. From the detailed budgets compiled during this survey, Cullen extracted considerable data regarding women's contributions, notably their income from pig and poultry keeping. None of the budgets included the unpaid work of women within the family, although significant time and labour was expended by women in transforming the family crop into a meal for the table.

12. Anne O'Dowd, 'Women in Rural Ireland in the Nineteenth and Early Twentieth Centuries—How the Daughters, Wives and Sisters of Small Farmers and Landless Labourers Fared', in *Rural History*, 5, 2 (1994), p. 178.

13. Daly, *Women and Work*, p. 22.

14. O'Dowd, 'Women in Rural Ireland', p. 174.

15. Quoted in Daly, *Women and Work*, p. 17.

16. Luddy, 'Women and work in nineteenth- and early twentieth-century', p. 47; Daly, *Women and Work*, p. 19.

17. Luddy, 'Women and work in nineteenth- and early twentieth-century', p. 55.

18. Mary E. Daly, 'Women in the Irish Free State 1922–1939: The Interaction Between Economics and Ideology', in *Journal of Women's History*, VOL. 6 NO. 4/VOL. 7 NO. 1 (1995), p. 104.

19. O'Dowd, 'Women in Rural Ireland', p. 175.

20. Caoimhín Ó Danachair, 'Marriage in Irish folk tradition', in Art Cosgrove (ed.), *Marriage in Ireland* (Dublin 1985), p. 110.

21. David M. Smith, '"I Thought I was Landed!": The Congested Districts Board and the Women of Western Ireland', in *Eire–Ireland*, XXXI, 3 and 4 (1996), p. 210.

22. Ibid, p. 213.

23. Ibid, p. 227.

24. Ibid, pp 223–4; also Bourke, *Husbandry to Housewifery*, p. 98.

25. Smith, 'I Thought I was Landed!', p. 225.

26. Rita Rhodes, *Women and the Family in Post-Famine Ireland* (New York and London 1992), p. 171.

27. Mona Hearn, 'Life for Domestic Servants in Ireland, 1880–1920', in Maria Luddy and Cliona Murphy (eds), *Women Surviving: Studies in Irish Women's History in the 19th and 20th centuries* (Dublin 1989), p. 148.

28. Ibid; see also Daly, 'Women in the Irish Workforce', p. 77.

29. Daly, *Women and Work*, p. 23.

30. O'Dowd, 'Women in Rural Ireland', p. 175. Luddy has pointed to the significance of the Factory Acts which applied to creameries, and restricted the hours women could work, Luddy, 'Women and work in nineteenth- and early twentieth-century', p. 48.

31. Bourke, *Husbandry to Housewifery*, p. 82.

32. Ibid, p. 190.

33. O'Dowd, 'Women in Rural Ireland', p. 175.

34. Bourke, *Husbandry to Housewifery*, p. 1.

35. Daly, *Women and Work*, p. 18.

36. Finola Kennedy, *Cottage to Crèche: Family Change in Ireland* (Dublin 2001), p. 74.
37. Ibid, p. 75.
38. Daly, 'Women in the Irish Free State', p. 101.
39. Joseph J. Lee, 'Women and the Church since the Famine', in Margaret MacCurtain and Donncha Ó Corráin (eds), *Women in Irish Society: The Historical Dimension* (Dublin 1978), p. 38.
40. Daly, *Women and Work*, p. 27.
41. Mary E. Daly, *Dublin—The Deposed Capital: A Social and Economic History 1860–1914* (Cork 1984), p. 44.
42. Daly, *Women and Work*, p. 28.
43. Hearn, 'Life for Domestic Servants', pp 151–3.
44. Ibid, p. 150; Hearn notes that the ratio of servants in Dublin was 50 per 1,000, in Cork 49 per 1,000, and in Belfast 22 per 1,000.
45. Quoted in Kennedy, *Cottage to Crèche*, p. 59.
46. Conrad M. Arensberg and Solon T. Kimball, *Family and Community in Ireland*, (3rd ed., Clasp Press, Co. Clare 2001), pp 364 and 373.
47. Daly, 'Women in the Irish Workforce', p. 76.
48. Ibid, p. 77.
49. Kevin C. Kearns, *Dublin Tenement Life* (Dublin 1994), p. 30.
50. Ibid, pp 79–80.
51. Ibid, p. 49.
52. Ibid, pp 90–92.
53. Ibid, p. 93.
54. Maria Luddy, 'The Army and Prostitution in Nineteenth-Century Ireland: The Case of the Wrens of the Curragh', in *Bullán, An Irish Studies Journal*, VOL. 6 NO. 1, (2001), p. 67.
55. Maria Luddy, 'An Outcast Community: the "wrens" of the Curragh', in *Women's History Review*, VOL. 1 NO. 3 (1992), p. 343,
56. Luddy, 'The Army and Prostitution', p. 68.
57. Kearns, *Dublin Tenement Life*, p. 54.
58. Ibid, pp 209–10.
59. Ibid, p. 69.
60. Ibid, pp. 69 and 209.
61. Luddy, 'An Outcast Community', p. 346; also Luddy, 'The Army and Prostitution', p. 67.
62. Luddy, 'An Outcast Community', p. 346.
63. Daly, *Women and Work*, p. 32.
64. Dermot Keogh, 'Michael O'Lehane and the Organisation of Linen Drapers Assistants', in *Saothar* 3 (1977), p. 35.
65. Daly, *Women and Work*, p. 39.
66. Bourke, *Husbandry to Housewifery*, pp 33–4.
67. Myrtle Hill and Vivienne Pollock, *Image and Experience: Photographs of Irishwomen c. 1880–1920* (Belfast 1993), p. 39.
68. Anne V. O'Connor, 'The revolution in girls' secondary education in Ireland,

1860–1910', in Mary Cullen (ed.), *Girls Don't Do Honours: Irish Women in Education in the 19th and 20th Centuries* (Dublin 1987), pp 50–52.

69. Ibid, pp 52–3.
70. Ibid, p. 54.
71. Daly, *Women and Work*, p. 39.
72. Quoted by Margaret Ó hÓgartaigh, 'Flower power and "mental grooviness": nurses and midwives in Ireland in the early twentieth century', in Bernadette Whelan (ed.), *Women and Paid Work in Ireland 1500–1930* (Dublin 2000), p. 135.
73. These included St Vincent's hospital in Dublin, established by the Sisters of Charity in 1834, and hospitals in Cork (1857) and Dublin (1861) run by the Sisters of Mercy.
74. Ó hÓgartaigh, 'Flower power and "mental grooviness"', p. 137.
75. Ibid, p. 138.
76. Maria Luddy, '"Angels of Mercy": Nuns as Workhouse Nurses, 1861–1898' in Malcolm and Jones (eds), *Medicine, Disease and the State in Ireland 1650–1940* (Cork 1999), p. 103.
77. Ibid, p. 107.
78. Quoted in Ó hÓgartaigh, 'Flower power and "mental grooviness"', p. 134.
79. Luddy, 'Angels of Mercy', pp 114–15.
80. Ibid, p. 115.
81. Tony Fahey, 'Nuns in the Catholic church in Ireland in the nineteenth century', in *Girls Don't Do Honours*, p. 15.
82. Daly, *Women and Work*, pp 39–40.
83. Bourke, *Husbandry to Housewifery*, p. 46.
84. Daly, *Women and Work*, p. 40.
85. Ó hÓgartaigh, 'Flower power and "mental grooviness"', p. 137.
86. Ibid.
87. Daly, *Women and Work*, p. 40.
88. Ibid, p. 41.
89. Ibid, p. 44.
90. Daly, 'Women in the Irish Free State', p. 102.
91. Ibid, p. 107.
92. Ibid, pp 107–8.
93. Ibid, p. 108.
94. Tony Farmar, *Ordinary Lives: Three Generations of Irish Middle Class Experience 1907, 1932, 1963* (Dublin 1991), p. 140.
95. Ibid.
96. Hill and Pollock, *Image and Experience*, p. 40.
97. Daly, 'Women in the Irish Free State', p. 108; also Mary Jones, *These Obstreperous Lassies: A History of the Irish Women Workers' Union* (Dublin 1988), pp 35, 36, 56.
98. Daly, 'Women in the Irish Free State', p. 109.
99. Daly, 'Women in the Irish Workforce', p. 77.
100. Pauric Travers, '"There was nothing for me there": Irish female emigration,

1922–71', in P. O'Sullivan (ed.), *Irish Women and Irish Migration* (London 1995), p. 149; Enda Delaney, *Demography, State and Society* (Liverpool 2000), p. 96.

101. Daly, 'Women in the Irish Free State', pp 109–10.

102. Daly, 'Women in the Irish Free State', p. 110; Daly, *Women and Work*, pp 45–6.

103. Liam O'Dowd, 'Church, State and Women: The Aftermath of Partition', in Chris Curtin, Pauline Jackson, Barbara O'Connor (eds), *Gender in Irish Society* (Galway 1987), p. 26.

104. *Report of Commission of Inquiry into the Civil Service 1932–35*, Official Publications R. 54 (Dublin 1935), p. 197, para. 1.

105. Ibid, p. 199, para. 14.

106. Ibid, p. 199, para. 12.

107. Ibid, p. 200, para. 17.

108. Ibid, p. 202, para. 28.

109. Ibid, p. 233, para. 164.

110. Ibid, p. 182, para. 3.

111. Quoted in Diarmaid Ferriter, *The Transformation of Ireland 1900–2000* (London 2004), p. 464.

112. Fergal Tobin, *The Best of Decades: Ireland in the 1960s* (2nd ed., Dublin 1996), pp 9 and 12.

113. Daly, *Women and Work*, pp 41–3.

114. Betty Purcell, 'Ten Years of Progress? Some Statistics', in *The Crane Bag*, vol. 4 no. 1 (1980), p. 43.

115. Daly, *Women and Work*, p. 45.

116. Margaret MacCurtain, 'Late in the Field: Catholic Sisters in Twentieth-Century Ireland and the New Religious History', in Mary O'Dowd and Sabine Wichert (eds), *Chattel, Servant or Citizen: Women's Status in Church, State and Society* (Belfast 1995), p. 39.

117. Daly, 'Oh, Kathleen Ni Houlihan', pp 114–15.

118. *Irish Times*, 2 November 1999.

119. Ferriter, *The Transformation of Ireland*, p. 496.

120. Daly, *Women and Work*, pp 48–9.

121. Mary Daly, 'Women, Work and Trade Unionism', in *Women in Irish Society*, p. 79.

122. Kennedy, *Cottage to Crèche*, p. 114.

123. Eoin O'Leary, 'The Irish National Teachers' Organisation and The Marriage Bar for Women National Teachers, 1933–1958', in *Saothar* 12 (1987), p. 51; Kennedy, *Cottage to Crèche*, p. 103.

124. *Irish Times*, 2 November 1999.

125. Tobin, *The Best of Decades*, p. 241.

126. Daly, *Women and Work*, pp 50–51.

Chapter 10 (pages 251–279)

1. *Irish Citizen*, September–December 1920 (the paper had just recently become a quarterly publication).

2. *Irish Citizen*, October 1919.

3. Helena Molony, 'James Connolly and Women', in *Dublin Labour Year Book* (1930), p. 31.

4. Maurice Manning, 'Women in National and Local Politics 1922–77', in Margaret MacCurtain and Donncha Ó Corráin, *Women in Irish Society: The Historical Dimension* (Dublin 1978), p. 92.

5. Quoted in Maryann Gialanella Valiulis, 'Defining Their Role in the New State: Irishwomen's Protest Against the Juries Act of 1927', in *Canadian Journal of Irish Studies*, 18, 1 (July 1992), p. 43.

6. Mary Clancy, 'Aspects of Women's Contribution to the Oireachtas Debate in the Irish Free State, 1922–1937', in Maria Luddy and Cliona Murphy (eds), *Women Surviving: Studies in Irish Women's History in the 19th and 20th Centuries* (Dublin 1989), p. 221.

7. Quoted in Valiulis, 'Defining Their Role', p. 44.

8. Report of Irishwomen's Citizens Association (IWCA), in *United Irishwomen*, VOL. 1, NOS 1–9 (1925–1926).

9. Ibid.

10. Maryann Gialanella Valiulis, 'Power, Gender and Identity in the Irish Free State', in *Journal of Women's History*, VOL. 6 NO. 4/VOL. 7 NO. 1 (1995), p. 123; Valiulis notes that in 1924 when a prospective woman candidate threatened legal action claiming that the government did not have the power to exclude on the grounds of sex, the Attorney General concurred. The following year the government introduced the Civil Service (Amendment) Act, pp 120–21.

11. Report of IWCA, p. 11.

12. Clancy, 'Aspects of Women's Contribution', p. 217.

13. Ibid, p. 218.

14. The Bill was delayed for twelve months after this defeat in the Seanad; Clancy, 'Aspects of Women's Contribution', pp 229–30.

15. Valiulis, 'Defining Their Role', p. 46.

16. Quoted in Valiulis, 'Defining Their Role', p. 50.

17. Quoted in Valiulis, 'Defining Their Role', pp 44–5.

18. Quoted in Valiulis, 'Defining Their Role', p. 45; Valiulis, 'Power, Gender and Identity', p. 122; also Clancy, 'Aspects of Women's Contribution', p. 223.

19. Quoted in Valiulis, 'Defining Their Role', p. 45.

20. Ibid, p. 48. See also Maryann Gialanella Valiulis, 'Engendering Citizenship: Women's Relationship to the State in Ireland and the United States in the Post-Suffrage Period', in Valiulis and O'Dowd (eds), *Women and Irish History* (Dublin 1997), p. 162; in this she argues that it was over the issue of jury service that 'women's relationship to the state was renegotiated'.

21. Quoted in Valiulis, 'Power, Gender and Identity', p. 123.

22. Quoted in Valiulis, 'Engendering Citizenship', p. 164.

23. Quoted in Valiulis, 'Defining Their Role', p. 53; newspapers cited by Valiulis include *Irish Independent, Dundalk Democrat, Evening Herald, Kilkenny People*.

24. Quoted in Valiulis, 'Defining Their Role', p. 54.

25. Margaret MacCurtain, 'The Historical Image', in Eiléan Ní Chuilleanáin (ed.), *Irish Women: Image and Achievement* (Dublin 1985), p. 49; also Tom Inglis,

Moral Monopoly: The Rise and Fall of the Catholic Church in Modern Ireland (Dublin 1987), p. 91.

26. Margaret O'Callaghan, 'Women and Politics in Independent Ireland, 1921–68', in Angela Bourke et al (eds), *The Field Day Anthology of Irish Writing*, VOL. V, (Cork 2002), p. 124.

27. Liam O'Dowd, 'Church, State and Women: The Aftermath of Partition', in Chris Curtin, Pauline Jackson, Barbara O'Connor (eds), *Gender in Irish Society* (Galway 1987), p. 19.

28. Ibid.

29. Daisy Lawrenson Swanton, *Emerging from the Shadow: The Lives of Sarah Anne Lawrenson and Lucy Olive Kingston* (Dublin 1994), p. 113. Underlying the Censorship debate, Clancy has argued, was a desire to control aspects of women's lives, and in particular their reading material. She notes as more significant, Part 3 of the Bill which proposed to ban the reporting of rape and sexual assault, Clancy, 'Aspects of Women's Contribution', p. 211.

30. J.H. Whyte, *Church and State in Modern Ireland 1923–1979* (2nd ed., Dublin 1980), p. 49.

31. Maryann Valiulis, 'Neither Feminist nor Flapper: the Ecclestiastical Construction of the Ideal Irish Women', in Mary O'Dowd and Sabine Wichert (eds), *Chattel, Servant or Citizen: Women's Status in Church, State and Society* (Belfast 1995), p. 172.

32. O'Callaghan, 'Women and Politics', p. 126.

33. MacCurtain, 'The Historical Image', p. 49.

34. O'Dowd, 'Church, State and Women', p. 20.

35. Whyte, *Church and State*, p. 26.

36. O'Dowd, 'Church, State and Women', p. 18.

37. Valiulis, 'Neither Feminist nor Flapper', p. 172.

38. Ibid.

39. Ibid, p. 173.

40. Ibid, p. 174.

41. O'Dowd, 'Church, State and Women', pp 20–21.

42. For further detail on this issue see Rosemary Cullen Owens, *Smashing Times: A History of the Irish Women's Suffrage Movement 1889–1922* (Dublin 1984 and 1995), pp 122–4.

43. Whyte, *Church and State*, pp 33–4.

44. Quoted in O'Dowd, 'Church, State and Women', p. 7.

45. Finola Kennedy, *Cottage to Crèche: Family Changes in Ireland* (Dublin 2001), p. 91; Kennedy notes that such campaigns were generally supported by feminists.

46. Quoted by Margaret MacCurtain, 'Fullness of Life: Defining Female Spirituality in Twentieth-Century Ireland', in Luddy and Murphy (eds), *Women Surviving*, p. 243.

47. O'Dowd, 'Church, State and Women', p. 13.

48. O'Dowd, 'Church, State and Women', pp 12–15.

49. Kennedy, *Cottage to Crèche*, p. 158.

50. Ibid.

51. Quoted in Kennedy, *Cottage to Crèche*, p. 132.
52. Carrigan quoted in Kennedy, *Cottage to Crèche*, p. 133.
53. Quoted in Kennedy, *Cottage to Crèche*, p. 159.
54. Kennedy, *Cottage to Crèche*, pp 160–61.
55. Clancy, 'Aspects of Women's Contribution', p. 212.
56. Ibid, p. 213; the age had been raised to 16 years in Great Britain and Northern Ireland.
57. Hilda Tweedy, *A Link in the Chain: The Story of the Irish Housewives Association 1942–1992* (Dublin 1992), p. 20.
58. Clancy, 'Aspects of Women's Contribution', pp 213–14.
59. Ibid, p. 214.
60. Caitriona A. Beaumont, 'Women and the Politics of Equality: The Irish Women's Movement, 1930–1943', in *Women and Irish History*, pp 178–9.
61. Clancy, 'Aspects of Women's Contribution', pp 214–15.
62. Kennedy, *Cottage to Crèche*, p. 163
63. O'Callaghan, 'Women and Politics', p. 128.
64. With changes in membership during the lifetime of the Joint Committee, groups in the early years included The Girls Friendly Society, The Girl Guides, Irish Countrywomen's Assoc., Irish Matron's Assoc., The Irish Save the Children Fund, Irish Women Workers' Union, Irish Schoolmistresses' Assoc., The Legion of Mary, The Mothers' Union, National Council of Women, Women Graduates Assoc. of Trinity College, Women Citizens' Assoc., Women's National Health Assoc., The Holy Child Assoc., Society for the Prevention of Cruelty to Children, University College Dublin Women Graduates' Assoc.
65. Report on *Fifty Years of the Joint Committee of Women's Societies and Social Workers, 1935–1985* (unpublished typescript in author's possession, courtesy of Nora F. Browne).
66. *Irish Citizen*, 9 January 1915.
67. Quinlan notes that the last member of this force retired in 1956; Carmel Quinlan, *Genteel Revolutionaries: Anna and Thomas Haslam and the Irish Women's Movement* (Cork 2002), p. 180. In 1936, Hanna Sheehy Skeffington contrasted the position of the few women police that existed in the IFS, with no power of arrest and no uniform, with that of Britain where there was a regular corps of women police under their own officers; quoted in Margaret Ward, *Hanna Sheehy Skeffington: A Life* (Cork 1997), p. 323.
68. Beaumont, 'Women and the Politics of Equality', p. 180.
69. Tweedy, *A Link in the Chain*, pp 32–3.
70. Eoin O'Leary, 'The Irish National Teachers' Organisation and the Marriage Bar for Women National Teachers, 1933–1958', in *Saothar* 12, (1987), p. 50. The other reasons cited by the Dept of Education were: maternity leave created difficulties for pupils and other staff; the average age of marriage for women teachers was 31–2 years, giving the State an adequate ten years service for its investment in training; after slight losses initially, the new regulation would be self-financing. Two other points, the undesirability of married women teaching in mixed schools and high absentee rate among married women teachers, were not

mentioned, although both were cited in Cabinet memoranda.

71. Ibid, p. 48.
72. Mary Daly, 'Women in the Irish Workforce from Pre-industrial to Modern Times', in *Saothar* 7 (1981), p. 79.
73. T.J. O'Connell, *History of the National Teachers' Organisation 1868–1968* (Dublin 1969), pp 284–5.
74. *Report of Commission into the Civil Service 1932–1935*, addendum C, p. 185.
75. My thanks to Vera McCarthy and Fr Dermod McCarthy for this information.
76. Kennedy, *Cottage to Crèche*, p. 91.
77. Valiulis, 'Neither Feminist nor Flapper', p. 178.
78. Mary Daly, 'Women and Trade Unions', in Nevin (ed.), *Trade Union Century* (Dublin 1994).
79. Mary Horkan, 'The Women Graduates' Association: Beginnings', in Anne Macdona (ed.), *From Newman to New Woman: UCD Women Remember* (Dublin 2001), p. xxii.
80. O'Dowd, 'Church, State and Women', p. 27.
81. Daly, 'Women and Trade Unions', p. 109.
82. Ibid, p. 111.
83. Quoted by Astrid McLaughlin in '"Received with politeness, treated with contempt", The story of the women's protests in Ireland against the regressive implications of sections of the Conditions of Employment Act (1936) and Bunreacht na hÉireann, The Irish Constitution of 1937' (unpublished M.A. thesis, University College Dublin, 1996), p. 18.
84. Quoted in Mary Jones, *These Obstreperous Lassies: A History of the Irish Women Workers' Union* (Dublin 1988), p. 124.
85. Ibid, p. 125.
86. *Irish Times*, 11 July 1935, cited in McLaughlin, 'Received with Politeness', p. 26.
87. IWWU, Executive Minutes, 5 September 1935.
88. For a detailed study of Bennett's involvement in this campaign see Rosemary Cullen Owens, *Louie Bennett* (Cork 2001).
89. These were Helena Concannon and Margaret Pearse (Fianna Fáil), Bridget Redmond (Cumann na nGaedheal).
90. Margaret Ward, *Unmanageable Revolutionaries: Women and Irish Nationalism* (London and Dingle 1983), p. 236.
91. Clancy, 'Aspects of Women's Contribution', p. 220.
92. Quoted in Kennedy, *Cottage to Crèche*, p. 82.
93. Ward, *Hanna Sheehy Skeffington*, p. 323.
94. McLaughlin, 'Received with Politeness', p. 33.
95. Whyte, *Church and State*, p. 86.
96. F.S.L. Lyons, *Ireland Since the Famine* (Great Britain 1971), p. 537.
97. Ward, *Hanna Sheehy Skeffington*, p. 324; McLoughlin, 'Received with Politeness', p. 140.
98. Cullen Owens, *Louie Bennett*, p. 97.
99. Ibid.
100. Maurice Manning, 'Women in Irish National and Local Politics', pp 94–5.

101. Whyte, *Church and State*, p. 51.
102. Ward, *Unmanageable Revolutionaries*, p. 238.
103. Ibid.
104. Ibid.
105. McLaughlin, 'Received with Politeness', p. 45.
106. *University College Dublin Women Graduates' Association, 1902–1982* (Dublin n.d.), pp 36 and 38.
107. Beaumont, 'Women and the Politics of Equality', p. 181.
108. Cullen Owens, *Louie Bennett*, p. 87.
109. NAI, DTS 9880, 21 May 1937.
110. Ward, *Unmanageable Revolutionaries*, p. 239.
111. J.J. Lee, *Ireland 1912–1985: Politics and Society*, p. 206.
112. Cullen Owens, *Louie Bennett*, p. 87.
113. Ward, *Unmanageable Revolutionaries*, p. 240.
114. Lee, *Ireland 1912–1985*, pp 206–7.
115. Cullen Owens, *Louie Bennett*, p. 89.
116. McLaughlin, 'Received with Politeness', p. 54.
117. Caitriona A. Beaumont, 'Women and the Politics of Equality, 1930–43', (unpublished M.A. thesis, University College Dublin, 1989), pp 19–20.
118. Joyce Padbury, 'Mary Hayden, First President of the Women Graduates' Association', in Macdona (ed.), *From Newman to New Woman*, p. xvi; also Beaumont, 'Women and the Politics of Equality', p. 184.
119. Author interview with Andree Sheehy Skeffington, RTÉ series *Moments in Time*, broadcast 26 December 1987.
120. Beaumont, 'Women and the Politics of Equality', p. 184.
121. Clancy, 'Aspects of Women's Contribution', p. 224.
122. Lee, *Ireland 1912–1985*, p. 210.
123. McLaughlin, 'Received with Politeness', p. 55.
124. Horkan, 'The Women Graduates' Association', p. xxiii.
125. Mary Robinson, 'Women and the New Irish State', in MacCurtain and Ó Corráin (eds), *Women in Irish Society*, p. 58.
126. Clancy, 'Aspects of Women's Contribution', p. 206.
127. Beaumont, 'Women and the Politics of Equality', p. 175.
128. Valiulis, 'Defining Their Role', p. 55.
129. Robinson, 'Women and the New Irish State', p. 63.
130. Beaumont, 'Women and the Politics of Equality, 1930–43', p. 3.
131. Robinson, 'Women and the New Irish State', pp 63–4.
132. Ibid, p. 64.
133. Ibid.
134. Mary Daly, 'Women in the Irish Free State 1922–1939: The Interaction between Economics and Ideology', in *Journal of Women's History*, VOL. 6 NO. 4/VOL. 7 NO. 1 (1995), pp 100–101.
135. IWCA *Report* in *United Irishwomen* (1925–1926).
136. Clancy, 'Aspects of Women's Contribution', p. 225.
137. Whyte, *Church and State*, p. 60.

138. O'Dowd, 'Church, State and Women', p. 33.

139. Daly, 'Women and Trade Unions', p. 110.

140. Beaumont, 'Women and the Politics of Equality, 1930–43', p. 8.

141. Clancy, 'Aspects of Women's Contribution', p. 225.

Chapter 11 (pages 280–316)

1. Maria Luddy, *Hanna Sheehy Skeffington* (Dublin 1995), p. 45.

2. Caitriona Beaumont, 'Women and the Politics of Equality: The Irish Women's Movement, 1930–1943', in Maryann Gialanella Valiulis and Mary O'Dowd (eds), *Women and Irish History* (Dublin 1997), p. 185 and fn 74, p. 321.

3. Women's Social and Progressive League (WSPL), Annual Report 1937–38, p. 1.

4. NAI, DTS 9880, 21 May 1937.

5. Cited in Luddy, *Hanna Sheehy Skeffington*, p. 48.

6. Ibid.

7. Quoted in Margaret Ward, *In their Own Voice: Women and Irish Nationalism* (Dublin 1995), pp 167–8.

8. Hanna Sheehy Skeffington, quoted in Ward, *In Their Own Voice*, p. 169.

9. Margaret Ward, *Hanna Sheehy Skeffington: A Life* (Cork 1997), p. 339.

10. Quoted in Luddy, *Hanna Sheehy Skeffington*, pp 49–50.

11. Ibid, p. 50.

12. Author interview with Rosaleen Mills, RTÉ series *Moments in Time*, broadcast 24 March 1987.

13. Luddy, *Hanna Sheehy Skeffington*, p. 50.

14. Ibid, p. 51; Rosaleen Mills recalled that late in the campaign, word was put around that HSSS was a lapsed Catholic, 'so that put paid to her chances'; Interview with Mills, RTÉ series *Moments in Time*.

15. Luddy, *Hanna Sheehy Skeffington*, p. 51.

16. Joseph Lee, 'Aspects of Corporatist Thought in Ireland: The Commission on Vocational Organisation, 1939–43', in Art Cosgrove and D. MacCartney (eds), *Studies in Irish History Presented to R. Dudley Edwards* (Dublin 1979), pp 324–46.

17. Finola Kennedy, *Cottage to Crèche: Family Changes in Ireland* (Dublin 2001), pp 105–7.

18. Caitríona Clear, *Women of the House: Women's Household Work in Ireland 1922–1961* (Dublin 2000), p. 39

19. Ibid, p. 40.

20. Ibid.

21. Minutes of Commission on Vocational Organisation (CVO), evidence of Irish Women Workers' Union, NLI MS 925 vol. 4, p. 1319.

22. Caitríona Clear, '"The Women Can Not be Blamed": The Commission on Vocational Organisation, Feminism and "Homemakers" in Independent Ireland in the 1930s and '40s', in Mary O'Dowd and Sabine Wichert (eds), *Chattel, Servant or Citizen: Women's Status in Church, State and Society* (Belfast 1995), pp 179–86. Clear notes that two of the Commissioners, Máire McGeehan and G.L.C. Crampton, pointed out in an addendum to the Report that 'homemakers' made

up 25 per cent of the adult population in the 1936 census, and that a minimum of 5 seats would be necessary to ensure proportionate representation on the suggested Assembly. These recommendations were ignored by government.

23. Andree Sheehy Skeffington quoted in Caitriona Beaumont, 'Women and the Politics of Equality, 1930–43', (unpublished M.A thesis, UCD, 1989), p. 39.
24. Interview with Mills, RTÉ series *Moments in Time*.
25. Quoted in preface to Kevin C. Kearns, *Dublin Tenement Life* (Dublin 1994).
26. Professor R. Collis, *To Be A Pilgrim: An Autobiography* (London 1975), p. 90.
27. James Deeny, *To Cure and to Care: Memoirs of a Chief Medical Officer* (Dublin 1989), pp 73–4.
28. Ibid, p. 93.
29. James Deeny, 'The Enteritis Epidemic of the 1940s', in Tony Farmar (ed.), *The End of an Epidemic: Essays in Irish Public Health 1935–65* (Dublin 1995), p. 64.
30. Deeny, *To Cure and to Care*, p. 103.
31. Hilda Tweedy, *A Link in the Chain: The Story of the Irish Housewives Association 1942–1992* (Dublin 1992), p. 11.
32. Ibid.
33. WSPL, Annual Report 1939–40, pp 9–10.
34. See Joanna Bourke, *Husbandry to Housewifery: Women, Economic Change and Housework in Ireland, 1890–1914* (Oxford 1993), pp 237–9, p. 248; also Kennedy, *Cottage to Crèche*, pp 104–5.
35. *Teach Ultain Inc.* 34th Annual Report, 1952, p. 17.
36. Kennedy, *Cottage to Crèche*, p. 104.
37. Tweedy, *A Link in the Chain*, p. 11.
38. Emmet O'Connor, *A Labour History of Ireland 1824–1960* (Dublin 1992), p. 137.
39. Deeny, *To Cure and to Care*, p. 98.
40. Tweedy, *A Link in the Chain*, p. 14.
41. Ibid, p. 16.
42. Ibid.
43. Cited in Kennedy, *Cottage to Crèche*, p. 107.
44. Tweedy, *A Link in the Chain*, p. 17; also interview with Hilda Tweedy, RTÉ series *Moments in Time*, 28 March 1987.
45. Tweedy, *A Link in the Chain*, p. 22.
46. Quoted in Ward, *Hanna Sheehy Skeffington*, pp 343–4; this article was published after Hanna's death in April 1946.
47. Interview with Andree Sheehy Skeffington, RTÉ series *Moments in Time*, broadcast 26 December 1987.
48. Tweedy, *A Link in the Chain*, p. 94.
49. Tweedy, *A Link in the Chain*, pp 95–7.
50. Seamus Cody, John O'Dowd, Peter Rigney (eds.), *The Parliament of Labour: 100 Years of the Dublin Council of Trade Unions* (Dublin 1986), p. 190.
51. Ibid, pp 190–91.
52. Tweedy, *A Link in the Chain*, p. 99.
53. Cody, O'Dowd, Rigney (eds), *The Parliament of Labour*, p. 192.
54. Tweedy, *A Link in the Chain*, p. 101.

55. Cody, O'Dowd, Rigney (eds), *The Parliament of Labour*, p. 193.
56. Tweedy, *A Link in the Chain*, p. 74.
57. Ibid, pp 68–72.
58. Interview with Andree Sheehy Skeffington, RTÉ series *Moments in Time*.
59. Ibid.
60. Tony Farmar (ed.), *The End of an Epidemic: Essays in Irish Public Health 1935–65* (Dublin 1995), Introduction by Ruth Barrington, pp 9–10.
61. Deeny, *To Cure and to Care*, p. 115.
62. Ibid, p. 116.
63. *Mother and Child, What the New Service Means to Every Family* (Stationery Office c. 1950), Foreword by Dr Noël C. Browne, Minister for Health.
64. Tweedy, *A Link in the Chain*, p. 73.
65. Ibid.
66. Ibid, pp 73–4.
67. Interview with Rosaleen Mills, RTÉ series *Moments in Time*.
68. Clear, *Women of the House*, p. 64.
69. Clear, 'The Women Can Not be Blamed', p. 184.
70. Tweedy, *A Link in the Chain*, p. 24.
71. Ibid, p. 28.
72. Ibid, p. 62.
73. She later joined Fianna Fáil and resigned from the IHA; Tweedy, *A Link in the Chain*, p. 63.
74. Tweedy, *A Link in the Chain*, p. 35.
75. Margaret MacCurtain, Foreword to Tweedy, *A Link in the Chain*, p. 7.
76. Esther Bishop (ed.), *Bantracht na Tuatha, Irish Countrywomen's Association*, (Dublin 1950), p. 3.
77. Bourke, *Husbandry to Housewifery*, p. 239.
78. Bishop, *Bantracht na Tuatha*, pp 3–4.
79. Ibid, p. 4; the training of nurses was later handed over to the Queen's Institute of District Nursing.
80. Ibid, pp 7–8.
81. Ibid, p. 9.
82. Diarmaid Ferriter, *Mothers, Maidens and Myths: A History of the ICA*, pp 33–4.
83. Ibid, p. 17.
84. Ibid.
85. Ibid, p. 9.
86. Ibid, p. 33.
87. Ferriter quoted in Kennedy, *Cottage to Crèche*, p. 108; Kennedy notes that this 1959 objective would be espoused by the Women's Liberation Movement in the 1970s.
88. Interview with Rosaleen Mill, RTÉ series *Moments in Time*.
89. Clear, 'The Women Can Not be Blamed', p. 183.
90. Clear, *Women of the House*, p. 40.
91. Mamo McDonald, Extract from address to 1984 EEC Seminar on Women in Agriculture and Self-Employment, quoted in Angela Bourke et al (eds), *The*

Field Day Anthology of Irish Writing, VOL. V (Cork 2002), pp 275–7.

92. Mary E. Daly, '"Turn on the Tap": The State, Irish Women and Running Water', in Maryann Gialanella Valiulis and Mary O'Dowd (eds), *Women and Irish History* (Dublin 1997), pp 206–19.
93. Ferriter, *Mothers*, p. 41.
94. Daly, 'Turn on the Tap', pp 206–7.
95. Ibid, p. 207; Ferriter, *Mothers*, p. 41.
96. Quoted in Daly, 'Turn on the Tap', p. 211.
97. Ibid.
98. Ferriter, *Mothers*, pp 41–2.
99. Daly, 'Turn on the Tap', pp 215–16.
100. Ibid, pp 214–16; Daly notes the opposition of the Department of Agriculture to any measure increasing taxation on farmers.
101. Ibid, p. 218.
102. Ferriter, *Mothers*, p. 43.
103. Ibid, pp 18 and 49.
104. Ibid, p. 45.
105. MacCurtain, Foreword to Tweedy, *A Link in the Chain*, p. 7.
106. See Maurice Manning, 'Women in Irish National and Local Politics 1922–77', in Margaret MacCurtain and Donncha Ó Corráin (eds.), *Women in Irish Society: The Historical Dimension* (Dublin 1978), pp 92–102.
107. Tweedy, *A Link in the Chain*, p. 13.
108. Mary E. Daly, 'Women and Trade Unions', in Donal Nevin (ed.), *Trade Union Century* (Cork 1994), p. 111.
109. Clear, *Women of the House*, p. 62.
110. Ibid, p. 212.
111. Ibid, pp 212–13; also Kennedy, *Cottage to Crèche*, p. 217. Kennedy notes that child benefit was eventually paid directly to women some thirty years later in 1974 when Cosgrave was Taoiseach.
112. Clear, *Women of the House*, p. 212.
113. Kennedy, *Cottage to Crèche*, p. 107.
114. Ferriter, *Mothers*, p. 10.
115. Ibid.
116. Ibid, p. 30.
117. J.J. Lee, *Ireland 1912–1985: Politics and Society* (Cambridge 1989), p. 377.
118. Quoted in Enda Delaney, *Demography, State and Society: Irish Migration to Britain 1921–1971* (Liverpool 2000), p. 243.
119. Quoted in Delaney, *Demography*, p. 186.
120. Pauric Travers, 'Emigration and Gender: The Case of Ireland 1922–60', in Mary O'Dowd and Sabine Wichert (eds), *Chattel, Servant or Citizen: Women's Status in Church, State and Society* (Belfast 1995), p. 190; the comparative figure for women from Dublin county or borough was 12.5 per cent, and for other urban districts 19.5 per cent.
121. Daly, 'Turn on the Tap', p. 206.
122. Ferriter, *Mothers*, p. 25.

123. Quoted in Delaney, *Demography,* p. 242.

124. *Irish Nurses Organisation 50th Anniversary Book* (1969), p. 12.

125. Joy Rudd, 'Invisible Exports: The Emigration of Irish Women This Century', in *Women's Studies International Forum,* VOL. 11 NO. 4 (1988), p. 310.

126. Margaret MacCurtain, 'Godly Burden: Catholic Sisterhoods in 20th-Century Ireland', in Anthony Bradley and Maryann Gialanella Valiulis (eds), *Gender and Sexuality in Modern Ireland* (Amherst, Mass, 1997), p. 251.

127. Ibid, p. 251.

128. Ibid, pp 253–4.

129. Daly, 'Turn on the Tap', p. 206.

130. Quoted in Pauric Travers, '"There was nothing for me there": Irish female emigration, 1922–71', in Patrick O'Sullivan (ed.), *Irish Women and Irish Migration* (London 1995), p. 154.

131. Travers, 'Emigration and Gender', p. 191.

132. Quoted in Kennedy, *Cottage to Crèche,* p. 225.

133. June Levine, 'The Women's Movement in the Republic of Ireland, 1968–80', in *The Field Day Anthology,* VOL. V, p. 184.

134. Eileen Proctor cited in *The Field Day Anthology,* VOL. V, p. 209; Marianne Heron, *Sheila Conroy: Fighting Spirit* (Dublin 1993), p. 142. In time, the NAWI expanded to 55 branches.

135. Levine, 'The Women's Movement', p. 184.

136. Author interview with Bríd Ní hÉigeartaigh, RTÉ series *Moments in Time,* broadcast 27 January 1990.

137. Kennedy, *Cottage to Crèche,* p. 212.

138. Interview with Bríd Ní hÉigeartaigh, RTÉ series *Moments in Time.*

139. Letter from AWCS to John Kelly TD, 30 April 1974 (copy held by author).

140. Guide to sources for Ireland and European Unity, p. 1, www.nationalarchives .ie/topics/EU/eu.htm

141. Tweedy, *A Link in the Chain,* pp 28–30; Tweedy notes that in 1992 with affiliated organisations in fifty-two countries and associated societies in ten countries, the IAW had consultative status B with the UN and permanent representation at the UN, including the ILO, WHO, UNESCO and FAO.

142. Tweedy, *A Link in the Chain,* p. 35.

143. Ibid, p. 37; also Levine, 'The Women's Movement', pp 177–8.

144. Tweedy, *A Link in the Chain,* p. 37.

145. Ibid, pp 38–9; Tweedy notes that in addition to requesting the establishment of a Commission on the Status of Women, this memorandum sought the signing, ratification and implementation of certain UN conventions of particular relevance to women, including conventions on Equal Pay, Abolition of Slavery, Traffic in Persons, Marriage (consent, minimum age etc.), and enforcement of maintenance obligations.

146. Ibid, pp 40–41.

147. NAI, Letter from the Office of the Minister for Labour to the Private Secretary, Department of the Taoiseach, 20 November 1968, Status of Women

International Conventions Equal Pay for Equal Work, Department of the Taoiseach, Cabinet File 96/6/184.

148. NAI, Letter from the Department of Finance to the Private Secretary, Department of the Taoiseach 13 August 1969, Status of Women International Conventions Equal Pay for Equal Work, Department of the Taoiseach, Cabinet File 96/6/184.

149. Levine, 'The Women's Movement', p. 178.

150. In January 2005 Ms Brigid McManus was appointed secretary general in the Department of Education, the fourth woman civil servant appointed at this level since Thekla Beere in the 1960s, *Irish Times*, 27 January 2005.

151. Author interview with Thekla Beere, RTÉ series *Moments in Time*, broadcast 8 March 1991; also Tweedy, *A Link in the Chain*, p. 42.

152. Interview with Thekla Beere, RTÉ series *Moments in Time*.

153. Ibid; Beere recalled with amusement a meeting with trade unionists for the confectionary trade, when she discovered that 'the women could make the cake, but when it came to decorating, the men had to do it'.

154. Levine, 'The Women's Movement', pp 178–9.

155. Levine, 'The Women's Movement', p. 179; Tweedy, *A Link in the Chain*, p. 50. Tweedy lists the seventeen organisations forming the first CSW in 1972: AIM, Altrusa, Association of Women Citizens of Ireland, Business and Professional Women's Clubs, Chartered Society of Physiotherapists, Cork Federation of Women's Organisations, Dublin University Women Graduates Association, Irish Countrywomen's Association, Irish Association of Dieticians, Irish Housewives Association, Irish Widows Association, National University Women Graduates Association, Soroptimists Clubs of Ireland, Women's International Zionist Organisation, Women's Liberation Movement, Women's Progressive Association (later Women's Political Association), ZONTA.

156. Levine, 'The Women's Movement', p. 179.

157. Thekla Beere, *Commission on the Status of Women: Progress Report* (1975), p. 46.

158. Tweedy, *A Link in the Chain*, pp 54–6, 60; Levine, 'The Women's Movement', p. 179.

159. Levine, 'The Women's Movement', p. 179.

160. Tweedy, *A Link in the Chain*, p. 49.

161. Ibid.

162. Ailbhe Smyth, 'The Women's Movement in the Republic of Ireland 1970–1990', in Ailbhe Smyth (ed.), *Irish Women's Studies Reader* (Dublin 1993), p. 254.

163. Ibid, pp 256–7; these included AIM, Cherish, Women's Aid, the Rape Crisis Centre, the WPA.

164. Tweedy, *A Link in the Chain*, pp 57–8.

165. Hanna Sheehy Skeffington, 'Women in Politics', in *The Bell*, VOL. 7 NO. 2 (Nov. 1943), p. 144.

166. Linda Connolly, *The Irish Women's Movement: From Revolution to Devolution* (Dublin 2003), p. 80.

Epilogue (pages 317–326)

1. Eavan Boland, *Night Feed* (Dublin 1982), p. 41.
2. Margaret MacCurtain, 'Godly Burden; Catholic Sisterhoods in 20th-Century Ireland', in Anthony Bradley and Maryann Gialanella Valiulis (eds), *Gender and Sexuality in Modern Ireland* (Amherst, Mass, 1977), p. 252.
3. Seanad Debates, VOL 47, 16 January 1957.
4. Diane Urquhart, '"The Female of the Species is More Deadlier than the Male"? The Ulster Women's Unionist Council, 1911–49', in Janice Holmes and Diane Urquhart (eds), *Coming into the Light: The Work, Politics and Religion of Women in Ulster 1840–1940* (Belfast 1994), p. 117.
5. Maurice Manning, 'Women in Irish National and Local Politics 1922–77', in Margaret MacCurtain and Donncha Ó Corráin (eds), *Women in Irish Society: The Historical Dimension* (Dublin 1978), p. 96.
6. Mary Clancy, 'Aspects of Women's Contribution to the Oireachteas Debate in the Irish Free State, 1922–1937', in Maria Luddy and Cliona Murphy (eds), *Women Surviving: Studies in Irish Women's History in the 19th and 20th Centuries* (Dublin 1990), p. 225.
7. J.J. Lee, *Ireland 1912–1918: Politics and Society* (Cambridge 1989), p. 380.
8. Ibid, p. 382.
9. Ibid, p. 376.
10. Ibid, p. 379.
11. *Report of Commission into the Civil Service 1932–35*, R. 54 (Dublin 1935).
12. *Report of the Commission on the Status of Women* (Dublin 1972), p. 12.
13. *The International Women's News*, Aug.–Sept. 1932, pp 143–4.
14. Ibid.
15. Olivia O'Leary and Helen Burke, *Mary Robinson: The Authorised Biography* (London 1998), p. 135.

BIBLIOGRAPHY

ARCHIVES

National Library of Ireland
Rosamund Jacob Diaries
Sheehy Skeffington Papers
Women's Suffrage Exhibition Collection
Minutes of Commission on Vocational Organisation

National Archives of Ireland
Chief Secretary's Office, Police & Crime Reports
General Prison's Board, Suffragette Papers
Department of the Taoiseach Files

Trinity College Dublin
John Dillon Papers

Irish Labour History Society Museum & Archive
IWWU Records

Museum of London
David Mitchell Collection

British Library of Political and Economic Science
WILPF Papers

University of Colorado
WILPF Papers

House of Lords, London
Lloyd George Papers

Archives Privately Held
Lucy Kingston Diaries
Robert Tweedy Collection

REPORTS

Irish Women's Franchise League, Report of Executive Committee 1913
Irish Women's Suffrage Federation, Annual Reports 1912–1917
Irish Women's Suffrage and Local Government Association, Annual Reports 1896–1918
Irish Women Workers' Union Annual Reports
ITUC Reports
Report of American Commission on Conditions in Ireland 1921
Report of Commission of Inquiry into the Civil Service (Dublin 1935–36)
Report of Commission on the Status of Women (Dublin 1972)
Report of Commission on Vocational Organisation (Dublin 1943)
Women's Social and Progressive League Annual Reports

JOURNALS/NEWSPAPERS

Bean na hÉireann
The Bell
Bullán: An Irish Studies Journal
Canadian Journal of Irish Studies
Catholic Bulletin
Catholic Standard
Church of Ireland Gazette
The Crane Bag
Dublin University Magazine
Éire-Ireland
The English Woman's Journal
Evening Telegraph
Freeman's Journal
History Ireland
International Woman Suffrage News
International Women's News
Irish Citizen
Irish Ecclesiastical Record
Irish Economist
The Irish Housewife
Irish Independent
Irish Journal of Psychology
Irish Press
The Irish Times
Irish Volunteer
Irish Worker
Journal of Women's History
Jus Suffragii
Labour History News

Labour News
The Leader
National Student
Republican Congress
Roscommon Herald
Rural History
Saothar
Sinn Féin
Social History
Studies
The Suffragette
United Irishwomen
Votes for Women
The Women's Advocate
Women's History Review
Women's Studies
Women's Studies International Forum
Women's Suffrage Journal
Workers' Republic

BOOKS/ARTICLES/THESES

Akenson, Donald H., *A Mirror to Kathleen's face* (Toronto 1973)

—*Education and Enmity: The Control of Schooling in Northern Ireland 1920–1950* (Newtown Abbot 1973)

Andrews, C.S., *Dublin Made Me: An Autobiography* (Dublin 1979)

Arensberg, Conrad M. and Kimball, Solon T., *Family and Community in Ireland* (3rd ed., Co. Clare 2001)

Atkinson, Norman, *Irish Education: A history of educational institutions* (Dublin 1969)

Barry, Rev. D., s.t.l., 'Female Suffrage from a Catholic Standpoint', in *Irish Ecclesiastical Record*, 4s 26 (September 1909)

Beaumont, Caitriona A., 'Women and the Politics of Equality, 1930–43', MA thesis (University College Dublin 1989)

—'Women and the Politics of Equality: The Irish Women's Movement, 1930–1943', in MacCurtain and Ó Corráin (eds), *Women and Irish History*

Bennett, Louie, 'With Irish Women Workers', in *Irish Economist*, vols 7–8 (August 1922)

—'Women and the Labour Movement', in *Dublin Labour Year Book* (Dublin 1930)

Bishop, Esther (ed.), *Bantracht na Tuatha, Irish Countrywomen's Association* (Dublin 1950)

Blackburn, H., *A Record of the Women's Suffrage Movement in the British Isles* (London 1902)

Boland, Eavan, *Night Feed* (Dublin 1982)

Bourke, Angela, Siobhán Kilfeather, Margaret MacCurtain, Geraldine Meaney, Máirín Ní Dhonnchadha, Mary O'Dowd and Clair Wills (eds), *The Field Day Anthology of Irish Writing: Volumes IV and V, Irish Women's Writing and Traditions* (Cork 2002)

Bourke, Joanna, *Husbandry to Housewifery: Women, Economic Change and Housework in Ireland, 1890–1914* (Oxford 1993)

Bradley, Anthony and Valiulis, Maryann Gialanella (eds), *Gender and Sexuality in Modern Ireland* (Amherst, Mass 1997)

Breathnach, Eibhlín, 'Charting New Waters: women's experience in higher education, 1879–1908,' in Cullen (ed.), *Girls Don't Do Honours*

—'Women and Higher Education in Ireland 1879–1914', in *The Crane Bag*, VOL. 4 NO. 1 (1980)

Brown, Terence, *Ireland, A Social and Cultural History 1922–79* (London 1981)

Bussey, Gertrude and Timms, Margaret, *Pioneers for Peace: Women's International League for Peace and Freedom 1915–65* (London 1965)

Cahalan, C., 'Women and the Irish Labour Movement', in *Dublin Labour Year Book* (Dublin 1930)

Clancy, Mary, 'Aspects of Women's Contribution to the Oireachtas Debate in the Irish Free State, 1922–37', in Luddy and Murphy (eds), *Women Surviving*

Clear, Caitríona, 'Walls Within Walls: Nuns in Nineteenth-Century Ireland', in Curtin, Jackson and O'Connor (eds), *Gender in Irish Society*

—'"The Women Can Not be Blamed": The Commission on Vocational Organisation, Feminism and "Homemakers", in Independent Ireland in the 1930s and '40s', in O'Dowd and Wichert (eds), *Chattel, Servant or Citizen*

—*Women of the House: Women's Household Work in Ireland 1922–1961* (Dublin 2000)

—'The Re-emergence of Nuns and Convents, 1800–1962', in *The Field Day Anthology of Irish Writing*, VOL. IV

Clifford, Mai, 'They gave us one week but we wanted two', in *Labour History News* (Autumn 1986)

Cody, Seamus, O'Dowd, John and Rigney, Peter (eds), *The Parliament of Labour: 100 Years of the Dublin Council of Trade Unions* (Dublin 1986)

Collis, R., *To Be A Pilgrim: An Autobiography* (London 1975)

Colum, Mary, *Life and the Dream* (New York 1947)

Connolly, J., *The Re-Conquest of Ireland* (Dublin 1917)

Connolly, Linda, *The Irish Women's Movement: From Revolution to Devolution* (Dublin 2003)

Cosgrove, Art (ed.), *Marriage in Ireland* (Dublin 1985)

Cosgrove, Art and MacCartney, D. (eds), *Studies in Irish History Presented to R. Dudley Edwards* (Dublin 1979)

Cousins, J.H. and M.E., *We Two Together* (Madras 1950)

Cullen, Mary, 'Anna Maria Haslam', in Cullen and Luddy (eds), *Women, Power and Consciousness*

—'Breadwinners and Providers: Women in the Household Economy of Labouring Families 1835–6', in Luddy and Murphy (eds), *Women Surviving*

Cullen, Mary (ed.), *Girls Don't Do Honours: Irish Women in Education in the 19th and 20th Centuries* (Dublin 1987)

Cullen, Mary and Luddy, Maria (eds), *Women, Power and Consciousness in 19th-Century Ireland* (Dublin 1995)

—*Female Activists: Irish Women and Change 1900–1960* (Dublin 2001)

Cullen Owens, Rosemary, *Louie Bennett* (Cork 2001)

—'Women and Pacifism in Ireland, 1915–1932', in Valiulis and O'Dowd (eds), *Women and Irish History*

—'Votes for Women', in Alan Hayes and Diane Urquhart (eds), *The Irish Women's History Reader* (London and New York 2001)

—'Louie Bennett 1870–1956', in Cullen and Luddy (eds), *Female Activists*

—*Smashing Times: A History of the Irish Women's Suffrage Movement 1889–1922* (Dublin 1984 and 1995)

Curtin, Chris, Jackson, Pauline and O'Connor, Barbara (eds), *Gender in Irish Society* (Galway 1987)

Dalsimer, A.M. (ed.), *Visualising Ireland: National Identity and the Pictorial Tradition* (Boston and London 1993)

Daly, Mary and Dickson, David (eds), *The Origins of Popular Literacy in Ireland: Language Change and Educational Development 1700–1920* (Dublin 1990)

Daly, Mary E., *Dublin—The Deposed Capital: A Social and Economic History 1860–1914* (Cork 1985)

—*The Famine in Ireland* (Dublin 1986)

—'"Oh, Kathleen Ni Houlihan, Your Way's a Thorny Way!": The Condition of Women in Twentieth-Century Ireland', in Bradley and Valiulis (eds), *Gender and Sexuality in Modern Ireland*

—'"Turn on the Tap": The State, Irish Women and Running Water', in Valiulis and O'Dowd (eds), *Women and Irish History* (Dublin 1997)

—'Women in the Irish Free State 1922–1939: The Interaction Between Economics and Ideology', in *Journal of Women's History*, VOL. 6 NO. 4/VOL. 7 NO. 1 (1995)

—'Women and Trade Unions', in Nevin (ed.), *Trade Union Century*

—*Women and Work in Ireland* (Dundalk 1997)

—'Women in the Irish Workforce from Pre-Industrial to Modern Times', in *Saothar 7* (1981)

—'Women, Work and Trade Unionism', in MacCurtain and Ó Corráin (eds), *Women in Irish Society*

Daly, Miriam, 'Women in Ulster', in Ní Chuilleanáin (ed.), *Irish Women: Image and Achievement*

Dangerfield, George, *The Strange Death of Liberal England* (London 1966)

Deeny, James, *To Cure and to Care: Memoirs of a Chief Medical Officer* (Dublin 1989)

—'The Enteritis Epidemic of the 1940s', in Farmar (ed.), *The End of an Epidemic*

Delaney, Enda, *Demography, State and Society: Irish Migration to Britain 1921–1971* (Liverpool 2000)

Diner, Hasier R., *Erin's Daughters in America* (Baltimore and London 1983)

Dooley, Dolores, 'Anna Doyle Wheeler', in Cullen and Luddy (eds), *Women, Power and Consciousness*

Doyle, Damien, 'Rosamund Jacob (1888–1960)', in Cullen and Luddy (eds), *Female Activists*

Dublin Labour Year Book (Dublin 1930)

Dudley Edwards, Ruth, *An Atlas of Irish History* (London 1973)

Evans, Richard, *Comrades and Sisters: Feminism, Socialism and Pacifism in Europe 1870–1945* (Sussex 1987)

Evans, Richard J., *The Feminists: Women's Emancipation Movements in Europe, America and Australasia 1840–1920* (London 1977)

Fahey, Tony, 'Nuns in the Catholic Church in Ireland in the Nineteenth Century', in Cullen (ed.), *Girls Don't Do Honours*

Fallon, Charlotte H., *Soul of Fire: A Biography of Mary MacSwiney* (Cork and Dublin 1986)

Fanning, R., Kennedy, M., Keogh, D. and O'Halpin, E. (eds), *Documents on Irish Foreign Policy*, VOL. 1, 1912–22 (Dublin 1998)

Farrell, Brian, 'Markievicz and the Women of the Revolution', in Martin (ed.), *Leaders and Men of the Easter Rising*

Farmar, Tony, *Ordinary Lives: Three Generations of Irish Middle Class Experience 1907, 1932, 1963* (Dublin 1991)

Farmar, Tony (ed.), *The End of an Epidemic: Essays in Irish Public Health 1935–65* (Dublin 1995)

Ferriter, Diarmaid, *Mothers, Maidens and Myths: A History of the ICA* (Dublin 1995)

—*The Transformation of Ireland 1900–2000* (London 2004)

Fitzpatrick, David, 'Marriage in Post-Famine Ireland', in Cosgrove (ed.), *Marriage in Ireland*

—'The Modernisation of the Irish Female', in O'Flanagan, Ferguson and Whelan (eds), *Rural Ireland 1600–1900*

—'A Share of the Honeycomb': Education, Emigration and Irishwomen', in Daly and Dickson (eds), *The Origins of Popular Literacy in Ireland*

Fox, R.M., *Louie Bennett: Her Life and Times* (Dublin 1958)

Fulford, R., *Votes for Women* (London 1957)

Garrett, Paul Michael, 'The abnormal flight: the migration and repatriation of Irish unmarried mothers', in *Social History*, VOL. 25 NO. 3 (October 2000)

Gaughan, A., *Thomas Johnson* (Dublin 1980)

Grieff, Mats, '"Marching Through the Streets Singing and Shouting": Industrial Struggle and Trade Unions Among Female Linen Workers in Belfast and Lurgan, 1872–1910', in *Saothar* 22 (1997)

Grieve, Norma and Ailsa Burns (eds), *Australian Women: New Feminist Perspectives* (Melbourne 1986)

Hazelkorn, Ellen, 'The Social and Political Views of Louie Bennett, 1870–1956', in *Saothar* 13 (1988)

Hearn, M., *Below Stairs: Domestic Service Remembered* (Dublin 1993)

Hearn, Mona, 'Life for Domestic Servants in Dublin, 1880–1920', in Luddy and Murphy (eds), *Women Surviving*

Hearne, Dana, 'The Irish Citizen 1914–1916: Nationalism, Feminism and Militarism', in *Canadian Journal of Irish Studies* 18, no. 1 (1992)

Heron, Marianne, *Sheila Conroy: Fighting Spirit* (Dublin 1993)

Hill, Myrtle and Pollock, Vivienne, *Image and Experience: Photographs of Irishwomen c. 1880–1920* (Belfast 1993)

Horkan, Mary, 'The Women Graduates' Association: Beginnings', in Macdona (ed.), *From Newman to New Woman*

Humphreys, Alexander J., *New Dubliners: Urbanization and the Irish Family* (London 1966)

Hynes, Christine, 'A Polite Struggle: The Dublin Seamstresses' Campaign, 1869–1972', in *Saothar* 18 (1993)

Inglis, Tom, *Moral Monopoly: The Rise and Fall of the Catholic Church in Modern Ireland* (Dublin 1987)

Jones, Mary, *These Obstreperous Lassies: A History of the Irish Women Workers' Union* (Dublin 1988)

Kearns, Kevin C., *Dublin Tenement Life: An Oral History* (Dublin 1994)

Kelleher, Margaret and Murphy, James H. (eds), *Gender Perspectives in Nineteenth-Century Ireland* (Dublin 1977)

Kennedy, Finola, *Cottage to Crèche: Family Change in Ireland* (Dublin 2001)

Keogh, Dermot, 'Michael O'Lehane and the Organisation of Linen Drapers' Assistants', in *Saothar* 3 (1977)

Kruse, Darryn and Sowerwine, Charles, 'Feminism and Pacifism: "Woman's Sphere" in Peace and War', in *Australian Women, New Feminist Perspectives*

Lawrenson Swanton, Daisy, *Emerging from the Shadow: The Lives of Sarah Anne Lawrenson and Lucy Olive Kingston* (Dublin 1994)

Lee, J.J., *Ireland 1912–1985: Politics and Society* (Cambridge 1989)

—'Women and the Church since the Famine', in MacCurtain and Ó Corráin (eds), *Women in Irish Society*

Lee, Joseph, 'Aspects of Corporatist Thought in Ireland: The Commission on Vocational Organisation, 1939–43', in Cosgrove and MacCartney (eds), *Studies in Irish History*

—*The Modernisation of Irish Society 1848–1918* (Dublin 1973 and 1989)

Levine, June, 'The Women's Movement in the Republic of Ireland, 1968–80', in *The Field Day Anthology*, VOL. V

Liddington, Jill, *The Long Road to Greenham: Feminism and Anti-Militarism in Britain since 1920* (London 1989)

Logan, John, 'The Dimensions of Gender in Nineteenth-Century Schooling', in Kelleher and Murphy (eds), *Gender Perspectives in Nineteenth-Century Ireland*

Luddy, Maria, '"Angels of Mercy": Nuns as Workhouse Nurses, 1861–1898', in Malcolm and Jones (eds), *Medicine, Disease and the State*

—'The Army and Prostitution in Nineteenth-Century Ireland: The Case of the Wrens of the Curragh', in *Bullán, An Irish Studies Journal*, VOL. 6 NO. 1 (2001)

—*Hanna Sheehy Skeffington* (Dublin 1995)

—'Irish Women and the Contagious Diseases Acts 1864–1886', in *History Ireland*, 1, 1 (Spring 1993)

—'Isabella M.S. Tod', in Cullen and Luddy (eds), *Women, Power and Consciousness*

—'Moral Rescue and Unmarried Mothers in Ireland in the 1920s', in *Women's Studies*, VOL. 30 NO. 6 (2001)

—'An Outcast Community: the "wrens" of the Curragh', in *Women's History Review*, VOL. 1 NO. 3 (1992)

—'Philanthropy in Nineteenth-Century Ireland', in Bourke et al (eds), *The Field Day Anthology of Irish Writing*, VOL. V

—'Women and Charitable Organisations in Nineteenth-Century Ireland', in *Women's Studies International Forum*, VOL. II NO. 4

—*Women in Ireland 1800–1918: A Documentary History* (Cork 1995)

—*Women and Philanthropy in Nineteenth-Century Ireland* (Cambridge 1995)

—'Women and Politics in Ireland, 1860–1918', in Bourke et al (eds), *The Field Day Anthology of Irish Writing* VOL. V

—'Women and Politics in 19th Century Ireland', in Valiulis and O'Dowd (eds), *Women and Irish History*

—'Women and work in nineteenth- and early twentieth-century Ireland: an overview', in Whelan (ed.), *Women and Paid Work in Ireland*

Luddy, Maria and Murphy, Cliona (eds) *Women Surviving: Studies in Irish Women's History in the 19th and 20th Centuries* (Dublin 1989)

Lyons, F.S.L., *Ireland Since the Famine* (rev. ed. London 1973)

MacCurtain, Margaret, 'Fullness of Life: Defining Female Spirituality in Twentieth Century Ireland', in Luddy and Murphy (eds), *Women Surviving*

—'Godly Burden: Catholic Sisterhoods in 20th-Century Ireland', in Bradley and Valiulis (eds), *Gender and Sexuality in Modern Ireland*

—'The Historical Image', in Ní Chuilleanáin (ed.), *Irish Women: Image and Achievement*

—'Late in the Field: Catholic Sisters in Twentieth-Century Ireland and the New Religious History', in O'Dowd and Wichert (eds), *Chattel, Servant or Citizen*

—'The Real Molly Macree', in A.M. Dalsimer (ed.), *Visualising Ireland*

MacCurtain, Margaret and Ó Corráin, Donncha (eds), *Women in Irish Society: The Historical Dimension* (Dublin 1978)

MacCurtain, Margaret and O'Dowd, Mary (eds), *Women in Early Modern Ireland* (Dublin 1991)

Macdona, Anne (ed.), *From Newman to New Woman: UCD Women Remember* (Dublin 2001)

McLaughlin, Astrid, '"Received with politeness, treated with contempt": The story of women's protests in Ireland against the regressive implications of sections of the Conditions of Employment Act (1936) and Bunreacht na hÉireann, The Irish Constitution of 1937', unpublished MA thesis (University College Dublin 1996)

McLoughlin, Dympna, 'Superfluous and unwanted deadweight: the emigration of nineteenth-century Irish pauper women', in Patrick O'Sullivan (ed.), *The Irish Worldwide, History, Heritage, Identity*, VOL. 4, *Irish Women and Irish Migration*

—'Women and sexuality in nineteenth-century Ireland', in *The Irish Journal of Psychology*, 15, 2 and 3 (1994)

—'Workhouses and Irish Female Paupers 1840–1870', in Luddy and Murphy (eds), *Women Surviving*

Malcolm, Elizabeth, '"The House of Strident Shadows": the Asylum, Family and Emigration in Post-Famine Rural Ireland', in Malcolm and Jones (eds), *Medicine, Disease and the State*

Malcolm, Elizabeth and Jones, Greta (eds), *Medicine, Disease and the State in Ireland 1650–1940* (Cork 1999)

Manning, Maurice, 'Women in National and Local Politics 1922–77', in MacCurtain and Ó Corráin (eds), *Women in Irish Society*

Martin, F.X. (ed.), *Leaders and Men of the Easter Rising: Dublin 1916* (London 1967)

Miller, Kerby A., with David N. Doyle and Patricia Kelleher, '"For love and liberty": Irish women, migration and domesticity in Ireland and America, 1815–1920', in O'Sullivan (ed.), *Irish Women and Irish Migration*

Molony, Helena, 'James Connolly and Women', in *Dublin Labour Year Book 1930*

Moriarty, Theresa, 'Mary Galway (1864–1928)', in Cullen and Luddy (eds), *Female Activists*

—*Work in Progress: Episodes from the history of Irish women's trade unionism* (Belfast and Dublin 1994)

Mulvihill, Margaret, *Charlotte Despard: a Biography* (London 1989)

Nevin, Donal (ed.), *Trade Union Century* (Cork 1994)

Ní Chuilleanáin, Eiléan (ed.), *Irish Women: Image and Achievement* (Dublin 1985)

O'Callaghan, Margaret, 'Women and Politics in Independent Ireland, 1921–68', in Bourke et al (eds), *The Field Day Anthology of Irish Writing*, VOL. V (Cork 2002)

O'Carroll, Ide, *Models for Movers: Irish Women's Emigration to America* (Dublin 1990)

Ó Catháin, Rev. Seán, S.J., 'Education in the New Ireland', in MacManus (ed.), *The Years of the Great Test*

O'Connell, Anne, 'Charlotte Grace O'Brien', in Cullen and Luddy (eds), *Women, Power and Consciousness*

O'Connell, T.J., *History of the National Teachers' Organisation 1868–1968* (Dublin 1969)

O'Connor, A., 'Women in Irish Folklore; the Testimony Regarding Illegitimacy, Abortion and Infanticide', in MacCurtain and O'Dowd (eds), *Women in Early Modern Ireland*

O'Connor, Anne V., 'Education in Nineteenth Century Ireland', in Angela Bourke, et al (eds), *The Field Day Anthology of Irish Writing*, VOL. V (Cork 2002)

—'The Revolution in Girls' Secondary Education in Ireland, 1860–1910', in Cullen (ed.), *Girls Don't Do Honours*

O'Connor, Emmet, *A Labour History of Ireland 1824–1960* (Dublin 1992)

Ó Danachair, Caoimhín, 'Marriage in Irish Folk Tradition', in Cosgrove (ed.), *Marriage in Ireland*

O'Dowd, Anne, 'Women in Rural Ireland in the Nineteenth and early Twentieth Centuries—How the Daughters, Wives and Sisters of Small Farmers and Landless Labourers Fared', in *Rural History*, 5, 2, (1994)

O'Dowd, Liam, 'Church, State and Women', in Curtin, Jackson and O'Connor (eds), *Gender in Irish Society*

O'Dowd, Mary and Wichert, Sabine (eds), *Chattel, Servant or Citizen: Women's Status in Church, State and Society* (Belfast 1995)

O'Flanagan, Patrick, Ferguson, Paul and Whelan, Kevin (eds), *Rural Ireland 1600–1900: Modernisation and Change* (Cork 1987)

Ó hÓgartaigh, Margaret, 'Flower power and "mental grooviness": nurses and midwives in Ireland in the early twentieth century', in Whelan (ed.), *Women and Paid Work in Ireland*

O'Hegarty, P.S., *The Victory of Sinn Féin* (Dublin 1924)

O'Leary, Eoin, 'The Irish National Teachers' Organisation and the Marriage Bar for Women National Teachers, 1933–1958', in *Saothar* 12 (1987)

O'Leary, Olivia and Burke, Helen, *Mary Robinson: The Authorised Biography* (London 1998)

O'Sullivan, Patrick (ed.), *Irish Women and Irish Migration* (London 1995)

Owens, Rosemary, 'Votes for Women, Votes for Ladies: Organised Labour and the Suffrage Movement, 1876–1922', in *Saothar* 9 (1983)

Padbury, Joyce, 'Mary Hayden, First President of the Women Graduates' Association', in Macdona (ed.), *From Newman to New Woman*

Pankhurst, Christabel, *Unshackled* (London 1959)

Pankhurst, E., *My Own Story* (London 1914)

Paseta, Senia, *Before the Revolution: Nationalism, Social Change and Ireland's Catholic Elite, 1879–1922* (Cork 1999)

Peckham Magray, Mary, *The Transforming Power of the Nuns: Women, Religion, and Cultural Change in Ireland, 1750–1900* (New York and Oxford 1998)

Prunty, Jacinta, 'Margaret Louisa Aylward', in Cullen and Luddy (eds), *Women, Power and Consciousness*

Purcell, Betty, 'Ten Years of Progress? Some Statistics', in *The Crane Bag*, VOL. 4 NO. 1 (1980)

Quinlan, Carmel, *Genteel Revolutionaries: Anna and Thomas Haslam and the Irish Women's Movement* (Cork 2002)

Raftery, Deirdre, 'Frances Power Cobbe', in Cullen and Luddy (eds), *Women, Power and Consciousness*

—*Women and Learning in English Writing 1600–1900* (Dublin 1997)

Raughter, Rosemary, 'A Natural Tenderness: The Ideal and the Reality of Eighteenth-Century Female Philanthropy', in Valiulis and O'Dowd (eds), *Women and Irish History*

Rhodes, Rita M., *Women and the Family in Post-Famine Ireland* (New York and London 1992)

Robinson, Mary, 'Women and the New Irish State', in MacCurtain and Ó Corráin (eds), *Women in Irish Society*

Rosen, Andrew, *Rise Up Women! The Militant Campaign of the Women's Social and Political Union 1903–1914* (London and Boston 1974)

Rossi, Alice S. (ed.), *The Feminist Papers* (2nd ed., New York 1974)

Rudd, Joy, 'Invisible Exports: The Emigration of Irish Women This Century', in *Women's Studies International Forum*, VOL. 11 NO. 4 (1988)

Schreiber, Adele and Mathieson, Margaret, *Journey Towards Freedom* (Denmark 1995)

Sheehy Skeffington, Andree D. and Owens, Rosemary (eds), *Votes for Women: Irish Women's Struggle for the Vote* (Dublin 1975)

Sheehy Skeffington, H., 'Reminiscences of an Irish Suffragette', in Sheehy Skeffington and Owens (eds and publs), *Votes for Women*

Sheehy Skeffington, Hanna, 'Women in Politics', in *The Bell*, VOL. 7 NO. 2 (Nov. 1943)

Smith, Brid, 'Cissy Cahalan, A Tribute', in *Labour History News*, NO. 8 (Autumn 1992)

Smith, David, '"I Thought I Was Landed!": The Congested Districts Board and The Women of Western Ireland', in *Éire-Ireland*, XXXI, 3 and 4 (1996)

Smyth, Ailbhe (ed.), *Irish Women's Studies Reader* (Dublin 1993)

—'The Women's Movement in the Republic of Ireland 1970–1990', in Smyth (ed.), *Irish Women's Studies Reader*

Steiner Scott, Elizabeth, '"To Bounce a Boot Off Her Now and Then ...": Domestic Violence in Post-Famine Ireland', in Valiulis and O'Dowd (eds), *Women and Irish History*

Swanwick, Helena, *I Have Been Young* (London 1935)

Sweeney, G., *In Public Service* (Dublin 1990)

Tobin, Fergal, *The Best of Decades: Ireland in the 1960s* (2nd ed., Dublin 1996)

Travers, Pauric, 'Emigration and Gender: The Case of Ireland 1922–60', in O'Dowd and Wichert (eds), *Chattel, Servant or Citizen*

—'"There was nothing for me there": Irish female emigration, 1922–71', in O'Sullivan (ed.), *Irish Women and Irish Migration*

Tweedy, Hilda, *A Link in the Chain: The Story of the Irish Housewives Association 1942–1992* (Dublin 1992)

Tynan, K., *The Years of the Shadow* (London 1919)

Valiulis, Maryann, 'Neither Feminist nor Flapper: the Ecclestiastical Construction of the Ideal Irish Women', in O'Dowd and Wichert (eds), *Chattel, Servant or Citizen*

Valiulis, Maryann Gialanella, 'Defining Their Role in the New State: Irishwomen's Protest Against the Juries Act of 1927', in *Canadian Journal of Irish Studies*, 18, 1 (July 1992)

—'Engendering Citizenship: Women's Relationship to the State in Ireland and the United States in the Post-Suffrage Period', in Valiulis and O'Dowd (eds), *Women and Irish History*

—'Power, Gender and Identity in the Irish Free State', in *Journal of Women's History*, VOL. 6 NO. 4/VOL. 7 NO. 1 (1995)

Valiulis, Maryann Gialanella and O'Dowd, Mary (eds), *Women and Irish History: Essays in honour of Margaret MacCurtain* (Dublin 1997)

Voris, Jacqueline van, *Constance de Markievicz in the Cause of Ireland* (Mass, USA 1967)

Walsh, Brendan M., 'Marriage in Ireland in the Twentieth Century', in Cosgrove (ed.), *Marriage in Ireland*

Ward, Margaret, *Hanna Sheehy Skeffington: A Life* (Cork 1997)

—*In Their Own Voice: Women and Irish Nationalism* (Dublin 1995)

—*Unmanageable Revolutionaries: Women and Irish Nationalism* (London and Dingle 1983)

Whelan, Bernadette (ed.), *Women and Paid Work in Ireland 1500–1930* (Dublin 2000)

Whyte, J.H., *Church and State in Modern Ireland 1923–1979* (2nd ed., Dublin 1980)

Wiltshire, Anne, *Most Dangerous Women: Feminist Peace Campaigners of the Great War* (London and Boston 1985)

Wollstonecraft, Mary, *A Vindication of the Rights of Woman* (1891 edition, E.R. Pennell (ed.))

INDEX